THE NEW NATURALIST
A SURVEY OF BRITISH NATURAL HISTORY

MAN AND BIRDS

The aim of this series is to interest the general reader
in the wild life of Britain by recapturing the inquiring
spirit of the old naturalists. The Editors believe that
the natural pride of the British public in the native
fauna and flora, to which must be added concern for
their conservation, is best fostered by maintaining a
high standard of accuracy combined with clarity of
exposition in presenting the results of modern
scientific research.

THE NEW NATURALIST

MAN AND BIRDS

R. K. MURTON, Ph.D.

COLLINS
ST JAMES'S PLACE, LONDON
1971

TO MY PARENTS

ISBN 0 00 213132 3

Printed in Great Britain
Collins Clear-Type Press
London and Glasgow

CONTENTS

PLATES

Except where indicated, all photographs are by the author

TEXT FIGURES

PREFACE

To find a suitable title for this book posed something of a problem. *Economic Ornithology*, which is what it is all about, seemed much too dull, *Birds on the Land* incomplete, and a more fanciful title out of keeping with the series. E. M. Nicholson wrote in 1951 at the end of his *Birds and Men*: 'Increased study and education, which enlarge our grasp and control of both direct and indirect influences upon birds, are, therefore, most important. Unless the human population should be exterminated the interests of birds must always occupy a subordinate place, except in a few localities where they can be overriding. Yet the close and growing similarity between the interests of birds and people in the shaping of the landscape encourages a hope that with intelligent and imaginative study Britain can be much improved as a habitat for both.' This statement is so much in accord with the theme of what I wanted to elaborate that *Man and Birds* emerged as the most appropriate title. The scope of what could be written under this title is enormous and so at the outset it is emphasised that the prime aim of this book is to deal with the truly economic aspects of man's interrelationships with birds, and virtually to ignore their study for the sake of pure knowledge or their important role in the inspiration of art, music and literature. Nevertheless, to maintain some balance I have attempted in the first chapter to give a chronological account of man's multifarious relationships with birds, with sufficient references to enable those so inclined to delve deeper into this fascinating subject.

Economic ornithology, in its wider sense, dates from the time when man first realised that birds could be good to eat, and such erudite writings as the *Boke of St. Albans* published in 1486 with its treatises of hawking, hunting and cote armour may properly be regarded as early text books on the subject. Sir Gervase Markham's *Hunger's Protection of the Whole Art of Fowling by Water and Land*, published in 1621, is pure economic ornithology. So, too, in its own way was W. H. Hudson's *Birds and Man* (1901), although in its pompous subjectivity and misplaced sentimentality it reflects an extreme attitude, a reaction against an earlier milieu of excessive exploitation of birds. There were probably as many birds pillaging the farmer's crops during the boom of agriculture in the mid-nineteenth century as there are today, but they posed few problems in an age when agricultural labour was cheap – so that every headland could be kept in weed-free neatness – and a surfeit of trigger-happy gamekeepers, and plenty of lads to rattle cans, provided the ideal psychological reassurance that something was being done.

It was not until the dawn of the twentieth century that man really sought to question his relationships with birds, whereupon economic ornithology in the limited sense emerged. For years, problem birds for the farmer were killed or scared with little thought of whether this did good, or of whether the expense was justified; and, by the same token, fluctuations in the productivity of game and other exploitable species were taken for granted. Between 1880–1883, Professor Stephen Forbes in the U.S.A. published seven papers on the relationships between birds and men, analysing the gut contents of birds to reveal their feeding habits, to be followed by W. E. Collinge in Britain. At the same time, E. Wilson, R. T. Leiper and A. Shipley were laying the foundations of a modern ecological approach in their studies of *The Grouse in Health and Disease* edited by Lord Lovat (1911). The early food inquiries had one undesirable consequence in that birds were classified as beneficial or harmful solely on the basis of the foods they ate. Fortunately the new science of ecology was also emerging at this time and by the late 1930s it was well appreciated that the diet of an animal could not be considered in isolation of its natural mode of life.

The enlightenment which now pervades economic ornithology results from three major developments:

First, the last two decades have seen a vast swing in public sympathy towards wild life, aided by the development of the mass media and by a growing need for escape from the human suffering wrought by two world wars and the increasing pressures of modern living. This has been reflected in the growth of such organisations as the British Trust for Ornithology, which was formed in 1932 and which exists to co-ordinate and guide the efforts of a growing army of serious amateurs. Government recognition of the need to conserve and manage our national wild life resources led in 1949 to the setting-up of the Nature Conservancy under a Royal Charter, as a research council under the supervision of the Privy Council (it is now incorporated in the National Environmental Research Council). One must at this point pay tribute to E. M. Nicholson. He was a driving force in the formation of both these organisations, as he has been in ornithology in general. To him is owed much of the credit for the fact that the hopes expressed in the quotation given above from his book are at last being realised.

Second, the 1939–45 war focused attention on the need for British agriculture to be self-sufficient. The slump and stagnation which had followed the golden years of the 1870s was over, and the whole pattern of farming changed, cereal production reaching record heights. Nothing could be allowed to interfere with 'productivity', and in response to requests from the Ministry of Agriculture, the Agricultural Research Council sponsored investigations into the status of the rook and wood-pigeon, entrusting the field work to the B.T.O., who by now had organised field helpers. Within the last twenty years other great agricultural changes have occurred as farming has become an increasingly mechanised, highly scientific and efficient industry, managed by hard-headed businessmen. There has been no surplus of cheap labour and everyone has had to operate to tight profit margins. The Government first gave financial support to farming by assisting sugar beet production in the 1920s, and the value of the elaborate system of agricultural support and guaranteed prices, negotiated at annual price reviews, was proved by the war and has continued since. These factors have inevitably made growers more conscious of their pest problems, and continual protests from farmers induced the Ministry of Agriculture in 1952 to begin an active programme of research into various bird problems. It is not always so much what or how much birds eat, as the fact that not all farmers suffer equally from their depredations, and when competition is tough nobody can afford to start off at a disadvantage.

Finally, increased opportunity for post-graduate research has led to a spate of ornithological studies at the University centres, notably at Oxford (the Edward Grey Institute founded in 1931 provides the lead), Aberdeen, Bristol, Cambridge, Durham and Exeter. These have often been of direct economic benefit or of indirect value in elaborating new techniques and principles.

This then is the background against which this book has been written. Since it first went to press there has been an upsurge in public sympathy for environmental studies, kindled by a growing awareness of the pollution problem and stoked by the publicity attached to European Conservation Year 1970. Already such words as 'conservation', 'ecosystem', 'environmental contamination' and most of all 'ecology' are becoming common vocabulary and it is vital that this concern is channelled into a useful direction.

Biological conservation is not synonymous with preservation or maintaining a *status quo*, but is instead concerned with sensible wild-life management in a dynamic environment constantly being altered by man. Animals must achieve the maximum reproductive output possible if their genes are not to be swamped and lost in competition with more fecund members of the population. In 'wild' nature this results in a density-adjusted, compensatory mortality and not a Malthusian population increase, and a balance with resources is accordingly maintained. Man by virtue of his sophisticated tech-nology has temporarily averted the need for an immediate regulatory mortality, and, as a consequence of his social and cultural inheritance, has a unique alternative. He can decide the level at which he is prepared to stabilise his population size, allowing his reproductive rate rather than mortality to be adjusted. So the fundamental issue in conservation is whether man should maximise his own numbers at the expense of wild-life, as he could so easily do, or whether he should regulate his numbers at a level which will allow him to enjoy something of his natural heritage.

There will probably be about 66 million people in Britain at the end of the century if data contributing to current projections are valid (for a valuable review see *The optimum population for Britain*, Institute of Biology Symposium No. 17 published by Academic Press 1970 and edited by L. R. Taylor). This is too many. Already Britain has a higher population density than China or India and it is quite untrue, as we so complacently think, that population control is something to be advocated for others and not for ourselves. In sophisticated societies such as Britain and the U.S.A. the birth of a new child provides a much, much higher potential demand on world resources than that of an Asiatic or African baby. This is because every western child will eventually make heavy demands on land for recreation and on resources to satisfy a rising standard of living and will, therefore, make a vastly more serious contribution to environ-mental pollution than the Asiatic, who can barely hope to exist.

The biotic (living) and physical (non-living) components of any area of country interact to produce an energy transfer system, the ecosystem, such that what is taken out is a function of what is put in.

The energy transfer occurs through food chains or food webs and only green plants, the primary producers, have the ability to fix the energy initially emanating from the sun. A prime concern of ecologists is to know to what extent the energy available in any system is being used most efficiently for man's welfare. We know that energy can be conserved more efficiently in complex ecosystems and that such systems are the most stable. They require the minimum of energy to maintain but are readily upset if too much energy is lost for any reason: defoliating tropical forest with herbicides amounts to criminal spoilation of resources. On the other hand, simple systems supporting short food chains are liable to large fluctuations with a high energy wastage unless this is harvested. Agriculture aims at shortening any biological food chain so that the energy initially fixed by plants is converted into human food as rapidly as possible without the existence of too many intermediate links which each can fix only a proportion of the energy and must waste much more. Western man who eats meat and thereby allows domestic animals to intervene between himself and the primary plant producers, is indulging in a luxury which cannot be tolerated in S.E. Asia where the minimum of wastage occurs between the plant stage (rice) and man the consumer. Biologically it must be advantageous for a consumer to cut out the middlemen as much as is feasible. Whales represent one of the few examples where a large top predator has truncated a food chain by feeding nearly at the primary trophic level (on small crustacea which in turn feed on the green algae). Man, too, has this capacity and in terms of natural selection is so justified if in the long-term the ecosystem is not irreversibly harmed; but this last condition is largely the crux of the problem.

Chapters 2 and 3 set out to examine the contribution made by ecological studies to understanding the complex problems involved in formulating conservation policies. The principles raised apply throughout the book and their significance immediately becomes apparent in Chapter 4 where the relationships between birds and forestry are reviewed. These chapters do unfortunately make the heaviest reading for those with little or no formal biological training. Nevertheless, it seemed worthwhile outlining the factors responsible for regulating and keeping bird populations in equilibrium from year to year and explaining how long-term increases or decreases in numbers may also occur. By understanding the nature of population fluctuations it can be appreciated that a species experiencing a long-term decline may, nonetheless, be producing a surplus of offspring each year, which could be killed without affecting the rate of decline. In such an event conservation of stocks ought to involve the identification of the factor responsible for population changes rather than any pious attempt to prevent mortality. In fact, the grey partridge presents a real example. Thus, although the species is suffering a long-term fall in total numbers, more birds could be shot for man's enjoyment each year without altering the rate of this decline; conversely to prevent decreases it is no use advocating the cessation of shooting. This is because the factors responsible for determining the level of the breeding population in spring are uncorrelated with the intensity of winter shooting. In discussing avian population dynamics I have singled out, in this way, species of economic importance, even though certain principles may have been better illustrated in birds which in the context of the present book are of more academic interest.

Chapter 2 also explains why apparently intensive shooting fails to reduce the numbers of pest species. Most birds produce such a large excess of offspring, which are surplus to the needs of a balanced population and are accordingly wasted, that intensive artificial slaughter, which is shown to replace and not augment natural loss, can occur without detriment to the stability of the population. Conservation is concerned with the best use being made of this wastage margin: in game-birds and wildfowl it may be cropped for sporting pleasure and be considered a farm crop and there is no contradiction in a conservationist advocating hunting; again the surplus may serve as food for a predator higher in the food chain, and be used to stabilise the whole ecosystem. The surplus in production could also be used to stock denuded areas elsewhere, either semi-natural sites or completely artificial ones in the form of zoological gardens. In this context it becomes important to know whether the production resulting from those wild birds nesting on farmland is necessary to fill other habitats outside farmland, or whether farmland merely absorbs, like a sponge, the surplus production from outside reservoirs. To answer such questions we have to provide a balance sheet of what exists on farmland – a consideration deferred until Chapter 5.

Work over the last fifteen years or so has highlighted the fact that in the main, animal populations can look after themselves and indeed can withstand fairly flagrant abuse, provided the habitat of the

animal concerned remains unchanged. But, of course, this is the
major problem because habitats are becoming changed, often extremely subtlety, so that only careful scientific measurements can
reveal the processes involved. Obviously, if a wood is chopped down
and replaced by a town the fauna will change, and whether this is
good or bad depends on the requirements of society. But, because
there are limitations on the way land can be deployed in an already
committed society, we have to decide on the optimum conservation
measures that can be adopted for any particular programme of land
development. Unfortunately there is little information, except from
empirical observation, of the minimum habitat requirements of
birds, or other animals, and it is not usually easy to make sound
predictions. For example, no observer alive in neolithic Britain could
have guessed that the result of deforestation and the creation of scrub
would provide ideal conditions for a small bird which was probably
once confined to Poland and Western Russia. The dunnock has
probably colonised the western Palearctic in comparatively recent
times and is the only representative in Britain of a genus which has
eleven species in the central Palearctic, extending from Russian
Turkestan and the Himalayas north to Siberia and east to Mongolia and Japan. All are insectivorous birds which live in the thin
scrub of the forest edge, particularly in montane habitats where
trees become shrubs; many even inhabit the gulleys on rough and
broken ground above the shrub line. Clearly, no group was better
pre-adapted to take advantage of the creation of artificial scrub in
the form of the patchwork of earthbanks, hedges and field boundaries.
Even today, dunnocks appear to be particularly successful in S.W.
England, where double hedgerows are associated with earthbanks
and dark gulleys, presumably conditions most approximating
ancestral habitat needs. Then again who could guess in advance that
gulls would prove the ideal birds to feed on Corporation rubbish
dumps? Can we be sure that an even better pre-adapted species is
not waiting round the corner? So in practical terms conservation is
concerned to define the smallest area that can be a viable habitat for
a species. A pile of brushwood with an adjacent nettle bed seems to
satisfy the wren; the log pile provides safety from large predators and
simulates the dense under-storey of natural habitats and the nettle
beds are rich in insect food. One could conceive a farmland monoculture broken by evenly distributed piles of logs plus nettle patch
and supporting a marvellously high wren population. This neglects

the aesthetic factor in conservation which is yet another intangible; one man loves a desert while another deplores such wilderness. However, the first requirement is to understand the factors which determine how many species exist in a particular habitat, and what limits species diversity, then we can decide which ones to have. Chapter 2 looks at these problems while Chapter 5 gives practical examples so far as farmland is concerned.

Chapters 6–9 examine the mode of life of those birds which typically live on farms or orchards. These are the species most impinging on man's immediate interests, and the manner in which their naturally acquired adaptations have enabled them to succeed at man's expense is of interest as well as importance. Time and again similar themes are repeated. For instance, economic damage is frequently caused, not by a species as such, but instead by the expendable post-breeding and displaced surplus of juveniles; this is true in the case of the crows and ravens which can harass lambing flocks of sheep, of the starlings and blackbirds which eat soft-fruit in orchards, and of many of the tits which open milk bottles. Many, perhaps all, birds have evolved adaptations which enable them to identify foods of highest nutritive content and this ability is particularly significant in the case of northern game-birds. The same capacity sometimes causes them to single out valuable trees in forest nurseries, especially those which have been well nourished with fertilisers. In mature woodland, the birds will often attack stunted or diseased trees as these have more nutrients in the leaf. Similarly, bullfinches select the buds of cultivated fruit trees in preference to less nutritious wild buds. Grey geese are attracted to fields specially fertilised to produce early spring-bite for feeding to lambing ewes, and the list could go on. Patterns emerge which must determine our basic approach to wild-life management.

Speciation and species diversity were discussed in Chapter 2. In Chapters 6–9 it is shown how various species can be forced into new relationships in man-altered habitats, where natural barriers to competition are often absent. Inter-specific competition has led, and continues to lead, to all kinds of status changes amongst birds, yellow and reed-buntings, various finches, house sparrow and gulls being singled out for mention; some birds are proving much more adaptable than others in the reshuffle which is occurring. In those bird populations which are expanding, mortality has been relinquished enabling more genetical diversity to be manifested. In a

strongly selected population, genotypes which carry bizarre features
are rapidly lost in competition with less handicapped individuals,
whereas if there is room for all progeny to live, unusual genotypes
may survive. We recognise the obvious manifestations of this
genetical diversity – for instance blackbird populations, which have
currently been very successful, contain an unusually high proportion
of birds with abnormal head feathers, while pied and albino
individuals are common. Such overt diversity, which is not apparent
in those species which are still being vigorously selected, is indicative
of a range of newly expressed physiological and behaviour traits less
readily recognised. Nonetheless, we note that expanding kittiwake
populations will now adopt unusual nesting sites, while sedge
warblers, reed-buntings, curlews, oystercatchers, linnets, display new
habitat tolerances and food preferences, and it is certain that even
less noticeable changes are in progress and will eventually be
measured. Man is the agent initiating these changes, this is evolution
in progress and we are witnessing natural selection at work. It is the
aim of the conservationist to understand such change, and certainly
not deplore change out of hand.

It is in our industrial society that the paradoxes in man's attitudes
to birds become most clear-cut and we are faced with having to
make the most difficult decisions. People love to feed pigeons, yet
these may be an important factor in disease transmission. Man the
aeronaut is sometimes in direct competition with birds for airspace.
This wide miscellany of problems has had to be condensed in
Chapter 11 to leave space for a brief consideration of the difficulties
involved in solving some of these problems, and for a reiteration of
Nicholson's plea that we learn to treat birds as an important component of our environment.

I am indebted to a great many people for helpful advice and encouragement and in particular to my wife who has read, criticised
and helped correct the various drafts and given me considerable
encouragement throughout. Various colleagues have allowed me to
quote their own work and have commented on my text, notably with
regard to Chapters 9, 11 and 12 and my thanks are owed to T.
Brough, D. D. B. Summers, and E. N. Wright. M. G. Ridpath, D.
Burgess, J. Gailey and S. Isbister helped with Chapter 3. Dr B.
Campbell helped with part of Chapter 4. Dr P. Dare, P. Davidson,
Dr D. A. Hancock and A. Mercer offered much valuable criticism
on the oystercatcher section in Chapter 10, and in addition Dr

H. A. Cole gave helpful advice on the whole of Chapter 10. I have
benefited from discussions with Dr D. W. Snow, K. Williamson and
other members of the B.T.O. staff, their knowledge being particularly valuable in the preparation of Chapter 5. Drs G. M. Dunnet
and I. Patterson at Aberdeen and Dr C. J. F. Coombs gave helpful
criticism of parts of Chapter 6, while Dr P. Bull advised on the New
Zealand situation, his data also being useful for the preparation of
Chapter 2. To all these people I offer my grateful thanks. My thanks
are also owed to Dr J. Berry and Dr H. A. Hyde for allowing me to
use their data in constructing Figure 1 and Table 16 respectively.
Mention of figures emphasises my indebtedness to Mr A. G. Jenson
for drawing most of the text-figures. Finally, it will be evident that
this book owes much to a large number of research workers in many
fields who are acknowledged in the text or bibliography. I have at
various times benefited from discussions or correspondence with
many of these people and they too deserve my gratitude. So do the
countless bird-watchers who participate in various organised schemes
for the common good, without their efforts achieving individual
recognition. It is largely through their efforts that British ornithology
can claim such a high place in the advancement of biological
knowledge and it is because of them that there is hope that man will
learn to live with and not compete against his heritage.

CHAPTER I

MEN AND BIRDS

WE can only speculate on the impact of the stone-age hunters of Europe on birds: they must have had some effect at least on those species which were easy to catch. Certainly the larger mammals seem to have felt the pressure of man the hunter as long ago as the Plcistoccnc. Using molar tooth rcmains, Socrgcl has calculatcd thc ages of Pleistocene elephants found at sites where either Heidelberg or Neanderthal man was present and at comparable sites where no human remains were found. In each case the age structure of the clcphant population is much lowci whcic man abidcd, suggcsting that he was cropping the populations sufficiently heavily to increase the need for a high rate of replacement by young animals. Some indication of the importance of birds to these ancient hunters may be gleaned from the cave drawings at Lascaux, France. Fisher and Peterson give good reason for believing that they depict a fauna existing in a warm inter-glacial, 100,000 years ago. Flamingo, spoonbill, geese, crane, eagle and raven are all shown, together with a dead hunter wearing a bird mask and sporting a hunting stick adorned with birds.

The earliest indications of man's interest in cereal culture date back in the Near East to about 8,000 BC. Remains of sickles, pestle and mortar have been found in mesolithic caves of Palestine, and arable farming had reached an advanced stage in the Near East by 3000 BC. This later neolithic culture did not spread to Britain until around 2000 BC and throughout the early and middle bronze ages men were still very much hunters rather than pastoralists, living a semi-nomadic life. Settlement brought man a new relationship with birds, because instead of loose contacts during hunting expeditions, conditions now existed for confining wild creatures and breeding them in captivity, leading to selective breeding and domestication. It is probably no coincidence, as the late F. E. Zeuner points out, that all the important domesticated birds are seed-eaters (pigeons and fowl), grazers or vegetable-eaters (geese and ducks), which could have gained an early association with man through their crop-robbing habits. Hence, the first use of birds was as a direct food substitute, their value as egg-producers and for pleasure and sport was not exploited until later. Nonetheless, as early as the Iron Age, in the Hallstatt culture which flourished on the Austrian shores of Lake Constance, there is evidence in the form of a crude carving that man had established a ritualistic link with what was probably a goose. The goose-herd survives as an important element in the rural economy of the Balkans today.

The ancient Greeks and Egyptians had domesticated grey-lag geese, and according to the *Odyssey*, Penelope owned twenty. Aesop's fable of the goose laying golden eggs symbolises the wealth enjoyed by these early farmers, by their counterparts the swan-owners of medieval England and the present-day turkey farmers. Furthermore, just as the modern broiler or battery industry is concerned with the most efficient conversion of vegetable food into protein, a fifth dynasty relief depicts captive geese being forcibly stuffed with food – perhaps these Egyptians were already·enjoying pâté de foie gras. In Britain, domestic fowl were doubtless kept before the arrival of the Romans, but little information exists until 1578 when Bishop Leslie describes how the birds were caught in nets when moulting, to be pinioned and tamed; at this time the grey-lag was a common breeder in the English fens.

Evidence of the domestication of rock doves goes back to 4500 BC in ancient Iraq, and it is possible that neolithic man had learned how to breed the species in captivity. Early inhabitants of Britain farmed the doo-caves, erecting extra ledges to facilitate the collection of the young, which were then used immediately or reared for breeding. The Norman lords had their dove-cotes, and the practice flourished in rural communities. Domestic fowl, which were probably kept in India as early as 3200 BC, were also associated with religious and sacrificial functions. The evolution of both the rock dove and fowl (and as will be mentioned below the house sparrow too) likely occurred in close association with the emergence of man, making them in a sense pre-adapted to domestication. Indeed, it is conceivable that these species would not have evolved in the absence of man the pastoralist. Recent studies by Collias and Saichuae of the jungle fowl *Gallus gallus*, the ancestor of the domestic fowl, in Thailand and Malaya, show that it depends on the man-altered habitat produced as a consequence of the cut, slash and burn type of shifting native husbandry. The bird thrives in the secondary scrub eventually produced when man moves elsewhere, and it seems to be poorly adapted to virgin forest. Furthermore, the behavioural patterns of these jungle fowl are virtually identical with those exhibited by domestic strains so that years of selective breeding have achieved relatively little modification in the species-characteristic behaviour.

A painting on the tomb of Haremhab at Thebes in the days of Thothmes IV (1420–11 BC) shows how men kept pelicans in enclosures and collected their eggs for food. Iron Age Glastonbury was less sophisticated, although pelicans and various other birds were caught and eaten by the local inhabitants. We have no idea why the pelican (Dalmatian Pelican) became extinct in Britain between then and the Dark Ages, and if we blame hunting man we have to explain why another great delicacy – the crane – managed to survive until about 1590. Bearing in mind the considerable changes in bird distribution which resulted from the improvement in climate from the late nineteenth century to about 1950, we may hazard a guess that climatic fluctuations also caused important faunal changes in these early years. Pelicans were still nesting in western Europe in the estuaries of the Scheldt, Rhine and Elbe in Pliny's time. The Dalmatian Pelican belongs to a group of birds which formerly lived on the edge of the Sarmatic inland sea which in Pleistocene times covered much of central Europe, and most of the typical members of this fauna are now relic species, (marbled duck, red-crested pochard, Mediterranean black-headed gull). The doom of these species could well have resulted mainly from the increasing desiccation which followed the wet Atlantic period; although there have been many ups and downs since, the process continues and the remaining strongholds of these birds are vanishing, as the lakes of the Asiatic steppes dry up.

One of these climatic fluctuations led, around 500 BC, to a much wetter period and probably gave an indirect boost to agriculture: Trow-Smith suggests that the resultant growth of scrub on the lighter cultivated soils forced the Celtic immigrants of the late Bronze Age to attend to the heavier lands, and stimulated the invention of the first early plough, the *aratrum*. Thus the irregular plots of neolithic farmers were replaced by straight furrows and the rectangular Celtic fields. Later, Belgic immigrants in about 75 BC brought the heavy plough *caruca* which resulted in the long Belgic strip cultivation, the precursor of the medieval system, and opened up land too in-

tractable for the prehistoric plough. The Roman occupation extended the scope of agriculture but did little to improve techniques
and it seems unlikely that these peoples did much to affect significantly our forest wild life. The population at this time was probably
around a quarter million and very much concentrated in south-east
England and East Anglia. The Romans, however, with their dykes
and causeways did start the settlement of the Lincolnshire and
Cambridgeshire fens. Land development was hindered by the arrival
of the Anglo-Saxons, although they continued the drainage of
marshes and used them as sheep pasturage. The process was in full
swing between 1150 and 1300 and eventually led to the loss of the
larger fenland species. The crane disappeared in about 1590, though
the spoonbill hung on until 1667 on the Orwell at Trimley, Suffolk.
Those other wetland birds, the bittern, Savi's warbler and black tern,
remained until the early nineteenth century (they have now returned
following intensive conservation efforts).

The Anglo-Saxons and their medieval descendants were free to
catch what birds they liked for food and their main problem was the
best means to adopt. Some idea of these methods can be gleaned
from the *Colloquy of Ælfric*, a tenth-century educational dialogue
between master and pupil quoted by Gurney.

Magister: What say you, Auceps? How do you beguile birds?

Auceps: I beguile birds in many ways; sometimes with nets, sometimes with snares, sometimes with bird lime, sometimes with a call,
sometimes with a bow, sometimes with a decoy.

With William the Conqueror came many of the inconsistencies
which still dictate the relationships between birds and men. William
introduced the special hunting forests where only the privileged
could take the better game animals, and the harsh, unjust forest laws
to enforce his ideals, foreshadowing the Game Act of 1831. With
William we see the beginnings of those illogical attitudes which
defined sport as the prerogative of gentlemen, as distinct from such
plebeian pursuits as shooting sitting birds, which though much more
humane, were associated with the illicit movements of the poacher
or serf. Sport in Norman days included hawking, first introduced to
England about AD 860, stag-hunting, hare-hunting and greyhound
coursing; and the idea developed of game as animals worth eating
and thus to be preserved. Deprived of hunting rights, the husband-
man had to find other means for amusement, and cock-fighting
provided one outlet. In ages when petty pilfering carried the death

penalty and the sanctity of human life counted for little, this must have seemed an innocuous enough sport. Sir Gervase Markham (1638) gives a good account of cocking: 'then you shall take his wings and spreading them forth by the length of the first feather of his rising wing clip the rest slipe wise with sharp points, that in his rising he may therewith endanger the eye of his adversary: then with a sharp knife you shall scape smooth and sharpen his spures.' Cock tournaments did not become illegal until 1849, and even today occasional legal proceedings are reported against some mains in north east England. Quite apart from the appeal of betting, cock fighting attracted a big following of people roused by sado-masochistic impulses – just as today many watch wrestling and boxing matches who can hardly be all that interested in the arts of self defence. Even at the beginning of the nineteenth century, fashionable ladies could foregather at Hurlingham to watch the gentlemen shoot pigeons released from cages; today trap shooting is harmless because clay discs replace a bewildered bird.

Inevitably there was pressure to find alternative meat supplies, to supplement the vagaries of hunting and to guarantee winter meat, and domesticated and semi-tame birds helped satisfy this need. But from William's time a host of rules and regulations restricted the number of persons able to enjoy such privileges. Richard II passed a statute forbidding artificers, labourers and persons not having lands of the value of 40s. a year from keeping greyhounds, or using ferrets for taking deer, hares or conies and other gentlemen's game. Edward IV enacted that, except for the sons of the King, only freeholders of land above a certain value could mark swans; swans on land below this value could be seized for the King.

Most north temperate birds have their breeding season proximately controlled by seasonal changes in daylength, and the deposition of post-nuptial migratory fat and other physiological events also have a photoperiodic basis. This was discovered empirically long ago and led to the practice of mewing – putting birds in the mews usually reserved for hawks, and then subjecting them to artificial light regimes. By being given extra light, muiten birds in Holland could be brought into breeding condition and made to sing in autumn, thereby serving as excellent decoys for the bird catchers trying to attract passing migrants. In Britain, the earlier process of keeping birds in the dark to fatten them was known, and to save on mew space it proved quicker simply to sew up the eyes of cranes and swans: the modern poultry farmer is doing nothing new in principle in regulating the light regime for his battery hens.

The Japanese and Chinese had learned in the fifth century AD that cormorants could be trained to catch fish for their masters – a fascinating use for which these birds are still employed in the East. Knowledge of the practice reached Europe and James I and Charles I both employed a Master of the Cormorants, who, at the royal bidding, travelled widely to display the skill of his charges.

Stone Age man had doubtless learned to take advantage of birds that had regular and predictable habits which made them easier to catch. The flightless condition assumed by wildfowl after breeding must early have attracted attention. Suitable ponds were being turned into decoys by the reign of King John (1199–1266) and were equipped with netted pipes into which the birds were driven, especially flappers in July. The more sophisticated Dutch technique, whereby dogs were employed to appear from behind a series of screens to arouse the curiosity of the ducks and so entice them up the pipes, was not introduced to Britain until the sixteenth century.

It was soon realised that certain dogs were more effective than others; those most resembling a fox in colour and shape seemed particularly useful, presumably because ducks have evolved responses to stimuli originating from natural predators because these have biological significance. The last commercial duck decoy at Nacton in Suffolk has only just ceased operating for profit and has been acquired by the Wildfowl Trust as a centre for the ringing and scientific study of wild duck. The regular migration of wood-pigeons through the valleys of the Pyrenees has enabled the development of a local trapping enterprise by the Basque bird catchers. Long nets are strung across the valleys into which the pigeons are decoyed by men stationed in towers sited along the valleys. These men throw white bats resembling table tennis rackets under the passing flocks, and the white flash stimulates a following response in the birds, causing them to fly lower and lower and finally into the nets.

The role of birds in culture up until Norman times followed a primitive urge to increase the fertility and ease of capture of prey, and was based to a large extent on superstition, fable and omen; the drumming of woodpeckers caused them to be accredited with rain-making abilities and black-coloured birds were associated with the devil. The Norman love of jousting and tournament combined with twelfth- and thirteenth-century religious influences to produce the heyday of heraldry – an extension of mystical symbolism, both in a military form with such subjects as the eagle and owl, and with the Christian dove and pelican. Bird art in Britain was also much in the hands of the ecclesiastics, and as Tudor points out, certain birds still featured mostly in religious symbolism, as they had in ancient Egyptian civilisations: the hawk was the emblem of Horus, the Sacred Ibis that of Throth, and they were much used for decorating illuminated manuscripts, psalters and breviaries. Between the Middle Ages and the late Baroque, and particularly in the Florentine schools of art, small birds occur as accessory symbols in hundreds of devotional paintings, over three-quarters being goldfinches. Gold wings and the bird's association with thistles (crown of thorns) made it a symbol of the resurrection and of the soul, but it has also featured as an augur of disease, particularly plague. Friedmann, who tells us this, notes that in nearly all cases the artist has depicted a docile bird; only Michelangelo (in a marble relief now in Burlington House) showed it in a realistic, albeit symbolic attitude fluttering and scaring the infant Christ. The freer use of birds in art came with the Renaissance – but that is outside the scope of this book. Readers interested in the role of birds in music, painting and literature are recommended to read the excellent pen picture provided by Fisher (1966) or specialist works, a few of which are mentioned in the bibliography.

Our knowledge of ornithology in the fourteenth and fifteenth centuries remains extremely scanty, though it is unlikely that man was doing much harm to wild life, especially after the ravages of the plague had reduced the population by nearly half. In 1348, when the Black Death started, the priors of the Monastery of Durham were finding rooks and crows sufficiently numerous on their manors to require thinning and they were enjoying young rooks in season. James I later passed an Act in Scotland in 1424 requiring them to be kept in check. Under-population and under-privilege for most country dwellers, and the decline of the monasteries and their dissolution were associated with agricultural stagnation; in 1500 there were about three sheep to each one of 2½–3 million people. Yet in the mid-sixteenth century emerged the farmers of foresight, who set the pattern of agriculture for years to come. Sir A. Fitzherbert's *Book of Husbandry* published in 1534 shows that his knowledge of land drainage and preparation, and of the culture of corn, could set

him on a par with the modern barley barons. Both he and Thomas
Tusser were among the earliest advocates of enclosure, both emphasising the wastefulness of the old open field system which prevented
the development of winter corn growing. Tusser (1573) writes:

> The flocks of the lords of the soil,
> Do yearly the winter corn wrong,
> The same in a manner they spoil,
> With feeding so low and so long
> And therefore that champion field,
> Doth seldom good winter corn yield.

It may be that this early enclosure was creating the right conditions
for the proliferation of the corvids. Henry VIII passed an Act which
having specifically stated that choughs (jackdaws), crows and rooks
had increased and were injuring corn, directed that all persons
possessing land were to destroy them. Parishes of at least ten house-
holds had to provide nets and facilities for catching the adults and
meet annually to agree how best to destroy all the young. Much of
the content of this Act was revived in another passed by Elizabeth I,
in which provision was made for destroying 'noyfull fowls and
vermin', including the corvids, buzzard, kite, osprey, harrier, woodpecker, kingfisher, shag, cormorant, bullfinch; and authority was
given to the churchwardens to pay a bonus for destruction of these
birds, ranging from one to four pence. The money came from taxing
the landowners. Henry, or his advisers, clearly had the wits to realise
that bonus schemes can be abused, because it was expressly forbidden
to make payment for these birds if taken in any park, warren or
ground employed for the maintenance of any game of conies, or for
any 'stares' taken in dove-houses or kites and ravens killed in and
around towns; but we do not know how these rules were enforced.
A Government subsidy of one shilling and later two shillings was
being paid on the tails of grey squirrels until stopped in 1958, and
there were those enlightened gentlemen who trapped the animals,
cut off their tails and released the creatures in hope that the progeny
would provide further remuneration.

The era of the country house dawned in the sixteenth century
and ornamental estates and parks blossomed in the seventeenth, and
it became increasingly fashionable to keep ornamental birds. Avi-
culture was not new, the Romans having long before indulged their
love of keeping exotic animals in captivity, one result being the

introduction of the pheasant *Phasianus colchicus* to Britain. Increasing travel and interest in science led in turn to more attention being paid to wild life. Charles II had his pelicans and other birds in St. James's Park, and the climate of opinion in which he founded the Royal Society was appropriate to experimental science, and led to the introduction of various exotic plants and animals, including the red-legged partridge (unsuccessful introduction attempted in 1673) and Canada goose. The rise of the squirearchy was also marked by the appearance of various game laws in the Restoration period, forcing the farmers and yeomen to make unpopular sacrifices in order that the squire could shoot, just as the King by means of the forest laws had supplanted all classes in preceding ages. The cross-bow, firing metal bolts, had been the important weapon until this time; but now the shot-gun replaced hawking as the gentleman's means of relaxation. It became more common during Charles II's reign, though not without much controversy, to shoot pheasants in flight instead of simply stalking perched birds or walking them up with dogs. Birds were caught for food with cross-bow, lime, snares, traps and nets, and nets were even used in sport. With the development of the shot-gun, it was gradually agreed that only certain species should be recognised as suitable for sport and be classified as game, and grouse and black cock were allotted to this category. The breech loading gun brought more controversy, just as double-barrelled guns and American repeaters were to do later, but it meant that birds could be driven over the guns and grouse shooting could emerge in about 1855, ensuring that from then on the nation's parliamentary business finished in time for the glorious 12th August. Actually in 1915, a bill was passed in the Lords authorising the shooting of grouse on 5th August, so that those for whom the war gave less spare time could be ensured their full share of enjoyment. It is to the credit of the Commons that they rejected the bill, amidst shouts of 'we want to shoot Germans not grouse'. So much have the priorities of men and birds become confused.

The arbitrary rules which grew up in connection with shooting are of interest and importance because they still govern much of our present-day approach to pest control. I have a good friend with a life-time's experience of both country sporting traditions and of pest control who was appalled at the suggestion that pigeons should be shot when sitting on their nests. He preferred to flush the bird first before shooting, in order to give it a sporting chance, despite the fact that my suggestion would give much greater prospects of a quick and humane kill. Game preservation and shooting have brought out some of man's worst attitudes to wild life. In the early days of the big country estates, poachers and gamekeepers were often engaged in open warfare; if hideous traps could be set for vermin it presumably seemed logical for man-traps to be set for poachers. Those days left a legacy of slyness, suspicion and conservatism which has been slow to disappear. The nineteenth century witnessed the worst excesses, with the ruthless slaughter of any predatory bird or mammal, and nothing was allowed to stand in the way of prodigious bags. William Cobbett in *Rural Rides* (1830) was contemptuous of these so-called sportsmen – especially those who claimed big bags. 'A professed shot is almost always a disagreeable brother sportsman. He must have in the first place a head rather of the emptiest to pride himself upon so poor a talent.' In 1903 the *Game Rearers Annual* stated: 'The hooded crows are most difficult to destroy and unless poison is used (which, by the way, is illegal) they cannot be successfully coped with. Where poison is used it is generally placed in the eyes of a dead sheep, which usually provides a fatal lure to the hoodies.' So much for the early Bird Protection Laws. Even today it is proving a slow uphill struggle to educate the more recalcitrant gamekeepers into accepting that such actions do not automatically improve game prospects, but there has been much progress.

Increasing demands for shooting at first led to the augmentation of pheasant stocks by hand rearing, a technique which has grown enormously in the last fifty years owing to a break up of large estates, and to the formation of shooting syndicates and the attraction of city business men, helped by improvements in transport and more leisure. This in turn has led to the scientific study of game-birds and the elevation of game biology to a highly respected place in the wider field of wild life conservation and management, and was heralded by the grouse inquiry (Lovat 1911) already mentioned in the preface. Following the growth of ecology, the Imperial Chemical Industries, Game Research Station (later Eley Game Advisory Station) was formed in 1933. Its ultimate aim was of course to improve prospects for selling cartridges, but under the direction of A. D. Middleton (himself a vital force in the growth of ecology at Oxford) it has set the standards for field ecology in a much wider sense, and made possible the formation of the progressive Game Research Association in 1960, which has subsequently become the

Game Conservancy since 1969. In the meantime, the study of grouse was recommenced when the Nature Conservancy inaugurated its Unit of Grouse and Moorland Ecology in 1959 at Aberdeen University. One hopes that the study and amenity of game will become even more integrated within the broader concepts of wild life management in Britain.

But we have moved on too far in time if we are to appreciate what man has done to the land as a habitat for birds. The rate of tree felling increased as the Tudor squires enclosed waste, common and woods, a process that accelerated after 1660 when the Government relinquished its opposition to private agreements negotiated by the landlords. All the same the pattern of the countryside as we see it to-day had only emerged in south-east England. Even by the eighteenth century there was abundant wilderness, about a quarter of the country being heath and moor, and much of the remainder was medieval with open fields of meadow and arable land adjoining gorse-covered common pasture; by 1760 less than a quarter million acres had been enclosed. One can picture the goose-girl tending her flock idly watching the goldfinches on thistle clumps or stonechats singing from some furze. Bustards were still stalking the chalk wolds of eastern England, white-tailed eagles were nesting on the Isle of Wight.

The big rural transformation came between 1750 and the General Enclosure Act of 1845, most of the open fields going in the sixty years of Farmer George III. Most of the earlier enclosures had been of common, waste and woodland, expensive to achieve but less disturbing for the community in that the old peasant system could still be based on self-sufficiency. The enclosures of the eighteenth and nineteenth centuries were based on economic necessity and were a national policy that brought much suffering and ill-will. In less than a century, they transformed peasant England into modern England. There were many protagonists. Pioneers of modern farming like Arthur Young, who did much to disseminate the latest results of experiments and supported all the agencies like farmers' clubs, ploughing matches and sparrow clubs which helped to diffuse ideas, claimed that enclosure brought more employment in fence mending and turnip husbandry, even though sheep were lost. Young was enthusiastic but he was inflexible and lacked judgement and others were less enchanted:

> The fault is great in man or woman,
> Who steals a goose from off a common,
> But what can plead that man's excuse,
> Who steals a common from a goose.
>
> (The Tickler Magazine, 1 February 1821.)

John Clare in 'The Village Minstrel' sums up some of the changes that must have grieved the ornithologist:

> There once were days, the woodman knows it well,
> Where shades e'en echoed with the singing thrush;
> There once were hours, the ploughman's tale can tell,
> When morning's beauty wore its earliest blush,
> How woodlarks carol'd from each stumpy bush;
> Lubin himself has mark'd the soar and sing:
> The thorns are gone, the wood-lark's song is hush'd,
> Spring more resembles winter now than spring,
> The shades are banish'd all – the birds have too to wing.

The population of England and Wales slowly increased from about 4 million in 1603 to 5½ million in 1714, held in check by a high death-rate. The explosion occurred with the Industrial Revolution, from 9 million in 1801 to 18 million in 1851. For a while the rate of increase was held down by a high urban mortality, through epidemics of cholera and other diseases of overcrowding. Improved hygiene in the latter half of the nineteenth century removed this check and the rate of natural increase was only halted in the 1920s (it fell from 10.4 in 1921 to 3.9 in 1931) as a direct consequence of contraception but by now there were 40 million people in England and Wales, reaching 52 million in 1959.

These demographic statistics serve two functions here. They illustrate for the human population some of the principles to be discussed in the next chapter in relation to birds. In particular, although the birth-rate was high in the seventeenth century (as it was earlier) the population was relatively stable due to a high reciprocal death-rate. Population size increased in response to improved environmental resources during the Industrial and Agrarian Revolutions. The data also emphasise the pressures that man had come to inflict on the land and, by inference, on its wild life. In the nineteenth century, bustard, bittern, avocet, ruff, black tern and roseate tern vanished, and large birds of prey like the goshawk became rare. Loss or fragmentation of their habitat was not the sole reason because some have since returned, and man's greed must be blamed to a large extent: there were those to whom the rarity of a bird made its capture imperative.

Those people living near large colonies of nesting birds have for long been able to harvest them for food. Fisher and Peterson have related how ancient sea-fowling communities in Greenland, Iceland, the Faroes and St Kilda had evolved a rational level of exploitation of the seabird colonies of gannets, fulmars and auks, ensuring that sufficient eggs or young birds were left to prevent declines in the future harvest. By trial and error they have found that about half the auks' eggs can be collected, as these species lay repeats, but fulmars do not and are better left alone to hatch their young. In a valuable review dealing with the exploitation of the eggs of wild birds throughout the world, Cott has emphasised how the factors governing the utilisation of wild birds' eggs are accessibility, palatability and availability. The first two are rarely limiting, but the size and concentration of the potential crop is important. Cott found that with the exception of the eggs of certain boobies, cormorants and pelicans, which are rank and fishy to a cultivated palate, there is a broad correlation between palatability, size and colonial grouping. For reasons which will become clear in Chapter 2, most adult birds and their eggs can withstand considerable cropping without the replacement potential being adversely affected, and, as with all wild food resources, the object is to achieve the highest annual cropping rate without detriment to the maintenance of a sustained yield. In the late nineteenth century this level was exceeded in species after species, with the same thoughtless greed with which the Victorians exploited other natural resources and the colonies. In 1884, 130,000 guillemot eggs were collected from Bempton (at the time, tons of eggs were sent to Leeds where the albumen was used in the manufacture of patent leather); in 1840, 44,000 black-headed gull eggs were taken from Scoulton Mere, and 89,600 puffin's eggs were taken from St Kilda in 1876.

The adornment of their ladies with feathers was another excuse for slaughtering wild birds. Quite apart from a scandalous trade in ostrich and egret plumes, a host of seabirds were massacred within the British Isles. Kittiwake wings were in demand for the millinery trade and a large industry existed at Clovelly in Devon and elsewhere; 9,000 are supposed to have been killed on Lundy in one fortnight. Coulson (1963) gives many other examples and relates how the species was also shot for sport and food, resulting in a decline from which it did not recover until the early decades of the twentieth century.

It is against the background of serious over-exploitation that the increase of a very wide range of seabirds in the twentieth century must be viewed and several examples will appear in later chapters – the great crested grebe (page 44), kittiwake (page 238), oyster-catcher (page 244). The eider perhaps should also be mentioned. One hundred years ago it was confined to the islands on the west coast of Scotland, and at one mainland site in East Lothian and in the Farne Islands. From this very restricted range it had spread to a wider range in coastal Scotland and to the Shetland and Orkney Islands by about 1890, and it became common by 1922. The bird has always been subject to intensive cropping both for its eggs and its down. While its down could be collected from the nest after the eggs have hatched, in the majority of cases the eggs and down have been lifted together, repeat layings often being harvested as well. On the Farne Islands the eider has always received a measure of protection owing to its association with St Cuthbert, but as long ago as 1397 the Bursar's roll of the Monastery of Durham, which contained the Shrine of Cuthbert, mentions the use of eider-down for stuffing and cushions. Several colonies in Scotland and the Farne Islands were reduced during the 1939–45 war when the birds were collected for food, but these have recovered. In addition, Tavener has documented a marked post-war rise in numbers of non-breeders round the British coast, associated with an increase in the Dutch population, and also increases in other parts of Europe and North America, all apparently resulting from protection. There has, however, been little southward extension of the bird's breeding range in Britain in the past 20 years. More recent studies by Dr H. Milne on the Sands of Forvie Nature Reserve, Aberdeenshire, showed that local numbers increased from about 3,000 birds in 1961–3 to around 5,000 during 1964–7 and that most of this increase resulted from a particularly good breeding season in 1963. Thus home-production rather than immigration apparently accounts for eider increases in Britain at least.

The excesses of the late nineteenth century roused the passions of a few men, and probably more women of suffragette spirit, and their campaigning led to the first Seabirds Preservation Act of 1869, hopelessly inadequate in its conception but a step in the right direction, to be followed by the Protection Acts of 1880–96. This same climate of moral indignation also led to the formation of the Society (later Royal Society) for the Protection of Birds in 1891. The Society went from strength to strength in the vanguard of the more enlightened attitude to birds characteristic of the start of the present century, doing immense good for ornithology, albeit sometimes for the wrong reasons. Today, the R.S.P.B. stands in the forefront of a scientific and imaginative approach to bird conservation.

With the outbreak of the First World War a new and widespread appreciation of birds was apparent. Birds were still used, but in an atmosphere of greater affection and regard. Canaries are about fifteen times more sensitive to poisonous gases than man, and they were accordingly kept in cages in the trenches to give advance warning of a gas attack, just as coal miners had used them in the mines. Soldiers enjoyed their companionship, and singing birds also were extensively used in ambulance trains. As pigeons had relayed the conquest of Gaul to Rome and had brought the first news of Napoleon's defeat at Waterloo to England, so they were put to extensive use in the war, old converted London buses being used as mobile pigeon lofts. In the Second World War, pigeons were again used extensively; for example, the underground movement in France employed them to send back messages to England. German gunners tried to shoot these birds down as they crossed the Brittany cliffs, and in Britain the authorities attempted to exterminate our south coast peregrines, for fear that they too might be successful in intercepting some vital message. The following appeared in *The Times* on 19 August, 1943:

A pigeon, released by a bomber crew from their rubber dinghy, has recently been responsible for their rescue in the Mediterranean. ... Realizing that something had gone wrong when there was no response to their first S.O.S., they had released their carrier pigeon from its container. As soon as the message it carried had been deciphered, an air-sea rescue launch put out, and the airmen were safely rescued.

In contrast with a report for 26 September, 1969:

'In what was called "the craziest strike of all", 44 men went on strike for half a day at the giant pressed steel Fisher Body plant in Swindon because of low-flying pigeons. The dispute was the latest of a series of labour stoppages which is costing Britain's car industry the loss of millions of pounds in exports. The workers who walked out were those who were caught in the crossfire of the "feeders", men who have been scattering bread crumbs and other bits of food to encourage the pigeons, and the "whangers", other workers who have been throwing nuts and bolts and other missiles to scare the birds away. "We were fed up with either being hit by nuts and bolts aimed by the whangers, or strafed by the pigeons diving for food," a press operator said. Meanwhile, a works management committee has asked the "whangers" to stop throwing missiles and the "feeders" to eat their sandwiches themselves.'

Some of the major developments in the relationships between men and birds since these years have been very briefly mentioned in the preface, but much more could be added for which there is no space. It would be pertinent to follow the growth of pet-keeping and other manifestations of an increasing public interest in living things. Similarly, we might examine the post-war boom in bird watching and the significance of such discoveries as the number of rare birds visiting sewage farms; the stampede to such sites was like an ornithological 'gold rush' once the initial discoveries at Nottingham were disclosed (Staton 1943). Has this widespread interest in wild life come too late?

The main hazards to birds today arise from the increasing pollution of the environment with the waste resulting from the sheer numbers of man; ironically man has become an indirect threat to the survival of wild life just when he seems to have learned to appreciate it. Mellanby has recently dealt with the pollution problem so admirably that I shall not attempt more than a passing reference here. But this should not detract from the severity of problems about which new facts emerge almost daily. For instance, we are still treading extremely cautiously so far as certain persistent agricultural chemicals are concerned. When the threat to wild life from organochlorine insecticides became really apparent in 1960–1, there was all manner of special pleading; agriculturalists claimed that food production must be the over-riding concern, manufacturers of chemicals naturally enough belittled the hazards to birds, bird protectionists made exaggerated claims, and Rachel Carson did the public at large a service with her deliberately biased book. In the years that have followed the initial hysteria, good sense has prevailed. Research has got under way and is producing facts where before there was only conjecture. When bird watchers first pointed out that birds of prey were breaking and eating their eggs and that this seemed to be associated with the decline in numbers associated with toxic chemicals, their suggestion was greeted with scepticism

by many people. Now, a careful study by Ratcliffe has suggested
some answers, for he has demonstrated that there has been a decline
in egg-shell thickness in the peregrine, sparrowhawk and golden
eagle since about 1950, and this explains why eggs are broken more
readily and are subsequently eaten by the parent birds. Thus, of
109 peregrine eyries examined between 1904–50 there were only
three instances of egg breakage, compared with 47 in 168 eyries
observed between 1951–66. Egg-breakage, decrease in egg-shell
weight, status of the breeding population and exposure to persistent
pesticides are correlated, and it would be unreasonable to suppose
that there is no causal connection, even if the exact factors and
mechanisms involved remain to be elucidated. Calcium metabolism
in birds is controlled by oestrogen and parathyroid hormone, and
there is evidence that pp D.D.T. will interfere with oestrogen-based
mechanisms in the Bengalese finch (Jefferies 1967).

Pollution of the environment by persistent, poisonous chemicals,
is the most obvious problem, firstly because small residues can be
accumulated in food chains, to give lethal dosages to the top predators, and secondly because they may produce unsuspected side-
effects. But pollution by detergents, oil, smoke and other waste
from man also present grave problems. Oil spillage at sea, either
accidental or resulting from the purposeful jettisoning, is a serious
hazard to seabirds against which the International Committee for
Bird Preservation and other bodies have long campaigned, to a large
extent successfully in the sense that the problem is recognised inter-
nationally. Bourne (1968), in a valuable review of the subject,
mentions that as long ago as 1907 the largest seven-masted schooner
built, the *Thomas W. Lawson*, was wrecked on the Isles of Scilly on
her maiden voyage. The release of her entire cargo of 'two million
gallons' of crude oil caused a vast slaughter of local seabirds, particularly puffins. In those days Annet is supposed to have supported
about 100,000 puffins, whereas to-day only about 100 remain. All
the colonies in the Western Approaches have been similarly reduced
(as Parslow 1967 has shown) and it seems likely that oil pollution
has been a major cause.

The loss at sea of oil-carrying vessels during the 1914–18 war
resulted in a large increase in the numbers of oiled seabirds. This
led the Royal Society for the Protection of Birds to publish figures in
1921 which played a large part in the introduction of the 'Oil in
Navigable Waters Act' soon after. In the Second World War most

tankers carried petroleum spirits, and the destruction of shipping presented less hazard. But this situation has changed as the needs of a modern industrialised world have led to an enormous expansion in oil traffic at sea; nowadays crude oil is carried to refinement plants near the destination in giant tankers. Constant pollution arises from ships washing-out at sea after a voyage and purposely releasing oil, while occasional accidents can have widescale repercussions. Thus, during the night of 18 September, 1966, the German tanker *Seestern* allowed 1,700 tons of crude diesel oil to escape into the Medway Estuary on a flood tide, polluting 8,000 acres of saltings. Probably about 5,000 birds died immediately. Certainly, 936 black-headed gulls, 927 great black-backed gulls, 184 dunlin, 165 herring gulls, 135 redshank, 98 common gulls, 90 oystercatchers, 65 curlew and various other birds (including an American pectoral sandpiper) were picked up. In this case the number of birds using the area had declined, by 20–100% depending on the species, in the following winter, but has since recovered so possibly no permanent damage has been done, yet for years an area could be denuded of suitable plant and animal food for birds and other wildlife. Only a small oil slick of about 87 tons hit the Tay estuary, the most important wintering ground for eiders, in March 1968. Fortunately, most of the birds had left, but between 7–26% of the national eider population was wiped out: the happy state of affairs pertaining to eiders and described above could soon be reversed. These modern incidents compare with R.S.P.B. estimates made for the 1940s and 50s that between 50,000–250,000 birds were being killed per year in home waters.

On 18 March, 1967, the *Torrey Canyon* ran on to the Seven Stones Reef and in all about 60,000 tons of crude oil were lost into the sea. At least 10,000 birds were collected, and many more must have died unbeknown, of which 9 out of 10 were guillemots. In the aftermath we now know (see special review by Bourne 1970, and Parslow 1967) that guillemots at some breeding colonies in Scilly and the north Cornish coast have been considerably reduced; in Cornwall, but not Scilly, fewer shags and herring gulls were breeding in 1966; kittiwake numbers at a colony within the worst polluted area were reduced in 1966. Only a few razorbills and apparently no puffins suffered in Britain, though these last are difficult to census. This was not the case in the Sept Iles in Britanny, the most important seabird colony in France, where careful protection had allowed a recovery in seabird numbers following the persecutions of the last century.

While aerial species such as the gannet had escaped damage, such divers as the shag had suffered markedly and the auks very severely: counts before and after the incident show that the number of pairs of guillemots fell from 270 to 50, of razorbills from 450 to 50, and of puffins from 2,500 to 400. This is the first incident where really detailed knowledge has been available, making a fairly comprehensive ecological survey possible so that wildlife interests are given more than passing regard. The public has been aroused at the prospects of ruined beaches and the 'overriding concern of the Government throughout has been to preserve the coasts from oil pollution and to adopt a course most likely to achieve this end'. Unfortunately the enormous quantities of detergents used for this purpose have done vastly more immediate and probably long-term harm to intertidal organisms than the oil itself. Whatever the pros and cons of the whole sad story, it illustrates the dilemma man finds himself in today. In some fields his technology has progressed far too quickly, while in others it has lagged, so that when accidents occur he is too often forced to resort to ill-conceived panic measures. Since this book has been in press there has been another major wreck of auks, this time in the Irish Sea in August 1969. At first attributed to gales, it seems that many birds came ashore under conditions of not particularly unfavourable weather. Analyses show the bodies to contain high levels of polychlorinated biphenyls, agents used in the paints and plastics industry. This new chemical hazard, unrealised when Mellanby prepared his book, highlights the complexity of the interaction of man and wildlife and the need for drastic measures if man is to avoid becoming the ultimate victim of this extensive environmental pollution, which wildlife is indicating.

CHAPTER 2

ECOLOGICAL CONSIDERATIONS

A THOROUGH insight into the relationships between birds and humans demands some understanding of population ecology, a knowledge of how animal numbers fluctuate and change through births and deaths and of the factors which determine these processes. Populations have dynamic properties and these cannot be neglected by people concerned with wild life management, whether as game preservers, conservationists, pest controllers or farmers. This chapter attempts to set out some of the basic principles with pertinent examples, but these same principles will emerge in later sections in various guises. Our knowledge of the subject was first collated and clearly enumerated by Dr D. Lack (1954) in a stimulating book *The Natural Regulation of Animal Numbers* since when more field studies have been made by various workers, which Lack (1966) has summarised in his *Population Studies of Birds*. Both books should be consulted by the reader who is really interested in this subject. In this account I have drawn on examples which, wherever possible, have direct relevance to economic ornithology.

Farmers tend to the pessimistic belief that all problem birds become more abundant every year. Yet careful counts of most such species living in stable environments usually show there to be no clear tendency towards a steady increase, or even decrease, though numbers may fluctuate from year to year. For instance, many farmers believe that the wood-pigeon has increased drastically during this century to become more of a pest, though in conditions of stable agriculture this is unlikely to be true. In fact, there is evidence of a decline since the early 1960s associated with a reduction in the acreage of winter clover-leys and pastures. Certainly the species has moved into newly developed marginal land; places like the east Suffolk heathlands, which have been ploughed and claimed for agriculture since the Second World War, have been colonised by wood-pigeons. Fig. 1 gives some indication of how wood-pigeon numbers have varied on a Scottish estate near Dundee since 1887, and it is evident that fluctuations have occurred within narrow

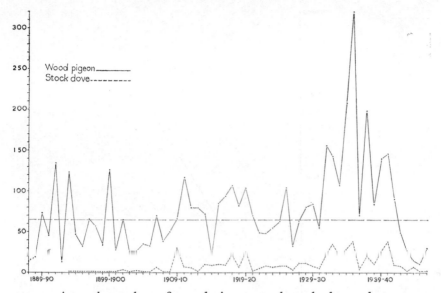

FIG. 1. Annual number of wood-pigeons and stock doves shot on an estate near Dundee. The data refer to an area which remained virtually unchanged during the period under review, and nearly all the birds were shot by one man who maintained a reasonably constant shooting pressure. They, therefore, probably provide a fair index of the total population. The autumn of 1909 was a disastrous one for the harvest owing to gales and rain from August until October so that much corn remained uncut. This resulted in an influx of wood-pigeons and the appearance of stock doves in large numbers. (Data by courtesy of Dr J. Berry.)

limits, with no evidence at all for a sustained rise or fall. In contrast, Fig. 1 also shows how the closely related stock dove has increased over the same period; this species first colonised in Scotland in 1866, reached Fife in 1878 and increased dramatically in Scotland in the next ten years. Every year each pair of wood-pigeons rears on average just over two young and it is evident that if all these survived to breed in their turn, population size would increase exponentially. That this does not normally occur indicates that some form of regulatory mechanism must be operating. Furthermore, this regulation must be density-dependent, that is, it must become proportionately more effective at high population densities and proportionately less effective at low ones. If the regulatory factor(s) operated without regard

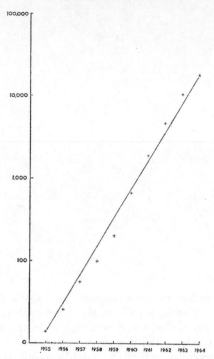

FIG. 2. Logarithmic increase of the collared dove in Britain. (Data from Hudson 1965).

to density, it is evident that population size could fluctuate widely without reference to a particular level – to the constant mean represented by the dotted line in the figure.

Sometimes bird numbers do in fact increase geometrically, as when a species moves into a previously untenanted region where there is scope for it to live; in biological terms where a vacant niche exists (see below). In this way the collared dove dispersed dramatically across Europe to reach Britain in 1952. It had spread to south-east Europe from northern India by the sixteenth century but had then remained static in its European outpost until 1930. It has subsequently spread north-west across Europe, reaching Jutland in 1950 and Britain in 1955; an expansion 1,000 miles across Europe in twenty-four years. Why this spread was so long delayed is not clear, though it is most feasible, as Mayr has suggested, that a genetical mutation occurred which suddenly rendered the species less restricted in its needs. (We can imagine a bird, though not necessarily the collared dove, to be restricted by a temperature tolerance which a single sudden genetic mutation could remedy.) Throughout Britain and Europe a vacant niche existed for a small dove living close to man; it is even possible that the decline in popularity of the dove-cote pigeon created this niche. Whatever the explanation, a high survival rate among collared doves has evidently been possible, and their potential capacity for geometric increase has been realised: see Fig. 2, which relates to Britain. The Syrian woodpecker may be on the brink of a similar explosion. It is considered to be a recently evolved species (post-glacial) which replaces the great spotted woodpecker in south-east Asia. It spread to Bulgaria to breed in 1890, to Hungary in 1949 and to Vienna in 1951. A significant feature of the bird's ecology in Europe is its confinement to cultivated areas which do not suit the great spotted woodpecker. If it proves to be better adapted to this man-made niche we can anticipate a continuing advance across Europe. Agricultural development in the Balkans may well bring other surprising range extensions.

Accepting* that populations are controlled in a density-dependent manner the next question to consider is the nature of these regulatory processes. Fundamentally, either the birth-rate or death-rate must be the factor of change. Wynne-Edwards and his supporters have argued that the reproductive rate is of much importance and that those animals with a high expectation of survival, such as many seabirds, have evolved low reproductive rates and *vice versa*. They have also claimed that a host of conventional behaviours have evolved as a means of regulating numbers. For instance, Wynne-Edwards regards the eating of eggs and young, practised by many raptors and also storks, as a device to limit their reproductive output; deferred maturity (gulls do not breed until three or four years old), territory formation, and various other behaviours are similarly regarded in this light. These views form part of his more general thesis that animal numbers in undisturbed habitats are at an optimum density and that maintaining this optimum has selective advantages. Special cases of this theme have

*There are a few authors who do not accept that density-dependent regulation is necessary nor that it frequently occurs. Andrewartha & Birch (1954) are such critics but I believe their arguments to be false and to have been sufficiently well dealt with by Lack (1966) to justify my not extending the scope of this book with detailed arguments.

attracted various supporters. E. M. Nicholson (1955) is one and he ascribes population control to density-dependent movements, rather than to mortality, while Lidiker (1962) goes further in seeing emigration as a mechanism enabling populations to have densities below the optimum carrying capacity of their habitat. Hence, Wynne-Edwards regards behaviours such as those listed above as homeostatic (self-regulatory) mechanisms, being induced by the population rather than by the environment.

Wynne-Edwards also drew parallels between bird and human populations, claiming that infanticide, taboos and other methods of reproductive restraint practised by so-called primitive societies were extensions of these same deep-rooted animal behaviours. In so doing he resuscitated some very early ideas of Carr-Saunders (published in 1922) which the well-known demographer did not subsequently repeat. Indeed, Mary Douglas, in criticising the idea of an optimum population, points out that there are many examples of human under-population. Considering certain primitive societies in detail, she makes it clear that they represent highly evolved and complex groups about which generalisations are meaningless. For instance, the Netsilik Eskimos live in a harsh environment where males suffer a very heavy mortality in hunting, and female infanticide is practised primarily to maintain an even sex balance. The Ndembu, a Lunda tribe in Zambia, grow cassava as their staple crop and live at a density of 3–5 people per square mile, whereas cassava could support a density of 18 people per square mile. The reason for the discrepancy is that the tribe passionately love hunting and move their villages to where game is available so that they never reach a stage where they are up against the ceiling imposed by their basic resources. As Douglas says: 'they live for the oysters and champagne of life not the bread and butter.' On the other hand, the Rendille are a tribe of camel herders in Kenya and live on the meat and milk of their sheep and camel herds. An optimum number of people is needed to maintain the camel herd, and when smallpox reduced man-power, stock had to be lost. In more normal conditions a balance of man-power is achieved by emigration, monogamy (herds are not divided but go only to the eldest son), while a measure of infanticide is practised (all boys born on Wednesdays).

In general terms, homeostatic population control in human groups depends on limited social advantages (the enjoyment of hunting by the Ndembu; education, motor cars and social prestige in western Europe) and not on any relationship to resources *per se*, as is the case with infra human species. Douglas could well be right in not attributing the increase in the Irish population between 1780–1840 to the adoption of potatoes as a staple diet, but rather to the ruination of Irish society by penal laws and English trade tariffs. Similarly she argues that the miseries of enclosures and the Poor Laws resulted in the population explosion which led to the Industrial Revolution, rather than that increased resources stimulated an increase in population. If true, this is quite different from the way in which animal populations are determined.

Animal populations cannot be directly compared even with the supposedly most primitive of human ones. Moreover, unequipped with any cultural tradition and means of communication, some special mechanism would have to be found to account for what amounts to altruistic behaviour. The Darwinian viewpoint is that if two animals (of the same or different species) are in competition, the one able to maintain the highest reproductive output must succeed at the expense of the other, all else being equal. This is the meaning of natural selection, which amounts to individual selection. What then would prevent the genes of parents which practise restraint from being at first swamped and then lost in competition with less socially inclined individuals? Wynne-Edwards surmounted this problem of explaining how individuals could acquire genes which cause them to behave in socially advantageous ways, sometimes at their own expense, by invoking the concept of group selection. In other words, in many situations survival of the group is more important than survival of the individual. Without entering into detail it must be said that the genetical basis for group selection is very restricted, and it can only be shown to be feasible in small isolated populations (birds do not satisfy the requirements of isolation as envisaged by geneticists) or in those, such as the social insects, where numerous genetically identical individuals are produced from one female, for which the term kin-selection is more appropriate. It seems to me that all the examples given by Wynne-Edwards can be answered (or will be when knowledge accumulates) more satisfactorily by individual selection and that to introduce group selection is unnecessary. This applies to two situations which I have studied closely – the peck order in birds and stress disease. I myself, therefore, reject the concept of an optimum population in this sense, together with the view that animals impose their own control over

population increase. I have discussed the subject at some length because it defines my approach to the subject of applied ornithology.
So far as reproduction is concerned I fully support Lack's thesis that
the reproductive rate has evolved as the highest possible; selective
disadvantages follow from the production of more or fewer young
than the optimum number. Disadvantages which accrue from over-
production include reduced survival chances for the offspring because they are undernourished, or impairment of the parents'
health; underproduction leads to a failure in intra-specific competition with more fecund individuals.

As most birds produce a large excess of young, the total post-
breeding population increases considerably, two-fold in the wood-
pigeon, up to six-fold in the great tit, but by less than half in the
fulmar. Various mortality factors, including disease, predation and
starvation, now remove surplus individuals so that a balance with
environmental resources is achieved, and a pattern of sharp fluctuations within each twelve-month period is superimposed on more
subtle changes in the breeding population from one year to another.
Lack has argued, and again I agree with his views, that the food
supply is usually, but not invariably, the most important factor
affecting these annual fluctuations *in birds*. While food could ultimately be the most important factor in all cases, other agencies, for
instance predators, may hold numbers below the level which would
be imposed by food shortage. The most important fact to appreciate
from the viewpoint of economic ornithology is that causes of death
are effective until the population is in balance with the environment,
and in the absence of one such factor another will take its place.
Conversely mortality factors are not usually additive – in the sense
that two together do not decrease numbers more than one alone.
The degree of stability seen in a population will, therefore, depend
primarily on that of the environment and not on any essential
characteristic of the population. By environment we not only mean
the food supply but include all the other components, biotic and
physical, which may interact to cause competition and mortality,
directly or indirectly.

Blank, Southwood and Cross have recently shown in a neat but
semi-mathematical way how the various causes of mortality contribute to the regulation of a partridge population on a Hampshire
estate which was studied from 1949–59. I shall illustrate less
elegantly certain aspects by using as an example another partridge

population living on a Norfolk estate, for which details of annual fluctuations in numbers have been given by Middleton and Huband (Table 1). Following breeding, numbers increase over tenfold but there immediately follows a period during which it is mostly the young which are lost, so that from a post-breeding average of nearly ten chicks to each adult the ratio falls to only 1.5 per adult by August, most of this chick loss occurring in the first few weeks of life. Jenkins (1961) had earlier claimed that this heavy loss of young, which is particularly heavy in cool, wet and windy summer weather, was the main variable determining the number of partridges later available for shooting. This was confirmed by Blank et al., who emphasised chick loss as the major contributor towards the total mortality occurring each year in partridges, and as the most important determinant of the September ratio of old to young. They found that about half of the variation in total mortality was due to fluctuations in chick loss, but that about half this chick mortality was unrelated to the size of the population at hatching. This means that the survival of chicks was partly responsible for *regulating* the autumn population (in the sense that autumn numbers were largely governed by how many young survived). However, because this survival was only partly determined by population size there was a margin of production which caused autumn numbers to fluctuate partly independently of population density. Thus 35% of the year-to-year fluctuation in the September population resulted from variations in chick mortality. In further studies Southwood and Cross were able to show that 94% of the variation in breeding success (they used the ratio of old to young birds in September as a measure of breeding success, this also being a measure of chick survival as explained above) could be accounted for by variations in general insect abundance in cereal and forage crops in June. They measured insect abundance by the use of suction traps and showed that the insects sampled were in the main those eaten by partridges, judged by analysing the crop contents of chicks.

The number of partridges finally surviving to breed in March depends on mortality factors operating in the winter, shooting being the most important. Shooting is contrived to operate in a density-dependent manner with proportionately more birds being shot when numbers are high, but this is, of course, an artificial situation which masks the effect of natural regulatory agents. These last are likely to reside in the nature of the environment, the amount and type of cover which in turn influence territory size and may result in surplus birds emigrating. They are considered in greater detail below (page 38) as they are involved as factors determining long-term changes in population size as distinct from annual fluctuations. To summarise, variations in chick survival dependent on arthropod food supplies are responsible for the marked ups and downs of partridge numbers from year to year. Density-related variations in chick survival, together with density-dependent winter losses, are responsible for keeping the spring breeding population within relatively narrow bounds from one year to another. Nevertheless, there has been a general long-term decline in this level which we shall consider below. It is to be noted that pre-hatching factors that influence the viability of eggs (the ability of the female to lay down yolk reserves could depend on spring food supplies and influence the viability of any eggs she laid), the hatching success of eggs, or any other cause of mortality, were not related to population size nor to variations in total mortality.

For the figures given in Table 1 it can be ascertained that the number of adults breeding in any one year was not at all related to the number breeding in the next year. In other words, a small breeding population could be followed by an increase or decrease in the following season and *vice versa*. But, as Fig 3a. shows, the percentage change in breeding population from one year to the next was positively correlated with the autumn ratio of young/old, this in turn depending on the survival of young during the summer. In Norfolk this post-breeding chick loss was not correlated with the size of post-breeding population. Thus for two quite separate populations of the grey partridge the major cause of changes in numbers from one breeding season to the next has been the death-rate of young in the summer months; when this has been low, breeding numbers have tended to increase. Annual differences in reproductive output have not contributed to the changes. In the Hampshire study the summer loss was dependent on the total partridge density, and this supplied the necessary regulation to keep fluctuations within relatively narrow limits. In addition, as we shall find, both populations experience density-dependent losses in winter, but the absence of any density related loss in summer among the Norfolk birds could be associated with the long-term decline this population is experiencing. (Fig. 26, page 176.) However, this last suggestion needs corroboration.

PLATE 1. The stonechat, *above left*, and whinchat, *right*, have declined since farmland replaced the gorse commons or waste they respectively require, although the whinchat survives on the rough hill grazing farms in the north and west of England. Red-backed shrikes, male, *below left*, female, *right*, have declined partly as a result of lost habitat, but also in response to a decrease in numbers of flying insects in the wetter and more cloudy summers since the 1950's.

PLATE 2. *Above*, nightjars rely on cryptic patterning and colour and are not easily located and flushed by a lone intruder into their breeding grounds on commons. However, they do suffer more disturbance when crowds of picnickers invade the wilder heaths and commons, and have locally declined as a result. *Below*, dartford warblers are on the edge of their range in Britain and favour a habitat where tall heather and gorse occur together. They are confined at present to the New Forest area and will have to be provided with a locally maintained habitat if the species is to survive in Britain.

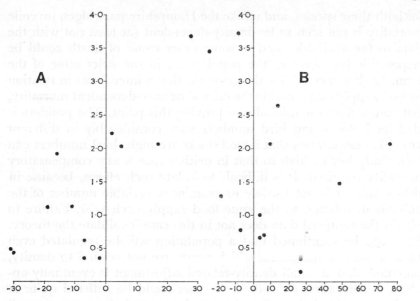

FIG. 3a. Percentage change in numbers of grey partridges between successive breeding seasons (abscissa) related to the corresponding autumn ratio of number of juveniles per adult (vertical scale). The correlation coefficient is statistically highly significant with $r_{11} = 0.822$.

3b. Percentage change in numbers of red-legged partridges between successive breeding seasons (abscissa), related to the corresponding autumn ratio of number of juveniles per adult (vertical scale). The correlation coefficient is not significant with $r_{11} = 0.367$. (Data derived from Table 1, from Middleton & Huband 1966).

Those mortality factors which, like chick loss, affect the size of the actual population, have been termed 'key factors' because they provide the key to predicting future population size, and are responsible for the year-to-year fluctuations in numbers. Perrins's work on the great tit and my own studies of the wood-pigeon had earlier demonstrated that, in these two species, the major factor influencing changes in numbers from one year to the next is the survival rate of young after the breeding season, not the reproductive output itself nor the adult loss. Juvenile survival has been proved to depend on the food supply in the case of the wood-pigeon, and there is good reason to believe that it is also involved in the case of the great tit. However, for both these species, and unlike the Hampshire partridges, juvenile mortality is not seen to be density-dependent (at least not with the data so far available) and so some other cause of death could be responsible for *regulating* the populations, in the strict sense of the term. Lack suspected, for the great tit, that winter losses in relation to food supply may provide the critical density-dependent mortality, but emphasised the difficulty of proving this point. The problem is that food stocks and bird numbers vary considerably in different years. It may happen that if food stocks are high, bird numbers can be already low or high so that in neither case is any compensatory mortality required. It is difficult to isolate such effects, because in field studies it is not feasible to examine a variable number of the animals in relation to the same food supply each year. Failure to obtain the required data does not in this case invalidate the theory. It should be mentioned that a population will be regulated even though most of the deaths which occur are not related to density, provided that a small density-related adjustment is eventually applied. For instance, 60%–80% of losses could be suffered quite at random provided that after these had occurred there was a small loss, say in the order of under 10%, which was related to density. Indeed, this is the more usual situation.

On the Norfolk estate under discussion, red-legged partridges have increased over roughly the same period that the grey have declined (see Fig. 26 and Chapter 7, p. 176). It is interesting that, in contrast to the case of the grey partridge, the autumn ratio of young to old has not been the factor which determines the subsequent spring population of the red-legged partridge (Fig. 3b). There were some years when more red-legs were shot in the autumn and winter on the estate than were actually known to be there at the beginning of the shooting season, and numbers sometimes were higher in spring than in the autumn. Clearly, something has been happening which has enabled immigrant red-legs to move into the area from surrounding farms or marginal land (see page 177). This suggestion highlights another facet of population control which must be considered, namely the role of immigration and emigration. In the case of the wood-pigeon, juvenile birds which are surplus to the carrying capacity of the area in the autumn do not necessarily die but may emigrate to other areas – to marginal habitats or even to France. A proportion survive to return in the spring. Although winter numbers may be directly related to the food supply – for the death-rate depends on how many surplus birds exist in relation to this food supply (in a poor year for food there is not necessarily any mortality if the population is already in balance with food stocks) – the number in spring will depend not only on local survival but also on how many of the emigrants survive to return. These complications do not invalidate the contention that in any area at the worst season numbers are regulated by the food supply (for the rest of the year there may be more food than birds to eat it, especially if breeding cannot be accomplished quickly enough), but they add to the difficulty of demonstrating clear-cut relationships, and are sometimes introduced in ill-conceived arguments as evidence against the theory.

Fig. 4 shows the autumn population, in decreasing order of size, of the grey partridge on the Norfolk estate against the percentage of birds dying in winter, either as a result of shooting or through natural causes. Similar data for the red log are also detailed, these being plotted against the appropriate years for grey and not in their own size order. The figure demonstrates in the case of the grey partridge that mortality due to shooting and other factors combined is positively correlated with the size of the autumn population, that is, it is density-dependent. The percentage of birds shot is even more strongly correlated with the numbers available for shooting and is also correlated with the total mortality. In contrast, natural mortality is not correlated with autumn numbers nor with shooting loss. That death by shooting should be adjusted to the autumn population is to be expected, since the people involved determine their activities according to the prospects; in years when autumn numbers are small, with a low young to old ratio, shooting is voluntarily abolished or curtailed. This attitude is mistaken for the simple reason that, in spite of shooting, additional animals have in any case to be lost to ensure stability in the spring, and if none are shot more disappear through other causes. This is well shown in Fig. 4 for the year 1954 when little or no shooting occurred and the level of natural mortality was raised. As a result the death-rate was at virtually the same level as it was in 1952 and 1955, when extensive shooting took place. Although enough animals are shot to ensure a density-dependent controlling effect on the winter population, this is only so because shooting obscures other causes of death. Because shooting may actually account for deaths it is not the reason why these occur: they would also occur in the absence of shooting. Jenkins reached this

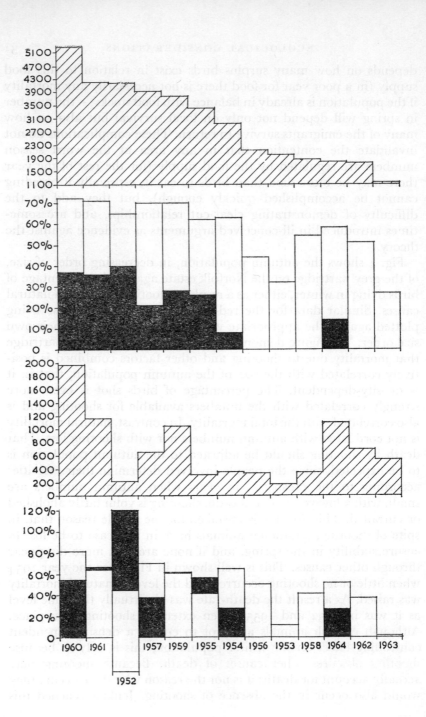

same conclusion for partridges he studied on Lord Rank's estate at Micheldever in Hampshire, and he and his colleagues (Jenkins, Watson and Miller) have more recently found that the same applies in the case of the grouse – the details are shown graphically in Fig. 5. The practical conclusion to be drawn from these studies is that people could as a rule enjoy more intensive shooting without detriment to game stocks – though this conclusion caused scepticism among many shooting men. It is ironical, therefore, that my colleagues and I found exactly the same principle to apply to a pest bird, the wood-pigeon. The number of these shot during organised battues in February was always less than the number which had to be lost to bring about stability in relation to clover stocks. We concluded that winter shooting was not controlling the population, nor in the circumstances did it reduce crop damage. Again this conclusion caused scepticism among many shooting men who could not appre-

FIG. 4. Relationship between the autumn population of the grey partridge (top hatched histogram) and red-legged partridge (third histogram from top, hatched) with the percentage of these populations lost between autumn and the following spring represented in the histograms below each. The percentage of birds lost is given by the open columns, and the percentage of these birds which were shot by the solid black. Loss due to other causes, is therefore, the difference between black and open parts of the columns.

[For the grey partridge the total mortality in winter is correlated with the autumn population being heavier in years of higher autumn numbers $r_{11}=0.827$. The percentage shot each winter is correlated with the autumn population $r_{11}=0.909$. The percentage shot is not correlated with the number lost for other reasons $r_{11}=-0.420$.

For the red-legged partridge the total mortality in winter is less correlated with the autumn population of red-legs, $r_{11}=0.583$, and more correlated with the autumn population of grey birds $r_{11}=0.747$. The number of red-legs shot bears no relation to the autumn population of red-legs but is related to the autumn population of the grey, $r_{11}=0.789$.]

The reason for some of the apparently anomalous results with the red-leg in which a higher proportion of birds was sometimes shot than was present in autumn is that the birds were moving into the area. Thus in 1952 the autumn population was 214, 259 birds were shot yet the spring population was 120, i.e. 121% of the autumn population was shot, there was a 77% loss not due to shooting (theoretically the difference between the total loss from autumn to spring=44%; with the loss due to shooting subtracted=−77%, and this has to be shown by drawing the column below the base line. (Data derived from Table 1, from Middleton & Huband 1966).

ciate that causes of death are compensatory, not additive. Only if more birds are shot than will be lost in any case can shooting become a controlling factor, in the sense that it will reduce numbers to lower levels in the next season.

The number of red-legged partridges shot on the Norfolk estate has borne only a slight correlation with the autumn numbers (Fig. 4). As the red-leg was much rarer than the grey, any decision on the numbers to be shot was made relative to the latter species, or more accurately to the total numbers of both species, rather than to the autumn population of the red-leg. For this reason the percentage of red-legs shot was fairly strongly correlated with autumn numbers of grey birds, while the total winter mortality (shooting plus natural) was slightly less strongly correlated. This illustrates how the amount of predation (in this case shooting) suffered by a species may be determined by the availability of similar prey. In such circumstances, the situation may arise where undesirably large numbers are lost by accident, even resulting in the extinction of a species.

Still considering Fig. 4, it is possible to imagine that this represented a species where the shooting had been done for pest control and not for sport, and that it was supported by a bounty. It becomes evident that a bonus scheme, unless it actually results in more animals being killed than would die in any case, would in this case prove a complete waste of money as a means of controlling numbers. It could only be justified if the animals concerned were killed before they caused damage. While the undesirability of a direct subsidy is fairly evident, there are often cases where grant-aid is paid in an indirect manner which obscures its futility. Variations in kill dependent on population size, and hence variations in subsidy, would be anticipated in different seasons – yet it usually happens that the amount claimed for a subsidy stays fairly constant. This is so in the case of the amount paid for wood-pigeon shooting. This suggests that only an arbitrary cull is being achieved; arbitrary in the sense that people now do roughly the same amount of shooting each year, and claim a fairly constant and acceptable level of support. It is extremely unlikely that this reflects realistically the variable level of crop damage caused by pigeons.

It is seen that most of the annual fluctuations which occur in the numbers of any bird depend primarily on juvenile rather than adult survival. Most adult birds die not through starvation but by accident – by predation, occasional disease, and pure accidents such as flying

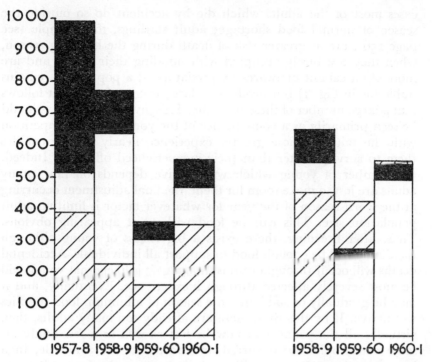

FIG. 5. The top of the columns represents the total number of grouse in different autumns on study areas in Scotland on low ground (left) or high ground (right). The number of these birds which were shot is indicated by the solid areas, the number lost through other causes by open columns and the number of grouse alive in the spring by hatching. The data show that more birds must die than are actually shot. On high ground in 1961 there were more grouse in spring and autumn, as a result of immigration. (Data from Jenkins, Watson & Miller 1963).

into a telegraph wire. In general, big birds are less prone to accident; they are less likely to be caught by a predator and so they tend to have lower death-rates, but there are many exceptions. Established adults must have already experienced a season of food shortage, which they have successfully survived in competition with other individuals. It is unlikely that they will suffer in subsequent years, unless a particularly lean season occurs. In other words, food shortage may only seriously affect an established adult in one year out of many (a hard winter is one example of this). Moreover, in many cases most of the adults which die by accident do so outside the season of normal food shortage; adult starlings, for example (see page 156), are at greater risk of death during the breeding season, when they are busily occupied with minding their young and are more often caught unawares by predators. If a population remains stable (as in Fig. 1) but produces a large excess of young, it follows that a large number of these must die. This juvenile mortality should be seen primarily as a consequence of the young birds' competition with the adults, whose greater experience nearly always enables them to survive better than their inexperienced offspring. Indeed, the number of young which will survive depends on how many adults are lost to make room for them, the final adjustment occurring at the worst season of the year for whatever factor is limiting adult population size. This can be food without it appearing obvious. Thus, after breeding, there exists a big excess of young although there may still be enough food to support all individuals. Accidental deaths will occur throughout this time, but it is likely that young will be most severely affected through inexperience. Eventually, and it may be gradually or suddenly, the season of minimum food supplies will arrive. If by this time there are already too many adults, then virtually all the young will now be lost as well as a few adults. If some catastrophe has occurred and no adults are available, then larger numbers of young will survive to restore the former balance between total numbers and environmental resources. But these two extreme situations will occur only rarely. The above account is slightly over-simplified, as in reality adults themselves do suffer a little from competition with their young, and the process is not completely one-sided. Removal of juveniles increases survival prospects for the adults. Furthermore, it will be appreciated that several factors influencing bird numbers may act simultaneously, so that adjustments are continuous – this is why animal populations are called dynamic.

Our studies of the wood-pigeon provide an example of some of these processes in operation. In 1959 the post-breeding population comprised 171 birds per 100 acres with 1.3 juveniles to every adult. In 1963 there were only 101 birds per 100 acres and 1.5 juveniles to each adult. The clover food supply, at the worst time of the succeeding winters of 1960 and 1964 was near enough the same and so the population was reduced to 34 and 35 birds per 100 acres respectively. But in the 1959–60 season the competition needed to bring about balance (171 down to 34) was clearly much greater than in 1963–4 (101 down to 33). The effect on the juveniles was striking. By the February of 1960 there were only 0.1 young to every adult against 1.1 in 1964. Hence, in both years total numbers reached the same level by winter, but juveniles suffered a 96% loss in 1959–60 against 74% in 1963–4. Adult loss in the first year was 59%, and 58% in the second season. These figures do of course illustrate a density-dependent loss of young. The term mortality has not been used, because some birds were lost through the emigration of both young and old, though it amounts to mortality so far as the carrying capacity of the land was involved in mid-winter. The true annual death-rate of adults was lower than the figures quoted.

This example shows how the age structure of a population may be altered without any change in its ultimate size. The red grouse provides another illustration of this effect, achieved by deliberate killing. It has already been noted that grouse numbers in spring are unaffected by shooting. Yet Jenkins and his team found that over the autumn the death-rates of adults and young were equal (at around 70% per annum), in sharp contrast to all other birds so far studied. This was because so many birds were shot that deaths from natural causes were not fully obvious; presumably shooting is not selective of either age group. If enough animals (old and young combined) are shot natural competition between adults and juveniles can be reduced. In an unshot population of white-tailed ptarmigan in Canada (Choate 1963) the juveniles did suffer a much higher death-rate than the adults. Again, young wood-pigeons are easier to shoot than adults until mid-winter, by which time they seem to have learnt to avoid men with guns and from February onwards are no more easily shot than old birds. But they still do less well than adults when competing for food (and at breeding sites later on) and for this reason suffer a higher death-rate. Clearly, the amount of winter shooting can alter the age structure of the population without affecting final numbers in summer.

As mentioned above, before any artificial killing can result in a reduction of population size, the total number of animals killed must exceed the rate of deaths from natural causes. In addition, as increasing numbers are killed artificially, natural mortality factors cease to operate and must be replaced by artificial ones if compensatory changes are to be avoided. Inability to reach the necessary threshold means failure so far as artificial control is concerned. If numbers need to be kept down it is best, all else being equal, to defer artificial killing to the season when natural factors have taken their toll. If such population control cannot be achieved artificially and numbers cannot be held below a natural optimum, it is vital to show that any cropping does prevent damage; it is of course feasible that artificial killing will remove animals before they would normally die, and so protects crops. But every case has to be taken on its own merits, and examples of wise and foolish applications will be found in later chapters.

The level around which a population fluctuates may be subjected to long-term changes not resulting from the key factors so far considered. Blank *et al.* have demonstrated that the number of breeding grey partridges (which have shown evidence of a general decline during the present century) is determined by the nature of the habitat. The favoured sites for nesting are an incomplete hedge, that is, a group of separate bushes often patchily arranged on a grassy bank, or a wide grass track. Jenkins (1961) also showed that a lack of winter cover (cereal crops as distinct from tall grass provide little cover) results in the formation of larger territories, because the males can see rivals at greater distances and this causes the breeding population to be lower; under these circumstances surplus birds move on to marginal habitats. It is conceivable that changes in land usage and farming techniques have harmed the partridge by causing the population to fluctuate around a lower level.

The well-documented decline of the corncrake seems to have resulted from farm mechanisation, which has eliminated the old hand cutting of hay and enabled the harvest of silage to take place earlier, to the detriment of nesting corncrakes. Once generally distributed throughout the British Isles, the species disappeared from East Anglia before 1900, from east midland and southern England by about 1914, and from Wales, northern England and east Scotland by about 1939. It remains common only in Ireland, parts of western Scotland and the Hebrides, Orkneys and Shetland – areas where the old methods of hay production to a large extent remain unchanged.

Britain has experienced several periods of radically altered climate which must have considerably affected bird distribution, particularly of those species at the edge of their range in northern Europe. Since the mid-nineteenth century changes in air circulation have caused a warming of the atmosphere particularly noticeable in northern areas; in central England, the decadal mean temperature of the summer months had risen about 2° C between 1900 and 1950, while a similar increase occurred in Finland and elsewhere. The temperature increases were particularly noticeable further north and at first were limited to the winter months (a 9° C increase in Spitsbergen), causing arctic ice to melt and polar seas to become warmer, but leading by the 1880s to increased temperatures during the northern springs, and to a summer increase in the 1920s.

Since about 1950 there has been a reverse trend in weather conditions which can be expected to bring about another southern displacement of the avi-fauna. Another complication is that the increase in mean temperatures has, in the maritime countries like Britain, resulted in distinctly wetter and cloudier summers. This is doubtless the reason why certain birds which depend on large flying insects have declined in recent years. Red-backed shrikes still produce more than enough offspring to ensure their increase, given the right conditions, but the bird has markedly declined in Britain and other parts of north-west Europe. Destruction of their habitat has sometimes been held to explain the decrease but this is by no means always the case, many areas now untenanted by shrikes appear to be unchanged, certainly in several Suffolk and Surrey localities that I know personally. Peakall, who has documented the decline, believes that a changing climate provides the explanation as flying insects become scarce on grey cloudy days. This was brought home to me very clearly when photographing red-backed shrikes on a Surrey heath in 1967 (see Pl. 1). During a six-hour session in a fully accepted hide when it was dull and overcast, the adults were clearly finding it difficult to get food. Even though they had large hungry young, each parent was visiting the nest about once every hour, bringing mostly ground beetles, until eventually they found a nest of young birds, and for a while flew back and forth with the nestlings. The following day was bright and sunny and the adults were feeding the young every five minutes or so, bringing dragonflies, butterflies, bees and lizards – in fact all the creatures which depend on sunshine to become active.

Other birds which depend on large flying insects, and which are at the edge of their distribution in north-west Europe and Britain, seem to be suffering a similar south-east contraction in range. Monk has shown that in 1850 the wryneck was very common in south-east England and the midlands and was scarce though regular north to the borders and west in Wales. By 1954, only 365 pairs could be accounted for and the total dropped to about 205 in 1958, since when it has fallen further. Moreover, well over three-quarters of the British breeding population is now confined to Kent. According to a survey carried out in 1957 and 1958 by Stafford, the nightjar is much more widely distributed in Britain, and although most common in southern England, it is frequent in the north of England and Wales though only irregular and local in Scotland. As it feeds on night-flying insects it has presumably been less adversely affected by cloudy summers. Even so, the survey showed that a decline has occurred during this century – though increased disturbance may be an important factor with this large and quiet-seeking species.

The stonechat, a bird of gorse commons, seems to have declined for a different reason. It feeds on large insects but catches them on fairly open ground, using a convenient bush as a vantage point. The ground and low herbage dwelling invertebrates on which it feeds can be found even in winter, so it remains a resident, like that exceptional Sylvid warbler, the Dartford warbler, which locally shares a very similar habitat. Magee, in a study of the stonechat in 1961, obtained breeding records from only twenty-three counties in England and seven in Wales, mostly only small numbers being involved. Only nine English, four Scottish and three Welsh counties had more than twenty pairs, whereas at the turn of the century the species bred in every English county. In 1961, 264 pairs were recorded in Pembrokeshire, 262 in Hampshire, 150 in Glamorgan, 104 in Cornwall, 96 in Devon and 51 in Dorset, after which Surrey with 39 pairs had the next highest English or Welsh county total. Magee pointed out that counties like Cornwall and Pembrokeshire have long stretches of coastline and still have extensive bracken and gorse headlands providing suitable conditions for the species. Otherwise poor gorse-covered commons or alternatively heath moor with numerous bushes have been largely lost as a habitat in Britain; the only extensive areas are to be found in those counties where tolerably high numbers still occur. Another complication is that severe winters hit stonechats very hard and it may take several years for numbers to recover. In this connection the coastal counties are probably less seriously affected, and Magee gives evidence that following any hard winter, recolonisation is usually first noticed in coastal areas from which birds then spread to inland habitats. In recent decades the predominantly mild winters between 1917 and 1939 allowed a fairly extensive re-occupation of inland habitats after the drastic reductions of the 1916–17 hard winter (41 consecutive night frosts at Hampstead) only to be followed by extensive reductions again with the hard winters of 1939–40 and subsequently. Hard winters are not regulatory factors in the accepted sense. Blanket snow cover or extended frosts affect wide areas irrespective of the number of animals present which must all suffer in a density-independent manner. A measure of density-dependence may be imposed if the animals are able to compete for restricted pockets of food; but this is a special case.

In south-west Europe, Cetti's warbler is one of a small group of resident warblers which are similarly sensitive to hard winters and this applies to the resident Dartford warbler which is on the edge of its range in southern Britain. Cetti's warbler spread north in France during the 1940s and 1950s with the period of mild winters and these also enabled a large proportion of Dartford warblers to survive in winter and then spread to other suitable habitats; a similar population increase and irruption to new areas occurred in the bearded tit for the same reason. The Dartford warbler formerly extended from Suffolk and Kent to Cornwall, but fragmentation of suitable heathland at the turn of the century has virtually restricted it to the New Forest, this being the only large enough area of suitable habitat, within its range, which can provide stability. Tubbs has demonstrated how during open winters the population can build up to occupy other heathland in Surrey and north Hampshire, where too small a population exists to withstand bad winters and where it has been exterminated two or three times since the 1940s – the winter of 1947 proving particularly disastrous. Tubbs has rightly emphasised the importance of maintaining the New Forest as a reservoir for the species. Here its numbers increased from around 80 pairs in 1955 to 382 pairs in 1961. Then came the snow of 1962 which exterminated the species in Surrey (the birds were trapped while roosting in tall heather by an overnight blanketing fall of snow) and left only 60 pairs in Hampshire. The following hard winter of 1962–3 virtually exterminated even the New Forest population, as well as causing a big retreat to the south of Cetti's warbler in France.

Apart from changes in range caused by weather, several species have recently increased in response to addition to available habitats, which are often man-made. In inland Eurasia the little ringed plover replaces the ringed plover and nests on the sand and pebbly shores of slow-moving rivers or inland lakes, predominantly near fresh water.

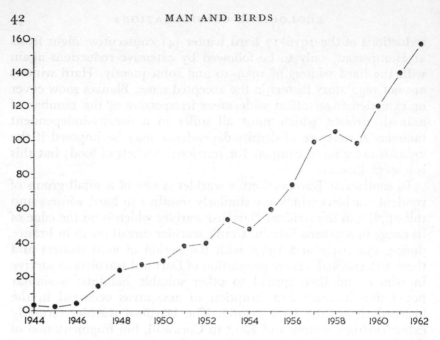

FIG. 6. Increase in number of pairs of little ringed plovers summering in Britain. (Data from Parrinder 1964).

A pair nested at the Tring reservoirs, Hertfordshire, in 1938 – the first nesting record in Britain. No further nests were found until 1944, when two pairs nested in another part of Hertfordshire, and one pair in Middlesex; the increase since then is shown in Fig. 6. By 1962 there were approximately 157 in Britain, nearly two-thirds being concentrated in the counties south of the Welland-Severn line and none extending further north than Yorkshire or west of Gloucestershire or Cheshire. Parrinder, who has documented these changes, points out that gravel pits provide over three-quarters of the nesting sites of little ringed plovers; sewage farms, reservoirs, brick pits and such places comprise the remainder. Most gravel-pits are centred in the areas where the species already occurs, except that a surplus of potential sites appears to exist in Lancashire, Northumberland and Durham and parts of Wales and these sites may next be occupied. Parrinder emphasises how gravel and sand production for building and road construction have increased with the post-war building boom and, as much of the material is derived from new workings, these have also increased. There can be little

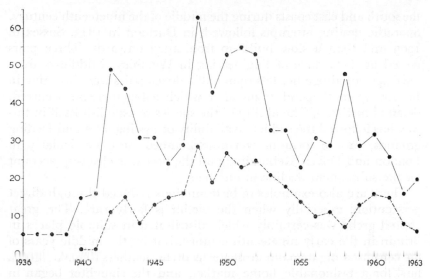

FIG. 7. Changing status of black redstart in Britain showing increase in number of territory holding males during the 1939-45 war with a decline following the final clear-up of war damaged sites after 1950. The solid line gives figures for the whole of Great Britain, while the dotted line is the contribution made by the City of London and Dover combined. (Data from Fitter 1965).

doubt that the creation of a new environment has favoured the species. It is interesting that our ringed plover has not been able to colonise these places, particularly as a local inland breeding population occurs in the East Anglian Breckland and the bird also breeds inland on some of the east Suffolk heathlands and in parts of north-east Scotland, for example in the Abernethy Forest.

The black redstart was originally a bird of the warm montane regions of the southern Palaearctic, like the rock thrush and crag martin, but spread northwards after the last glaciation. It has adapted itself to a man-made environment, using buildings for nesting sites in lieu of cliff faces, and in parts of Germany it replaces the robin as the familiar follower of man. Its northward spread was still in progress across Germany during the last hundred years, and it only reached Jutland in the second half of the nineteenth century, and Scandinavia in the early 1940s. There is no record of it in Britain before 1819, though it became a regular passage migrant on the south and east coasts during the middle of the nineteenth century. Sporadic nesting attempts followed, in Durham in 1845, Sussex in 1909 and then a slow build-up from 1923 onwards. Three pairs nested at the Palace of Engineering in Wembley, Middlesex from 1926–41 but altogether less than half a dozen pairs were breeding in Britain up to the mid 1930s after which a big increase occurred, detailed in Fig. 7. The ability of the species to establish itself in this way has followed the sudden availability of nesting sites and feeding grounds, in the form of war-time bombed sites, particularly in London and Dover. Rebuilding and the post-war clean-up account for the subsequent decline in numbers.

There are also examples of bird numbers reduced through direct persecution, especially when the victim is fairly rare. The great crested grebe was certainly widely distributed in suitable places in Britain in the early nineteenth century, but by the middle years of the century a big demand arose for its breast feathers to make 'grebe furs' for a fashionable home market, and the slaughter began in 1857. By 1860, the species was reduced to 42 known pairs and was only saved by the sanctuary afforded by private estates, while further help came with the Bird Protection Acts of 1870–1880. Nevertheless, some increase was under way by 1880, before protection could have been very effective, and Harrison and Hollom (1932), who record these early changes, consider that human persecution came at the start of a period of long-term cyclical increase. By 1931, there were around 1,150 breeding pairs (with non-breeders, about 2,650 adults) in England and Wales and about another 80 pairs in Scotland. A sample census by Hollom (1959) showed that about the same number of adult grebes existed in Britain in the 1940s, but that an increase then began. When Prestt and Mills undertook a census in 1965 there were approximately 4,500 adults in Britain. This increase seems to have been favoured by man's activities in creating numerous new reservoirs and gravel pits, just as the little ringed plover benefited. The 70% increase of the population in about twenty years can be compared with an increase of 84% in sand and gravel production between 1948 and 1957. That an increase followed the creation of new habitats also indicates that saturation had previously been attained and that the bird was regulated in the sense already discussed.

For a species to extend its range and take advantage of newly developed habitats it would be helpful for it to possess some kind of

PLATE 3. Two new species which have become established in Britain as a result of man creating suitable habitats, albeit unintentionally. *Above*, little ringed plovers photographed at the Queen Elizabeth II reservoir while under construction. *Below*, black redstarts increased as nesting birds in the conditions provided by war-time bomb sites.

PLATE 4. *Above*, great crested grebes were almost exterminated in the late nineteenth century when their skins were in demand for the plume trade. Protection enabled them to return to their previous level and a further population increase followed as a result of the construction of new reservoirs and gravel pits. *Below*, sand martins have also benefitted from the nesting places provided at sand and gravel pits and in the banks of reservoirs.

exploratory behaviour rather than rely on chance movements. It is becoming clear that immediately after breeding, many species, which normally migrate south, first indulge in northerly flights. The large-scale ringing of sand martins has shown that birds breeding at a colony in the south of England may move north to have their second brood, and juveniles marked in southern England have been found again in roosts in the north in the same season. Wood-pigeons also display northerly flights in September and October, before adopting a southerly orientation later in the autumn. Collared doves ringed in Europe as nestlings have moved north to Britain in the same autumn, and numbers of serins have turned up in south-west England in recent autumns. These movements seem adaptive in that young individuals which are surplus to the needs of the area in which they are born will stand more chance of finding new places to settle if they first explore north. The same principle applies to those birds of south-east and east Europe which might be expected to move north-west or west. I suspect that this factor may account for big arrivals of red-breasted flycatchers, woodchat shrikes, barred warblers, melodious and icterine warblers – all predominantly juvenile – into Britain in September 1958 and in subsequent years. Williamson showed that red-breasted flycatchers and icterine warblers arrived in Britain in clear anticyclonic weather with light winds, and as both migrate south-east to Asia, their movement several hundreds of miles off-course is remarkable. The explanation that they drifted in with down winds seems unlikely, and instead I wonder whether the existence of anticyclonic weather facilitated a normal adaptation after breeding in the form of a deliberate dispersal north-west, a process possibly truncated in years of less favourable weather.

Man has done so much in a passive way to alter the avifauna of Europe that it seems reasonable to take active steps to reintroduce lost species. Any reservations that this would be unnatural, should be tempered by the thought that the environment we have created is in any case artificial. Probably more pleasure than harm has been derived from the reintroduction of the capercaillie. It would seem laudable to follow up a recent suggestion and attempt the reintro-duction of the bustard to parts of the East Anglian Breckland, and to encourage black terns to stay and breed. It is quite a different matter to introduce alien species to a new country, especially without sound biological knowledge. In Britain, some of these introductions, red-legged partridge, various pheasants, little owl, Canada and

Egyptian goose and Mandarin duck have on balance improved our bird-life, but the same could not be said of the introduction of the house-sparrow and starling to Australia and North America.

Perhaps a more interesting question to ask here is why the majority of introduced species are unsuccessful. This is part of the much bigger question of what factors determine faunal diversity and enable some habitats to support more species than others. The concept of a niche, which refers to the animal's place in the biotic environment and its relations to food and predators, should now be widely appreciated. It is a fundamental tenet of ecology that no two species can occupy the same niche in any one habitat, because both cannot be equally well adapted. R. and J. MacArthur (1961) examined numerous habitats at different latitudes for their plant species composition and foliage profile and 'species diversity'. They found this last to be a more useful measure than the actual number of species because their calculations allowed at a habitat containing 50 of species A and 50 of B to rank a higher diversity than one with 99 of A and 1 of B. (The latter tends to be the farmland situation, the former that of tropical forest.) It turned out that neither the variety of plant species nor the latitude affected the amount of species diversity which instead depended entirely on the variation in foliage height, probably because birds mostly respond to different configurations of vegetation in different layers. This means that habitats of the same structural profile have the same diversity of bird species. In any area, a bird might either feed on all food of a suitable size within a narrowly defined habitat or, alternatively, be selective of food but collect it throughout a wider range of habitats. In other words, birds could partition their food or their habitat. The former has occurred because feeding specialisation brings the greatest advantages and has been favoured by natural selection. Partitioning the habitat would necessitate birds moving from one suitable micro-habitat (say a species of tree) to another, and it would depend on the pattern of the total habitat how much time would be wasted in the process. But adaptation to a comparatively broad habitat structure, for instance, to arboreal or ground feeding, must in turn impose physical limitations which restrict the diversity of feeding adaptations; in practice, bill size and shape is about all that can be much modified to suit the collection of different foods.

From the viewpoint of zoo-geography, the Palaearctic has existed as an entirety for sufficient time to ensure that most niches are filled by highly efficient species. Furthermore, man and birds have lived side by side since Neolithic times, so that the new habitats created by agriculture and man's other activities have been occupied by the species best suited to them. The same is not true of Australia and New Zealand, which were cut off from the main centres of evolution at an earlier stage, one result being that primitive marsupial mammals were not replaced by the better adapted placental mammals. Birds are less insular, however, and the native avifauna of Australia seems to be the best fitted to occupy the niches available. Thus of at least 24 bird species deliberately introduced into Australia in the past, only 12 have become established. It is significant that only the blackbird has managed to invade native forest, the remainder existing in areas of recent agricultural development or urbanisation. But introduced birds like the feral pigeon, starling and house sparrow are better equipped to occupy the man-made niches than the native fauna, simply because these are species which have already been selected to occupy a man-made environment. New Zealand has an impoverished avifauna compared with Australia on which it has depended for colonisation, and the process is still incomplete. In consequence, fewer niches are saturated in New Zealand, so more exotic species have been successful. Of 130 species originally introduced, 24 have become established, although apart from the black-bird, chaffinch and redpoll which appear to be filling unexploited niches, most are again restricted to man-made habitats. Hawaii, which is even more isolated, and not saturated by a wide diversity of species, must have even more vacant niches, for, according to Elton (1958), of 94 birds introduced 53 have become established, some deep in the native forest.

According to Middleton, the European goldfinch has been successful in Australia and New Zealand only in the man-made agricultural areas, to which none of the native Australian Ploceid finches were adapted. In contrast, the European goldfinch has not been a successful bird in North America because it has virtually the same ecological requirements as the fitter endemic American goldfinch. Only one small colony of European goldfinches became established near New York, though these have since vanished when their habitat was destroyed for building purposes. Again the European house-sparrow has been highly successful in Australia, over roughly the same range as the goldfinch, whereas the introduced greenfinch is more restricted as it has rather more conservative ecotone requirements. It is interesting that this reflects a trend occurring today in Britain; the greenfinch is declining with the loss of hedgerows and woodland edges, while the goldfinch and linnet are increasing.

To return to New Zealand, it is noticeable that the birds which have become pests in agricultural areas, apart from being introduced species as one would expect from the comments above, present the same kinds of problems as they do in Britain. I am grateful to Dr P. C. Bull for allowing me to give details. As we shall see, skylarks (page 208) are locally troublesome in Britain to young seedling crops such as lettuce. Near Hastings, N.Z., they and house sparrows have together been responsible for damaging asparagus and other seedlings. Both blackbird and song thrush and also the starling, resort to orchards in the dry season after breeding and cause considerable damage to all kinds of fruit, ripening pears, cherries and grapes. Redpolls do considerable damage to apricot blossom in their search for insects, and blossom searching is a habit which is increasing in Britain (page 222). Locally in Britain, linnets peck out the seeds from strawberries (page 227), while in N.Z. goldfinches do the same.

Various attempts were made to introduce the rook into N.Z. from 1762 onwards but only 35, liberated near Christchurch in 1873, seem to have thrived. The species occurs in five localities on the yellow-grey earths in the east of the county, generally where cereal growing occurs. Rooks at first increased very slowly but there was a rapid increase between 1935 and 1950, and a final levelling off with the density of birds in their favoured areas becoming virtually the same as that in Britain (around 16 nests per square mile). At Christchurch, the population increased from 1,000 birds in one rookery in 1925 to 7–10,000 in 1947 (13 rookeries), since when the numbers have remained roughly constant with 19 rookeries in use. Until 1926, the rookeries were in eucalypts, probably the favourite tree, but following a disease epidemic which killed these trees the birds changed to pines. Bull points out that the rate of increase of rooks has been slower than that of other introduced passerines and attributes this to their gregarious nesting habits and their need for group stimulation, and to an early shortage of suitable habitats. A feature of N.Z. rookeries is their very large size compared with British ones (rookeries of over 1,000 nests are quite common), and the traditional return to the same nesting sites may partly explain the slowness of expansion. (The large size of rookeries, and difficulties in getting sufficient food locally may also explain why the birds seem to lay, on average, smaller clutches in N.Z.; 3.4 eggs against 4 + in Britain, (see page 145), though more data are needed to establish the point.) Frequently, only when man actively disturbed these large rookeries did they become fragmented in surrounding areas, often with a rapid increase in total bird numbers in the district. As in Britain, rooks uproot seedling peas and corn, take ripening peas (and pumpkins) and maize and are also partial to walnuts.

The number of closely related birds which can live in the same habitat without competing for food depends to a large measure on the degree of stability within the environment. Marked fluctuations occur on English farmland, not only because of the changing seasons, but also because ploughing, harvesting and other farm operations impose drastic changes. As a result, the farmland birds occupying the various niches available for ground-feeders show a wide character displacement, we find a plover, three passerines (rook, starling, lark), a partridge and a pigeon, other species being only transient visitors, or primarily dependent on other habitats. No bird can afford to be too conservative in its niche requirements in a fluctuating environment, while the need for each species to show more tolerance reduces the number of ecologically isolated forms. Therefore, we should expect modern farm mechanisation, which enables whole farms to be ploughed within a fortnight, to be detrimental to bird life compared with the old methods which ensured some degree of stability by leaving land fallow and by transforming stubbles into bare ground more gradually. Klopfer and MacArthur (1960) have similarly emphasised that the major factor accounting for a decrease in the number of species away from the tropics, while the number of individuals of each species increases, does not result from a decrease in habitat complexity, but to a decrease in the similarity of co-existing species. The principle can obviously be extended to any situation where man simplifies the environment.

An important feature of complex ecological communities is that interactions between members damp out oscillations in the numbers of any one species (see page 61) and so help to introduce a high degree of stability and energy utilisation. For one thing, available food is more fully exploited, which is not the case in arctic environments for instance, where considerable seasonal changes occur. Hence, the amount of energy needed to maintain a stable community is less than that required for an unstable one. Man's activities have tended to reduce complexity and introduce monotony, through monocultures of crops, uniform stands of trees, or rows of similar houses. In consequence, the animals inhabiting these environments usually fluctuate much more than those of more complex ecosystems, often to the extent of becoming pests (see page 61). One feature of stabilisation is that natural selection can favour anticipatory functions – for example, the breeding season of northern birds has become approximately geared to seasonal daylight changes – in unstable environments opportunism must set more of a premium. Because more energy goes into maintaining fluctuations in simple ecosystems, often short-term fluctuations, these systems offer more scope for rational exploitation, giving more production per unit of biomass. In general, pestiferous birds and game species can be cropped very intensively, but the corollary also applies in that the energy needed to counteract fluctuations, the efforts of pest control, must often be so considerable as to be impracticable. On the other hand, mature and complex ecosystems can be disturbed relatively easily. In the Eltonian food chain the predators at each level become rarer and larger, because the energy passing from link to link is only in the region of 10%–20%. This not only sets limits on the number of links in a food chain (five seems to be the maximum) and rules out the possibility of a super-predator but makes the top predators particularly vulnerable to small but cumulative changes in the food chain. The loss and increased rarity of so many of the birds of prey depends not so much on persecution, but on the reduced complexity of the environment through human 'progress'. Clearly our future policies should not concentrate too much on bird protection *per se*, but rather on the creation and maintenance of as much diversified habitat as possible.

The long-term or ultimate value to a species in settling in an appropriate habitat will depend on the bird's ability to find suitable food and produce surviving progeny, and this ability will be conditioned by the structural and behavioural adaptations of the species. The immediate or proximate factors which determine how a bird chooses an appropriate habitat are unlikely to involve these same factors. Instead, natural selection has enabled each species to respond to immediate signals, which can be reliably taken as indicators that other more basic needs will be satisfied. In this way a bird which lives in oak woodland might respond to the configuration of an oak tree, because natural selection will favour this appropriate response provided it leads the bird to find in the oak woods all the various foods which are appropriate to its needs and feeding adaptations. Natural selection can favour the emergence of appropriate proximate responses which are anticipatory.

In practice, it is generally agreed that birds respond to a range of releasing stimuli which combine to provide the best cues. A meadow pipit may respond innately to open country, thereafter to specific elements of the habitat, such as the height of grass, the presence of song posts and nest sites. These considerations are important when man radically alters the habitat, without necessarily altering its food value. As various features of the environment combine to produce a response, they need not always be present in the same proportions, and some may even be absent, for a response still to occur. Species vary in the capacity to respond when some stimuli are absent. Within any area intraspecific competition ensures that the most favourable sites are filled at the start, after which less complete habitats can be occupied. At low population densities, when, for example, a species is at the edge of its range, only the best habitats are occupied (stenotopy) whereas when population explosions occur, marginal areas are also utilised (eurytopy). This is well illustrated by the wide range of nesting sites accepted by the various gulls which have undergone a spectacular population explosion in Britain – nesting colonies occur on rocky and sandy sea shores, estuarine and fresh-water marshes, inland lakes, and on moors and fells.

It becomes clear how an originally montane bird like the house martin should come to accept the sides of houses for its nest site instead of cliffs. Similarly the absence of a species from what appears to be a suitable habitat may be attributable to the absence of some apparently trivial factor which must be satisfied. Already in south Europe it is known that the presence of electric and telephone pylons and cables in otherwise open country facilitates colonisation by species like the collared dove and various shrikes.

The psychological response of the reed bunting to a limited range of habitat cues seems to have been the only reason for its past restriction to wetland habitats and its ecological isolation from the yellow-hammer. But, as will emerge later, this segregation is no longer maintained and the invasion of yellowhammer habitats by the reed bunting is possibly the result of a genotypic change which has removed this psychological restriction. Another explanation is also tenable. Although most habitat recognition is innate, birds are able to reinforce or even modify, to a variable extent, these innate responses by learning processes. By this means, adults often return to traditional areas, even though these change drastically, whereas young birds breeding for the first time avoid entering habitats which do not release appropriate responses – either innate or acquired by imprinting in early life. For instance, Peitzmeier (1952) found that in a study area in Germany the curlew typically nested only in boggy areas and avoided surrounding cultivated land. When the marshes were drained and cultivated, the adults not only remained faithful to the area, but after learning its new characteristics, also spread to other tilled land which before they had avoided. It could be that this situation has applied in the case of the reed bunting. Peitzmeier attributes the further spread of curlews in arable environments to the imprinting of young which have been reared in these new habitats. Such processes explain why local populations of birds come to acquire unusual habitat associations – for example, the stone curlews which used to nest on the shingle of Dungeness and Norfolk beaches, or yellow wagtails which breed in fields of growing potatoes. Peitzmeier accounts for a remarkable and fairly sudden change in the nesting habitat of the mistle thrush in the same way – originally confined to continuous woodland dominated by conifers it began, in 1925, to nest in parkland-type habitat, and in small groups of deciduous trees in cultivated country. That very recent changes may have occurred in the habitat of an animal must always be remembered when trying to understand their adaptations – they may have evolved in conditions quite unlike those in which the birds are seen today.

CHAPTER 3

SOME PREDATORS AND THEIR PREY

THE last chapter was primarily concerned with the factors governing bird numbers and distribution, showing some of the ways in which man does or does not influence the natural balance. The importance of the food supply was stressed. In many cases the food supply can be considered as an independent variable. For example, the quantity of beech-mast varies in different years in response to climatic and other factors and is not initially determined by the birds which use it as food. Nevertheless, the availability of beech-mast profoundly affects the numbers of those species which have to depend on it for food. More bramblings winter in Britain in good beech-mast years. On the other hand, when short-eared owls feed on voles they may themselves become an important factor determining vole numbers. Watson (1893) quotes an interesting example chronicled for 1580. In that year a vole plague developed in the marshes near South-minster, Essex, which so depleted the grasses that cattle died and men were powerless to take any preventive action. The situation was supposedly saved by the arrival of 'such a number of owls as all the shire was not able to yield; whereby the marsh-holders were shortly delivered from the vexations of the said mice'. When a reciprocal interaction exists between an animal and its food supply, it is termed a predator–prey relationship. The principles involved in such predator–prey interactions are fundamental to almost all aspects of economic ornithology, from the daily routine of the game-keeper to the effects some forest birds may have on various insect pests. In discussing certain economically important examples it seems desirable to outline some of these principles.

A complex range of variables determines the nature of predation. For one thing the availability of other foods in the environment influences the extent to which a predator concentrates on any par-ticular prey. This also depends on how specialised the predator has become in feeding on restricted categories of prey; kestrels are better equipped to catch ground-living rodents in open country than are sparrowhawks, and these in turn are more efficient at catching small birds in flight in wooded areas. Prey-species have evolved an enormous range of anti-predator devices, the more so if they are subject to intense attack. These protective devices vary from breeding in colonies to the various forms of camouflage and cryptic behaviour and the possession of special defence organs. Some invertebrates and the eggs of some birds are distasteful to predators, and the list could be longer. Whatever anti-predator adaptation has evolved, it is likely that this is also subject to limitations. For example, camouflage can only be effective if sufficient concealing backgrounds are available and when these are saturated surplus animals may derive no benefit from being cryptically coloured. Accepting the existence of all these modifying influences, there are two basic aspects to the response shown by a predator to changes of its prey (Solomon 1949). First, there is the response of the individual predator to changing numbers, or, better, to the changing density of its prey (food), this being the *functional* response of the predator. Second, predators may respond to increases of prey density by increasing their own numbers through immigration or by breeding, and *vice versa*, and the change in population size of the predator is the *numerical* response.

The simplest functional response shown by a predator to changes in food density is depicted in Fig. 8 based on the number of cereal grains eaten per unit time by wood-pigeons according to grain density on stubbles or sowings. The response is simple because the birds have little or no other food choice when they search the stubbles; unlike the related stock dove they do not normally respond to the presence of weed seeds. It can be seen that once grain density reaches a particular threshold the birds' intake rate cannot be increased; this limitation is imposed because a constant amount of time is needed to pick up, manipulate and swallow each grain. The stock dove's ability to find weed seeds on stubbles and sowings probably depends on it having shorter legs so that it is nearer the ground. In such ways birds have evolved different feeding mechanisms which are efficient in a limited range of feeding situations.

In most circumstances predators have a choice of prey and the particular item they select depends not only on prey density but also on learned individual preferences. This learning ability introduces a sigmoid stage to the functional response curve as shown in Fig. 9. This type of response curve is much more common among vertebrates and has, for instance, been found to apply to the predation by titmice on forest insects (Tinbergen 1960, Mook 1963), and has been

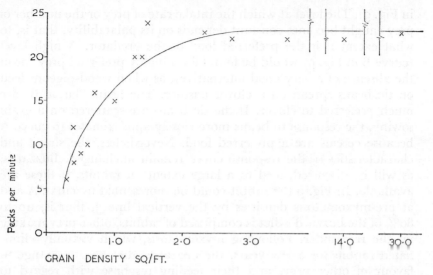

FIG. 8. Number of cereal grains eaten per minute by wood-pigeons depending on grain density. Note that the scale on the abscissa and the actual graph are broken to save space. (From Murton 1968).

produced experimentally with mammals in the laboratory by Holling (1965). The same curve is also found when bait, in the form of beans or peas, is spread on a grain sowing where wood-pigeons are feeding. This characteristic curve has been explained, as follows, by Leopold in 1933 and more recently by L. Tinbergen. At very low densities of the specific prey (density 1 for curve A in Fig. 9), few or none are found, and the food of the predator consists entirely of other items (100% other prey). As the specific prey density increases, a point is reached when some individuals are found by chance (density 2 in Fig. 9) and for a while the curve rises with density as chance encounters increase. But at some stage, which varies with the attractiveness of the prey, the predator learns that this particular food is available and makes a special effort to find it. The food is now found more often than by chance alone, and this causes the sigmoid stage to appear in the response curve (between densities 2 and 3 in Fig. 9). In the terminology of Tinbergen the bird now adopts a specific searching image for the prey in question. At even higher prey densities the predator again introduces variety into its diet and from now on the prey is taken at a constant rate (from density 3 onwards for curve A in Fig. 9). The level at which the intake rate of prey or the number of prey caught becomes constant depends on its palatability, that is, to what extent it is the preferred food of the predator. A high level (curve B in Fig. 9) would be found for a highly preferred prey (or in the absence of a very good alternative), as when wood-pigeons feed on tic beans spread on a clover pasture. The beans (curve B) are much preferred to clover. If the tic beans are scattered on a grain sowing, the response to beans more closely approximates to curve A because cereals are a preferred food. Nevertheless, the shape and characteristics of the response curve remain unchanged. Buzzards, as will be discussed, feed to a large extent on rabbits, if these are available. In Fig. 9 the rabbit could be represented by curve A and at pre-myxomatosis densities by the vertical line 3, that is, up to 80% of the buzzard's diet is comprised of rabbits, other prey making up the remainder. Following myxomatosis, which virtually elimi- nated rabbits for a few years, the buzzards' diet had to change in favour of other prey, and their feeding response with regard to rabbits could now be represented by the vertical line 1. As with the simple response already considered, it is important to note that above a certain point increase in prey density still does not result in a higher proportion being eaten. There is no reason why the activities of a pest-control operator or a gamekeeper would not obey curves of this kind. When an operator can kill only relatively small proportions of a pest animal, it is necessary to ensure that he does not switch from one pest to another depending on the ease of catching. For example, a rabbit catcher might undesirably be ignoring rabbits at low den- sities, to concentrate on catching and killing moles, pigeons and other species.

Any numerical responses shown by bird predators to changes in the density of their prey can most rapidly be achieved by emigration or immigration; more permanent changes dependent on reproduc- tion must necessarily be slow and delayed, because birds have restricted breeding seasons. Figure 10, based on Mook (1963), shows how the numbers of bay-breasted warblers which settled to breed in certain Canadian conifer forests, after they had returned from migration, varied according to the density of the third instar larvae of the spruce budworm *Choristoneura fumiferana*. The response did not depend on the reproductive rate of the warblers: it resembles the behaviour of certain arctic birds of prey, like the snowy owl, which settle to breed in the Canadian arctic and in Scandinavia in those

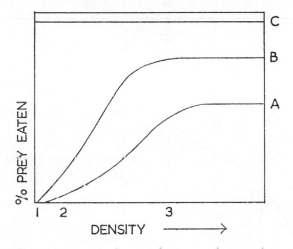

FIG. 9. Functional response of a predator to changes in prey density. The horizontal line C represents the total food of the predator equal to 100%. The proportion of a specific prey, either A or B, eaten by the predator is also shown, depending on changing density of A or B. Consider a predator eating B. At density 1 none is found and the predator's diet is composed of 100% of C (this could be many different items considered *in toto*). At density 3, 80% of the diet is composed of B and 20%, i.e. C—B, of other things again making a total of 100%C. (Based on Holling 1965).

years when lemmings are abundant, and is similar to the behaviour of the short-eared owls already mentioned. There are, however, many cases in which a bird predator shows no numerical response to a specific prey component. An example is discussed below (page 244) where it was found that numbers of wintering oystercatchers showed little variation over several seasons, although their preferred prey, second year cockles, fluctuated widely in numbers. This was because in seasons when second year cockles were scarce the birds fed on cockle spat and the older age groups, so that while oyster-catcher numbers may have been related to the total cockle population they were not related to this one specific age group.

The synthesis of the numerical and functional responses shown by a predator determines the nature of predation and its significance for the prey concerned, the main possibilities being represented in Fig. 11. Because bird predators must in most cases take time to respond to changes in prey density, any interaction must usually be

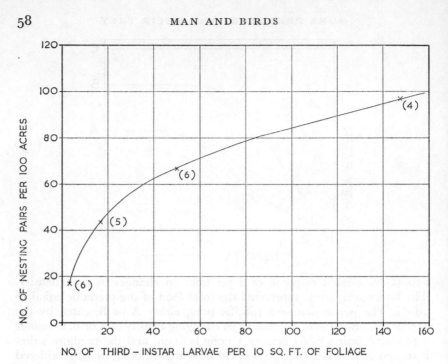

NO. OF THIRD – INSTAR LARVAE PER 10 SQ. FT. OF FOLIAGE

FIG. 10. Numerical response of predator to changes in prey density as shown by the number of nesting pairs of bay-breasted warblers per 100 acres of forest in relation to the number of third-instar larvae of the spruce budworm per 10 sq. ft. of foliage. (From Mook 1963).

delayed. The classical predator-prey relationship is shown at A in Fig. 11. Here the predator increases when prey is abundant, causing the prey to decrease. This results in a decrease of the predator, followed again by an increase of the prey. This ideal balance was first demonstrated in laboratory cultures of the protozoan *Paramecium* by Gause (1934), and was derived theoretically by Lotka (1925) and Volterra (1926). It is rare to find such perfect examples in wild populations, usually because predators have other prey which they turn to when their major source becomes scarce. An apparent case is shown in Fig. 12 which refers to the number of barn owls and kestrels ringed each year, and which may be taken as an index of their actual abundance. Snow (1968) has shown that most of the peaks of kestrels depend on high numbers being ringed in the north of England and south Scotland and they reflect fluctuations in the number of families ringed, not differences in the size of broods. There is no

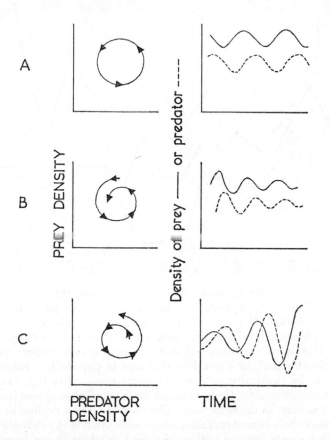

FIG. II. Three possible interactions between a predator and its prey. On the left the numbers of predator are plotted against numbers of prey and successive points on the time scale chosen (months, years, etc.) joined in chronological order. In the right hand graphs the numbers of prey (solid line) or predator (dotted line) are plotted against time.

A. An increase in prey numbers if followed by an increase of predators which eat the prey, causing a decline in the prey which is followed by a decline in the predator so that with time a steady balance is maintained.

B. Predator density increases relative to prey density so that the regular oscillations shown at A become damped.

C. Prey density increases relative to predator numbers and the system become unstable with violent oscillations.

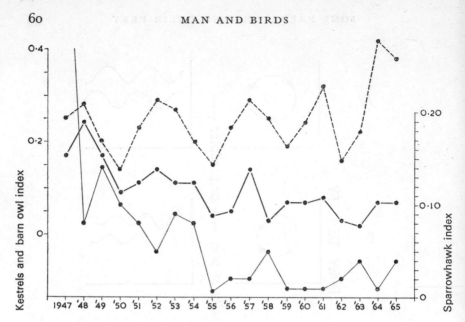

FIG. 12. Number of nestling kestrels (top) barn owls (middle) or sparrow-hawks (bottom) ringed each year as a percentage of all nestlings ringed under the British Trust for Ornithology scheme. The ease with which observers find nestlings to ring is assumed to be an index of the populatuon at risk. The kestrel and barn owl feed on the same small rodent species and it is noticeable that their numbers fluctuate in parallel in a manner reminiscent of the classical predator-prey curve depicted in Fig. 11a. In contrast, the sparrowhawk feeds on small birds (see Table 3) and its numbers do not fluctuate in the same way. The suggestion of a decline in sparrow-hawk numbers is almost certainly a true indication of the changed status of the species due to contamination of its food supply with persistent organochlorine insecticides. The risks of such contamination are very much less for species feeding on small rodents.

evidence for similar periodic fluctuations in southern England. Moreover, there is good evidence that the vole *Microtus agrestis* has been particularly abundant in the north of England in the same years that large numbers of kestrels have been found for ringing. But the curves seem to represent a numerical response of the predator, more kestrels settling to breed when vole numbers are high. There is no evidence that the survival rate of nestling or adult kestrels has varied in the different years in a way that would be expected in a classical predator-prey situation.

PLATE 5. Two woodland predators. *Above*, sparrowhawks declined drastically in the 1950's and early '60's as a result of ingesting toxic chemicals from their prey. This pair, photographed in Surrey in 1966, laid six eggs of which one disappeared and three were broken by the female. One of these carried high residues of D.D.E. In 1967 only two eggs hatched out of five laid. *Below*, jays are very efficient at finding and eating the eggs and small young of other woodland birds.

PLATE 6. *Above left*, ravens occasionally attack ailing lambs especially at parturition, and arouse the wrath of shepherds. More often they depend on sheep carrion. Carrion and hooded crows are commoner and are more often implicated in these attacks on live sheep and lambs. *Right*, this ewe was experiencing difficulty in the birth of her lamb and while laying helpless on the ground had her eye removed by a crow. *Below*, lambs attacked by carrion crows. The frequency of such incidents is much less than one per cent of the animals at risk, but the sight of such attacks obviously arouses strong emotions in the shepherd concerned with the welfare of his flock.

Simple systems of this kind are theoretically liable to change to the kind shown at C in Fig. 11, where the oscillations between predator and prey become self-destructive and lead to the extinction of one or the other. Feeding patterns like those shown above density 3 in Fig. 9, where increased prey density is not compensated by an increased predation (in practice more animals would usually move in to take advantage of such good feeding conditions), tend to produce violent fluctuations. One reason that such oscillations rarely occur depends on the complexity of natural ecosystems as was discussed in the previous chapter (page 49). Prey is effectively isolated in groups so that if one group is accidentally exterminated it is re-populated in a density-dependent way according to its own food supply; predators tend to be less efficient at very high prey densities; and some prey have refuges enabling them to escape predation. These factors plus the existence of more than one kind of predator all help to dampen the kind of expanding oscillation seen in Fig. 11c.

When the percentage of predation at first increases with rising prey numbers, there is a high probability that oscillations will be damped as in Fig. 11b. If the numbers of an insect increase, a proportional increase in the amount of predation by birds could bring the system back to its old level. There is good evidence from L. Tinbergen's researches that this is what certain insectivorous birds may achieve in preying on forest insects in the manner shown in the sigmoid part of Fig. 9; fluctuations in prey density can be reduced and predator-prey oscillations damped, so reducing the risk of an infestation developing. But it is clear that if insect density rises beyond the level where the predation curve is S-shaped in Fig. 9, that is, if the prey achieves densities where a smaller proportion is taken with rising density, then the predator could not be held to have a regulating effect. As will be discussed in Chapter 4, birds cannot control an insect plague once it has developed, but they may help prevent it developing in the first instance. From the point of view of pest control or conservation one general lesson following from the above is that predator–prey interactions will be most stable in environments with a diverse structure supporting a wide variety of predators and prey, as for example, natural undisturbed oak woodland. Monocultures of introduced conifers would be expected to provide unstable conditions. Voute's (1946) observation that outbreaks of insect pests are commoner in pure than in mixed stands of

trees is, therefore, of considerable interest and adds weight to the
suggestion that forestry policy should aim at intermixing deciduous
trees in conifer woods (see page 95).

It can often happen that a predator takes only a fixed number of
the prey with which it is in contact, satisfying its food requirements
and allowing the surplus prey to escape. Again, this is an unstable
situation which cannot last, either because predator numbers would
eventually increase leading to new relationships, or because if the
same predators persist in their attacks they will eventually exterminate the prey. Examples are the temporary concentration of birds
seeking the invertebrates disturbed by a farmer ploughing a field,
the gathering of swallows and martins to feed on the insects blown
from a wood in strong wind, and the birds which gather round a
locust swarm. Here, the number of prey eaten depends on the
number of predators that chances to arrive on the scene, and is not a
function of prey density. The scale of losses inflicted by birds on
locust swarms seems usually slight. Around a small locust swarm in
Eritrea, which covered about ten acres, Smith and Popov noted
two or three hundred white storks, many great and lesser spotted
eagles, and several hundred Steppe eagles, as well as smaller numbers
of black kites, lanner falcons, marabou storks and other species. Shot
and dissected storks each proved to have eaten up to 1,000 locusts.
But most observers agree that this scale of predation has a negligible
effect. More important is the suggestion (e.g. Vesey-Fitzgerald 1955)
that birds may be useful in preventing a rapid build-up of locust
numbers. Recent evidence from the Rukwa Valley indicates that
this is not the case. First, because the preferred feeding habitat of
the birds mostly concerned – white stork, cattle egret and little egret
– is the short grass area of the lakeshore, whereas the locusts prefer
and breed in the long grass associations covering much of the plains.
Second, locusts are most abundant from March–June, when bird
numbers are low, and decrease for other reasons in July when large
numbers of immigrant birds arrive.

When man preys upon wood-pigeons by shooting them on their
return to their roosting woods, the number he kills increases slightly
when the total population increases, but the percentage shot declines.
Each man shoots at the passing flock but can potentially kill only
two birds because he uses a double barrel 12-bore gun. More flocks
pass when pigeon numbers are high, enabling a higher total of birds
to be shot, but the flocks are also much larger and a smaller pro-

portion of each can be killed. Hunting methods impose a limit on a man's kill, and the only way to achieve a higher rate of predation would be for more men to shoot or for each man to use a faster firing, or otherwise more efficient gun. The first possibility is limited by social considerations; the number of men interested in shooting, either for sport or for monetary gain, is restricted because today there are so many more outlets for pastoral relaxation and the financial reward for shooting pigeons is low. The battue shoots did not usually begin until the end of the pheasant shooting season, in late January and early February, because only then were game-owners prepared to let pigeon shooters wander over the estates. They ended in early March when shooting at dusk on the longer days interfered with the other attractions of evening, the village dance or local hostel. The alternative of using a more lethal weapon would be opposed to the arbitrary code of sportsmanship current in Britain today, a code which imposes operose conditions on the ways animals can be 'taken' – a euphemism for 'killed'. In days when cumbrous muzzle-loading guns prevailed, shooting birds sitting on the ground was acceptable, but fashion changed to 'shooting flying' during the eighteenth century as guns improved, and today shooting a sitting bird is unthinkable. Today a similar pretentious scorn is poured upon the American repeater, just as it was upon the double barrelled 12-bore when it first appeared. As Markland (1727) says in *Pteryptegia* or *The Art of Shooting Flying*:

> he who dares by different means destroy
> Than nature meant, offends 'gainst Nature's law.

A viewpoint all right in sport but with no place in serious pest control.

Sometimes predators take all, or at least a large proportion of, a prey species only when the prey exceed a certain minimum number. This minimum may result from a fixed number of safe refuges, physically or behaviourally determined, in the environment; or may occur because the predator finds it unrewarding to search for prey below a fixed density and moves off elsewhere. Errington showed that a given area of range in Iowa could support a relatively fixed number of bob-white quail in winter irrespective of the autumn population, while the surplus birds were taken by predators. A similar story applies to the red grouse in Glen Esk which have been studied in great detail by D. Jenkins, A. Watson and G. R. Miller.

It has already been noted that a territorial system relates grouse numbers to the carrying capacity of the habitat, forcing excess birds to move into less favourable marginal areas. Most of this dispersal takes place during two distinct seasons, from November to December and from February to April, the displaced birds suffer much more from predators than those resident in territories. Knowledge of a territory presumably enables the individual to find hiding places when danger threatens. Of 383 birds individually tabbed which had territories in November the remains of 2% were later found killed by predators, whereas of 261 tagged birds known to be displaced from territories in November as many as 14% were found killed. On high ground (700 m. and above) eagles and foxes accounted for about half the grouse preyed upon, while on low ground (500 m. and below) foxes and hen harriers were about equally responsible for the losses. Table 2 also shows how grouse suffered much more from predators in years when the number known to be dispersing was high. The number of raptors actually hunting in the study area also increased in such years, although roughly a similar total was present in the general area each year. Jenkins *et al.* presume that the grouse were but one of a number of suitable foods and were only taken when they were particularly vulnerable. In this case the number of predators was not determined by the availability of the specific prey studied; their numbers may have been related to the abundance of all prey animals combined, but this is at present unknown. There are times when it is only the birds dispersed to marginal habitats in ways like those outlined above, that cause economic problems – one case is given below (page 77).

At Glen Esk gamekeepers persecuted the predatory birds and mammals at every opportunity. In spite of this, Jenkins *et al.* showed that slaughter was not controlling these predators because a similar number appeared every year. They point out that the number of predators expected to be killed on the moors of Perthshire and Kincardineshire today are similar to figures quoted in 1906 by Harvie-Brown. Keepers may well reduce breeding numbers slightly, or prevent the breeding of some individuals in early summer, but the relatively large number of young produced on the estates in question and near by, is always sufficient to make good these losses. In other words, gamekeepers merely crop an expendable surplus of predatory birds and mammals, in much the same way as these predators crop their prey – as a man does when he shoots grouse. In the circumstances, it is probably a waste of time for the keepers to set their traps and patrol their estates in search of so-called vermin. As far as grouse are concerned, the most useful employment for the keeper would be to lend a hand with heather burning and help to improve moor management, for this is really what affects grouse numbers, not predator control.

It would be a sophism to infer from this account that the activities of gamekeepers have never been detrimental to the birds of prey, but it is likely that in many cases the senseless slaughter has at most accelerated processes brought about by more fundamental changes, particularly in land use or loss of habitat. Once a species declines and becomes restricted in range through lack of habitat it is far more vulnerable to persecution by man. The osprey was probably always rarer as a breeding bird than some authors have implied, as it was restricted by a need for large lochs with good fish populations, but man's greed and his continuous persecution eventually caused its extinction in Britain at the turn of the century. The marsh harrier, too, has long been persecuted. In one Suffolk locality two or three pairs regularly nested up to 1951, in spite of egg-collectors (the mentality of one of the men concerned is shown by the fact that in one day he took nine clutches of shoveller from the level where the harriers bred to demonstrate clutch and egg-size variation) and shooting by the keeper of a nearby estate. But it was drainage of the marsh to improve cattle grazing that spelt the final doom for the harriers at this site in the mid 1950s; not just persecution, senseless though it had been.

Unlike the marsh harrier, the hen harrier has proved remarkably adaptable in its habitat requirements: indeed in the Americas it is the only harrier and occupies the combined niche of all the Old World species. In the north of Britain it has increased, despite fairly heavy persecution, and is doing particularly well in the new conifer plantations of Scotland, which are rich in ground rodents. On the whole, the hen harrier seems to be making good the ground it lost in the nineteenth century, when an even more intensive slaughter banished it from the Scottish mainland as a breeding species. In eastern Europe, the pallid harrier has expanded and increased its range from the Russian Steppes, in close association with the spread of agriculture. Thus human disturbance alone does not necessarily disturb birds of prey. This is shown by the distribution and breeding of the osprey on the eastern end of Long Island Sound in coastal

Connecticut and New York with little regard for human activity; it nests on artificial man-made platforms as does the stork in Europe.

The difficulties of measuring the contribution of habitat change and the persecution of gamekeepers, skin and egg-collectors to the decline of the raptors is well illustrated in the case of the buzzard. The changing status of this bird has been very carefully documented by Dr N. W. Moore following a survey sponsored through the British Trust for Ornithology. Until the early nineteenth century the buzzard was to be found over virtually the whole of the British Isles. Then a serious decline occurred in East Anglia, the Midlands and much of Ireland in the mid-nineteenth century, followed by some recovery in the twentieth century. Today densities of 1–2 pairs per square mile can be expected in suitable habitats. The decline cannot be attributed directly to the spread of agriculture during the nineteenth century because the species underwent increases and decreases both during times of agricultural advance and recession. Also during this period the rabbit, one of the main foods of the buzzard, became more common. Similarly, more urbanisation took place between 1915 and 1954 when the buzzard was increasing, than during the years 1800–1915 when it was decreasing. Furthermore, in the 1954 survey, which indicated a British population of 20–30,000 birds, the highest buzzard density was recorded on mixed agricultural moorland, rather than in pure forest or on extensive moorland, where nesting sites seem to be in short supply. In fact, Moore attributes the early decline of the buzzard to the game-preservation which boomed from 1800–1914. Convincing evidence is provided by his maps, which show an inverse correlation between areas of intensive game-preservation, judged by the number of gamekeepers per square mile, and the distribution of buzzards. His view is also supported by the fact that the biggest recovery took place during the two world wars, when there was much less game-preservation, and many keepers were fighting a different adversary. However, the early decline of the buzzard in the nineteenth century is also temporally related to a marked decline of sheep farming, particularly in East Anglia, and, as discussed below in the case of the raven and carrion crow, the associated loss of carrion may have provided the initial cause, being only accelerated by keepers. Nor does persecution account for the disappearance of the buzzard from Ireland.

Myxomatosis was confirmed at Edenbridge in October 1953, and from two original outbreaks it rapidly spread until by early 1955 rabbits throughout the mainland of Britain were infected with a 99% lethal strain of the virus (Armour and Thompson 1955). The 1954 buzzard survey was carried out before there had been widespread reductions in rabbit numbers, but already many poultry farmers and shooting men were afraid that the bird would now turn to other forms of prey, particularly chickens and game-birds. The same concern was accorded the fox, but fortunately an investigation of this animal's feeding habits had been made before myxomatosis by Southern and Watson (1941) and this was repeated by Lever (1959) on behalf of the Ministry of Agriculture in 1955. The results showed that in the absence of rabbits, foxes concentrated on other small rodents which would normally have been their second most important prey; the incidence of poultry or game-birds in stomach remains did not increase. This turned out to be roughly what happened in the case of the buzzards. Deprived of rabbits, they turned to other small rodents, but took no more game-birds or poultry than before. In the normal course of events the buzzard is not a very specialised feeder and takes a wide range of prey, including rabbits, small rodents, birds and invertebrates, so that their response to a density change in one prey species was as discussed above (page 56). Although the buzzard could turn to other prey, it proved much more difficult for the birds to obtain enough food. The immediate consequence of myxomatosis was that many pairs failed to breed, while those that did attempt to nest laid fewer eggs and were much less successful than usual at rearing the young.

The deforestation in north-west Scotland which caused the loss of the roe deer, great-spotted woodpecker and other species (see page 95), also opened up the Western Highlands for sheep grazing (around 1800); at first good on the rich woodland soil, but subsequently poor as a result of soil degeneration and moor burning. Muirburn resulted in the loss of woody, nourishing and palatable plants leaving only those species resistant to fire. Associated with this spoliation of the habitat, the numbers of all local animals decreased, including grouse, mountain hares, woodcock, snipe and red deer. These last die in large numbers in winter because the impoverished habitat provides much too poor a food supply at the critical time – ideally, good management should ensure a better balance between summer and winter resources. For roughly the same reasons, many sheep die each winter and few lambs survive. A good deal of carrion therefore exists in the form of deer, lambs and ewes already doomed to die and this provides food for golden eagles in the area. Dr J. D. Lockie, who has examined the problem in detail in Wester Ross, has taken great care to discover to what extent eagles prey upon live sheep. Lambs taken as carrion have often lost their eyes as a result of crow attack, or have had limbs or ears bitten off by foxes. In catching live lambs the eagle's talons cause considerable haemorrhage and bruising of the back, which can be recognised at a post-mortem. It is, therefore, fairly easy to distinguish the two sorts of prey by examining lamb carcases in eyries, and for 22 remains found at one eyrie between 1956 and 1961, 10 could be so categorised. Three of these lambs had been killed by eagles and seven taken as carrion. What could not be determined was how many of the live captures were weakling animals or twins – an important consideration in the case of attacks by ravens and carrion crows (see below). Nevertheless, the anti-eagle policy adopted by so many shepherds is understandable. Lockie was able to show that the percentage of lamb in the eagle's diet averaged about 46% in years when lamb survival was average or poor, that is, when conditions for lamb rearing were poor; but it fell to 23% in years of high lamb survival. Hence, when lamb was not abundant the eagles compensated by turning to other prey. Clearly, sensible sheep management is the answer to any eagle problems, and it is not fair to attribute poor lamb seasons directly to eagle predation.

On the Isle of Lewis, complaints that eagles had been attacking sheep in 1954 were investigated by Lockie and Stephen on behalf of the Nature Conservancy. Here the main prey comprises rabbits, lamb and sheep carrion, supplemented by a few hares, grouse, rats, golden plover and hooded crows. Occasionally the eagles do attack live lambs and a pair which were seen to attack 5 lambs sparked off the complaints. Actually, out of thirteen local farmers and crofters interviewed, only two had seen eagles in the act of killing lambs, though two others believed that eagles did attack lambs. The eagle has increased on Lewis since about 1946, coincident with a decline in mountain hares, grouse and rabbits, but an increase in sheep. As the eagle density is now, if anything, higher on Lewis than in other areas of Scotland, where a much richer wild fauna exists, it seems that the high density is maintained by the sheep carrion, of which there is an excessive amount because sheep mortality is high. Overgrazing occurs and deficiency diseases are frequent. In one two-mile walk on 20 April, 28 carcases were counted. Again the basic problem is one of land management, the inefficient farmer being the one who suffers most.

The Western Highlands are mostly deer-forest where, with the exception of some shepherds, the hand of man is not specially directed against birds of prey. The attitude is that if these eat grouse they do good because an accidentally flushed grouse frightens deer and hinders the stalker. The attitude varies again in north-eastern Scotland. In parts of the southern Cairngorms, where Watson found about 12 eagle pairs in 220 square miles of suitable country, sheep are rare on the hills in winter and their density in summer is also low compared with Wester Ross and Lewis. Here eagles are rarely disturbed. Their food in summer comprises about 60% red grouse and ptarmigan and around 30% mountain hares and rabbits. On lower ground, which is grouse moorland, and also on the grouse moors of the southern Grampians, any bird with a hooked bill is considered a potential competitor with man for the grouse stocks – a totally unjustified view as we have seen. The effects of persecution are well-illustrated by a study made by Sandeman of breeding success among eagles in the south Grampians. Successful birds reared on average 1.4 young per year, but making allowance for non-breeders, or birds whose eggs or young were destroyed, gives a figure of 0.4 young per pair per year for the whole area. In the northern part of the area studied by Sandeman the land is primarily deer-forest and sheep ground, where eagles are little disturbed. Here the average success was 0.6 young per pair, which compares with a production of only 0.3 young per pair on nearby areas predominantly given over to grouse-management and sheep-grazing, and where persecution is considerable. The consequences of killing adult eagles are also reflected in the number of immature birds mated to old birds. In 24 territories on deer ground which were occupied over the years 1950–56, no member of any pair was ever immature and no bird was without a partner. In contrast, on the grouse and sheep moors where 51 occupied territories were watched over the same period, immature birds were paired to adults in four territories, while in eight territories only one member of the pair was present. Males or females mated to immature birds either did not breed, or if eggs were laid these were often infertile; killing could thus result in a suppression of breeding success in following years among the survivors. Immature birds were replacing lost adults and, although this replacement may have been insufficient as to saturate the pre-breeding population, it is possible that post-breeding numbers were little below par due to immigration. It is perhaps surprising that intensive killing had so little effect on this slow breeding species, but the area in question probably relied on immigration from areas with a higher breeding success, and were it not for the existence of such reservoirs killing would certainly have depressed total numbers. In the southern Cairngorms, Watson found that the average number of young leaving a successful nest was similar to the above at 1.3 young per pair. However, more pairs were successful and five which were closely studied by Watson reared 0.8 young per year. It is presumably from areas such as these that excess birds are produced which can replace the losses inflicted by man on the grouse estates.

The population of eagles in the deer-forest country of the remote North-West Highlands has probably long been near the maximum carrying capacity of the habitat, in spite of constant harrying by man in supposed defence of his sheep. It required the more subtle action of toxic insecticides to upset this balance, it being suggested that these derived from sheep dips containing organo-chlorine insecticides, particularly dieldrin. These chemicals contaminated carcases and were then accumulated by feeding eagles, with the result that their breeding efficiency was seriously impaired. Lockie and Ratcliffe (1964) found that the proportion of non-breeding eagles in western Scotland increased from 3% in 1937–60 to 41% in 1961–3, and the proportion of pairs rearing young fell from 72% to 29% in the same periods.

There is much stronger evidence that the peregrine has suffered drastically since toxic chemicals were introduced. In 1961 and 1962 Ratcliffe undertook a survey of the species for the B.T.O., primarily because pigeon fanciers had claimed that the species was increasing and threatening their interests. As it happened quite the opposite was found. The average British breeding population from 1930–9 had been about 650 pairs with territories, but in 1962 only about half these territories proved to be occupied, and successful nesting occurred in only 13% of 488 examined. There had been some deple-tion in the south of England during the war years of 1939–45, because the bird was outlawed as a potential predator of carrier pigeons with war dispatches, and was rigorously shot by the Air Ministry; it was almost exterminated on the south coast. Subse-quently there was a rapid build-up in numbers in southern England, which were nearly back to the pre-war level by the mid-1950s. Then the second much more drastic and this time national decline took place, associated with a fall in nesting success and the frequent breaking and disappearance of eggs which the birds appeared to be eating themselves (page 17). While the evidence that toxic chemicals were responsible was necessarily circumstantial, it was such that no reasonable person could wait for cut and dried scientific proof while there was a grave risk of losing much of our wild life in the meantime, and a voluntary ban on the use of these chemicals was agreed. All the same, the recovery of dead peregrines and their infertile eggs containing high residues of organo-chlorine insecticides, together with the coinciding of the decline with the increased usage of the more toxic insecticides, seems to indicate that pollution from these chemicals does account for the loss of these birds. In fact, fifteen infertile eggs from thirteen different eyries in 1963 and 1964 all contained either D.D.T., B.H.C., dieldrin, heptachlor or their metabolites. The distribution and residue level of these insecticides in adults and eggs shows that birds at the top of the food chain are highly susceptible to contamination. A sample of 137 of those territories examined in 1962 was again checked in 1963 and 1964. In 1962, 83 of these were occupied and in 42% of these young were produced (this is the best measure of nesting success), in 1963 only 62 of these territories were occupied but 44% produced young while 66 were occupied in 1964 and 53% produced young. There thus seems some hope that the alarming decline in numbers has been halted and that breeding success is returning to a more normal level. To complicate the picture, though certainly unconnected with the effect of toxic chemicals, there is some evidence that there has been a gradual fall in the peregrine population of the Western Highlands and Hebrides since the start of the century. Whether or not this decline followed the depletion of vertebrate prey in the region already referred to, is not at all clear.

Peregrines capture live prey, usually in flight, and, as Table 3 shows, domestic pigeons form a large proportion of the food in the breeding season. The peregrine is called duck hawk in the United States, and it can sometimes be seen on the estuary in winter instilling panic into wigeon and teal flocks, although duck form a relatively unimportant prey in the summer. It is surprising that the wood-pigeon is not taken more frequently, but it is likely that the adults, which average 500 gms, are too big; domestic and racing forms of the rock dove weigh 350–440 gms. In fact, the only wood-pigeons I have seen killed by the peregrine, and this was in S. E. Kent, were juveniles about 2–3 months out of the nest. In this area of Kent, peregrines seemed to do much better in autumn by concentrating on the flocks of migrants, particularly starlings, which pour into the country over the cliffs at Dover. It is not known to what extent peregrines take domestic or racing pigeons which have become lost and have joined wild populations and as a result are of no value to their owners. Ignoring this factor, but making various allowances for breeding and non-breeding birds, Ratcliffe estimated that the pre-war peregrine population (650 pairs) would consume about 68,000 pigeons per annum, while the depleted population in 1962 would eat about 16,500. This latter figure represents about 0.3% per annum of the total racing pigeon population of Britain, numbering about five million birds. To put this in proportion, there are about 5–10 million wood-pigeons in Britain, depending on the season, which are widely regarded as a pest of mankind – yet mankind happily finds food for 5,000,000 domesticated pigeons. In Belgium, the home of racing pigeons (one-third of the world's pigeon fanciers are Belgian and one-fifth are British), the Federation of Pigeon Fanciers was offering a reward of 40 francs for evidence of the killing of red kite, sparrowhawk, peregrine or goshawk, in spite of the fact that Belgium has ratified the International Convention for the Protection of Birds under which such subsidies are forbidden. While education is again the answer to this kind of attitude it is slow to take effect. A big problem arises because pigeon racing, like greyhound racing, provides a relaxation which can be coupled with betting. As some pigeons are fairly valuable, and the loss of a race through a bird failing to home results in lost prizes or betting money, it is all too easy to lay the blame on a bird of prey.

There is much evidence that predators select ailing prey, and when this additional allowance is made it seems ludicrous to claim that peregrines can really do significant harm to racing pigeon interests. Rudebeck observed 260 hunts by peregrines. Of these only 19 were successful and in three of the cases the victim was suffering from an obvious abnormality. For 52 successful hunts by four species of predatory bird (sparrowhawk, goshawk, peregrine and sea eagle) he recorded that obviously abnormal individuals were selected in 19% of the cases – a much higher ratio of abnormal birds than would normally be expected in the wild. Thus when Hickey (1943) examined 10,000 starlings collected at random he reckoned that only 5% showed recognisable defects. M. H. Woodward, one time

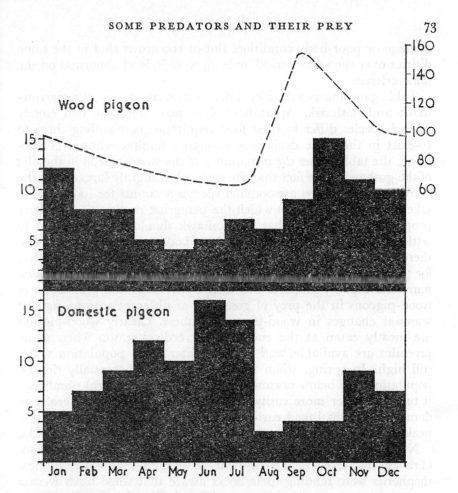

FIG. 13. Seasonal changes in the number of wood-pigeons (top figure) or domestic pigeons (lower figure) in the diet of the goshawk in Germany. The dotted line is based on Murton, Westwood & Isaacson 1964 and represents seasonal changes in the population size of the wood-pigeon. Goshawks take more pigeons when the population size of their prey is swollen by a post-breeding surplus of juveniles, domestic pigeons having their peak breeding season earlier than wood-pigeons. (Based on data in Brüll 1964).

secretary of the British Falconers' Club, quotes the case of 100 crows killed in Germany by trained falcons belonging to Herr Eutermoser. Sixty of these crows were judged to be fit, but the remainder were suffering from some sort of handicap, such as shot wounds, feather damage or poor body condition. But of 100 crows shot in the same district over the same period, only 23 were judged abnormal on the same criteria.

Table 3 summarises the diet of two other birds of prey, the sparrow-hawk and goshawk. Apart from demonstrating how two closely related species differ in their food requirements, enabling them to co-exist in the same deciduous woodland habitat without compe-tition, the table shows the importance of the wood-pigeon in the diet of the goshawk. The fact that the goshawk is slightly larger than the peregrine and is also a woodland species accounts for its ability to take those larger pigeons which the peregrine rarely utilises. Many people have suggested that the goshawk should be encouraged to settle in Britain to help control the wood-pigeon population, but there is no evidence that it would take a sufficient toll to be effective, for the same reasons that eagles and harriers do not control grouse numbers. Fig. 13 supports this view by showing the proportion of wood-pigeons in the prey of goshawks at different seasons, against seasonal changes in wood-pigeon numbers. Clearly wood-pigeons are mostly eaten at the end of the breeding season when many juveniles are available, and in mid-winter when population size is still high. In spring, when the goshawk could potentially depress population size below normal – and hence really control numbers – it turns to other more easily captured prey. In contrast, feral and domestic pigeons breed earlier in the year and have a population peak in June; this is when they are most often caught by goshawks.

Neolithic husbandmen were doubtless familiar with the presence of ravens and crows near their domestic animals, long before biblical shepherds were tending their flocks aware that these birds were a potential menace to a young or weakly animal – *the eye that mocketh at his father . . . the ravens of the valley shall pick it out* (Proverbs 30: 17). Predacious habits and black plumage, burnt by the fires of hell, long ago made the crows prophets of disaster. A suspicion of such augury still persists among those who today think it appropriate to hang corvids and birds of prey on some barbed wire fence or makeshift gibbet; while these crucifixions may well release human frustrations, they do nothing whatever to deter the survivors (see Chapter 12).

Ravens are no longer widely distributed throughout Britain as they were in medieval and even more recent times, but there are still frequent complaints from hill farmers and shepherds in parts of Wales, northern England and Scotland that ravens, and hooded or carrion crows, sometimes kill or maim lambs and even weakly ewes. According to Bolam (1913) sheep, mostly in the form of carrion, comprise the major part of the diet of ravens in Merionethshire, sheep remains being found at least three times more frequently in castings than remains of any other food item (these including rabbits, rats, voles and mice, moles, birds, seashore and other invertebrates, snails and large beetles and some vegetable remains of cereals and tree fruits). Similarly, E. Blezard (quoted by D. Ratcliffe 1962) found sheep remains in over half the castings he examined from birds in northern England and southern Scotland, the next most important item being rabbit, which occurred in only a quarter of the castings. The examination of castings probably underestimates the importance of rapidly digested invertebrates or vegetable foods, but it is clear that sheep (probably as carrion) are an important food source, although the raven, like the crow, is very much an omnivore and carrion feeder. There is no reason to doubt that the raven had similar food habits in the past, when it occurred throughout lowland Britain; in fact, we know that shepherds in Suffolk around 1850 were bitterly hostile to the bird – 'five were among Mr Roper's sheep at Thetford in August 1836'. Like the buzzard, the raven was a reasonably common breeder in Norfolk and Suffolk until about 1830, but it declined markedly thereafter, coincident with the rise of intensive keepering, and it had vanished by the end of the nineteenth century. While continued persecution was doubtless responsible for the final elimination of the bird, and was also probably responsible for making the carrion crow very rare in the second half of the nineteenth century, other factors doubtless contributed to the initial decline. Loss of carrion is usually given as the cause, and it seems likely that it was specifically the loss of sheep carrion that was responsible. In Norfolk and Suffolk this coincided with the period of active enclosure, particularly that of waste land and sheep walks from 1800 to the mid-nineteenth century. According to Arthur Young, half Norfolk yielded nothing but sheep feed until the close of the eighteenth century, when with enormous speed – enclosure was mostly achieved in twenty years – the land was covered with fine barley, rye and wheat. The rapidity with which enclosure was completed is manifested in west Norfolk by straight roads and compact villages, the result of planning on a large scale, whereas in the east of the county the winding lanes, isolated churches, farms and homesteads derive from centuries of slow economic evolution.

Although improvements in hygiene, a lack of carrion and the extensive use of firearms may have eliminated the raven from most of lowland Britain, in relatively undisturbed areas, like the Welsh and Scottish Highlands, its density has probably been altered less. But even in such areas man has much reduced the upland forest habitat of the species and caused it to depend on cliffs for breeding. For more recent times, Ratcliffe (1962) has been able to show that breeding populations in four areas he studied have not dropped by more than 14% since 1945, and average only 6% below the maxima ever recorded. Some increases may even have occurred in areas where the bird previously suffered intensive persecution; in the Scottish borders tree-nesting, but not rock-nesting, has increased since 1945, indicating an increase in local populations which are again able to exploit traditional nesting sites. In Ratcliffe's four inland study areas the average size of a raven's territory ranged from 6.6 to 17.6 square miles (in these same areas the breeding density of the raven was about 2½ times that of the peregrine) but higher densities may occur in favourable coastal areas, for example, four pairs in two miles of cliffs in Anglesey. In Pembrokeshire, R. M. Lockley estimated the raven population at 80 pairs in 1949. In 1953 M. G. Ridpath (Report to Ministry of Agriculture, Fisheries and Food, 1953) searched 25 miles of cliff, in the 140 miles of apparently suitable coast-line, and found an average of one breeding pair every two miles.

Ridpath spent three weeks (220 hours) between 9 and 30 March, 1953, watching a lambing flock of about 1,500 sheep in the Prescelly Mountains, Pembrokeshire. During this period he saw two lambs killed by ravens, and in addition nine other attacks on lambs and eight on adult ewes. Attacks on lambs were concentrated on the eyes, lips, umbilical cord and anus. In one case two ravens persistently attacked a four-day-old lamb in spite of the mother's efforts to defend it. At first the ewe managed to ward off the birds, but eventually one of them managed to peck at the lamb, at which point the mother walked away leaving the birds to finish the kill. In many other cases when attacks were first witnessed, the ewes were active in defence of their young and successfully repulsed the birds.

One of the local farmers, an experienced observer, showed Ridpath a young lamb which he had seen killed by a raven as it was being born. By weight and appearance it did not seem to have been a weakling. Both ravens and crows are certainly attracted by the after-

PLATE 7. Those birds which feed on the larvae of forest insects may help reduce outbreaks of pest species. Coal tits, *above left*, are the most important in coniferous woodland with willow tits, *right*, of minor value while blue tits (not shown) and great tits, *below*, predominate in broadleaved woods.

PLATE 8. *Above*, Capercaillie can sometimes cause considerable damage to newly planted pine plantations and nursery beds. *Below left*, great spotted woodpeckers occasionally cause damage to sound trees in seeking sap and in the absence of suitable dead trees may sometimes excavate a nest hole in telegraph poles. *Right*, Cedar shingles of a Surrey church damaged by green woodpecker.

births at lambing time, and sometimes newly born lambs are not readily distinguished. Lambs are most vulnerable during the moment of delivery (especially if parturition is at all difficult, or twin births occur) when the mother cannot guard them, and for two or three days afterwards. Weaklings are attacked most often, as they are easier to kill than healthy lambs, which make vigorous attempts to escape. Ravens and crows (and for that matter golden eagles in Scotland) rely mostly on carrion, which is fairly common owing to the larger number of sheep which perish in the rigorous hill environment (see below). Attacks on sheep are most frequent at lambing time and during the winter months when parties of ravens or crows are attracted to the supplementary feed put out in the vicinity of the sheep flocks. There is reason to believe that much of the trouble is caused by non-breeding or immature individuals of either species. Thus during Ridpath's study up to nineteen ravens were seen associating with the sheep, but though paired they seemed to be non-breeding birds, and were probably immatures not yet holding territories. Ratcliffe considers that established pairs keep very much to their own territories and do not associate in flocks in this way. It is very likely that these bold attacks on lambing sheep are largely made because birds excluded from the large territories, which must normally contain ample stocks of carrion, are short of food.

Good shepherding in the hills of Britain is a tradition that goes back for centuries. It has always included burying carcases which attract predators and cause disease, the regular and frequent surveillance of lambing flocks and help for ewes in difficulties and for weakling lambs – bad cases are even brought down from the hills. Ridpath concluded that any trouble could be greatly reduced by returning to these practices. If and when control is really needed (the raven is rare and is protected by law) it should be aimed only at the birds causing the damage. It should not involve indiscriminate killing of all the corvids in the area, most of which probably cause very little harm.

Unlike the raven, the carrion crow has increased considerably throughout Britain after suffering a marked suppression from the 1860s until the early twentieth century. A decline in the intensity of game-preservation after two world wars has certainly been a big factor, but it is clear that the crow's feeding habits have enabled it to become re-established in areas now unsuitable for the raven. It seems likely that it has benefited from changes in agriculture and is the best adapted avian scavenger of the new farm environment. That its numbers are still increasing over most of Britain is shown by a B.T.O. inquiry recently conducted by Prestt (1965) for the period 1953–63. It is probably significant that the only region where no increase has occurred over the last ten to fifteen years is East Anglia, where game-preservation remains most intensive.

Burgess (unpubl.) recently organised a survey of carrion crows over an area of 6,000 acres, near the confluence of the North and South Tyne rivers in Northumberland. This is predominantly a pasture area, lying 2–300 feet above sea level, and consists of large fields surrounded by untrimmed hedgerows with many mature trees. The survey involved the destruction of all occupied nests that could be found in mid-May and a repeat of this operation in late June and August, partly to check for repeat nests or those previously overlooked. The first search for nests was begun in April. For the whole area, including those overlooked in the first operation, there were about 103 occupied nests in May 1961, 134 in May 1963, 128 in 1964 and 137 in 1965 (old nests which were never used were noted and totalled about as many nests again in each year). The results indicate a breeding population averaging one pair to about 50 acres, excluding an unknown number of non-breeding individuals. They also suggest a remarkable constancy in the size of the breeding population in different years, a feature also noted for the raven by Ratcliffe. Population fluctuations in birds of prey, including some corvids, seem to depend largely on the number of non-breeding individuals, partly because the size of a breeding territory seems less flexible than in many bird species, and sets a relatively constant limit on the size of the breeding population, which thus remains stable over long periods. This is not to deny that if long enough periods are considered, or different habitats, the size of the territory is ultimately adjusted to the food supply available. As virtually all successful breeding was prevented in 1961 by the nest destruction, it is clear that this had no depressing effect on the subsequent breeding population, a result in keeping with other similar studies and to be expected.

Because of their smaller size, crows seem less of a danger to ewes at parturition and to young lambs, but because of their large numbers and wider range they provide a greater potential threat to the sheep flocks. In Wales, Ridpath saw two carrion crows kill a ewe and her lamb during delivery, and during his three-week watch he also recorded 30 abortive attacks on sleeping lambs, where the crows crept up to the animal and then pounced at the head or tail base.

It is most distressing for a shepherd to contemplate such savage attacks; to see his defenceless lambs with their eyes pecked out obviously rouses deep emotions which make it hard to keep the problem in perspective. It is difficult to obtain objective and un-exaggerated estimates of damage. Burgess (1963) did try to overcome this problem and organised an inquiry covering 155 selected hill-farms in Cumberland and 59 in Westmorland in 1962, after a good deal of publicity to ensure that all incidents would be reported. These farms between them supported some 82,000 ewes and in all 16 attacks on ewes were reported (0.02%). In nearly all cases the ewes attacked were in some difficulty, trapped in snow drifts or hedges, lying on their backs or giving birth. About two-thirds of the attacked ewes did not survive, but a little over half of these were already sick, many suffering from staggers. On the same farms there were 69 attacks reported on lambs, approximately 77,000 being at risk. About half the attacks were made on live lambs (0.04% of lambs at risk) while half again were fit lambs that should have survived. Allowing for unreported cases, the loss of lambs due to crow attack must be well under 0.5% of those at risk.

A pilot survey was conducted in Argyllshire between May and July 1964 (Gailey *in litt.*) by officers of the Department of Agriculture and Fisheries for Scotland. On 50 farms holding 48,390 ewes and 36,292 lambs*, losses attributable to hoodie crows were 192 ewes (0.4%) and 366 lambs (1%). Losses due to all predatory birds (including eagles, ravens and great black-back gull) amounted to 1% of the total sheep stock, hoodies being responsible for 0.65% of this total. Again, this is a very low percentage of damage particularly as this area of Scotland is generally reckoned to suffer the highest level of crow damage. In Argyll, the average mortality of ewes is 7.4% from November to July and 1.6% from July to November, according to McCreath and Murray (1954). These authors give lamb losses as 13% between birth in April and marking in June, and 5% between marking and sales in September. The sheep stock for the county of Argyll is approximately 450,000 breeding ewes and 338,000 lambs. The application of these results to the whole county

*This gives a lambing percentage of 75 per 100 ewes which is close to the average figure of 80 given by McCreath & Murray 1954 for Argyll.

would mean a loss of 2,926 ewes and 2,195 lambs to hoodies, which at £5 and £3 per head respectively at first suggests £21,000 worth of damage. But this is the kind of calculation made by the farmer and is quite unjustified. It can be calculated from McCreath and Murray's mortality data that around 16,000 ewes (3.6%) and 60,800 lambs (18%) would die in the county between April and the September sales, a level of normal wastage far above that of the damage attributable to crows.

The level of damage to sheep seems to be markedly similar in widely separated areas. A survey in Radnorshire, Breconshire and Montgomery in 1969 showed that under 0.01% of 114,751 ewes at risk were attacked by crows, while 0.6% of 119,680 lambs at risk were attacked, the figure becoming 1.4% if only farms where attacks actually occurred are included (K. Walton, in litt.). In Australia, Smith reckoned that avian predators were responsible for the death of less than 2% of the lamb crop, and other Australian studies indicate that the live lambs attacked are already ailing; many have no milk in their stomachs and seem not to be receiving proper maternal care. The work of Alexander *et al.* (1959) in Australia has shown that sheep in their lambing flocks react relatively little towards foxes, more towards crows and most of all towards dogs. Unlike foxes, crows make very determined efforts to attack lambs.

As already discussed (page 34), losses are not additive in these circumstances and it is likely that deaths caused by predatory birds simply improve the survival chances for the remaining animals, so that the final yield is unaffected. There would have to be a very much lower death-rate of sheep and lambs from natural causes before it could be accepted without qualification that predatory birds were depressing the output. The survival of sheep must depend largely on the carrying capacity of the hill, and an effective reduction in sheep mortality would best be obtained by improvements in land management. In large areas of Britain overgrazing and bad land management have been responsible for much sheep carrion, and this in turn supports the predator population. It is this sort of problem that needs evaluation and the immediate answer is not an out-and-out war on the birds. In some circumstances these birds may indeed be troublesome, even allowing for natural losses – but biologists cannot accept the extrapolation of damage costs, as in the example above.

In Britain it is common to see starlings, jackdaws, and less often magpies, associating with livestock and even perching on the backs of the animals. They catch the insects flushed from the ground by the animals' movements or those attracted to the beasts, such as various flies. In addition, they sometimes search the fur for ticks and other parasites, like the tick-birds of Africa. The habit does not cause trouble in this country but in the U.S.A. magpies (a sub-species of the European form, which has a ring distribution extending all round the world) sometimes become more adventurous. Schorger (1921) and Berry (1922) have described how the birds learned to peck open a small hole in the sheep's back, which they gradually enlarged until they located the kidneys which provided a favoured delicacy. Unshorn sheep on open range were sufficiently protected by the thick fleece, and it was only after shearing, when the animals were confined to untended paddocks, that the trouble began; possibly the birds were originally attracted by small wounds left by the shearers. Even small sores provide sites for secondary attack by blowflies. This kind of damage is reminiscent of the attacks of the kea parrot of New Zealand.

The progression from a commensal to a parasitic association between bird and mammal host is well seen in the red-billed ox-pecker in Kenya. These birds feed on the ticks and other insects gleaned from the larger game animals, and help the host by warning it of impending danger. Occasionally, they also make the most of blood clots and fragments of skin from any abrasion or wound and will purposely open up a sore with hammer-like blows to eat the serum and blood discharged. Van Someren (1951) comments that the wounds inflicted on the livestock are smooth saucer-like depressions, 1–3 inches in diameter, which do not suppurate, perhaps because the birds keep them clean. Oxpeckers feed on open sores by nibbling with a scissor-like motion as if squeezing out the blood and scrum. The attacked animals seem untroubled and their wounds rapidly heal if protected from bird attack. The dependence of the oxpecker on ticks is emphasised in districts where insecticide dips are extensively used. In these places the bird has declined drastically rather than become more prone to flesh feeding as some people feared. The European starling has also been recorded as inflicting extensive wounds on cattle in Texas, by pecking at warbles (McCoy 1941). Apparently the birds were first stimulated to attempt this mode of feeding when more normal food supplies were inaccessible through frozen ground.

CHAPTER 4

BIRDS AND FORESTS

To see oak woodland today in anything like its natural state, with a field layer of bluebells, bracken and brambles, and a shrub zone of holly and other small deciduous trees, one must seek out places like the New Forest or the Forest of Dean, or search for other isolated remnants, mostly derived from secondary plantings, which are scattered in small patches throughout the land. Oak in something like this condition had covered much of Britain for around 4,000 years, to be almost totally destroyed since the enclosures of the last 300 years. At sites in Breckland, pollen analysis reveals a decrease of tree pollen in about 3,000 BC followed by the appearance of grass ling and heather and there seems no doubt that Neolithic man was able to clear some quite extensive areas, to produce the heathland that exists today; that this has been maintained does of course owe much to sheep and rabbit grazing. These early efforts at forest clearance, though effective, were certainly made on a very local basis. The open nature of oak woodland allows the development of a rich associated flora of shrubs and herbs supporting a consequently diversified fauna; this diversity has also been facilitated by a long period of establishment enabling a wide variety of plants and animals to reach Britain from Europe. In contrast, beech woodland only spread to Britain at the end of the Atlantic climatic period, roughly at the time when the English Channel was formed and the land bridge with Europe was severed. With the beech came the sweet chestnut, hornbeam and various poplars, and a few other species. None of these have become so widely established as the oak, partly because they are more demanding in their physiological and ecological requirements. In times of much more severe preboreal climate birch was the dominant vegetation, and large areas reminiscent of these ancient times still survive in many parts, particularly in the north of Scotland. Native Scots pine, which preceded the southern deciduous forests, is now confined to the 'black woods' of the Highlands. This, like birch, provides a more uniform habitat than oak and supports a less rich, but none the less interesting, avifauna.

After systematically spoiling almost all the native woodland, man has replanted the landscape with comparatively few small stands of hardwoods, a fairly considerable acreage of trees in orchard and hedgerow, and an increasing area of exotic conifers, from the Japanese larch to the north American Sitka spruce and Douglas fir. These new woods have been colonised in varying degrees by our native sylvan birds. Deafforestation, reafforestation (often with new and exotic species) and afforestation (the planting of trees where none previously grew, at least in recent times) have certainly altered the bird fauna, as we shall see in the next chapter. Here our task is to discover whether the birds have any clear effect on man's interests. The more general question of the role played by birds in the ecosystem is much more difficult to answer, because the interactions involved are complex and not readily measured. There have been many general statements made about the whole plant and animal community, which can be neither refuted nor proved. For example, it is often claimed that some birds, by eating forest seeds, may hinder natural regeneration and, conversely, that birds actually help to distribute seeds and fruit. While it is undoubtedly true that many plants have evolved dispersal mechanisms which rely on animals (the mistletoe is a good example), no quantitative data on such inter-relationships are available. Turček considers that jays, which are specialist feeders on acorns, are practically the only agents able to move acorns uphill. Mellanby (1968) has also considered the role of animals in this respect and disagrees with the many ecologists who consider that most animals prevent natural regeneration of oak woodland. Those animals which destroy the most acorns by feeding on them also appear to be of most importance in causing oak regeneration. Turček also has data to show the importance of birds, particularly jays and blackbirds, in disseminating the sweet cherry in some spruce forests in the central Slovakian mountains. During the summer a mean of 18 casted seeds and 7 seedlings were found per square metre, most within 50 metres of the fruiting tree. Similarly, nutcrackers transport the seeds of *Pinus cembra* and have been responsible for the recolonisation of open pastures, both above and below the tree line, according to Holtmeier (1966).

The case of the jay is particularly interesting and it has been explored by Bossema in Holland. When acorns are freely available in the autumn, the birds devote much time to hoarding them, and carry up to six at a time (one in the bill, and the remainder in the oesophagus) from oak to hiding places in the forest floor. Many of these are later recovered and augment other winter food supplies, in the same way that the nutcracker retrieves hazel nuts which it buries in the autumn. Many acorns are not found and germinate instead, and Bossema considers that the size of an acorn which is not too big for jays to swallow has been specially evolved to provide them with a good food source. By April and May only a few buried acorns can be found, and the proportion of these in the bird's diet falls from more than three-quarters in January to less than a fifth. Surprisingly, the birds again find many fresh looking acorns in June, at a time when most have rotted or been eaten, or have otherwise produced young seedlings. The jay can recognise these young plants and can even distinguish them from the seedlings of other species and the offshoots of roots. On finding a newly germinated seedling, the jay digs down and removes the cotyledons, which are still as fresh as the acorns in autumn. The jay does not damage the young oak tree in the process. It presumably benefits from this food source at a time when it has young just out of the nest, though it does not feed its nestlings on acorns. It lays its eggs mostly in May, which is later than the other British corvids – especially the magpie, which gives its young a similar diet but lays in April. According to Owen (1956) the jay feeds its young primarily on lepidopterous larvae, particularly *Tortrix* spp. which it finds in the foliage of oaks, whereas the magpie collects its food from the ground particularly at the woodland edge and along forest rides. About 41% of the food collected by magpies consists of defoliating caterpillars blown off trees, half of which are again the *Tortrix* spp., while the rest of its food is mainly Coleoptera (21%) such as the Carabid beetles, and Diptera (16%). Ground invertebrates become available earlier than those living in trees, and this could account for the earlier breeding of the magpie. None the less, as most of the species which feed their young on defoliating caterpillars lay in late April and early May (the robin and the tits) it is tempting to attribute the later season of the jay, at least partly, to anticipation of the June acorn supply. To what extent a true symbiosis exists between the jay and the oak is more of a problem; the jay may rely on the oak, but testing for any reciprocal dependence poses enormous problems because of the time-scales involved in the development of an oak wood.

As hinted in the last chapter, many forest workers believe that birds remove harmful insects in sufficient quantities to prevent infestations developing, and therefore consider the provision of nest-boxes a good thing. Indeed, studies at Wytham wood, Oxford, by members of the Edward Grey Institute and by Kluijver in Holland, have shown that the provision of nestboxes may increase the density of great and blue tits, which may be restricted in summer by the availability of suitable natural holes. The numbers of coal and crested tits do not similarly increase, since these species, particularly the coal tit, are able to use a wider range of natural holes, including ones in the ground. To decide whether or not nestboxes are bene-ficial in the control of pest insects raises many interesting problems. Before dealing with these it is worth digressing to consider the difficulties of study techniques that have to be overcome before any facts can be ascertained – difficulties that are common to all objec-tive field assessments of the true economic status of problem species. One must first define the normal diet of the bird concerned. Some-times it is possible to identify food remains in the gizzards of shot samples, but care must be taken to ensure that the sample adequately covers the different seasons, and caters for possible geographical or diurnal variations in diet. In practice, large numbers are usually needed, a problem if the bird in question is uncommon or protected. Difficulties may arise in identifying macerated food remains from a gizzard, and the problem that different foods may be digested at different rates usually arises. It is none the less surprising how accu-rately plants and animals can be identified from a single hair, scale, or fragment of leaf or seed capsule; there is plenty of scope for forensic science in this field. To supplement gizzard analyses, it is usually vital to make observations of the birds in the field and so establish the preferred feeding sites, because a knowledge of these can provide valuable clues, and sometimes direct evidence, of the foods being exploited. Sometimes, the food brought to the young can be collected in the gape of an artificial nestling, or tight collars can temporarily be placed round the neck of a nestling, preventing it from swallowing and enabling the observer to collect the sample after the parents leave the nest. There are countless ingenious methods, depending on the species studied, and every worker normally develops a suitable technique for the species under con-sideration. Royama, for example, modified a time-lapse cine camera and electronic flash gun and mounted them at the back of a nesting box, the lens looking into the box through a glass window. An in-genious trip mechanism and circuit caused the adults to take their own full-face portrait as they entered their nest hole, and inspection of the exposed film showed the species of caterpillar, spider etc. which the birds were bringing to their young. Royama included frame counting and double exposure preventing devices in his circuit and suspended a watch inside the nest box so that a record of the time was included with the bird's picture. Fortunately, tits bring only one food item at a time in their beak to their young, making it easier to identify and estimate the size of the species. The tedium prevented by this method can be gauged by the fact that great tits may make up to seven hundred visits with food to the nest per day, and Royama collected comprehensive data on several pairs for the whole of the time they were feeding young. L. Tinbergen used a similar method, but relied on watching the birds himself from a hide placed behind a glass-backed nesting box. He devoted long hours to this study, but it yielded some extremely rewarding results.

Apart from knowing what, and how much birds eat, one must also know the number of insects available in a particular area of forest. Again, sampling techniques can be used, designed for the specific insect concerned, but satisfactory results usually entail extremely tedious efforts. To estimate the number of insects which were potential prey for titmice in Breckland conifer forest, Gibb and his helpers cut branches from various parts of the trees, later cutting these into smaller sections. These samples were anaesthetised and the immobilised insects removed by beating the twigs inside a metal cannister; they could then be counted, weighed, and identified. Finally each twig had to be searched for scale and other insects not dislodged by the beating process. In spring and summer, an index of the abundance of certain defoliating caterpillars can be obtained by measuring the rate at which their faeces accumulate on fine muslin trays placed below the trees (frass counts). Care has to be taken to avoid windy days and corrections can be made to allow for the growth of the caterpillars. A discussion of such techniques would occupy many pages but enough has been said to indicate the kind of difficulties involved.

Studies making use of some of the above methods were made by Dr Monica Betts in the Forest of Dean, to compare the diet of various titmice, particularly great and blue tits, with the numbers of defoliating caterpillars living in this mature oak woodland, which is now about 150 years old. Betts reckoned from frass counts in 1950 that there were 1,299,000 defoliating caterpillars per acre in one part of the forest (at Nagshead, where there were 63 oak trees per acre) and 932,000 per acre in another part (at Barnhill, with 31 trees per acre). In 1951 these plots had, respectively, 45% and 36% fewer caterpillars. Certain approximations had to be made in these estimates – for example, it was impossible to include small shrubs. However, the estimates could be checked again by counting the number of larvae on samples of 100 leaves collected in the two years; a reduction of about 38% was found. Larvae of the winter moth *Operophtera brumata* accounted for nearly three-quarters of these caterpillars. Nestboxes were sited in the Nagshead plantation, though not in Barnhill, and as a result, the number of tits was doubled. In fact, the total population of adult and young titmice at the time of maximum caterpillar abundance was calculated (from careful census counts of singing males, from the number of nestboxes occupied and from the average number of young per brood) in Nagshead at 19 per acre in 1950 and 15 in 1951, and 6 per acre in both years at Barnhill. With a knowledge of the feeding rate of nestling tits, the proportions of different food items in the diet, and on the assumption that adults ate the same amount as their young (probably an underestimate), the average intake of each individual tit could be calculated as 1,344 lepidopterous larvae during the nestling period. This may seem a large quantity, but it means that in 1950 the average tit population removed only 1.4% of the caterpillars from Nagshead and 0.9% from Barnhill, comparable figures in 1951 being 4.8% and 3.2%. To examine the effect on *O. brumata* alone, it was calculated that in 1950 the birds removed 0.5% from Nagshead and 0.3% from Barnhill and 2.6% and 1.7% respectively in 1951.

It is a very tedious task to obtain data such as these. They are subject to reservations, but nevertheless give a valuable idea of the nature of bird predation on insects. Such a low level of predation could not make any significant check on the outbreak of a pest infestation, especially as the reproductive rate of the birds must be much slower than that of their insect prey. It is enlightening also to consider that a doubling of tit numbers by the erection of nestboxes caused only a slight increase in insect predation. This is a little misleading because Nagshead did support more trees and a higher insect population, while the provision of nestboxes also increased the numbers of pied flycatcher, redstart and nuthatch whose food intake and rate of predation was not measured.

Caterpillars of the winter moth pupate in the ground, and the wingless females emerge between late November and late February and climb the trees where they lay their eggs. On average each female lays about 200 eggs and, as Betts found that there were up to 443 individuals per tree, the potential caterpillar population for 1951 in Nagshead was 5 million. She was impressed by the fact that there were many more adult moths per tree in Nagshead (443) than in Barnhill (350) in spite of more predation by birds in Nagshead; this observation could be explained if factors other than predation by birds determined the survival chances of the larvae. The caterpillar population in 1951 was only one-tenth of its potential so it is possible that bird predation on adult moths, when the insects ascended the trees to lay, may account for the discrepancy. Actually, the predation rate on the adult female moths was probably about 20% which, though fairly high, does not entirely account for the inconsistency (there should still have been 1 million potential larvae instead of the estimated 558,000). In December, when these observations were made, the tits were able to use a very good alternative food supply of beech mast, a crop which was not available in 1948 and 1949 when the birds concentrated their feeding much more on the oaks. This implies that in some years the predation rate may become high enough to dampen fluctuations in caterpillar numbers. All the same, it is always dangerous to speculate too far in situations of this kind. If potential caterpillar numbers were not limited by winter tit predation, some other factor(s) must have been involved; it is known that caterpillars compete with each other for suitable feeding places, and the weather may well be a factor in egg hatching, quite apart from predation from other sources. In cases like this, the problem is whether the potential eggs from the 20% of females which were eaten would have produced viable caterpillars had they been laid; this cannot be automatically assumed.

Similar results were obtained in another summer study by Gibb and Betts (1963), this time working in the Breckland pine plantations of the Forestry Commission at Thetford Chase, on the borders of Norfolk and Suffolk. The forest consists of large acreages of evenly spaced trees, mostly Scots pine *Pinus sylvestris* with some stands of Corsican pine *P. nigra*. Coal tits are the most numerous tit in conifer woods, where in the absence of natural sites they may nest in holes in the ground or at the base of trees. In the Breckland pines, great and blue tits were also induced to nest by the provision of nestboxes. The monotony of the forests is relieved by occasional forest rides, and the edges of the larger rides are fringed with deciduous trees which served as protection when the forests were first planted. Sometimes more than half the food of coal, great and blue tits was collected from these sites and they clearly offered a more rewarding source than the conifers in spite of their small area. Moreover, more nestboxes were occupied in areas adjacent to the broad-leaved trees, probably because they were so near a good food source. Caterpillars of such genera as *Evetria*, *Thera*, *Ellopia* and *Panolis* made up about half the diet of both early and late broods of all the tit species considered together, although each species of tit favoured different sizes and proportions of these foods. Again, with a knowledge of the adult and nestling diet and of bird and insect densities from sampling, it was calculated that the number of caterpillars eaten was usually less than 3% of those available, except that in May and early June 1956 coal tits alone took about 20% of the stock of *Evetria*.

The replacement, rather than additive, effects of predation were well illustrated by the case of the coal tits, which were feeding on *Thera* larvae that had been parasitised by the encyrtid *Litomastix* sp. (Hymenoptera, Chalcidodea). The parasitic larvae cause the normally cryptically coloured green *Thera* first to become more immobile and a conspicuous silvery grey-green, and then an inflated yellow skin full of the chalcid pupae. Up to 42% of the *Thera* larvae collected were parasitised in this way.

Kendeigh (1947) estimated that only 4% of a plague population of the spruce budworm *Archips fumiferana* was eaten by birds, though a higher proportion was taken after the plague when insect numbers were decreasing; at such times Dowden, Jaynes and Carolin have recorded birds taking between 20% and 40% of the available prey. In Canada, an infestation of spruce budworm synchronised over an area of some 30,000 square miles resulted in a twelve-fold increase in bay-breasted warblers *Dendroica castanea* (Morris *et al.* 1958), and this was insufficient to control the outbreak. On the other hand, Keve and Reichart found in Hungary that house-sparrows killed 98% of the fall webworm moth *Hyphantria cunea* before it could lay its eggs. Reichart (1959) also studied a plague of the gypsy moth *Lymantria dispar* in the oak–hornbeam forest of Hungary. The moth deposits its eggs in piles under a protective web. Great tits, blue tits, nuthatches and tree-creepers were between them attacking up to three-quarters of the egg heaps present in the forest, destroying between one and two-thirds of the eggs in large piles and 80%–100% in smaller ones.

In 1949, M. V. and A. D. Brian conducted an interesting experiment on an oak tree near Glasgow. They carefully caged ten branches in early April with half-inch wire netting sleeves to prevent access by birds, principally chaffinches, willow warblers, blue and great tits, known to be feeding on caterpillars in the area. Two months later, in June, ten unprotected control branches of comparable size supported 17 defoliating caterpillars, whereas there were 63 where the birds had been prevented from feeding. The most important species were the winter moth and oak roller moth *Tortrix viridana*. Furthermore, the variability in insect numbers was greater in the protected samples, suggesting that the birds had reduced caterpillars proportionately more where numbers were high, by feeding in a density-dependent manner. Work of this kind is always difficult and open to the criticism that the cages would provide protection from rain, frost or other insect predators which would cause an increase in insect numbers even in the absence of birds. Allowing this, the experiment is still suggestive of a real effect through bird predation.

The impact of birds on insect numbers outside the insect breeding season may be rather different from their usually ineffective attention in summer or during plagues. Gibb found that in winter the tits and goldcrests living in Thetford Chase were eating up to 235 gm of invertebrate food per acre (where the average stock present throughout the winter was 395 gm/acre). Moreover, the total demands over the winter exceeded the amount of insect food present at any one time, so that the birds might have eaten themselves completely out of house and home, but for a certain amount of insect breeding and replacement during even the coldest winters. Under these conditions, the numbers of tits varied in different winters in direct relationship to the density of invertebrates – evidence that the food supply regulated the number of birds. Altogether the birds ate about 25%–30% of the entire original stock of invertebrates but some species suffered a much higher predation. In particular, there was a eucosmid moth larva *Ernarmonia conicolana* living in pine seeds, of which the birds ate 45% each winter, but up to 70% in some localities in certain years. *Ernarmonia* is not an economically important species; if it was, there might be grounds for attributing a beneficial role to the birds. However, the situation is complicated because in the case of *Ernar-*

monia the tits concentrated their feeding on this source when its numbers were high in relation to those of other insects in the environment – conditions under which the birds found it particularly easy to find *Ernarmonia* (see Fig. 14).

In Japan, tree sparrows and grey starlings *Sturnus cineraceus* were estimated to take 40–50% of the adult moths of *Hyphantria cunea* as these emerged before dusk. Hasegawa and Ito (1967) describe how the predation ceases at dusk and how the moths ended their sexual flights in the mornings, before the sparrows emerged. Although the moths need daylight to perceive the visual cues necessary for copulation, it seems that pressure from birds has been sufficient for them to limit their day flying activities as much as possible.

As was discussed on page 56, if there is a choice of foods, a bird's consumption of one particular species of prey does not necessarily increase in proportion to increasing numbers. Provided they can obtain sufficient food, birds seem to prefer a mixed diet. This has been shown particularly well in studies made by L. Tinbergen and his colleagues in Dutch pinewoods already partly referred to (page 61) and illustrated in Fig. 9. These workers ascribed a 'risk index' to the different species of caterpillar living in the pinewoods. This index related the density of caterpillars in the environment to the number caught by the birds during a unit period of hunting. The 'risk index' of a caterpillar depends on various factors, including its size, palatability and cryptic properties. Tinbergen made the important discovery that when a new species of suitable prey appears in the environment, its risk is at first low and then increases suddenly. This phenomenon led to the hypothesis that tits, when searching for prey, concentrate on only one or two species at a time and through some sort of learning process adopt 'specific searching images' of these species. By analogy, if silver sixpences and brown pennies are dropped on the carpet it is easier to look for either one or the other at a time; one gets one's eye in for a particular coin. To carry the analogy further, we should probably pick up the sixpences first, because these are the coins we prefer. Factors affecting the adoption of a 'searching image' are various, one of the most important being the density of the particular food. Tinbergen found that the percentage of prey in a bird's diet was lower than would be expected on the basis of chance encounters when the prey was at low densities, higher at medium densities and below expectation again at high densities. The results are explained by assuming that the birds do not adopt 'specific searching images' for food which is scarce but find it solely by chance, while at high densities they again cease to use this hunting method in order to obtain a more varied diet, when specialisation is no longer essential to survive.

If birds feed on any particular insect in such a way as to produce the sigmoid response shown in Fig. 9, their predation rate must be density-dependent. Gibb showed that this was happening when blue tits in particular were feeding on *Ernarmonia conicolana*. His diagram demonstrating this has become something of a classic, and is reproduced as Fig. 14. Tinbergen and Klomp (1960) have calculated that given predation of this kind, with the birds taking usually more than a quarter of the insects at risk, oscillations in prey numbers can be damped in accordance with Fig. 11b. Within these strictly defined conditions insectivorous birds may be considered beneficial in helping to control pestiferous insects. But once insect numbers reach their usual summer level or plague proportions, the percentage eaten falls below the critical level for effective control; moreover, the feeding rate of the birds is no longer influenced by density (Fig. 9), and in such circumstances they cannot make any significant impact on their prey.

Now that we have considered in detail certain important relationships between birds and forest insects we may return to our original question of whether nestboxes help to reduce insect pests. Baron von Berlepsch in Germany convinced many foresters with his observation that a wood with nestboxes remained green during an insect plague, while a nearby one without boxes was defoliated, and the subject has attracted much attention in Germany. Bruns (1960) has reviewed much of the literature on the subject and reports a study in progress at Steckby-on-the-Elbe, where there are periodic plagues of the pine looper moth *Bupalus piniarius*. Some forest compartments have been provided with nestboxes (1 or 2 per acre), while others have not, and over 33 years the nestbox areas have always remained relatively undamaged during each insect plague (Hähnle 1946, Herberg 1959). In another area at Neustrelitz, Mansfeld has reported how there were only 50 caterpillars of *Bupalus piniarius* per tree in a seventy-acre area with two nestboxes per acre, as against 5,000 caterpillars per tree in adjoining areas.

Similar studies are currently in progress in the Forest of Dean, Gloucestershire, at Cannock Chase in Staffordshire, under the auspices of the Forestry Commission, and in the Culbin forest,

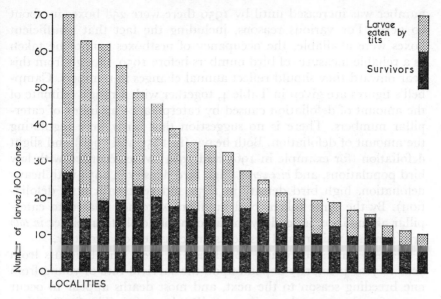

FIG. 14. Number of *Ernamonia conicolana* larvae per 100 Scots pine cones in 21 localities of Breckland pine forest in winter 1955-6. Density-dependent predation by blue and coal tits is evident in the proportion of larvae eaten by these birds. (After Gibb 1958).

Morayshire, by M. Crooke. Work started at Culbin in 1961 but has been hindered through difficulties in making an accurate assessment of the numbers of coal and crested tits. The provision of nestboxes in one plot did not increase coal tit numbers (as might be expected from page 85), nor did it induce coal tits to use boxes instead of ground holes, though it did encourage a few pairs of blue tits to nest in the woods. However, the total bird density seems to have been little affected, and there was no significant difference in the number of pine looper moth pupae in plots with nestboxes and in those without, during the years 1962–5.

The best series of figures in Britain arise from the persistent energies of Dr Bruce Campbell, who since 1946 has inspired various helpers to run a nestbox study in the Forest of Dean, a scheme originated in 1942 by W. L. Taylor in the Nagshead plantation to encourage insectivorous birds. I have already referred to the intensive studies of Dr Monica Betts who used the facilities of this area. In 1942 there were 84 nestboxes in about 37 acres, but this number was increased until by 1950 there were 258 boxes in about 60 acres. For various reasons, including the fact that insufficient boxes were available, the occupancy of nestboxes cannot be taken as a reliable measure of bird numbers before 1950, though from this year onward they should reflect annual changes in numbers. Campbell's figures are given in Table 4, together with a rough estimate of the amount of defoliation caused by caterpillars – an index of caterpillar numbers. There is no suggestion that birds were regulating the amount of defoliation. Both heavy (in 1955 and 1956) and slight defoliation (for example in 1963 and 1964) were recorded with low bird populations, and *vice versa* (high bird density in 1954 with heavy defoliation, high bird density in 1957 and 1961 with little defoliation). By the same token, bird numbers were not related to caterpillar abundance, judged by the amount of defoliation, either *in toto* or if summer visitors and residents are considered separately.

Changes in the breeding population of great and blue tits from year to year primarily depend upon the survival rate of young from one breeding season to the next, and most deaths appear to occur soon after the young leave the nest (Perrins 1965). The final critical adjustment of numbers occurs in winter, and in the case of the coal tit there is good evidence from Gibb's (1960) work that the winter food supply is the important factor involved. As the birds cannot anticipate the summer stock of food, it is purely a matter of chance whether their numbers are high when a pest outbreak occurs. There is therefore no relationship between the number of tits at the end of one breeding season and the number entering the next as Table 4 also demonstrates. Any increase in the number of nesting pairs after nestboxes have been provided must therefore depend on birds which are attracted to the woods for breeding from outside habitats. By winter many of these excess birds must disperse again. As compensatory deaths also occur, a real increase in numbers is not achieved at the season when birds can make significant inroads into their prey. This conclusion does not invalidate the earlier statement that birds may damp down oscillations in insect numbers, but their impact must be less than it would be if their own numbers fluctuated in more direct relation to summer insect numbers. Nor do the results lessen the possibility that some species of birds may respond more directly to insect numbers and settle to breed at a higher density when insect numbers are high, as in the case of the bay-breasted warbler and spruce budworm (Fig. 10). Nonetheless, there is no suggestion

from Table 4 that more birds settled to breed when insect numbers
were high.

In conifer woodland the provision of extra feeding places in the
form of deciduous trees could be of far greater value than the
erection of nestboxes. It could lead to a bigger tit population in
winter, capable of eating more insects in the conifers, because the
birds would be helped by extra food reserves of no economic importance. As Gibb pointed out, tits living in deciduous woodland
use a variety of feeding stations, from branches to trunk, moving in
turn from one category of feeding site to another as different insects
are exploited. Such versatility is denied to birds living in the pure
stands of a coniferous forest, but it could arise if belts of deciduous
trees were planted to break up the pure stands, using as wide a range
as possible of trees like beech, oak, hazel and birch. Not only would
this make for a greater amenity value but it could also increase the
general diversity of wild life.

Breeding numbers of the pied flycatcher and redstart, which are
summer migrants, fluctuated independently of those of the tits in
the Forest of Dean (Table 4). Presumably their numbers were
determined by different factors though it is not known what these
were. Unlike the tits, the size of their breeding populations may be
affected by the more permanent provision of nestboxes. According
to Campbell, pied flycatchers require highland wooded areas where
the shrub layer is not too dense, where oak or similar trees provide a
good food supply of defoliating caterpillars, and where old trees
exist to give natural holes for nesting. These conditions are most
generally found in sessile oak woodland and the peculiar local
distribution of the species in England and Wales follows the distribution of these woodland types. The pied flycatcher has considerably
increased its range in Britain over the last 100 years, and in many
localities this can be attributed to the provision of nestboxes. It is
still very sporadic in Scotland, which is surprising in view of its
habitat requirements. Campbell considers it possible that the bird is
limited to within the 50° F May isotherm of average mean temperature which does not include Scotland. But he thinks it more likely
that the pied flycatcher previously did exist in Scotland, and that
like the red squirrel, roe deer, capercaillie and great spotted woodpecker it became extinct, or very rare, following deforestation in the
eighteenth and early nineteenth centuries. These other species have
only recently recolonised Scotland, following the reafforestation with

conifers and the natural regeneration of the hardwoods. The great spotted woodpecker was the last of these species to recolonise the highlands and has spread since 1887 when it bred in Berwick, to Perthshire in 1907 and Inverness-shire in 1921. It is possible that the pied flycatcher has followed the woodpecker, making use of old woodpecker holes for nesting; indeed the distribution of the fly-catcher in 1952 was extremely similar to that of the woodpecker in 1908. Two other hole-nesting species with habitat requirements similar to those of the pied flycatcher in England and Wales are the redstart and coal tit. Both extend well to the north in Scotland, which runs counter to the suggestion above. But as Campbell points out, the pied flycatcher is the latest breeder and has to establish a nest site after these other species have had first choice; on this account it could be expected to be slow to recolonise the Highlands. It should be mentioned that the pied flycatcher has now penetrated to the far north of Scotland.

Mention of woodpeckers raises the issue that they occasionally cause concern to foresters by damaging healthy trees, although most of their attentions are devoted to dead or decaying branches, which provide insect food or nest sites. The habit of ringing trees and eating the exuding sap is typical behaviour of some New World wood-peckers, in particular the sap-suckers. The American Picidae show a wider ecological divergence than their Old World relatives and indulge much more in habits like seed storing (the Acorn wood-pecker), catching insects on the wing, and egg-stealing, while these activities are rare in the European species. Nevertheless, certain of the European woodpeckers do ring trees to obtain the sap, and while not such a common habit as in America, it has frequently been recorded from March until summer when the tree sap, rich in carbohydrates, is rising. Turček (1954), who has studied the subject, found that in central Europe first the great-spotted woodpecker and then the black woodpecker were the species most involved, while the three-toed woodpecker in conifer woodland, and the middle-spotted woodpecker and lesser-spotted woodpecker in deci-duous woodland, were also implicated to a smaller extent. Among the conifers, *Pinus silvestris* is the preferred tree; while oak and lime are the hardwoods most often used. However, a wide range of trees including larch, yew, douglas fir, birch, beech, elm and sycamore may also be visited. Turček watched a great-spotted woodpecker make several horizontal punctures down to the cambium in a maple,

PLATE 9. Woodland birds that do not succeed as breeding birds on farms without well developed hedgerows and occasional stands of mature timber, although immigrant chaffinches do find much food on stubbles in winter. *Above left*, chaffinch. *Right*, longtailed tit. *Below*, greenfinch. Nest sanitation is less efficient in those finches which only make infrequent visits to the nest.

PLATE 10. Goldfinches declined at the end of the nineteenth century but are currently increasing on farmland. The female is regurgitating food for the young and bears a B.T.O. ring. In finches both sexes often visit the nest at the same time to reduce the risk of exposing the site to predators.

and visit the tree several times during the next three hours to drink the sap which oozed out. During these visits it made new punctures on various parts of the trunk and branches. Marsh tits, long-tailed tits, great tits and blue tits also came to the tree and took the sap which the woodpecker released. It is interesting to note that woodpeckers usually ring an odd tree species (mixed-in trees) growing among other types, or damaged or stunted trees. Thus of 177 cases involving sixteen species of tree, 18 were stunted and overshadowed by surrounding trees, 37 were injured in some way, 164 were 'mixed-in' and only 19 could be classed as normal healthy specimens. It is not clear if such abnormal trees are characterised by a more nutritive sap content or whether the timing or quantity of their sap flow differs. Tree ringing is not an economic problem, and it is only occasionally that a healthy, commercially valuable tree is damaged when subjected to repeated attack. Continuous puncturing may lead to the formation of callus or other deformity above the wound, and sometimes secondary infections from insects or fungi may gain access to the tree. In conifers, resinous vacua may sometimes be formed in the wood which spoil it for plank making purposes. Woodpeckers sometimes damage timber structures outside forest areas, and these problems are discussed again in Chapter 11.

Two leaf and bud feeders, the capercaillie and black grouse (the female is termed grey-hen) have feeding habits which sometimes bring them into conflict with forestry interests, though in general their shooting and amenity value outweighs any damage they do to forest culture. Voous, unlike earlier authors, places the black grouse in the same genus as the capercaillie, since a fertile hybrid, the *Rakkelhuhn*, is often produced. Black grouse also interbreed with willow grouse and ptarmigan and these sympatric species are best regarded as only slightly differentiated, although for the most part they remain ecologically isolated. In areas of range expansion, capercaillie hens arrive first and in the absence of a caper cock often mate with a black cock. The capercaillie is a highly specialist feeder on the buds, shoots and cones of *Pinus sylvestris*, while the black grouse depends on birch buds and shoots, particularly at the most critical time of the year for food supplies. In fact, the tetronids show a very interesting ecological separation with each species adapted to concentrate on one major food plant at the worst season of the year. In Europe, the red grouse takes heather shoots, while its conspecific continental form, the willow grouse, eats the buds and catkins of

Salix species; the hazel grouse prefers alder buds and catkins. Black game frequent a mosaic of wet heath and moorland with *Calluna vulgaris* and a thin covering of birch and pine, and even mature open pine forest with a thick undergrowth. At the turn of the century, the bird occurred in suitable habitats over a great part of Britain, including such counties as Norfolk and those from Hampshire west to Cornwall. A general decrease in range has not only led to lower numbers in Scotland but to the bird's disappearance from most English localities. Today the population may again be increasing, particularly in the new conifer forests of Wales. These changes could be part of a long term trend associated with climatic changes: gamebird records indicate peaks from 1860–70 and again from 1910–15 (Mackenzie 1952).

The caper is very much more restricted in its habitat range; it does frequent highland birch woods and other broad-leaved forests in Europe, but in Britain it is virtually confined to the old open pinewoods with a thick undergrowth of heather, blaeberry and juniper. It begins to colonise pine plantations when these are about 15 to 20 years old. In days of a different climate the capercaillie was well distributed throughout Britain, but as natural pine forest became more restricted to the north the range of the bird declined until it was finally exterminated from the woods of Inverness-shire in about 1770. The present British stock depends on introductions from Sweden first successfully made into Perthshire in 1837 and 1838, but since repeated at least 25 times according to Dr I. Pennie. Today the bird is distributed in suitable pine woods from Fife and Kinross to Moray, Nairn and Inverness. Isolated pockets exist in Ross-shire and Sutherland, and from Argyll and Arran in the west to Stirlingshire. Outside these areas it occurs only sporadically. In winter and early spring the entire diet consists of the needles and to a lesser extent the buds, shoots, cones, and seeds of Scots pine and larch, and to a much smaller extent those of spruce and other conifers. Zwickel, studying the bird in Kincardineshire, found that capercaillies shifted from ground to tree feeding and from woods without much pine (many were in large plantations in September and October) to those dominated by pines in November when the first snow of the winter fell. In spring young blackberry shoots and leaves are taken, and the birds exploit a wider range of shoots, buds and berries, cranberry, crawberry, bilberry, grass and sedge seeds, acorns and cereal grain from stubbles and stooks.

In summer the black grouse has a diet similar to the summer diet of the caper, to judge from Kaasa's work in Norway (1959). It collects the shoots and berries of *Vaccinium* and *Empetrum* species and also the flowers, leaves and seeds of various herbaceous plants and birch buds. Later in the season juniper berries increase in importance while heather shoots and bilberry twigs are also taken. Observations by Johnstone in Scotland agree with these records but show that heather is an important food throughout the year in Glen Dye. In winter black game come to depend much more on birch buds and twigs and also on the catkins in years when these are available; in Scandinavia they have a much more exclusive diet of birch than in Scotland.

The fact that these two game-birds each rely primarily on a single food plant in mid-winter has led to some interesting adaptations. In Finland, Seiskari (1962) has shown that the oesophageal crop is a vital storage organ enabling the short-winter feeding day to be extended. Even so, the capercaillie can collect only half the amount of food in mid-winter that it takes in the spring when the feeding day is longer. In mid-winter the capercaillie can fill its crop with food, but this, with what is already ingested, is not enough and the birds gradually lose weight at this time. In Scotland, Zwickel also found that capercaillie lost weight between December and January. The total intake of food is difficult to assess, but a full crop can hold up to 30 gm. In the wood-pigeon a full crop at dusk represents only 10%–14% of the total intake of food, which suggests that capercaillie may eat 300 gm of pine shoots in a day. This seems quite possible since the females of this large grazing species weigh nearly 2,000 gm and the males almost twice as much. A full crop does appear to represent a sufficient rate of food intake for the black grouse and this species does not collect more food in spring than it does when the days are shortest. Female capercaillie begin to restrict themselves to winter food earlier in the autumn than the males but in spring begin increasing their range of foods sooner. The marked differences in structure and size between the sexes lead them to have different preferences in their winter feeding habitats, and the flocks of males and females remain completely segregated. Males will feed in the tops of trees, whereas the females prefer the lower branches where they have more protection from predators. The best feeding conditions for the capercaillie are provided by fairly open pine woods, where there is plenty of young growth to provide maximum nutritive yields, but for roosting the birds require deep soft snow into which they can tunnel. The deepest snow is found in open areas and the birds move to these to roost.

Capercaillie show preferences for certain trees and even for certain pine needles which suggests that their nutritive value is important. Sparse needle clusters are taken most, possibly because the birds find them easier to manipulate, but also because they often come from stunted plants; in Finland these include trees infected with a fungal disease, the pine blister rust (*Peridermium* sp.). Such trees form about 15% of the total according to Lindroth and Lindgren (1950) who suggest that these needles have a higher nutritive value than normal ones. These authors also point out that capercaillie prefer trees which have stopped growing in height and which have rounded profiles so facilitating perching. In North America, the blue grouse (*Dendragapus obscurus*) has been shown to select those trees – it feeds on the needles of the white fir *Abies concolor* – which have a 1%–2% higher content of protein than surrounding trees (Hoffman 1961). Black grouse also seem to select those birches supporting large catkin crops. Because catkins are more abundant on the forest edge, where the amount of light is greatest, black game feed most often in these places. It is interesting that in certain Finnish forests birches were purposely killed by foresters by peeling off their bark, to prevent regrowth after cutting. Assimilation products remained in the tops of the trees and produced bigger catkin crops than normal, which in turn attracted large flocks of wintering black grouse.

Helminen (1963) states that between 40% and 60% of capercaillie and black game die per annum. Considering the capercaillie, it is difficult to understand how the availability of pine needles could ever limit numbers, as the branches of one full grown pine could satisfy the food requirements of a pair of capercaillie for about 20 days. But if very slight variations in nutritive value or the accessibility of needles is critical in determining whether birds find enough food, it is probable that food shortage may indeed exist. That some sort of competition occurs is also suggested by the fact that different types of woodland support different densities of game, and a parallel could exist with the red grouse in Britain, where the condition of the heather is monitored through a territorial system, and determines the number of grouse an area will support (Jenkins, Watson and Miller 1963). Siivonen, who has inspired much interesting work on these northern game animals, has summarised some important features of the biology of these birds. In particular, fluctuations in the number of tetronids in the autumn can be traced to feeding conditions in the previous winter. A low nutritive value of the winter food leads to excessive loss of weight, which the female birds must make good before they can accumulate sufficient reserves for egg-laying. They are therefore dependent on the spring temperature as this affects the rate of snow thaw and makes their spring food available. The females turn to the first cleared patches much earlier than the males – an adaptive necessity, as only they have to lay eggs. Hence, the spring diet is decisive in restoring the female's condition and it determines when and how many eggs she can lay, their fertility and hatching potential, and the young birds' chances of survival. The reproductive output, then, directly determines the autumn population, which of course depends to a large extent on how many young survive. A similar story applies to the red grouse, as the condition of the heather in winter predetermines the later hatching success of any eggs laid, the number laid and the survival chances of the young. This may be a general feature of game-birds whose females produce large numbers of eggs, because Southwood (1967) finds that the partridge may respond in the same manner, but to a lesser degree. Thus if partridge eggs show a low hatchability in captivity, the corresponding survival of the young produced is also low, presumably because they lack sufficient reserves. Unlike the case of the grouse, this effect is masked by field conditions, because other factors have a more profound influence on chick survival.

Because the capercaillie and black game have a relatively direct relationship with their winter food supply, conditions are ideal for marked fluctuations in numbers to develop between the predator (capercaillie and black grouse) and prey (pine needles and birch shoots). These marked population oscillations are a feature of northern game-birds, and have led to the claim for the existence of cycles of 4 or 10 years' duration, although the actual periodicity of the cycles is now known to be largely an artifact.

The balance between the capercaillie and mature pine may be upset when man decides to plant nursery stock or to transplant young seedlings near established forests. Such a bountiful supply of young and succulent plants can attract severe damage, and Pennie quoted one case in Ross-shire where a single capercaillie was seen to eat 150 seedlings in a nursery bed at one feed, and beds of 50,000 young plants were stripped. Johnstone, who has recently investigated the problem, examined 76 naturally regenerated and 89 planted trees in the Black Wood of Rannoch and found that capercaillie had removed the leader from 44% of the planted trees, but from only 14% of the naturally regenerating ones. The planted trees were more conspicuous, but it is quite possible that they had more nutritive value, as they had been previously treated with fertiliser. Most damage caused by browsing occurs in late winter and spring and at the least prevents growth. Black game can also cause similar damage, but they usually remove only the single terminal bud, rather than the whole terminal shoot with a cluster of buds and needles, as the caper does. Zehetmayr reported that Scots pine in the Cheviots, which had been protected from black game by wire cages, grew 50% more than unprotected trees during the first 10 years of growth. Near Elgin, only 4% of pines protected from black game died, as against 12% of the unprotected trees. Johnstone considered that the worst game damage he had seen was in Glen Dye, where for two years 80% of the trees had leaders removed by black game, while capercaillie had taken 70% of the leaders in a wood at Rannoch. The general level of damage is apparently in the order of 30%–50% in areas where either bird is common, and of course removal of a leader causes malformation of what should be a straight stem, even giving the pines a bushy shape in some cases. Young conifers become immune once they reach a critical size because neither bird can effectively remove buds much above 60 cm from the ground.

Apart from shooting, when game numbers get too high, methods of preventing damage range from the use of repellents to the judicious siting of newly planted trees. It is even better to plant unfavoured food species like spruce and Douglas fir in areas where game damage is particularly severe, than to invite damage to pines. Johnstone reports an experiment by Nef in Belgium, in which a suspension of lime was applied by brush to vulnerable buds and reduced the number of trees which had the leader removed from 85% to between 2% and 20%.

CHAPTER 5

BIRDS ON THE FARM:
THE COMMUNITY

FROM being a country originally covered with deciduous forest, Britain, in the early 1970s, has reached the stage where woodland occupies only 8% of the land surface, while just under a third remains reasonably wild in the form of commons, moor or heathland. The remainder is either urban (8%) or can broadly be classed as farmland – about 32% arable (including orchards) and 22% permanent grass. The slow evolution of the landscape has taken 1,500 years, beginning with the Anglo-Saxon settlements of the fifth century, and until the turn of the present century much of this transformation had been achieved without serious detriment to a full and varied flora and fauna. By the late nineteenth-century the English pastoral scene, though almost entirely artificial, could still instil a sense of tranquillity and beauty, a feeling captured so effectively, if wistfully, in the works of Thomas Hardy:

'The old barn embodied practices which had suffered no mutilation at the hands of time. Here at least the spirit of the ancient builders was at one with the spirit of the modern beholder. Standing before this abraded pile, the eye regarded its present usage; the mind dwelt upon its past history, with a satisfied sense of functional continuity throughout' – (*Far from the Madding Crowd*).

Since then our so-called heritage has been littered with the 'fagends' of two world wars and systematically mutilated in the name of progress. The barbed-wire fences, concrete slabs, acres of ribbon development, electric pylons, make-do corrugated iron erections, dumped mattresses, massacred hedges, the list could go on *ad nauseum*. I remember a poignant moment as I sat in a hide in a cornfield by the nest of a woodlark. Mixed with occasional snatches of song from what is without doubt our most subtle songster, came the raucous music of the loudspeaker system on a nearby polo ground bringing strains of 'Some enchanted evening'. Farmland, though we may deplore much of its modern ugliness, is now the biggest bird habitat left. It is a habitat entirely manipulated by man and it

therefore behoves us to examine in detail his attitude to the remaining
wildlife it supports, and its effect upon him.

The need to assess the farmland environment has been urgent for
many years, but until recently ecologists have preferred to work in
more natural and less disturbed habitats. Fortunately, this need is
now being met. The advent of toxic chemicals and the devastating
effects these began to have on wild life stimulated the Nature Conservancy, in 1960 under Mr Max Nicholson, to make a more detailed
study of farmland wild life. One result was the provision of funds for
a 'Common Bird Census' to be run by the British Trust for Ornithology. Under this scheme, begun in 1961, skilled voluntary observers
throughout Britain make regular censuses of the birds of their own
farmland study areas, although other habitats are also being
examined. The original aim was to provide an index of population
fluctuations of the commoner birds, enabling the effects of agricultural change and practice to be monitored; for example, the consequences of replacing hedgerows by wire fences, or the impact of
new insecticides on bird life. Preliminary results show that these
objects can be realised within limits, at least for selected species, but
the project also provides for the first time an objective balance-sheet
of the bird population of various types of farmland. Moreover, it
should eventually prove possible to isolate and measure the significance for a given species of particular components of the habitat;
to test the importance of a ditch, the kind and number of hedgerow
trees, the value of evergreen cover, or the consequences of crop
rotation – analyses far more sophisticated than anything which
could be attempted before.

In evaluating past census work, problems arise because different
workers have used different methods to make bird counts, because
some species are more easy to record than others and because some
habitats are more easily assessable. The technique adopted for the
Common Bird Census involves counting singing males and plotting
their territories on a large-scale map, and this is one of the most
reliable methods of showing changes from year to year. Its limitations
are that it is confined to the census of territory owners in the breeding
season and can, therefore, take no account of non-breeding individuals, those birds that do not regularly advertise their territory by
singing, and non-breeding immigrants. Recorders are expected to
make at least eight visits to their study areas. Independent checks on
the method carried out by staff of the B.T.O. and reported by Snow

PLATE II. Kestrel – the raptor of farmland. In some areas, particularly in hill districts where voles comprise the main diet, the population of this species oscillates in parallel with the numbers of voles.

PLATE 12. The willow warbler, *above left*, here in aggressive display is the Phylloscopid warbler of farmland while its congener the chiffchaff, *right*, prefers woodland conditions. Similarly, of the Sylvid warblers the whitethroat, *below left*, prospers in agricultural habitats while the blackcap, *right*, needs mature trees in its environment.

(1965) show that, for most of the species counted, eight visits discovered 60%–70% of the number revealed with twice as many visits. For the carrion crow, magpie, blackbird, robin, dunnock, sedge warbler, chaffinch, linnet, yellowhammer, and possibly wren and tree sparrow, eight visits produced a considerably higher percentage of accuracy. But the method is unreliable for some birds, in particular those which may have extremely large territories on farmland (song thrush), those which forage over large areas (tits, skylark), those which sing sporadically before laying (*Sylvia* warblers) or those which frequently breed late and have no well-defined territories (greenfinch, bullfinch). Furthermore, certain difficult species are not even attempted by the census workers, notably woodpigeon, starling, house sparrow and rook.

To give some idea of the structure of the farmland bird community based on C.B.C. returns, data for 1962 referring to 49 sample areas covering a total of 9,980 acres of all kinds of farmland are given in Table 5, taken from results presented by Williamson and Homes (1964). Some later results analysed by Williamson are also included in the table, and these refer to a more limited sample of 28 returns (5,432 acres) of 'typical' farmland in the central English lowlands. All the original figures have been doubled on the assumption that each singing male had a female, but discrepancies may arise for the reasons mentioned above.

As Table 5 gives no indication of the winter bird population, two further sets of data are presented in Table 6. One gives the results of studies made on an Oxfordshire farm between 1926 and 1935 by members of the Oxford Ornithological Society, which was reported by Alexander in 1932 and by Chapman in 1939. The workers concerned relied on counting every bird seen during systematic transect walks. The other figures are for a Cambridgeshire farm (Fig. 15) where N. J. Westwood and I have made observations since 1958. Again, an absolute count of all the birds in the area was made during standard walks undertaken throughout the year; we relied on the relative lack of cover to ensure that not too many individuals were overlooked. We certainly underestimated the total bird population, especially at some seasons, but probably no more than if we had used the C.B.C. method; for large field species like the rook and wood-pigeon the figures are very reliable. These figures from Carlton represent the average number of birds present during the winter and summer, hence they take into account birds moving through the area on passage in spring and autumn. But it would be wrong to consider either Table 5 or 6 as giving more than an indication of the order of numbers and the relative abundance of the different species, especially as farmland can be so variable, and the 49 C.B.C. areas cover a wide range of farm conditions. Thus discrepancies in the various sets of data arise partly because different methods have been adopted, and partly from differences in land use.

In spite of the sparseness of the countryside at Carlton there exist 49 breeding species which represents a greater variety than the C.B.C. average for farmland. Blackbird density at Carlton is low because there are few hedges, this being part of a region where more than anywhere else in the country hedges are cut down in the interest of farm mechanisation. On the other hand, skylark densities are high because arable farming suits the bird very well, especially when root crops are grown. Williamson found that in the Midlands bird numbers per 100 acres of farmland (actually he converted his figures to numbers per 100 hectares, equalling 247 acres, which increases the species diversity) varied from 110 pairs made up of 22 species (on a farm in Worcestershire) to 499 pairs of 33 species (at a site in Hertfordshire). The most productive farms, as one would expect, are those with a wide diversity of habitat containing straggling hedgerows, tall trees, streams and ditches, orchards and other 'rough corners'. A small ditch or pond seems enough to encourage the moorhen, and it is surprising how far from water the bird is prepared to wander. I have on many occasions found the birds nesting in some dry hedge bottom and even up to 14 feet from the ground in old wood-pigeon nests. The sedge warbler may similarly occur well away from its natural marshland habitat, nesting in dry hedgerows near some ditch but even occurring right away from such water sources. This trend is comparatively recent and is possibly consequent on change occurring on farmland. It could be that the sedge warbler is more at home in farmland now denuded of trees and hedges than the basically woodland-loving blackcap and garden warbler, i.e. the sedge warbler could be taking the place of some other warbler.

Farms which are not generally reckoned to be in the forefront of 'modernisation' are the best for birds, and one site in Suffolk, where, incidentally, farmland can still be pleasing to the eye, produced 43 breeding species. At another site in East Suffolk, the following could be added as breeding species to the birds listed in Table 6: redpoll, redstart, nightingale, nuthatch, sand martin,

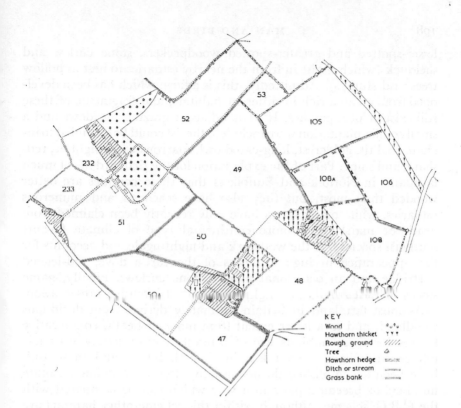

KEY
Wood
Hawthorn thicket
Rough ground
Tree
Hawthorn hedge
Ditch or stream
Grass bank

FIG. 15. Part of a farmland study area of about 200 acres at Carlton, Cambridgeshire which has been regularly censused for birds. The area is typical of many of the farms which harbour a high proportion of our wild birds and which are being studied under the B.T.O., Common Bird Census Scheme. For discussion see page 105. Field utilisation in December 1961 was: plough, fields 47, 48, 50, 51, 233; winter wheat, 49, 50A, 105, 106, 232; clover-ley, 52, 108A; beans, 108; pasture 53. In June 1962: fallow, 47; wheat, 49, 50A, 105, 106, 232; spring barley, 48, 51, 233; clover-ley 52; beans, 108; sugar beet, 50; pasture 53; plough, 108A. The birds of this area are listed in Table 6.

Enclosure was effected in 1799 by the local rector, when 1050 acres of heath, waste-land, common and common-field was dealt with. Before enclosure there were around 300 acres of wheat in the district, this total immediately falling to 70 acres. This was a temporary set back it being the general experience that once a Parish expected enclosure it did nothing about the land, so that a decline in productivity occurred. As the Rev. W. Gooch explains, it then took a few years to put into good cultivation lands exhausted by cropping, deluged by water, matted with spire grass and filled with weeds.

lesser-spotted and greater-spotted woodpeckers, stone curlew and shelduck (which flight in from the nearby estuaries to nest in hollow trees and stumps). Admittedly, this is a farm which has been developed from an area rich in different habitats, and fragments of these still exist as local patches. If some adjacent grazing meadows and a small conifer plantation were included, the list could be extended to include coal tit, goldcrest, long-eared owl, sparrowhawk, nightjar, redshank and snipe. Part of the explanation for the rich bird life of much farmland in Norfolk and Suffolk is that these counties are better wooded than most, but they also have seacoasts and numerous estuaries, while many farms have only recently been claimed from heath or marsh. The more continental type of climate favours southern species like the woodlark and nightingale and accounts for the appearance in high numbers of the turtle dove, red-legged partridge and an occasional pair of stone curlews. Finally, game stocks in East Anglia are high, the result of intensive preservation.

As most farmland in Britain ultimately derives from deciduous woodland, and to a lesser extent from moor or heath, comparative figures for these habitats are of interest. Unfortunately very few full censuses have been taken in these habitats, and those that have been accomplished do not usually attempt to define absolute numbers or breeding pairs in a way which can be compared with the C.B.C. scheme, although within this scheme other habitats are being studied. One of the first woodland censuses was organised on behalf of the B.T.O. by Lack and Venables (1939). Observers were asked to make slow standard walks through their selected woodland areas, recording every bird encountered. The inquiry provided useful comparative data on the bird composition of different kinds of woodland – but with some reservations, because not all species are equally easy to record. Colquhoun (1941) followed this inquiry with an extensive study of the birds of Savernake Forest, Wiltshire, an area of mature pedunculate oak, and he recorded his results as numbers encountered per 10 hours of slow walking. He, like many other workers since, was concerned to find the best census technique and was still devoting much of his time to applying correction factors for the varying conspicuousness of different species, when war put an end to this work and he concentrated on his valuable wood-pigeon investigations for the Agricultural Research Council. W. B. Yapp has made censuses of various types of woodland in a similar manner, using a line-transect method which enables the relative frequency of species to be calculated (see Table 7). Some of the best data for mature pedunculate oak woodland come from 40 acres studied in Surrey over fifteen years by Bevan and members of the London Natural History Society. Their method has been based on counts of singing males, and so some of the rarer species, or those which do not sing, have been omitted. The mean number of birds per 100 acres in the breeding season (assuming again that each singing male had a female) is given in the composite Table 7 below, together with figures derived from a few woodland censuses (265 acres examined) done by C.B.C. workers and published by Williamson and Homes, and some preliminary result for an area of mixed woodland in Berkshire, studied by Williamson (1964). This last site contained several open spaces and, like certain of the localities studied by Yapp, held more of the species typical of open parkland (starling, jackdaw and tree pipit) or of the scrub zone of disturbed woodland (dunnock), than would normally be found in mature oak woodland. With these reservations, the figures give a good indication of the bird fauna before forest clearance.

Colquhoun and Morley (1941) have examined bird density on Berkshire downland, which is mostly short tufty grassland. Counts in the breeding season in May yielded bird densities per 100 acres of:

skylark	14
meadow pipit	6
partridges	5
lapwing	4
wheatear	1
rook	0.3
carrion crow	0.3
starling	0.3

In February and early March rook, starling and lapwing densities were higher at 2, 5 and 6 respectively, due to the presence of wintering immigrants. The total bird population on such downland (32 birds per 100 acres) is somewhat lower than that on heath and moorland in general, where a wider range of vegetation and ground cover is encountered. Lack (1935) obtained a figure of 67 birds per 100 acres during a B.T.O. investigation in 1934, when nearly two thousand acres of heath and moorland were examined in the breeding season. Most areas in the sample were in southern England (from Devon to Suffolk) and varied from areas of short grass turf to dry heather moorland, but heather moorland in Yorkshire and Shetland was also included in the sample.

From studies of this kind three important generalisations can be made about the birds of farmland. First, the diversity of the farmland bird fauna is at least as varied, if not generally more so, than that of the wood, heath or moor which have been replaced. Second, more than three-quarters of the bird species on a farm are from woodland, many from the scrub ecotone where woodland gives way to open country. In effect the creation of small coppices and numerous hedgerows has greatly extended this valuable habitat and the scrub species have prospered as a result. Third, because agricultural development has resulted mainly in vast monocultures of single crops which support relatively few niches, only a minority of species are more common on farmland than in their ancestral habitats. These few common birds, like the wood-pigeon, rook and starling, exhibit a high degree of specialisation for living under such conditions and this enables their population density to be high.

If, instead of numbers, the weight of birds is considered, the predominance of one or two species becomes even more noticeable. Of the total summer numbers at Carlton, the wood-pigeon represents 14% of all birds present. On a weight basis it constitutes 40% of the bird fauna, and clearly, in terms of energy demands on the ecosystem, it is the predominant bird component; with numbers of rabbits still low after myxomatosis, it is probably the most important component of the biotope after man and his domestic animals, although in terms of energy transfer within the environment, the earthworm and other soil invertebrates are more important. At Carlton, the rook comprises 31% of the total avian biomass followed by the house sparrow and skylark at 2% each. But the percentage of these three in terms of *numbers* is 12, 11 and 10 respectively, a very different story. In summer, three-quarters of the total mass of birds on farmland are formed by only four species, and this figure is not likely to be far out for farmland elsewhere in Britain. In winter more species are abundant, because of the influx of winter visitors which exploit a winter peak of soil invertebrates. In winter, the composition of the avifauna by percentage numbers and percentage weight (in brackets) respectively is then wood-pigeon 10, (36); rook 6, (18); house sparrow 9, (2); skylark 14, (4); lapwing 6, (11); starling 8, (5) and these six species account for three-quarters of the total biomass. At Carlton, there is an average of 303 birds per 100 acres in summer and 465 in winter, the biomass averaging 53 kg/100 acres in summer and 65 kg/100 acres in winter. Alexander reckoned that there were between 126–320 birds/100 acres in different winters on the Oxfordshire farm mentioned above, which had a higher proportion of pasture than Carlton. He also reckoned that both biomass and numbers declined in winter (a mean of 127 birds in summer declining to 114 in mid-winter). This is true if separate months are considered instead of the average six-monthly situation, the reason being that passage birds are included if a six-month average is taken. During a cold spell – which in normal years may only last a fortnight – many ground-feeding species disperse to clear areas and for a short period the totals may be very low. The average situation gives a truer impression of the demands made on the environment, and Alexander also commented that bird numbers in winter were very similar to those found in summer.

Judging by Bevan's data supplemented with those of Lack, Venables and Colquhoun, and the information given in Table 7, the total bird population per 100 acres of oak woodland in summer may be in the order of 500–550 birds per 100 acres. But the total biomass is probably much less than on farmland. Even trebling the biomass calculated from Bevan's figures to allow for uncounted species, including heavy ones like the pigeons, it is only of the order of 37 kg. The difference is primarily due to the high density of the woodpigeon and rook on farmland. Breeding bird densities on heath or moor are considerably lower than on farmland and the total biomass lower still.

Presumably the reduced stability of the farmland monoculture enables energy to fluctuate between different trophic levels (as discussed on page 49), and this is reflected in the high biomass of birds on farmland. On the other hand, the woodland habitat is more stable with energy conserved in many more components of the food chain. Indeed, to draw a better analogy, we should imagine the wildlife community on farmland as being represented by a relatively simple *food chain* with much energy getting to the top end of the chain and being lost due to the death or exploitation of the animals concerned (rabbit, pigeon, partridge), whereas in woodland a *food web* is more apparent. The complex interactions occurring within a food web enable energy to be conserved more effectively.

Farmland can be very diverse, ranging from rough hill-grazing to areas of intensive arable cultivation, while the vegetation cover and its composition can be equally variable. Williamson compared bird densities on farms which were mainly arable (that is if more than 60% of the cultivated area was under root crops and cereals) or mainly pasture. There was little or no difference between the two categories as far as the hedgerow loving species were concerned. But partridges, skylarks and reed buntings had two or three times the density on arable farms that they had on pasture, while the density of the wren, robin, willow warbler, chiffchaff and chaffinch was lower than in pasture areas. Corn buntings possibly favour corn areas, but too few returns were obtained for the results to be statistically valid.

Because farmland is varied, it is difficult to define a typical farm bird community. Fortunately the structure of the habitat seems to be more important than the species composition of the vegetation, so that, by confining our observations to lowland farms with less than a tenth of their area covered by woods or hedgerows and composed half and half of arable and pasture, some generalisations are permissible. About half the common summer birds are divided roughly between true woodland (blue and great tits) and scrub species (dunnock and warblers), and the wood-pigeon, blackbird and dunnock dominate from these groups. The other half is divisible into three groups: first, birds like the stock dove, jackdaw and tree pipit which favour more open parkland; second, the truly field species such as the partridges, lapwing and skylark; and third, birds which belong typically to quite different habitats. This last category includes water birds like the various gulls, moorhen, pied wagtail, mallard and the house sparrow which has probably evolved in close association with man. Many of the stragglers to farmland such as the heron, the snipe, and the brambling and redwing from northern birch forests, belong in this group. Figures 16 and 17 show how farmland birds are distributed among the habitats available. Williamson has suggested that in a typical farm bird community the blackbird and skylark occur in the proportion of two, three or four to one, together making up 15%–40% of the total bird population; but this excludes the pigeons and corvids.

A high proportion of farm birds are fully resident (Table 6) and there is no very noticeable immigration of summer visitors, as those that do arrive occupy woodland and scrub. This is primarily because the true farmland environment, unlike woodland, does not produce a very good flush of spring and summer insect food, but partly because the habitat has been saturated only by the most highly efficient and flexible species. In autumn, however, a superabundant seed supply both from cultivated cereals and from associated weed species, enables a population increase greater than that possible for resident birds. Accordingly, many graminivorous species, like the linnet, visit farmland in large numbers on their autumn passage south, while some immigrants from continental Europe like the chaffinch regularly make farmland their winter home. Similarly a winter peak of soil invertebrates makes possible an immigration of birds like the lapwing, rook, starling and various thrushes. These topics are examined more fully in the next two chapters.

Unlike the true woodland birds, which need mature trees for feeding or nesting, birds favouring the scrub belt, which flourishes where light penetrates woodland clearings on the forest edge, have benefited from forest felling and from the creation of a patchwork of hedges with grassy banks and wood filled ditches. One cannot deny the importance of hedges for many species living on the farm, and the enormous amount of enclosure completed between 1750 and 1850 (almost all the open fields being dealt with in George III's reign) must have had a profound effect on bird distribution. In many places, particularly on the south and east coasts of England and in Devon, the change from open fields, with narrow strip cultivation, grassy footpaths, headlands and winding lanes, to the chequerboard pattern of small square fields surrounded by hedges had already taken place. But Moore, Hooper and Davis have emphasised for three manors in Huntingdonshire how hedgerows increased in the late eighteenth century. Between 1364 and 1550 the total length of hedgerows on four thousand acres increased only from 20 to 32 miles, but then rose rapidly to 46 miles in 1680, 58 in 1780 and 76 in 1850. The situation then remained virtually unchanged until 1946, since when the increasing farm mechanisation has caused a reduction to the level of 1364. In the church warden's accounts dealing with field-reeves records for the Midland villages during the late 1700s, the marked increase of small birds, which sung in countless numbers from the new hedges, is often commented upon. Hawthorn, which derives its name from the old English *haga* meaning a hedge or enclosure, and which had been in use since Saxon times for making impenetrable stockades, was the almost universally planted hedge shrub.

Some idea of the effects of enclosure can be obtained by comparing

FIG. 16. Percentage distribution by habitat of the birds living on the farm shown at Fig. 15, in winter.

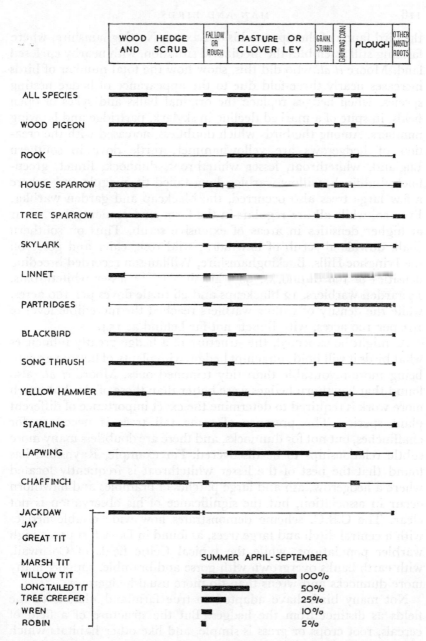

	WOOD AND SCRUB	HEDGE OR SCRUB	FALLOW OR ROUGH	PASTURE OR CLOVER LEY	GRAIN. STUBBLE	GROWING CORN	PLOUGH	OTHER MOSTLY ROOTS

ALL SPECIES

WOOD PIGEON

ROOK

HOUSE SPARROW

TREE SPARROW

SKYLARK

LINNET

PARTRIDGES

BLACKBIRD

SONG THRUSH

YELLOW HAMMER

STARLING

LAPWING

CHAFFINCH

JACKDAW
JAY
GREAT TIT

MARSH TIT
WILLOW TIT
LONG TAILED TIT
TREE CREEPER
WREN
ROBIN

SUMMER APRIL- SEPTEMBER

100%
50%
25%
10%
5%

FIG. 17. Percentage distribution by habitat of the birds living on the farm shown at Fig. 15, in summer.

the bird fauna of the open fields of Laxton, Nottinghamshire, where farming still resembles the mediaeval situation, with nearby enclosed land. Moore *et al.* who did this, show how the total number of birds increases nearly three-fold due to the appearance of hedge nesting species, when hedges replace the original balks and sykes of open fields, in spite of a marked decline in skylark, partridge and lapwing numbers. Among the birds which doubtless increased with the creation of hedgerows are yellowhammer, turtle dove in southern England, whitethroat, lesser whitethroat, dunnock, linnet, greenfinch, bullfinch, willow warbler, long-tailed tit, magpie and, where a few large trees also occurred, the blackcap and garden warbler. Even so, while all are regulars in the farm environment, they occur at higher densities in areas of extensive scrub. Thus on southern chalk downland scrub of hawthorn, wild rose, elder and gorse on the Ivinghoe Hills, Buckinghamshire, Williamson recorded breeding densities of 108 dunnocks, 90 whitethroats, 14 lesser whitethroats, 14 garden warblers, 12 blackcaps and 26 turtle doves per 100 acres, while the density of willow warblers reached the incredible level of 194 per 100 acres, with linnets not far behind at 154.

As might be expected, the structure of a hedge greatly influences what birds it will hold; unkempt hedges with plenty of bottom growth being more favourable than tidy trimmed ones. Moore *et al.* also found that hawthorn hedges were better than those of elm but much more work is required to determine the exact importance of different plant species. The presence of some tall trees is necessary for chaffinches, but not for dunnocks, and there are doubtless many more subtle relationships to be discovered. For example, Raynsford has found that the nest of the lesser whitethroat is frequently located where a hedgerow, ash and large patches of brambles and hawthorn occur in association, but the significance of his observation is not clear. The C.B.C. scheme demonstrates how wide double hedges with a central ditch and large trees, as found in Dorset, support high warbler populations, while the typical Celtic fields of Cornwall, with earth banks overgrown with gorse and bramble, support many more dunnocks and wrens than do more usual hedgerows.

Not many birds have adapted to true farmland, that is to the fields as distinct from the hedges. But the structure of a field of cereals, root crops or grass is simple, and like other habitats which can be regarded as comparable, it apparently contains the maximum number of species possible. Cody has shown that different kinds of grassland in widely separated regions, from the heath tundra of Iceland to the prairies of Chile, each contain three–four passerines, one or two wader type birds, a grouse or pigeon-type grazer and a raptor. Some examples are:

Type of grassland	Passerines present	Wader	Grazer	Predator
			Non-passerines present	
Heath tundra Iceland	Meadow pipit Wheatear Snow bunting	Golden plover Whimbrel	Ptarmigan	Merlin Gyr falcon
Rocky Mt. Colorado	American pipit Rosy finch Horned lark	Spotted sandpiper	White-tailed ptarmigan	Merlin Golden eagle
Wet grass prairie Minnesota	Bobolink Savanna sparrow Le Conte's sparrow	Upland plover Marbled godwit	Prairie chicken	Marsh hawk Red-tailed hawk
Highland heather moor Scotland	Meadow pipit Twite Reed bunting	Golden plover (Lapwing, Curlew)	Red grouse	Merlin Hen harrier or Golden eagle
Chalk downland England	Skylark Wheatear Starling (Rook)	Lapwing	Grey partridge (Wood-pigeon)	Kestrel (Carrion crow)
Arable/grass farmland England	Skylark Rook Starling	Lapwing	Wood-pigeon Grey partridge	Kestrel (Carrion crow)

The last three examples are additional to those given by Cody, and emphasise that the newly created habitats of downland or farmland have been filled secondarily by the rook and starling which can be considered recent (on the geological time scale) arrivals to Britain from the Asiatic Steppes. The wood-pigeon has secondarily adapted to grassland from a woodland origin, to replace the partridge as the most efficient grazer. On upland pastures where winter frosts prevent feeding by probing, the waders can still excel, the curlew on the wetter hill farms, and the oystercatcher increasingly on upland farms where unexploited earthworms are available. In Surrey and Hampshire many of the curlew frequenting the wetter commons may actually nest on arable fields, flighting to nearby boggy areas to feed; without these wet areas it is doubtful whether the curlew would survive as a farm bird.

A raptor preying regularly on birds might have been expected on English farmland, judging from the table above. The goshawk has not been able to move away from continuous woodland to live in the fragmented tree cover of the farm, as have some of its prey species. It depends on catching its victim by surprise in the manner of the sparrowhawk and open country would militate against such hunting behaviour. But a kite or harrier ought to feature in the agricultural scene. In Britain, Montagu's harrier was an inhabitant of East Anglian marsh or heath, but now remains predominantly a heathland bird throughout most of the south of England to Cornwall, often favouring the young conifer plantations owned by the Forestry Commission. It does occasionally nest in growing corn, in Hampshire for instance, and could potentially find its food on farmland and nearby wasteland as it does in many parts of France. Intensive persecution in areas where game preservation is practised and the precariousness of being on the edge of its range in Britain seem to account for its failure to become a more regular bird of farmland. In Poland, male marsh harriers during the breeding season hunted over farmland and mainly caught short-tailed voles and other rodents, while the females spent most of their hunting time over wet marsh near the nest and caught mainly small birds such as the skylark and sedge warbler. In winter in S.E. Kent I have noticed the marsh harrier spending much hunting time over farmland adjacent to its coastal marshes.

The kestrel feeds more on small birds in East Anglia than anywhere else in its British range, as it is essentially a specialist on small rodents, particularly short-tailed voles. The barn owl takes very much the same diet, but catches its prey at night; similar food habits doubtless explain why the numbers of these two birds appear to fluctuate in parallel (Fig. 12). On farmland, the barn owl takes a variable proportion of brown rats, but these rarely make up more than a third of its diet in weight so it is unlikely to be having much regulatory effect on this component of its prey. Indeed, Glue (1967) has shown how, when the kestrel, barn owl and tawny owl shared a common feeding ground of rough grazing in Hampshire, the kestrel and barn owl had the same diet three-quarters composed of short-tailed voles and virtually no rats, while half the tawny owl's diet consisted of brown rats with voles only accounting for a fifth of the intake.

The little owl was artificially introduced to Kent and Northampton in the late nineteenth century, increased and spread rapidly until the 1930s and slowly thereafter. Its success has been striking in farming areas, but it has not been able to compete successfully for a place in woodland. It was once feared that the little owl would become a serious predator of game chicks and small birds but Miss Hibbert-Ware who conducted the *Little Owl Enquiry* (report produced 1936–7) showed these fears to be unfounded. Roughly half of its diet is composed of small rodents (vole and field mouse) and nearly half of large insects (beetles) and earthworms, while birds are not an important prey. To some extent, the diet resembles that of the barn owl and is obtained from similar places although the hunting methods of the two species differ. The little owl is also able to exploit earthworms and insects which become active on the soil surface at dusk, a niche otherwise not filled (the stone curlew does feed nocturnally on surface-living invertebrates, but it is local and frequents a rather different habitat).

The corvids are well represented on farmland, especially the rook, which is discussed in detail in the next chapter. All feed to a large extent on cereal grain, and only the jay, which is essentially a woodland bird, is well segregated in its plant food preferences. As already discussed (page 83) it specialises on acorns. The corvids also show considerable overlap in their animal food diet. Ecological competition is partly avoided by slight differences in food preference, but particularly in the habitat each prefers. Unfortunately, it is the availability of clearly defined habitats which is most affected by the drastic changes occurring on the farm and appropriate adjustments in distribution and status of the corvids are occurring in consequence. The raven was once a scavenger of large food items throughout much of woodland Britain, but is now confined to the upland farms and moors where dead sheep and other animals occur. The carrion crow can manage on lesser fare and it remains the scavenger of farmland, where fragments of woodland remain, supplementing any shortage

of carrion with an ability to collect insects, earthworms in soft
ground, and small mammals and birds. The rook is well emancipated from woodland, except it needs high trees for nesting, and is
the only really efficient prober. Probably originally a bird of short
pastures, it has been well able to exploit the soil invertebrates of
arable farmland. The jackdaw also feeds extensively on grassland
insects, but Lockie (1956) showed that it takes mostly different and
usually smaller species than the rook, and it is equipped to catch
many of the more active kinds living in long grass. Its predominance
in parkland seems to depend primarily on the fact that long grass
is most often found in such areas. The magpie is a bird of the woodland edge, its long tail doubtless facilitating movement through low
unstable branches, and it collects many insects, snails (an important
food judged from data collected by Holyoak, 1968), small mammals,
eggs and nestling birds when available. Fragmentation of woodland
must have initially favoured the magpie and it was a characteristic
bird of nearly every farm, associating with those spinneys and hedges
where a few tall trees exist. It has lost ground with the extensive
removal of hedges and cover from the farm.

Of the field birds, skylarks have prospered from an extension of
their preferred habitat. On heathland or moorland their density
averages 13 per 100 acres, while Colquhoun recorded 14 per 100
acres on open downland, and for farmland the C.B.C. scheme showed
13 per 100 acres. Skylarks prefer a fairly thin ground cover of grass,
and arable farming with cereals and root crops simulates these
particularly suitable conditions. In areas of intensive arable farming,
such as at Carlton, densities may be extremely high, and there are
some specially favoured areas in the fens and parts of Essex and
Thanet where intensive market gardening occurs and where densities
of up to 60 per 100 acres have been noted. Not surprisingly, complaints of damage have been forthcoming from such areas (see page
208). The meadow pipit favours thicker ground cover than the skylark, with bracken or heather present, and only rough headlands
suit its requirements on the farm. Its density on heath and moorland
in general, at 36 per 100 acres (Lack's data), is considerably higher
than that Colquhoun found on grass downland (6 per 100 acres) or
that the C.B.C. recorded for farmland (1 per 100 acres). A break-
down of Lack's figures shows that in areas with much short grass,
skylark density was 22 as against 10 for the meadow pipit. In areas
of long grass and bracken, or on heather moor, only 5 skylarks but

16 meadow pipits were found per 100 acres. Venables (1937) was also struck by the association of skylarks with grass and meadow pipits with heather on the Greensand heaths of Surrey.

The wheatear is a typical downland bird which is conspicuously absent from farmland, except during passage. It requires very short turf, in country broken by rabbit holes, boulders or small rock out-crops, where it can find nesting sites; organised playing fields and the like do not, therefore, satisfy its needs. It feeds on the small ground-surface invertebrates, particularly small Coleoptera and Diptera larvae. This food supply, unlike most other soil invertebrates, reaches a peak in spring enabling the wheatear to be one of the earliest arriving summer visitors, in contrast to the whinchat which feeds on those insect species which depend on full grass growth for peak emergence. Upland grazed pasture as in the Lake District or the York-shire Dales provides good conditions for the wheatear. The whinchat is conservative in its need for coarse vegetation, preferring not only long grass with a high insect population, but a scattering of large plants, such as the Umbelliferae or small bushes, to provide hunting perches. Much of its food consists of the insects which are attracted to these plants. It still does well in farmland areas of rough neglected pasture, as in parts of Northumberland, where low posts supporting wire fencing are acceptable as hunting perches. The stonechat prefers rough commons with more bushes than the whinchat, and because it feeds less often from grassy vegetations requires more open ground and drier conditions. It is not nowadays a farmland bird in Britain. The relative status of these two birds in Europe is interesting because their habitats overlap to a certain extent. Only the whinchat occurs in north Scandinavia and parts of central Europe, and it seems likely that its presence here excludes the stonechat. In contrast, the whin-chat is absent from Asia and north Russia, and here the stonechat occurs in all the habitats normally occupied by both species in Europe, though it migrates from these high latitudes to the Mediter-ranean region for the winter. The whinchat seems to have prospered from agricultural development and road building in western Siberia and has pushed its range further to the east in consequence.

The blackbird is now the commonest song-bird in Britain. Originally a woodland bird, it has penetrated a very wide range of habitats from city centres (where densities of 6 per 100 acres can be recorded) and suburban gardens, to open moorland and isolated stretches of rocky coast in northern Scotland and the Scottish islands, where it is also typical of the small crofts and farmsteads. It is often the commonest species on the farm. Thrushes are liable to suffer during summer droughts, when ground invertebrates become scarce (a topic discussed in greater detail in the next chapter), though individuals living in woodland can partly compensate by turning to other foods. Moreover, woodland leaf litter is less liable to dry up in summer than open pastures, so the invertebrate fauna is less seriously affected during a short dry spell. Both the blackbird and song thrush have a long breeding season for invertebrate feeding species, each rearing three and sometimes more broods between March and June, and even July in some years. Earthworms are an important food for first broods, but those reared in May and June are fed primarily on caterpillars, which are collected from the ground when they descend to pupate. Both the blackbird and song thrush find it more difficult to rear young after May, and the number of eggs laid per clutch shows an adaptive variation, beginning low in March, rising to a peak in May and declining thereafter (Snow 1955). Clutch size may also be lower than normal in a dry spring. Although both species are affected by drought, the song thrush usually does better than the blackbird, because its smaller size enables it to exploit caterpillars and other insects to better advantage, and, unlike the blackbird, it has learned how to open snails on anvils; this gives it an important source of extra food to which it turns at any time of the year, when other foods become scarce. The song thrush, therefore, has a slightly longer breeding season than the blackbird with a higher percentage of egg-laying in July (up to 2% of all clutches laid as against 0.5%–0.7% for the blackbird). Both these birds have been successfully introduced by man to New Zealand and both show the same breeding relationship to the southern spring and summer – the song thrush again having a slightly longer season.

The song thrush and blackbird suffer greatly, especially in their native woodland, from the predation of jays on their eggs and young. These losses, together with those brought about by desertion and other factors, result in the hatching of young from only 41% of blackbird nests and 36% of song thrush nests, these figures being national averages from Snow (1955) and covering all habitats. The song thrush suffers more from total failures, perhaps because its timidity renders it more vulnerable to predators and other disturbances, including those of man. It compensates to some extent by incubating more efficiently when not disturbed and, because it is better at finding food for its young, it rears more nestlings from each successful nest and so has a slightly higher overall productivity.

In summer, the song thrush and blackbird have such similar ecological requirements (see for example Fig. 17) that they might be expected to compete. The blackbird is a more aggressive and dynamic species and almost invariably wins in any inter-specific contest, in fact song thrushes are subordinate to all *Turdus* species when feeding in such mixed company (Davies and Snow 1965). The ability of the song thrush to exploit snails, and even berries, during times of food shortage seems to offset this disadvantage. In the first three decades of the twentieth century it was commoner than the blackbird, judging by the relative number of birds marked by contributors to the B.T.O. ringing scheme (Fig. 18). At that time it suffered a lower juvenile mortality than the blackbird (when Lack 1946 analysed the B.T.O. ringing recoveries, 65% of song thrushes captured in the Aug.–Dec. period were in their first year of life, and 74% of blackbirds were similarly juveniles), but compensating for this the adult death-rate was higher (45% as against 40%). This suggests that the wider choice of invertebrate food favoured by song thrushes benefits juveniles, as well as nestlings, causing more to survive and compete with adults, thereby reducing adult survival. Since the 1940s the song thrush has become less common than the blackbird. This is partly because the blackbird suffers much less during hard winters, as Ticehurst and Hartley (1948) were able to demonstrate for the hard winter of 1946–7, and partly because the blackbird seems more adaptable to the changes wrought by man and occurs at a slightly higher density on farmland than does the song thrush.

Fig. 18 does not necessarily prove that the total, as distinct from relative, number of blackbirds has increased, but this does seem possible, as the species has been generally expanding its range in Europe. In this connection it is interesting that Snow (1966), from a long series of B.T.O. records, has been able to show that the annual adult mortality of the blackbird has dropped from around 50% in 1951–2 to 32% in 1960–1. Over this period clutch size and hatching success have remained fairly constant, except that nesting success showed a small decline from 1956 to 1961, with a return to normal in 1962. The recruitment rate has not fallen to compensate for the reduced mortality, so there are grounds for believing that a higher blackbird population exists, though the small, inadequate number of field studies made does not resolve this point. The relative increase in recruitment over mortality has, however, been too high to account for all the range expansion and population increase observed, and so much of the increased production must have been compensated for by an increase in juvenile deaths. Juvenile mortality fluctuates considerably in different seasons in relation to conditions; for example, in the drought year of 1959 it was double that of 1960 or 1961.

In Britain, a proportion of the song thrush and blackbird populations emigrates for the winter, although many more song thrushes do so than blackbirds, which again reflects the greater sensitivity of the song thrush to hard winters and the adaptive advantages of moving. This is reflected in Table 6, where it can be seen that song thrush numbers were considerably lower at Carlton in winter, while blackbirds showed an increase. Immigrant song thrushes and blackbirds, mainly from Holland, enter Britain for the winter and to some extent must compete with resident birds. At Carlton, as in many other parts of Britain, the arrival of song thrushes hardly offsets the loss of the summer visitors, and a total decrease in numbers occurs, whereas roughly the opposite holds in the case of the blackbird. Figs. 16 and 17 show that in winter blackbirds occupy woodland far more than in summer, and this probably means that immigrants also enter woodland. On the other hand, song thrushes are found to a lesser extent in the woods, and the reduced population, including immigrants, shows a far greater preference for pastures, from which the blackbird is relatively absent. Large numbers of fieldfares, from Scandinavia (mainly Norway) and redwings, mainly from Finland (Ashmole 1962), also occur on pastures in winter. The biggest danger for these wintering thrushes comes with periods of hard frosts. At such times ecological differences become noticeable, and Hartley (1954) has demonstrated that the song thrush specialises most on yew berries, the fieldfare and redwing on haws, while the fieldfare unlike the other species except blackbird will tackle crab apples. In keeping with its liking for woodland, the blackbird shows at all times a preference for a wide range of tree fruits. Myrtle Ashmole (1962), in examining the migratory movements of the thrushes on a broad European basis, demonstrated from ringing recoveries that competition is reduced in the blackbird, mistle thrush and song thrush, because populations from various parts of their range winter in different areas to varying extents, whereas

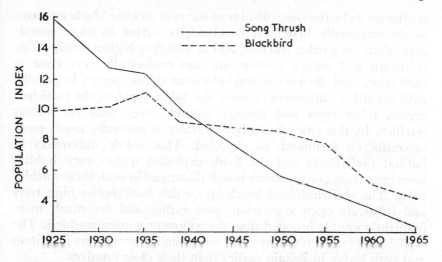

FIG. 18. Number of blackbirds and song thrushes ringed as nestlings under the B.T.O. scheme as a percentage of the total nestlings of all species ringed. The apparent decline of both species is an artifact primarily dependent on a gradual increase in the number and variety of other species ringed. The data, are, however, valid for comparing the *relative* status of these two species and emphasise how the blackbird has become more common than the song thrush.

wintering fieldfares and redwings from widely separate breeding localities overlap each other considerably. The last two species have evolved a high degree of nomadism and can change their wintering areas in different years and even within a season, depending on food resources.

The warblers provide some interesting puzzles. For instance, the garden warbler and blackcap are ecologically and behaviourally very close, so close that in the absence of a distinctive song the latter has evolved a black top to its head for sexual isolation. Both species take insects, but the blackcap seems better able to subsist on berries and fruits in the autumn, which enables one or two birds to over-winter in Britain; all the same, many of the records of wintering blackcaps submitted to the editors of county bird reports turn out to be marsh or willow tits. The garden warbler feeds at a lower zone in the vegetation than the blackcap, will tolerate areas of fewer and lower trees, and breeds slightly further north in Europe; all in all it appears to be the more flexible of the two. Yet the blackcap seems to do marginally better on farmland, occurring in more sample areas than the garden warbler, and at a slightly higher density. The chiffchaff and willow warbler are also ecologically very close to each other, and often occur and behave as sibling species. In parallel with the slight differences between the *Sylvia* warblers, the chiffchaff prefers taller trees and thinner ground cover than the willow warbler. In this case, the willow warbler is generally much more successful on farmland, as expected. That subtle differences in habitat preferences and the foods exploited within each habitat have important consequences is well illustrated in both these warbler pairs. The chiffchaff and blackcap (which both prefer high trees and relatively open vegetation) nest earlier and are much more frequently double-brooded than the willow or garden warblers. The chiffchaff, like the blackcap, also occasionally overwinters in Britain and both arrive in Britain earlier than their close relatives.

We must also consider the whitethroat and lesser whitethroat. The former (the hay-jack of many countrymen) is the most successful warbler of farmland, enjoying low scrub, nettle banks and overgrown ditches, and it is only on a few highland farms, particularly where birch is a prominent component of the habitat, that it is out-numbered by the willow warbler. The lesser whitethroat frequents more scrubby areas, shows a decided preference for high coarse bushes, and tends to avoid grassier sites. It breeds slightly earlier than the whitethroat, following the pattern of those other warblers which do not rely on the growth of grass and small herbage to provide insect food. It might be expected to favour farmland at least as much as the blackcap, but it is definitely found there less frequently.

Dunnocks, like the other scrub species, occur at lower densities than in less well managed habitats. As they and meadow pipits are the chief foster parents to the cuckoo in Britain, their low density on farmland may partly account for the scarcity of the cuckoo in agricultural areas. The evolution of good mimicry of the host's eggs depends on reproductive isolation in the various cuckoo gentes. This is possible in undisturbed natural areas, such as still exist in parts of the continent, and cuckoos parasitising a particular prey rarely inter-breed with individuals favouring other hosts. But fragmentation of the habitat by agricultural development makes it far more likely that a dunnock specialist will interbreed with a pipit favouring

gente. Where genetic isolation cannot be maintained, all cuckoos
tend to produce the same kind of egg, which is the reason why a
high degree of egg mimicry is not found in the British cuckoos. The
poorer the resemblance of the cuckoo's egg to that of its host, the
greater the probability that it will be deserted. It is not known how
far the breeding success of cuckoos in agricultural habitats differs
from that under ancestral conditions.

The ecotone belts of scrub or parkland must in the past have
moved geographically and changed with long-term climatic variations so that they represent unstable conditions. In consequence,
they have been centres for a relatively high level of evolutionary
change in their flora and fauna, compared with the stable conditions
of their constituent habitats. Furthermore, the birds recently evolved
in ecotones may be expected to be relatively adaptable. The buntings,
tree-pipit, and many of the scrub species can be included in this
group; but three species particularly successful on farmland today
are the starling, jackdaw, and rook – they will be dealt with again
in the next chapter. These three are all typical birds of the grassland
steppes of central Europe and Russia, and probably spread to
Britain from this region in the past – in fact large numbers of immigrants from this source winter in Britain every year. All are grassland
feeders which are still tied in some form or another to woodland for
nesting purposes, although the jackdaw and starling will now secondarily use man's buildings or rock crevices. They show various con-
vergent adaptations to their new environment, into which they do
not merge, unlike the cryptically coloured skylark, lapwing and
partridge, which are true field species. This makes them specially
vulnerable to predators, especially as they all have to feed with their
heads to the ground. Most feed in a markedly gregarious manner,
an adaptation which must have evolved to give mutual warning of
danger. All form very large flocks in the post-breeding period of food
shortage and respond very positively to individuals which have found
a good feeding source. This is important, because in large tractless
country food distribution may be patchy and an individual searching
alone might not encounter worthwhile feeding grounds quickly
enough. All return to safe roosting sites at night in tree cover, although the starling now accepts buildings. Because gregarious
feeding has evolved primarily as an anti-predator device, many
other biological functions have to occur in the flock including the
mechanism by which population regulation is achieved through the

social hierarchy. But these are secondary consequences of flock-
ing rather than the cause. Other farmland birds which probably
originated in a parkland ecotone include the kestrel, little owl, barn
owl, green woodpecker, stock dove and, on the continent, the white
stork.

The woodpecker of the farm is the green woodpecker, the familiar
yaffle of countrymen. It obtains much of its food from the ground,
particularly specialising on ants. It is much more a bird of open
country than its European congener the grey-headed woodpecker,
which has a wider range in the Palaearctic, but which feeds far less
on the ground in areas where the green also occurs; presumably to
avoid inter-specific competition. The green woodpecker, therefore,
is adapting to a niche quite unlike that occupied by any other
European woodpecker. It well illustrates the compromises that have
to be made by animals in the course of natural selection and the
haphazard process of evolution. At first thought, a walking bird like a
pipit or plover might be expected to become adapted to ant-feeding.
But a long tongue is advantageous and the only group which has
been subjected to sufficient pressure to evolve prehensile tongues are
the woodpeckers and one of them has been in the best position
secondarily to invade and occupy this particular niche.

In suitable areas farm livestock may be beneficial to some birds.
Grazing meadows in low lying river valleys are the habitat of the
yellow wagtail, whose distribution in Britain has been well documented by Stuart Smith. The highest densities occur in the grazing
marshes of Cheshire through to Staffordshire, south Lancashire, the
Lake District throughout the Yorkshire Dales and then again from
the Lincolnshire fens, the Wash and a coastal strip from Norfolk to
Dorset. Ideal habitats seem to be provided where grazing stock
provide plenty of droppings and the meadows abound with flies.
A host of dipterous flies including blow-flies *Calliphora*, house-flies
Musca, crane-flies *Tipulidae* and hover-flies *Syrphidae* provide the
bird with its main food, supplemented with ground living beetles
and weevils. The bird usually catches these by running through the
grass and picking them from the air as they are disturbed, occasionally
making short aerial chases. Occasionally, too, the bird will dart
after flies from some perch, like a flycatcher. The distribution of the
yellow wagtail is well explained by the knowledge of its feeding
ecology, including its liking for sewage farms. The big problem,
however, is to explain why in a few areas, notably in the Brecks and

PLATE 13. Waders on the farm. *Above left*, lapwings succeed as breeding birds on farmland but are much more common as winter visitors. *Right*, redshanks can breed in the wetter grazing meadows of some farms. *Below*, locally the stone curlew has adapted itself to the lighter farmland on southern downland and parts of East Anglia, when this has replaced its more natural habitat.

PLATE 14. Two species whose status on farmland is improving and which appear to be involved in inter-specific competition with other closely related species. *Above*, red-legged partridge. *Below*, reed-bunting nesting in a dry farmland habitat.

other parts of East Anglia and in the New Forest area, the bird occurs on dry heather and bracken heaths in country normally dominated by the meadow pipit. Arable fields near marshland often provide a sought after habitat. But the same occurs on inland farms far away from water, for instance an arable farm in Suffolk still had yellow wagtails nesting among potato crops which had replaced an original heathland ten years earlier. It would be interesting to know whether these 'dry-nesting' wagtails have modified their feeding habits.

The pied wagtail is also catholic in its choice of habitat, ranging from mountain streams and riverine meadows to the farmyard. Like the yellow wagtail, it is adapted to living off the large flies which frequent streams, canals and meadows, and has found conditions around the farmyard (and sewage farms) to its liking. Man-made structures like barns, outhouses and stone walls appear sufficiently similar to natural boulder-strewn streams to make acceptable nest-sites, and the large fly population around cow sheds and stable yards provides a suitable food source. Away from farm buildings the pied wagtail is not common in agricultural country, though its greater tolerance of short grass and bare ground makes it more common on arable farmland than its congener and it will follow the plough.

The aerial feeding swallow is certainly encouraged by pasture farming, particularly where cattle are kept, and it is the character-istic hirundine of farmland, as the house martin associates more with man in cities and built-up areas. Swallows generally hunt nearer the ground than house martins, for which their long tails are probably advantageous, and they manoeuvre skilfully round feeding cattle to collect the insects disturbed from the grass. The short-tailed house martin, like the swift, is more efficiently built for high flying and is thus able to exploit the insects drawn up in the warm thermals found near large areas of buildings. Man is probably changing the status of both these birds in consequence of modern progress. A loss of horses for draft, the confinement of cattle to ultra-hygienic indoor factory farms has meant the disappearance of the old-style farmyard, with its animals and muck. These changes are detrimental to the swallow. On the other hand, industrial plants pollute the air near big urban centres, resulting in a reduction of airborne invertebrates and of house martins. It is encouraging that the clean air measures taken in some centres, notably in London, are resulting in a return of such insect feeders as the house martin.

The biology and economic importance of some farm birds is discussed in the next three chapters, but to end this survey of the community it is appropriate to compare the breeding success of the same species living in its native woodland, on farmland, and in suburban gardens. This has been done by Snow and Mayer-Gross (1967) and some of their figures are set out in Table 8. If breeding success is considered as the number of nests started which produce one or more fledged young, it is an inverse measure of the incidence of total failures, which, in the species considered, is overwhelmingly the result of predation. Predator numbers on well managed farmland are much lower than in woodland, partly because of greater activity by gamekeepers and partly because the density of the jay—the worst egg-thief in woodland—falls to a low level in open hedgerow country. Consequently, predation losses for a given species are lower on farmland, and lower still in suburban gardens where there are even fewer nest predators. Snow and Mayer-Gross found that clutch and family size were about the same on farmland as in the rural habitats, except in the case of the blackbird where they were lower. In the absence of predation, the birds' ability to rear their young was usually greater in woodland and farmland than in suburban and urban habitats, but this increased productivity could not offset losses caused by predators, even allowing for repeat layings. Hence, several species of birds may well rear more young per pair in habitats altered by man. This paradox does not, of course, mean that there will necessarily be more adult birds in the man-made habitats: as discussed in Chapter 2, population size is not a function of the reproductive rate. It does however imply that either the mortality rate is higher in man-made habitats, or that dispersal takes place from these areas to less favourable ones.

CHAPTER 6

BIRDS ON THE FARM: THE ANIMAL FEEDERS

TRUE farmland supports three major food sources for birds; the soil invertebrates, and to a lesser extent the herbage invertebrates, the green vegetation of growing plants and grain or seeds derived from or associated with farm crops. The seasonal availability of these three sources of food varies in quite different ways, imposing fundamental differences on the pattern of migration, breeding seasons and population dynamics of the birds which have adjusted to them. It is convenient to discuss these adaptations here and in the next two sections, beginning with the birds which are dependent on soil invertebrates, and singling out for detailed consideration a few species which in a sense were pre-adapted to fill the niches created. The foliage of farm crops, unlike that of woodland herbage, is a poor source of invertebrates. This is partly because exotic or man-created species are cultivated which lack a natural fauna; if one does develop, it is frequently composed of pest species to be quickly dealt with by an appropriate insecticide. The foliage feeding insectivores rarely stray from hedgerows to feed, and it is mostly rooks, starlings, lapwings and wintering thrushes, gulls and plovers that are able to tackle the soil fauna proper in open areas.

The total biomass of arthropods varies in different habitats and crops, and Southwood and Cross obtained the following figures for the live weights of arthropods in kilograms per hectare using a suction apparatus to collect samples: downland 4.6, uncut grass 3.2, grass and clover ley 1.8, hedgerow 1.2, pasture 0.80, cereals 0.50. However, treatment of cereal fields with herbicide reduced numbers by one-half and biomass by one-third of their value in fields where weeds were not controlled. Arthropods of importance in barley crops include aphids and jassids, various Staphylinid and larger carabid beetles, collembola, particularly *Sminthrus viridis*, some lepidopterous larva and such pests as sawfly larvae. The low numbers of these animals provide sufficient explanation for the paucity of insectivorous birds in such crops.

Davis (1967) made a useful study of bird feeding preferences in different crops in an area near Huntingdon. He found ground beetles, particularly *Feronia* spp and *Harpalus rufipes*, made up the biggest biomass of invertebrates caught in pitfall traps in crops and pasture. Although these insects were eaten by skylarks, he reckoned that they were too large to serve as food for most bird species, and in any case they are primarily nocturnal. Smaller genera such as *Bembidion*, *Trechus* and *Agonum* were likely more important. His results are of interest in measuring the density of birds feeding in different crops, thereby reflecting the value of these as sources of food. Considering hedgerow and open-field species, namely blackbird, chaffinch, dunnock, linnet, red-legged partridge, skylark, whitethroat, yellow hammer, and adding all these together, the following indices of density were obtained:

Beans	Pasture	Rape	Peas	Wheat
8.9	8.0	6.8	6.8	1.2

For the flock-forming species, lapwing, sparrow, starling and wood-pigeons, the results were:

Peas	Pasture	Rape	Beans	Wheat
25.8	12.6	4.3	1.6	0.9

The value of broadleaved pea, bean and rape crops is particularly noticeable compared with the cereal fields; these crops become noticeably more used by birds as they grew and their insect faunas developed. A tree sparrow collected when feeding in a pea field had eaten many aphids, and it contained also the remains of eight beetles, including the weevils *Sitona lineatus* and *Phytonomus* sp. and the ground beetle *Bembidion lampros*. Two skylarks had also eaten large numbers of *Sitona*. Much more information of this kind is needed to define precisely what food items farmland birds require and how the different species partition the resources.

Sir John Russell in his book *The World of the Soil* gives a very full account of the animals living in the soil. Most are too small to be eaten directly by birds, though they may be important constituents in food chains, and the important ones are the various earthworms, tipulid larvae, beetles and molluscs. Earthworms constitute one of the most important dietary items of the rook and, in general, *Allolobophora nocturna*, *A. caliginosa*, *A. (Eisenia) rosea*, *A. chlorotica* and *Lumbricus terrestris* are the species most often eaten by these and other birds. Evans and Guild (1948) in their classic studies of earthworm biology, and Gerard too (1967), have shown that numbers in the soil vary throughout the year, the latter author dealing extensively with the vertical distribution of the worms. Peak numbers and biomass occur in April and May and from September to December – the mild wet months – smaller numbers being found from January until early March when low soil temperatures occur; even fewer worms can be found in the June to August period which corresponds with summer droughts. In summer many worms aestivate. Some worms, including *L. terrestris*, have deep burrows and come to the soil surface at night to feed on vegetable matter lying near the burrow entrance. On wet mornings *Lumbricus* may be surprised by a bird predator before it can retreat; the early bird catches the worm is an apt axiom. Its total abundance in the soil is not, therefore, a true measure of its availability to birds.

Other soil inhabitants which can be important as food sources for birds include the enchytraeid worms, which are mostly small (5–10 mm long), and fluctuate violently in numbers from a summer minimum to autumn peaks. Several Coleoptera larvae undergo their early life history in the soil, notably wireworms which are the larvae of the click beetles *Agriotes*, mostly *A. lineatus* and *A. obscurus*. Their natural home is permanent grassland, where they do relatively little harm in feeding on grass roots. However, they are polyphagous and when, during the Second World War, much grassland was converted to arable the wireworms readily turned to cereal roots or potato crops as a source of food, causing considerable damage and stimulating intensive research. They are one of the soil pests which led farmers to use fertilisers containing 0.2% aldrin as an insurance policy – a practice now fortunately banned. Other notable beetle larvae in grassland are the root-feeding white grubs of the chafer beetles, the adult cockchafer *Melolontha melolontha* which emerges in May or June and the closely related *Amphimallon solstitialis* or summer chafer in June. Even more numerous are the larvae of certain of the dipterous flies, particularly leatherjackets *Tipula paludosa* much favoured by the starling. Each female insect lays over 250 eggs on grassland in late August and September. The eggs hatch after about ten days and the tiny larvae feed intensively in the following spring, continuing until they are fully grown in July, when pupation occurs and new adults emerge in late summer and autumn. They prefer moist conditions, and up to 3 million larvae of some Tipulid species may occur per acre in marshland in March, though pasture numbers are usually below the 100,000 per acre level. Centipedes of the genera *Lithobius* and *Geophilus* and the millipede *Blaniulus guttulatus* are also common inhabitants of the upper soil. The latter may reach densities in the region of 6½ million per acre. I must also mention the slugs and snails. *Agriolimax reticulatus* the grey field slug is the commonest field species, particulary when much compost is added to a field. The snails are more typically found in woodland, though the small *Helix memoralis* and *H. horgensis* are common in forage crops and amongst tall grass including cereals.

A major problem in studying soil animals involves finding efficient sampling procedures; these have been much criticised and reassessed in recent years. Most soil zoologists are concerned to know the total invertebrate population of the soil, whereas an ornithologist is usually content with a reliable index of the changes rather than an absolute figure. Furthermore, he is concerned only with the larger species available at any time in the top layers of the soil. Basically two techniques can be adopted. First, chemical methods can be used which involve pouring standard quantities of potassium permanganate or formalin solutions on to the surface and waiting for active species like the worms to come to the surface. Varying results are obtained depending on soil porosity, which affects the depth and speed of penetration, and on the water content of soil, which modifies the dilution rate and the time taken for an effective reaction. In addition, each species of worm responds differently to these various treatments. Raw (1959) has examined these problems, and his findings are worth consulting for background information. Second, for studying all the different larger soil invertebrates that may be eaten by birds, the old method of flotation-washing and of han d sorting sample cores 'dug' from the ground is still the best, even though it is subject to fluctuations caused by the worker's ability to spot his animals. Again, for comparative, rather than absolute work, these problems can be surmounted by restricting the number of people sorting the material and by taking care to keep methods standard.

Data from soil core analyses have been used in the preparation of Figs. 19 and 21. Many soil invertebrates vary in size throughout the season; for instance, one leatherjacket eaten in June may be equivalent in weight to nine eaten the previous September, so that biomass is usually a more satisfactory measure for quantitative work and is used in Fig. 21 for earthworms. But, it is also important to appreciate

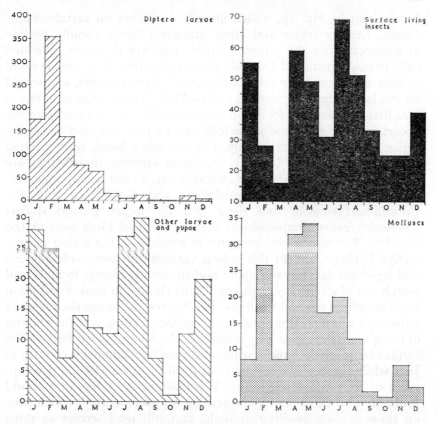

FIG. 19. Seasonal changes in the status of various soil animals in fields on and adjacent to the area depicted at Fig. 15, these animals being important constituents in the diet of various farmland birds. The figures are based on sample soil cores collected monthly each being 4″ × 2″ deep, 26 being collected on arable and 29 on pasture. The diptera larvae are mostly leatherjackets. Beetles and spiders, comprise the main surface dwelling component while other larvae and pupae include mostly wireworms, beetle and weevil larvae, and lepidopterous larvae and pupae.

that a bird may respond to small items if they occur at a satisfactory density, whereas fewer larger animals, though equivalent in weight, may not provide an adequate stimulus to initiate search behaviour. As it proved too tedious to separate and weigh all the constituents of the soil fauna the total number of various invertebrate groups has been given in Fig. 19, which gives information on certain major trends. Leatherjackets and other dipterous larvae rapidly decline in numbers after the winter (larger numbers than are indicated exist from August until December but at this time they are too small to isolate and count by the sampling technique adopted, and would mostly be too small for birds to find and eat). This decline in numbers is at first compensated for by an increase in size, so that peak biomass occurs in May and June to be followed by pupation and the emergence of the adult flies in July. On the other hand, surface-living invertebrates show far less of a decline in summer, though they are harmed by winter frosts. The common beetles are mostly members of the families *Carabidae*, *Staphylinidae* and *Scarabaeidae* and the Curculionid weevils, and these and the larger ground spiders (*Araneida*) feature frequently in the diet of field birds such as the lapwing. The insects can be active in summer in the shelter of protective herbage, and at this season various dipterous, coleopterous and lepidopterous larvae pupate and the adults emerge to mate and search out places to lay their eggs. This change in food distribution explains why rooks and starlings are observed to change their feeding pattern in summer, from probing to surface feeding and the chasing of imagines. It explains why immigrant lapwings, which feed on the surface far more than the starling and rook, can enter this country in July while the last two species wait until October and the development of the genuine soil fauna. Were details available, they would probably also explain why species like the pied wagtail, which prey on these surface dwelling animals, can still tend second or third broods in July and August, long after the probers must cease to breed.

The nature of the soil and its vegetation profoundly influences the soil fauna, and must equally affect birds depending on these food sources; but details are lacking. For example, sandy soils are known to support more invertebrate animals which are active at night than do loam soils. It is also known that temperature extremes are more drastic on sandy soils, so that on warm nights they hold more, and on cold nights fewer, insects than loam (Tischler 1955). Winter crops allow a rich biotic community to develop on the surface, but summer crops do not, as the fields must be disturbed during spring cultivation, when ploughing selectively reduces those Carabid beetles which hibernate as adults; larval hibernators, however, are less seriously affected. There are a host of considerations of this kind which must be very important as far as birds are concerned which

PLATE 15. *Above*, skylarks have prospered on arable farmland and in some areas are the most abundant farmland bird in winter. *Below left*, house sparrows favour the buildings and surrounds of the farmyard but when nesting in hedgerows build large, untidy, domed nests. *Right*, the introduced little owl has succeeded on farmland where it does not face competition from a better adapted indigenous predator.

PLATE 16. Two nesting rooks photographed from the same hide on the same day late in May. *Above*, an established adult with young nearly ready to fledge. *Below*, a female, attempting to breed for the first time but having built a nest and laid one egg much too late in the season to produce viable young. This egg was later deserted.

need investigation and would doubtless explain many empirical observations that birds favour certain fields and avoid others.

Birds like the rook and starling, which depend largely on invertebrates living within the soil, must breed in spring to coincide with the early peak in food availability, and breeding is then followed by a peak in numbers. But the worst season for food occurs in midsummer, and this is when maximum adjustment of bird numbers in relation to food supplies must occur. This too is when juvenile mortality is at a maximum. As the species concerned have breeding seasons which are proximately controlled by daylength (photoperiodic), their reproductive organs must enter a refractory phase to prevent unseasonal breeding attempts at a time when daylight remains stimulatory. In autumn, soil invertebrates become freely available again, the refractory period ends and there may be a short period during which the pituitary can be stimulated to produce enough hormones to initiate a partial development of the gonads. This process quickly becomes halted as daylengths fall below a stimulatory level with the onset of winter. Nevertheless, the birds may show signs of a sexual recrudescence as, for instance, in rooks by nest building, and in the starling by territorial singing and the reoccupation of nesting holes. However, as no real breeding can be accomplished before the following spring, because winter frosts and short days make it impossible to collect enough extra food to rear a family, population size must remain lower than is potentially supportable by the food supply. There is scope for an immigration of winter visitors, and for this reason large numbers of continental rooks, starlings, lapwings and thrushes arrive to take advantage of the surplus food which cannot be fully exploited by the resident population. These generalisations can now be examined in more detail for the starling and lapwing, and particularly for the rook.

THE ROOK

The rook's economic status has been disputed ever since 1424, when James I of Scotland introduced an act for their destruction. The medieval drawing reproduced in Fig. 20 shows what are undoubtedly rooks harassing a spring corn sowing, and indicates an early approach to the problem of control. In 1533, a further act 'to destroy choughs (jackdaws), crows and rooks' was passed because of their alleged damage to corn, and parishes had to set nets to capture the birds or else pay a fine of ten shillings for every day when no nets were erected. Robert Bloomfield (1799), the Suffolk poet says:

> But still unsafe the big swoln grain below,
> A fav'rite morsel with the Rook and Crow.
> From field to field the flock increasing goes
> To level crops most formidable foes
> Their danger well the wary plunderers know
> And place a watch on some conspicuous bough.

Countrymen today still believe that nuisance birds have the altruistic ability to place sentries on guard. In *A Society of Gentlemen* (1766) rooks are claimed to do considerable damage to sprouting corn but 'they never moleft the wheat which is fown about Michaelmas; because fo much grain of the late harvest then lies scattered about fields, that they find it much eafer to pick up that, than to fearch for corn under ground in new-fown lands.' Devices used to frighten them away included feathers stuck up, the limbs of rooks scattered about the ground, dead rooks hung on sticks, the gun, a boy to halloo and throw his hat or to toss a dead rook up in the air. In contrast, William Marshall (1787) in his *Rural economy of Norfolk* says that rooks are not often shot as the notion prevails that they are more beneficial than harmful in picking up worms and grubs 'especially the grub of the cockchaffer.'

The arguments for and against the rook were still being debated when early in the second world war the Agricultural Research Council, mindful of possible food shortages, sponsored a national investigation into the status of the bird. The task was allotted to the British Trust for Ornithology with James Fisher as the organiser and the late W. B. Alexander as adviser. The A.R.C. were transmitting a request from the Ministry of Agriculture and Fisheries who specifically asked (a) whether the population of the rook was increasing significantly, and (b) whether there had been any significant change in the rook's feeding habits during the war. The question of whether rooks were harmful to agriculture was not formally raised, but presumably it was tacitly assumed. I am grateful to James Fisher for allowing me to quote some of his unpublished figures.

The 1944–6 national census of nests embraced about 90,000 square miles, and by extrapolation indicated a total adult rook population for Britain of just under 3 million birds. This probably represented a general increase of about 20% since a previous census was taken in

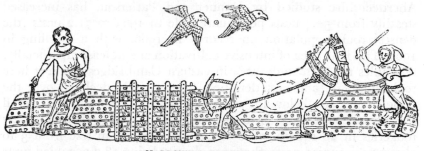

HARROWING, C. A.D. 1340.
Loutrell Psalter.

FIG. 20. This medieval drawing illustrates rooks about to harass a farmer's corn sowing and an early attempt at pest control.

the 1930s. Certainly in Oxfordshire, which was fully studied in both decades, the number of nests increased by 17% between 1931 and 1944–6. An analysis of the census result suggested that England supported 1¾–2 million rooks, Scotland ¾ million and Wales about 200,000. These figures suggest an average rook density of nearly 35 adults per square mile (5/100 acres). Censuses in Holland also indicated a 21% increase between 1936 and 1944 when there were 47,568 nests and the average rook density stood at eight adults per square mile. In 1944, as now, there were considerable variations in rook numbers within and between counties. For instance, densities of occupied nests varied from only 1.2 per square mile in S.W. Monmouth to 47 per square mile in Huntingdonshire and Upper Teesdale (mean of 17.6 per square mile, Fisher unpubl.). It is more interesting to find actual reasons for the rook numbers and the changes occurring in a certain area but this is, of course, a much greater problem. There is no obvious feature associated with areas of increase, areas where numbers remained stable, and areas where decline occurred. In very general terms, decreases were noted where agriculture was declining (West Highlands and Islands) or urbanisation was spreading (Middlesex), while no decrease occurred where agriculture was intensive (Orkney). Although such a relationship might be expected, details of the precise factors which could have been operating within the broader spectrum of agricultural change are simply not available.

Today, a population of rooks in the Ythan Valley of coastal

Aberdeenshire studied by Dunnet and Patterson, has increased steadily from 52.4 nests per square mile in 1963 to 71.2 nests (the densest rook population on record) in 1966, with a levelling in 1967. This is an area of intensive cultivation and at least superficially, resembles my own study area in eastern Cambridgeshire. Yet here rook numbers (and nest densities) have steadily declined over the same period (see below for suggested explanations) and the overall size of the population is always smaller. In 1965, there were 27 rookeries in 28 square miles of country varying in size from 3 to about 70 occupied nests, the mean density being 18.3 occupied nests per square mile. By 1966 the total dropped to 13.5 occupied nests per square mile. Near Penryn, Cornwall, Coombs has recorded a decline in nest numbers of 39% between 1945 and 1953, and a further reduction of 36% from 1953 to 1965. Again it is impossible to detect from a superficial examination any change in the local agriculture which would account for the decline.

In contrast, Dobbs (1964) has shown that the number of rooks in the Trent Valley continued the increase mentioned above until 1958, when there were 20.2 nests per square mile. His figures are set out in Table 9, because between 1928 and 1958 the numbers have clearly not been correlated with the acreage of grass, which has in fact declined, but they tend instead to have increased with the acreage under grain. Dobbs has suggested that increased tillage may have improved supplies of earthworms and that the increasing availability of cereals has been of secondary benefit. In 1962 rook numbers declined to the 1944 level, and he gives evidence that this was caused by the extensive use of organo-chlorine seed dressings (a factor known to have reduced other bird species, including wood-pigeons in my study area, Murton and Vizoso, 1963). This explanation, if true, is of passing interest as it demonstrates that artificial population control is feasible provided a sizable effort is made in relation to the population at risk – though no one would advocate employing these particular chemicals.

In nearby Derbyshire rooks have declined by 22% between 1944 and 1966, though numbers may have been higher in the 1950s than at the start of the period (Lomas, 1968). A slight increase in grain acreage has apparently not helped the rook in this area. Similarly, in the Wirral and West Cheshire, Mary Henderson (1968) shows that numbers have fallen since 1944, particularly between 1955 and 1960, and she attributes the cause to a loss of farmland through increasing

PLATE 17. *Above*, wood-pigeon – the most serious bird pest of agriculture – coming to drink at water tank. *Below*, wood-pigeon damage to cabbages.

PLATE 18. *Above*, bullfinches – the most serious bird pest of horticulture. Male and female visit the nest together to reduce the risk of exposing the site to a predator. *Below*, orchard attacked by bullfinches. The buds of the trees on the left have been eaten by bullfinches; the variety on the right is rarely attacked. The absence of blossom is the result of bullfinch feeding earlier in the year.

urbanisation and industrialisation. Evidently more details are needed to evaluate these various changes.

It seems likely that annual and geographical variations in rook numbers will ultimately be explained in terms of food supplies, but adequate details are at present lacking. The absence of the rook from southern Europe and the Mediterranean probably results from the long dry summers which must inhibit feeding by probing; closely related species feeding on surface-living insects would not be restricted in this way, and the jackdaw does penetrate much farther south.

The rook has evolved from a crow-like ancestor, becoming more and more specialised as a prober, and at the same time presumably moving from the woodland edge to the open grassland of the steppes. According to Lockie, carrion crows eat a wide range of insect larvae, nestling and small birds, small mammals, carrion and earthworms. They obtain earthworms from the moist litter of the woodland floor, and this seems to have been the origin of a feeding habit which led to the development of a highly specialised digging and probing bill. Had rooks been long evolved in the open environment they now inhabit, they would be expected to have cryptic plumage like the skylark, lapwing and other field species, though uniform black plumage represents a more highly evolved condition. It is of interest that the completely unrelated black crow *Corvus capensis* of South Africa has evolved from a distinct corvid stock to fill the same sort of niche on open grassland and secondarily on arable farmland – like the rook it has a great propensity to dig up the farmer's maize crop. It also has acquired an elongated bill remarkably similar in size and shape to that of the rook, but unlike the rook it nests solitarily and is much less gregarious throughout the year. Today the rook is very much associated with arable farmland, often in preference to grass, but in many districts it is noticeable that at the worst seasons of the year for food, in summer and again in mid-winter, it resorts to grassland to use the food source for which it is best adapted.

Dunnet and Patterson have demonstrated that rooks prefer to frequent grain sites whenever these are available on stubbles or sowings and that they prefer cultivated fields in spring and autumn. It seems that when the adults have only themselves to feed, grain suits them very well, but they do need to resort to freshly cultivated land and pasture in order to get earthworms and other animal food when feeding their young (and possibly to give themselves extra reserves during the breeding season). In mid-summer, when no grain is available and no cultivation is turning up the worms, they must again return to the pastures. At this season they are quick to visit a freshly mown hay, clover or other silage crop, where farming operations expose a host of invertebrates normally hidden under the foliage. Lockie (1956) has shown that during May and June, and again from August to October, rooks, and to an even greater extent jackdaws, often feed by jumping at flying diptera and that during this season rooks are forced to dig instead of probe into hard ground to get food.

During Fisher's war-time studies, numerous (about 138) voluntary observers throughout Britain noted the places where they saw rooks feeding and in this way over ½ million birds were recorded. From the figures the percentage seen on different feeding grounds could be calculated each month. This percentage not only shows where most rooks feed, but must also be a function of the time spent on different feeding grounds. In general rooks spend more time on grassland with a peak of 77% in June declining to 43% in September, 37% in October, and 35% in March. In March there are more birds (24%) on plough, and hence more time is spent there, whereas in September only 6% of the birds are on plough and 34% are now found on stubbles. Estimation of the most important foods by gizzard analysis is unfortunately liable to bias from differential digestion. Cereal husks tend to remain undigested in the gizzard while soft earthworms are rapidly assimilated and only their keratinous chaetae remain, which can only be seen under a low power microscope. It is therefore easy to over-emphasise the importance of cereal food. For the whole year the rook investigation, judged from volume of food eaten, indicated a diet of 5% animal material (and earthworms were not properly included), 9% root crops, potatoes, acorns and legumes, and 86% cereals. Animal food was at its lowest in January and February and at its highest from April until July, with a peak in June. In spite of the small amount of animal food recorded, at least half the birds examined had eaten some. How far the earthworm component of the diet was underestimated was not known until Lockie re-examined the problem. (That earthworms could not be quantitatively estimated in gizzard remains was known to Fisher and his colleagues and they deliberately omitted them from several calculations. This does not detract from certain of their comparative conclusions.) Knowing the proportion of different feeding actions in various situations and the average weight of animals within each of these feeding places, Lockie showed that earthworms were by far the most important food, comprising over 95% of the animal food in winter. Other animal food eaten in the appropriate season includes dung beetles, weevils, wireworms, click beetles, ground beetles and rove beetles, muscid flies, caterpillars, moths, leatherjackets and crane-flies.

In evaluating the 1944–5 rook investigation, Fisher was able to demonstrate that corn featured more prominently in the diet than it had in any earlier investigations and he attributed this to the large increase in cereal growing during the war. For example, from Collinge's studies in 1913–16 only 35% by volume of the diet was found to be corn, as against 86% in 1944–5. Fisher compared three studies using the method which records the percentage of frequency of occurrence (based on the number of birds examined which contained the food in question) and showed that Gilmour (1896) had recorded a 60% frequency of corn in 1894–5, when corn growing prospered, that Leigh (1916) recorded only 34% from 1908–15, when there was a depression in corn growing, while he himself found 50% of the rooks to have eaten corn in 1944–5. These figures are not absolute, but are valid for comparative purposes. The size of the samples examined by these workers and the number of different studies giving the same low intake of corn in the early 1900s, seem to justify Fisher's conclusion and it is interesting to consider these results in the light of Dobbs's studies mentioned above. Of the corn eaten in 1944–5, 36% was from stubbles and 38% was vulnerable corn from a sowing, corn stack or germinating plant. It was concluded that, on balance, the rook was harmful to agriculture and that the British rook population ate an estimated 26,500 tons of vulnerable corn per year. However, we now appreciate that this does not necessarily mean a corresponding loss to the farmer (for example, yields from surviving plants usually increase to compensate for a low seed rate at sowing) and the figure has to be related to an estimated total of 650,000 tons of corn planted and 13–14 million tons harvested in the U.K. today.

When rooks do cause serious damage it is usually on a very local scale, and certainly it is no longer reasonable to regard them as universally harmful to agriculture. Their liking for maize sometimes makes them troublesome to growers in S.W. England, where some farmers claim that they are the chief reason for the restricted growth of this crop. Again there is no evidence to show that more than a few individual growers ever suffer to the extent of having their final yields reduced. The same arguments apply to damage to newly sown peas, and the only careful experiments made (in connection with wood-pigeon damage) show that the seed rate has to be reduced very considerably before final yields are affected – even allowing for the fact that rooks can excavate buried seed. Rooks have been recorded digging down to the tubers of growing potatoes, but fortunately such behaviour is usually very local and does not occur every season. Here and there the rook may be a real nuisance, but it pays to recognise the exact nature and location of any damage, rather than waste time and money waging a war against a bird which for most of the year, and in most situations, can be safely ignored.

Rooks have long been known to begin breeding earlier in mild springs and Lockie showed that the breeding season around Oxford was timed to synchronise with a peak in earthworm abundance. When he did his work, from 1952–4, there was little annual difference in the timing of the breeding season, although on extending Lockie's observations at the rookeries to 1957, Owen found that the season in 1956 was unusually late, the mean date for egg-laying being the 23rd March, while 1957 was unusually early, the mean laying date being 7th March. Unfortunately Owen did not continue the sampling of earthworms, and so could not correlate his results with their availability. He did, however, show that for six years (1952–7) the mean date for egg-laying was correlated with air temperature; in 1956 the spring was unusually cold, while 1957 was unusually mild. As temperature affects earthworm activity, it remains to be proved whether it is primarily the ease of finding suitable food or temperature itself, which provides the main stimulus initiating egg-laying; the fact that high temperatures may be associated with drought might make it dangerous for rooks to rely on this as the signal.

The average number of eggs laid by rooks also varies in different years and at different times during the season, the most frequent clutch size being either four or five eggs. However, in some years there are more birds than usual laying more or fewer eggs, so that while Lockie and Owen were carrying out their studies at Oxford the mean clutch size varied over six years from 4.2 to 4.7 for eggs laid in March, the overall mean being 4.4. Some further data for the Carlton area are set out in Table 10 and they suggest that the mean clutch in March was below average when earthworm numbers were low. More birds laid only two eggs than in the other years, and clutches of five were uncommon. Further records will be needed to test the possibility that clutch size in first layings is related to earth-worm availability. The same does not apply to repeat and late clutches which seem always to be smaller irrespective of the food supply as Table 11 shows. Food supplies are usually good when April eggs are laid, indeed usually better than in March, but any young produced from such eggs must fledge nearer the summer when earthworm stocks decline, so that their post-fledging survival is likely to be lower on this account. If this is so, it is probably adaptively advantageous always to lay fewer eggs in late or repeat clutches, a situation also pertaining to the great tit (see Lack 1966). Young rooks breeding for the first time lay later in the season than older individuals, and the young individuals of several species are known to lay fewer eggs than older birds. The decline in clutch size is thus probably caused by the reduced size of repeats and the fact that inexperienced females also lay eggs.

Lack long ago advanced the view that the commonest clutch size of any species was the one which, on average, produced most surviving young, and he explained the existence of more than one clutch size by the fluctuating success of these in different years or under different conditions. He has since added that the optimum clutch size may not always be achieved if the female is unable to accumulate sufficient body reserves. For the rook, Lockie established that the percentage of eggs hatched did not vary with clutch size, and Owen subsequently demonstrated that broods of four or five produced more young than broods above or below this size. The same is indicated in Table 12 where it is seen that, although a higher proportion of young were successfully reared in early clutches of three eggs, there were actually more young produced per pair in clutches of four or five, these being the most economical clutch sizes. Neverthe-less, in late layings, clutches of three seem to have been at a much greater relative advantage. These data from Carlton are insufficient to prove the superiority of smaller broods late in the season but suggest that such a trend exists. If post-fledging survival were also considered, the differences might be more striking. For instance, in Holland, van Koersveld did find that broods of one or two suffered a lower mortality *after* leaving the nest than broods of three. In 1964, when the April food supply was good at Carlton (see Table 10) twelve clutches of four eggs produced an average of 2.7 young as opposed to 2.6 young from seven clutches of five eggs. In 1966, when earthworms were scarce in April, seven clutches of four produced an average of 3.4 young per pair where five clutches of five averaged only 2.6 young. When rooks lay their eggs in March, it is unlikely that they could predict what conditions in April would be and, therefore, could find themselves with over-large or unnecessarily small clutches. Their ability to rear young would then depend on the relation between the food supply and the number of young they had produced, without being perfectly anticipatory. It would, of course, take a long series of years to eradicate chance fluctuations of this kind, but on average one should expect rooks to produce the number of eggs which most often proved appropriate to the average prevailing conditions. Owen has shown, in greater detail, that the most productive brood size varies in different years, but he does not relate his figures to the food supply (this added refinement does not matter for the purposes of the present argument), finally it is possible that a clutch of five is generally the most productive, and clutches of four are produced, not because they are relatively more productive, but because in some years the adults simply cannot produce more.

Table 13 shows that the ability of rooks to hatch their eggs does not seem clearly related to the year or season, while Lockie has already shown that it does not depend on clutch size. At present I am unable to account properly for these variations, which are caused by a combination of predation by other rooks – even though the females remain near their nests some egg stealing does occur – as well as desertion and infertility. Examination of both early and late nests in Table 13 suggests that the larger the breeding population the fewer the eggs hatched, and it is conceivable that more social interaction and egg stealing occurs at high population density. It is also evident that the overall proportion of young fledged (breeding successes) was not directly related to the total food supply primarily because clutch and brood size varied, to a large extent independently; success was higher in early broods in 1965 than in 1964 because the parents had fewer young to care for. (It is because so many factors contribute to the story that it is necessary to have information for many years.) Whatever the variable interactions existing between the adults and their food supply and whatever their resultant ability to rear young, the day of reckoning comes with the onset of the early summer droughts. In 1966 a very poor earthworm supply in June caused the juveniles to suffer badly and few were recorded in the feeding flocks. The earthworm food supply in June 1964 was slightly better than in 1965, yet a lower proportion of young was seen than in 1965. But as Table 13 shows, 1965 had been a much more productive breeding season and if the percentage of young lost is considered (this may include emigration) – this is a truer measure of how severely the population was affected – it is seen to be proportionately higher in 1965 than in 1964, and was highest in 1966.

Understanding the way in which rook numbers vary throughout the year and in different years is complicated by the different behaviour of various age groups. Birds of one year in age and under can generally be identified in the field by their lack of white face; these birds occasionally breed at one year. Individuals in their second year can usually be identified in the hand until August but not usually thereafter, and when these birds reach their third April or May (end of their second year) they sometimes breed. Thus there are three major age groups contributing in different ways to the size of the total and the breeding populations, but only two age groups (first year or older) can be readily identified in the field.

Some preliminary figures for the Cambridgeshire study area are set out in Fig. 21 with the number and percentage of first-years indicated, that of second-years being unknown. This study area covers 2,647 acres, and the main roost is three miles away. After breeding, many birds withdraw from the area and scatter over a much wider area of the surrounding countryside. The area does not seem to be particularly favoured in winter, when we find more birds nearer the central roost. Winter numbers in two of the three years were lower than breeding numbers, the juvenile ratio falling at times when total numbers decreased, which suggests a departure of young. In January 1965 the high population may have depended on the presence of continental immigrants, although these normally seem to live and feed much nearer the main winter roost and are not often found in our study area. In Aberdeenshire, Dunnet and Patterson have been able to examine a bigger study area which includes a roost. They consistently find an increase in winter numbers plausibly attributable to immigrants, but whether from Europe or other parts of Scotland is not known. Otherwise, the seasonal variations in population size are similar in pattern at Carlton and at Aberdeen.

Also shown in Fig. 21 is the seasonal and annual change in the abundance of earthworms. Bearing in mind that outside the June–July period rooks find many food sources, the figure demonstrates a fair degree of correlation between earthworm abundance and rook numbers in the area. Over four years there has been a decline in the index of the breeding population as shown in Table 13. This index is estimated from counts of all the *occupied* rooks' nests in the area, and some accessible nests were climbed to find the proportion of empty nests. The birds from one rookery included in our study area mostly feed and live outside the area covered by the circuit counts, which causes the estimate of the breeding population to be higher than the total derived from direct counting. There has also been a decline in the population counted by direct means at breeding time, except for an anomalous high figure in 1966 (see Fig. 21). This high figure was the result of an intensive control campaign at a rookery outside the area, which caused many birds to disperse, and some to enter the area. The gradual decline in the resident breeding population seems directly attributable to a steady worsening of the summer food supply and to an increasingly poor survival of young birds. Comparison of Fig. 21 with Table 13 shows that between 1964 and 1965 there was a high survival of first-year birds and the breeding population remained constant (between 1964 and 1965). Earthworm stocks were poorer in the summer of 1965 and, in spite of a higher breeding success in 1965 compared with 1964, the post-fledging survival of young was much lower between June and the following breeding season of 1966 than it had been between 1964 and 1965. It is reasonable to suppose that second-year birds would also have suffered directly in relation to decreased food stocks but to a lesser extent, while adults may or may not. It is also reasonable to expect a decreasing availability of sub-adult animals to balance the natural adult wastage and cause a decline in recruitment potential. The breeding season of 1966 was good and the number of young produced might have brought the population back to the 1964 level, if the worst May and June on record for food had not caused an almost complete loss of these young causing the 1967 breeding stock to decline even more. Over four years, recruitment (including that from the second to third year) has progressively declined, and while adult mortality may have been adversely affected in parallel, the lack of recruitment to replace accidental mortality could well account for all the changes.

Over three years, field counts of black-faced birds, have shown the average percentage of first-year birds surviving in the March population to be 13%. Assuming the total population to be stable

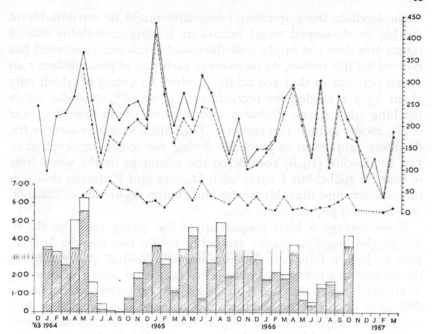

FIG. 21. Variations in the number of rooks in a Cambridgeshire study area and the number of earthworms in samples of soil cores,—total rook population, - - - number of birds older than one year, . . . number of first-year individuals. The hatched areas of the histograms refer to the dry weight of earthworms in 29 soil samples, each 4″ × 2″ deep, from pastures and the unshaded areas to the weight of worms in 26 similar samples from arable fields. The shortage of worms on disturbed fields is clearly apparent.

and taking this as the average recruitment rate into adult population (making the further assumption that recruitment of first-years into the second-year age group will equal the recruitment rate of second-years to adult status) would imply an adult mortality rate of around 13% per annum. Dunnet and Patterson reckoned adult mortality to be 7.5–11% based on the survival of marked adults from one year to the next while Coombs (1960) estimated that it was around 16%. This is a very low figure for a passerine and presumably depends on the large size of the rook and freedom from predation (this does not mean that the bird would not evolve anti-predator behaviour). Some of the freedom from accidental mortality might be attributable to the highly developed social behaviour leading to stability but of course this does not imply that the social behaviour concerned has evolved for this reason. As on average each pair of rooks fledges 1.20 young per year so that 100 adults produce 60 young of which only about 13 are needed for recruitment, 47 or 78% must die before reaching adult status. Probably most of these die in their first year of life, mostly in their first summer. That this is so is indicated by the declining proportion of juveniles during the season represented in Fig. 21. Lockie (1956) considered the winter to be the worst time of year for rooks, but I agree with Dunnet and Patterson that it is the summer, and that this is when maximum regulation of the total post-breeding population occurs.

If on average a high proportion of the young rooks produced during the breeding season are going to die two months later in June or July, it follows that it is pointless to destroy young birds at the rookery as a control measure. The traditional 'sport' of shooting 'branchers' which has been practised for centuries can make no difference at all to the level of crop damage occurring after July and cannot be justified. Looking at the matter from another viewpoint, Dunnet and Patterson have compared lightly shot and heavily shot rookeries (where nearly all young were eliminated) and show that shooting has no effect on the change in rookery size in subsequent years. On the other hand, shooting young rooks for rook pie provides a good protein food without harming the population that is cropped. People who slaughter young rooks do neither good nor harm and the only criticism to be levelled is the moral one of whether it is right to derive enjoyment from pointless killing when one is once faced with the facts.

THE STARLING

Like the rook, the starling seems to have evolved in the Asiatic Steppes, moving from wooded parkland to utilise the soil invertebrates of open grassland and riverine valleys. In so doing it must also have become more exposed to predators, particularly when feeding, and it has evolved intensive gregarious roosting and feeding habits to give mutual protection. The complicated movements made by groups of starlings leaving or returning to roost with sudden swoop dives are typical of the movements made when a flock is chased by a sparrowhawk. An impressive anti-predator behaviour is apparent when the members of a flock flying at height suddenly drop towards the ground with fluttering wings giving the appearance of leaves falling from a dark cloud.

As long as Britain remained an intensively wooded country the starling was a rare bird, and it has only become common in many parts of western and northern Britain within the last hundred years or so. In the mid-eighteenth century it just penetrated the south-west lowlands of Scotland and was only a winter visitor to Wales and peninsular England. The first breeding in Devon was recorded in 1830, and in Cornwall in 1855. Similarly in Wales, the starling only arrived as a breeding bird between 1830–60. Davies (1949), in examining its status in south Wales covered eighty square miles in south Cardiganshire in the spring of 1947 and could find no breeding birds. In an intensive follow-up survey in 1948 throughout Cardiganshire, Carmarthenshire and Pembrokeshire less than 100 pairs were accounted for in Carmarthenshire, though Lloyd (1950), in extending the records, gives evidence of a general increase in west Wales in the second decade of this century, which has since continued (Parslow 1968).

In the more distant past, colonisation of western Europe is likely to have depended on migrants from central Europe moving to the milder maritime countries in winter in the face of frozen ground and food supplies in the east. A group of drifted migrants must have landed in the treeless Orkneys and settled to breed in isolation giving rise to the distinctive sub-species now resident. This must have been an early fluke before the species really colonised the west of Europe, or at least Scotland, for otherwise one would have expected them to intermix with a mainland population. L. S. V. and U. M. Venables (1953) describe a similar but recent event in the case of the rook. Until 1952 the rook was a passage migrant and a rare winter visitor to Shetland. There was an unusual influx in February 1952 which resulted in nine pairs settling to breed in the spring, the number increasing to eleven nests in 1953. The nearest rookeries to this isolated population, which still remains, lie 100 miles south in mid-Orkney and about 180 miles east in Norway. British starlings have been separated from continental birds long enough to acquire a distinct physiological difference in breeding response; they respond to lower levels of daylight and so come into breeding condition earlier and also show sexual recrudescence in the autumn, enabling them to hold territories at this time. This physiological distinctiveness has not made them eligible to be regarded a valid taxonomic sub-species.

Today Britain supports a large immigrant winter population, part of which, like the immigrant rooks, originates from ancestral homes in Russia, the Soviet Baltic, Poland and Germany, while the rest comes from Sweden, Norway, Finland, Denmark and the Low Countries. Goodacre (1959) has shown from ringing recoveries that birds from Scandinavia mostly winter in northern Britain, and those from central Europe in the south of England. Moreover, starlings from furthest east in Europe winter mostly in the east of England, while those from areas nearer to Britain travel further west through the country to winter in the west and in Ireland. The movement is basically a lateral displacement.

The starling is essentially a grassland feeder, and its long bill facilitates the collection of invertebrates living in grass roots – grass and herbage are parted by gaping movements of the bill – or in the top soil layer. For a population he studied in Aberdeenshire, Dunnet showed that leatherjackets were by far the most important food during the starling's breeding season, with the addition of a few earthworms. At Aberdeen leatherjackets were also the main food taken at other seasons, but they were supplemented by large amounts of oats and smaller quantities of weevils from September and throughout the winter. Less important foods were various Carabid beetles, wireworms, small molluscs and spiders. Dunnet considered the late summer, particularly August (July could probably be included in the south of England) to be the worst season of the year for food. By this time leatherjackets have pupated and emerged and the new generation of larvae which hatch in August are too small to provide a good food supply. In addition, starlings cannot get grain until harvesting begins later in the month, and show evidence of feeding difficulties by adopting less typical feeding behaviour such as hawking after flying insects, just as the rook does.

The introduction and subsequent spread of the starling in various parts of the world testifies to its success as a species. In the United States the place for a bird filling a similar niche on open grassland was occupied by the meadowlark *Sturnella magna*, a species similar in build and bill adaptation, but belonging to the New World family, the Icteridae. This bird is viewed benevolently by American farmers because it eats large numbers of soil pests such as cut-worms, various caterpillars and grasshoppers, but like the starling turns to various seeds and cereal grain in winter. The meadowlark must be highly adapted for this field environment because in Africa a totally unrelated pipit, the yellow-throated longclaw, *Macronix croceus*, which also lives by foraging and probing in grassland, is almost identical to it in colour, detailed markings and external shape (but not in internal anatomy). Such remarkable convergence indicates that these two isolated species have been subjected to the same selective pressure presumably resulting in almost ideal adaptations to their mode of life. It is, therefore, surprising to find that the starling has managed to find a place alongside the meadowlark in the eastern United States and become in many places equally abundant as the data in Table 14 show. Table 14 also helps to emphasise that agricultural development has led to a reduction in faunal diversity, with a few species becoming particularly abundant in order to maintain roughly the same total of individual birds. Like the rook, the starling in Britain may have benefited from a general increase in cereal production which provides a valuable supplement to the diet in late summer, when soil invertebrates are still scarce.

The introduced starling population of the United States has been intensively studied by Kalmbach (1922), and its diet in North America in 1916 has been compared with Collinge's 1918 figures for Britain. In Britain at that time animal food comprised half the diet and cereals made up 21% of the remaining vegetable half. In the U.S.A. more animal than vegetable food was eaten (57% as opposed to 43%) and of the vegetable component cereals comprised only 1%, wild fruits and weed seeds being taken to a much greater extent. These differences could well mirror the temporal changes in feeding habits that have occurred within Britain, where cereals have gradually assumed more importance.

The starling is a great food opportunist in other ways, taking bread in back gardens or processed poultry and animal food mash. It can cause considerable economic damage where poultry and other livestock are fed from open hoppers, and large numbers congregate to compete with the farm animals for food. On one large commercial poultry farm it was calculated that starlings were stealing about 1,000 tons of animal food a year. At another farm, where bullocks were intensively fed from open tumbrils, starlings were said to be consuming four hundredweights of food per day worth 23s. per cwt. When such enormous losses occur, the only satisfactory answer is to feed the livestock in bird-proof surroundings – but this can admittedly be difficult and initially expensive and may even lead to complications. At one turkey farm starlings were entering brooders through 2 in. wire netting to steal the turkeys' food. On intensive commercial poultry farms the turnover rate of stock, the feeding schedules and profit margins are so efficiently geared, that a change in routine, enough to cause a delay of only a day or two in the rearing time may seriously upset the whole economy of the enterprise. Other examples of the damage caused by starlings are given in Chapters 9 and 11. Such damage is serious, but altogether may be not enough to justify attempts to reduce starling numbers on a national scale because these would prove to be even more expensive than the damage caused, if one assumes that conventional control techniques would be employed. The problem is made more difficult by the large number of immigrants involved.

Dunnet has shown that the starling manages to rear two broods at the time when leatherjackets are most abundant (Fig. 22). In this respect the starling is less restricted than the rook, but in order to rear first broods at the right time, it lays many eggs in partial antici-pation of the peak in food supplies. To achieve the necessary syn-chronisation, starlings are geared to respond first to appropriate increases in daylength, while further adjustment may be brought about by a direct response to temperature. Certainly Dunnet found that in a year when the spring temperature was low the birds laid late, and conversely laid early when the average spring temperature was high (actually the 'warmth sum' obtained by totalling the mean daily temperatures from 1st January to the season of egg-laying was used as a measure of the total spring temperature). It might be claimed that natural selection would favour such a response to temperature, if temperature also affected the activity and growth of the soil invertebrates – which it does. In the great tit a correlation between spring temperature and the date of egg-laying has been established in much greater detail, and it results in young being hatched at about the time when food is most plentiful (see Lack 1966 for details). Perrins has shown that there are many great tits which have young when food supplies are not optimal, and these birds rear fewer young than they might otherwise do. He postulated that the birds begin laying as soon as possible after the females have acquired sufficient reserves. Their ability to do this must depend on the immediate food supply which is directly correlated with tempera-

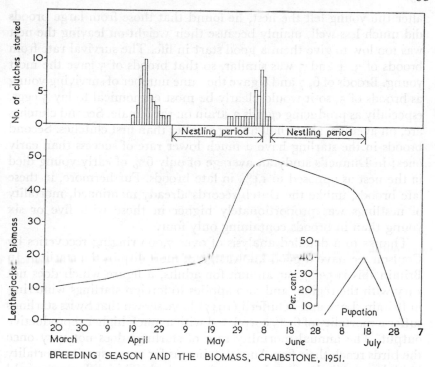

FIG. 22. Breeding season of starling in relation to the availability of leatherjackets in a study area in Aberdeenshire. (After Dunnet 1955).

ture, so that food rather than temperature, would seem to be the most important factor. By laying eggs as soon as possible when the food supply is rising and improving, the birds tend to produce their young at the most propitious season, although the relationship is by no means perfect. In the starling, one would expect response patterns similar to those already discussed in the case of the rook, where with hindsight it would be possible to adjust the season of breeding and clutch size more advantageously in relation to the whole seasonal change in food stocks.

Lack (1948) showed for Dutch and Swiss starlings that the average number of young fledged per starling brood was proportionately the same for a wide range of brood sizes (3–8), so that large broods were not penalised at the nestling stage. When Lack examined survival after the young left the nest, he found that those from large broods did much less well, mainly because their weight on leaving the nest was too low to give them a good start in life. The survival rate from broods of 3, 4 and 5 was similar, so that broods of 5 gave the most young. Broods of 6, 7 and 8 gave the same number of surviving young as broods of 5, so it would clearly be most economical to lay 5 eggs, especially as producing eggs is a strain on the female. Second clutches are, on average, about half an egg smaller than first clutches. Second broods in the starling have a much lower rate of success than early ones; in Dunnet's study an average of only 6% of early young died in the nest as opposed to 14% in late broods. Furthermore, in these late broods, unlike the Dutch records already mentioned, mortality of nestlings was proportionately higher in those with five or six young than in broods containing only four.

Thanks to a detailed analysis of over 7,000 ringing recoveries by Coulson we have a good knowledge of mortality in the starling. In Britain this is 53% per annum for adults, a figure which does not vary with the region, and also applies to foreign starlings wintering in Britain. Lack and Schifferli (1947) have shown that Swiss starlings suffer a mortality of 63% correlated with a much higher reproductive output. The annual mortality rate of starlings does not vary once the birds reach their first August, whereas for many species mortality is higher until the first January is reached. This difference could depend on the big improvement in food supplies once the harvest begins, because, as stated, the worst food season for starlings comes in late July and early August. Indeed, Coulson was able to show that in July in particular, and to a lesser extent in August and September, the proportion of juveniles dying was much greater than that of adults, presumably as a result of poor food supplies. On the other hand, a smaller proportion of first-years than adults died in the succeeding April–June, and this reduced wastage balanced the earlier higher mortality of young. The reason is that many first-year birds do not breed. During the period from fledging to their first winter there is little or no difference in the death-rate of male or female starlings. But, in the period between their first March of life and the attainment of adult plumage in the next autumn, males suffer a 39% mortality while females experience a 70% loss. This results in a combined mortality of 56%, and produces an unequal sex ratio in later life, males outnumbering females by about two to one. The explanation seems almost certainly to be that whereas

PLATE 19. *Above left*, bullfinch in act of eating apple bud. *Above right and below*, distress call apparatus set up to repel starlings from an orchard.

PLATE 20. Bird damage in horticulture. *Above left*, linnets can locally damage certain soft fruits and can sometimes be troublesome to seed growers. *Right*, strawberry, the seeds of which have been eaten by linnets. *Below left*, rose pecked by tits searching for insects, annoying but of no commercial significance. *Right*, jay damage to beans.

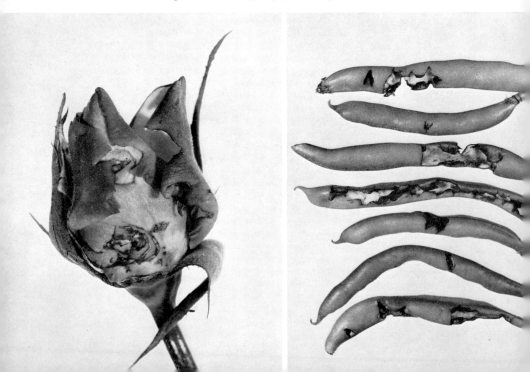

most first-year male starlings do not breed, first-year females often do.

The circumstances and season in which ringed starlings are recovered may or may not be a true indication of the seasonal pattern of natural mortality. Thus, if many starlings are recovered in the breeding season, it could be that they come nearer to human habitation at such times. Nevertheless, the pattern of all recoveries in Britain suggests that adult deaths in Britain reach a peak during the breeding season, whereas in the U.S.A. the peak of recoveries occur in January, February and March. The difference could depend on the much more severe winter climate of the eastern U.S.A. causing feeding difficulties in frozen ground. When the adult mortality in different years in Britain was compared, Coulson did find a slightly higher mortality in winters with above average snowfalls and a smaller increase associated with the amount of winter frost. It is of interest to note that while all recoveries in Britain reach a peak in the breeding season this is even more marked for recoveries made when the adult is killed by a cat. It seems reasonable to suppose that, when feeding young, the adults spend more time searching for food on the ground and run a greater risk of being caught napping by a ground predator. Ideally they would do better to feed in flocks at this time to avoid such risks, as they do at other times. Presumably social feeding is not compatible with successful breeding though it is often noticeable that starlings in the breeding season, like many other birds, will still try to maintain a certain level of gregariousness on the feeding ground if other birds are already present. Deaths from shooting reach a peak in December. These results are of interest in emphasising how the worst season of the year for food may not be the time when most adults die, yet it is the time when juvenile loss is greatest, bringing the population into balance with resources (see Chapter 2 page 36).

THE PLOVERS

The lapwing is yet another component of the grassland fauna of central Europe which in the past has benefited from agriculture and the creation of open country with sparse vegetation. Farming coupled with better weather conditions enabled it to spread in western Europe; notably in the Faroes and Iceland during this century and today in Norway (Myrberget 1962). The lapwing's relationship with agriculture has been the subject of several intensive investigations, notably a B.T.O. inquiry organised by E. M. Nicholson in 1937 and a follow-up by M. D. Lister in 1960–1. It has long been felt that recent changes in agricultural practice may have been detrimental to the species, in particular the war-time reduction in grassland at the expense of arable, and increasing mechanisation since the 1930s, which has resulted in many more farm operations being performed on fields during the breeding season. One might expect the mechanics of spraying herbicides, the development of strip grazing, the more rapid maturation of leys and meadows permitting the cutting of silage as early as May, to have been detrimental. Yet there is no concrete evidence forthcoming. The adult mortality rate of British lapwings is 34% per annum (Lack 1943, Haldane 1955), that of Dutch birds slightly higher at 40%, according to Kraak, Rinkel and Hoogerheide (1940), possibly because these birds suffer a greater risk through being more migratory. Allowing for the fact that not all birds breed in their first year of life, an output of $1\frac{1}{2}$ young per pair should be easily sufficient to maintain population size. As the normal clutch is four, and as nests lost early are replaced, actually up to five clutches may be laid if losses occur soon after the laying of the fourth egg (Klomp, 1951), the reproductive potential seems more than adequate to withstand a fair degree of agricultural disturbance. Like the partridge (see page 176), the lapwing is one of the few species of farmland birds which, according to the Common Bird Census, does not seem to be recovering as rapidly as it should from the hard winter of 1962–3. As with the partridge, the resident population seems to be experiencing sharp fluctuations in numbers within each year, resulting from the production of young and their subsequent mortality, but superimposed on this pattern there is a steady decline of adults linked with some factor associated with breeding dispersal. In other words, lapwings are declining not because they cannot produce sufficient young, but because smaller numbers of adults can manage to breed in any given locality. It is unlikely that the lapwing suffers from a shortage of nesting places, and the most plausible explanation is that food supplies during the breeding season have changed in such a way that fewer adults can settle in any area. Unfortunately, no detailed information is available on the adults' food during the breeding season, nor that of the young during their early life.

Lister's inquiry indicates that lapwings prefer conditions in which

surface invertebrates can be expected to be most numerous. For
instance, bird densities are higher between 250 and 499 ft. above
sea-level during the dry months of June–September, but not in
March, April and May; they prefer light soils to heavy clays and
shales, though definitely do not require good drainage. On farmland, areas with more pasture than arable are favoured during the
nesting season, but areas of predominantly arable are rather
suddenly favoured in August, and then to a variable extent until
mid-winter. In August, as I have mentioned, many soil invertebrates reach low densities but as soon as early ploughing of the first
stubbles begins a previously inaccessible supply of food is made
available. The long-term effect of soil cultivation is to decrease the
numbers of soil invertebrates, so that by spring arable land provides
a far less attractive source of food. Food supplies may account for
much of the lapwing's distribution, but it is also clear that the birds
have certain preferences in nesting sites, and these may not be in
exactly the same areas as the most abundant supplies of food. A need
for rough meadows may account for the preference shown during the
breeding season for ley grass, including clover and lucerne crops,
rather than for the generally shorter permanent grassland; permanent grass is noticeably preferred at all other times.

The problem of the lapwing's status is complicated by the fact
that most areas support a larger immigrant than resident population,
which arrives at the end of June as can be seen in Fig. 23. Furthermore, the number of summer and autumn immigrants does not
appear to be declining, which leads one to suppose that autumn and
early winter food supplies are not limiting. This summer immigration
at first comprises moulting adults from Holland, the birds having
arrived there from Scandinavia, Germany, the Baltic states, Poland
and the U.S.S.R.; the exodus from eastern Europe starts at the
end of May. Basically, these movements take the birds away from
areas of hard winter frosts to the milder maritime conditions of the
Atlantic seaboard including Ireland; the lapwing is one of the best
indicator species of frost, and its hard weather responses are well-
known to bird watchers. Some explanation for the behaviour of the
lapwing can be made by comparing Figs. 23 and 19. Bearing in
mind that the lapwing is not a prober, it is apparent that the immigrants arrive in time to enjoy the summer peak of surface-living
insects. The onset of hard weather in November results in a further
influx, these birds moving off at the turn of the year, probably south

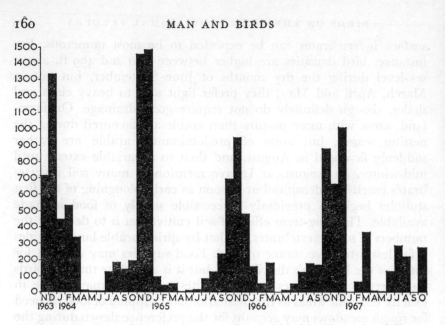

FIG. 23. Number of lapwings on a Cambridgeshire farm in different years. Data refer to an area of 2,647 acres.

to Europe. Unfortunately not enough soil samples are available with which to compare different years individually.

Lapwings begin breeding in March, staking out their territories by delightful acrobatics and haunting *pee-wit* calls. Surface invertebrates are now relatively scarce, and this may explain why only a few individuals stay to breed, while the rest, like so many of the waders, return to richer feeding grounds further north and east in Europe. This does not explain why resident lapwings do not wait until, say, July to begin breeding, when food supplies are better. The growth of vegetation could well prevent them finding food, even though plenty was present, or it could be that the young have a very specialised food requirement which can be obtained only in April and May. The breeding biology of the lapwing would well repay study.

In the past the lapwing suffered a marked decline, not to be confused with the present decrease, through the intensive collection of its eggs as a delicacy. This trade persisted throughout the nineteenth century, repeat clutches being taken whenever they could be found.

Stevenson records how a single 'egger' at Potter Heigham, Norfolk, took 160 dozen eggs from the adjacent marshes in 1821, while in 1834 a Yarmouth game-dealer used to send between 600 and 700 eggs to the London markets every week during the season, including as 'plovers'' eggs those of redshank, reeve, snipe and black tern. In 1845 prices rarely dropped below 3 shillings a dozen (8d. each for early eggs), until by 1870 Stevenson records that eggs were fetching four shillings a dozen in the Norwich market, the supply having decreased so much through persecution. With high demand and short supplies, black-headed gulls' eggs were then sold as plovers', a deceit that is often practised today. On one estate near Thetford about 280 dozen lapwing eggs were taken annually in the 1860s, but by the 1880s the annual take had fallen to 60 dozen, in spite of the fact that none were collected after 1st May. The decline continued until only 6 dozen were collected in 1902 and only 20 pairs were still thought to be nesting in 1915. On the other hand, there were other places where no decline in status was recorded. In view of such intense exploitation, it is impossible to isolate the harmful effects of a changing agriculture, but it is notable that lapwings again increased and spread in a spectacular manner with the passing of the 'Lapwing Act' in 1926.

The golden plover is another common winter visitor to farmland, and is so similar to the lapwing in size, bill shape and feeding habits that it would seem to be a potential competitor in winter. A super-abundance of food may allow the two species to co-exist in winter, but more study is needed. For breeding the golden plover is restricted to upland moors in Britain, generally preferring peat-mosses where its yellow-brown flecked plumage is cryptic, but it also frequents more grassy areas and patches of burnt heather, especially on grouse moors and the highland fells of west Yorkshire. In such habitats it is probably better adapted than the lapwing, although in many places the two species may nest very near each other. The breeding distribution of the golden plover in Europe is surprisingly restricted and has the characteristics of a relict species which was probably at its peak during the immediate post-glacial periods. It has retreated in range northwards while the lapwing has been expanding; this could well be a direct consequence of climate changes rather than true inter-specific competition. Like the lapwing, it is an early breeder, but post-nuptial dispersal is not nearly so marked in early summer – perhaps because upland moors are less subject to summer droughts.

Stevenson records how a single 'expert' at Potter Heigham, Norfolk, took 160 dozen eggs from the adjoining marshes in 1835, while in 1841 a Yarmouth gun-dealer used to send between 100 and 300 eggs to the London markets every week during the season. Indeed in 1815 prices rarely dropped below 9 shillings a dozen till early in early 1890 by 1890 Stevenson records that eggs were fetching

CHAPTER 7

BIRDS ON THE FARM: THE SEED-EATERS

THE seeds and fruits of weeds and trees mostly develop during the late spring and summer, and reach peak abundance in summer and autumn when they are shed. From this time onwards they are only available to birds which are able to collect them from the ground, and stocks decline throughout the autumn and winter as there is no replenishment until the following year. In contrast to soil invertebrates, there is generally a single seasonal peak in seed production and this harvest then becomes steadily depleted through soil movements, weathering, germination and, to a larger extent, through the feeding activities of various animals. This situation causes seed-eaters to continue breeding later in the year than comparable insectivores, and the post-breeding numbers which are now at their peak experience worsening feeding conditions throughout the autumn, the worst season of all being winter or early spring. But many graminivorous birds must make use of animal food when feeding their young in order to supply sufficient protein during the early rapid stages of nestling growth. These birds may therefore be restricted in their breeding season by the availability of this animal component. There is little scope for an influx of winter seed-eaters and almost none for summer immigrants; exceptions are the crossbills, equipped with bills enabling them to extract the seed from conifers. Invasions of the common crossbill occur frequently in late June and July when the spruce seed crop on which they depend fails in Europe. Occasionally, as in 1962, we also get visitations from the larger parrot crossbill of Eurasia which is a pine specialist; but the two-barred crossbill, a larch feeder, is a very rare visitor to Britain.

The so-called irruption birds illustrate in an exaggerated way processes that occur on a smaller scale among our own seed-eating birds. The production of fruit by trees is far more liable to fluctuate than the number of soil invertebrates. Many trees, including the ash and beech, effectively bear fruit only once every two years so that good crops are followed by bad ones, with some years producing bumper yields and others complete failures. The basic reason for biennial cropping is that the tree cannot manage to accumulate enough physical reserves to bear fruit every year, but a second consideration is that individual trees become synchronised in their fruiting periodicity. This synchrony is usually imposed by climatic agencies so that if, for instance, very severe frosts inhibit all the trees in an area one year, they will all tend to produce good crops in phase in the next cycle; over a long period close synchronisation results. Species like the crossbill, the waxwing, nutcracker, pine grosbeak and great spotted woodpecker, which inhabit north European forests, have adapted to this variable food supply by evolving the irruptive types of migration. They have the capacity to migrate every year and may even begin to move, but they only continue to do so if the food supply fails. It often happens that a good breeding season produces too many birds in relation to food stocks, and this led past workers to consider that population pressure was the initiating factor in irruption. Svärdson (1957), however, has shown in a very full study of the subject that this is not so. In contrast to irruption behaviour, regular annual migration is an adaptation which takes birds away from an area where food supplies will certainly fail – swallows will not find flying insects in the English winter, although they can be found in South Africa.

British wood-pigeons, and probably many of our other seed-eating species, display irruptive type behaviour. Every autumn wood-pigeons lay down reserves of migratory fat and adopt flight patterns typical of true migrants; Ridpath and I said that they displayed a latent migratory urge. But this 'urge' to migrate is only realised if the cereal and beech mast crop fails; if it does, a small proportion of the British wood-pigeon population emigrates to France, otherwise the birds stay at home. Many finches stay in Britain if plentiful seed stocks occur in autumn, but move out of Britain for the winter months. Spencer has been examining the ringing recoveries of the linnet and finds that, like the wood-pigeon, it only moves to southern France and Spain in certain years, behaving a little like the more spectacular irruption birds. Similarly, Evans (1966) has shown that more redpolls leave Britain in years of poor birch seed than when a good crop occurs.

Compared with the masses of fieldfares, redwings, starlings, rooks and lapwings which reach our shores – a movement well-illustrated by numerous recoveries of foreign ringed birds in Britain (see Hudson 1965 for a useful summary) – very few continental greenfinches, linnets, bullfinches, goldfinches, yellowhammers or sparrows move in; indeed, as already stated, the main tendency is for our own birds to move out. Virtually no continental stock doves or wood-pigeons winter with us, and the only graminivorous birds which may be rated as regular immigrants in sizable numbers are the chaffinch and brambling, both of which come to us from Norway and Sweden, and the redpoll and siskin. Immigrant chaffinches from European deciduous woodland, and bramblings (the ecological replacement of the chaffinch in northern birch forests) have both secondarily accepted farmland proper as a wintering habitat. However, they will both take advantage of the glut of woodland beech mast in years when it occurs. Segregation between the chaffinch and brambling is also maintained by differing migration patterns. Whereas most chaffinches return to the same wintering grounds year after year, individual bramblings may winter in places several hundred miles apart in succeeding years depending on where beech mast is most available. Newton has shown that the immigrant chaffinches remain well segregated from the resident stock by frequenting the open fields and feeding on a restricted diet of seeds, particularly cereals, charlock *Sinapis arvensis*, fat hen *Chenpodium album* and persicaria *Polygonum persicaria*. Agricultural development may well have helped these winter visitors, whereas our resident stock, which relies on woodland, may have suffered. Nonetheless, higher breeding densities of chaffinches occur in woodland than in the hedgerows and isolated copses on open farmland (see Chapter 5). In winter, resident chaffinches living in woodland roost singly and subsist on a wider range of seed foods and cereals than do the immigrants, and they also consume a lot of invertebrate food in the form of weevils, beetles and their larvae, and earwigs. Thus, as in the case of the thrushes, immigrant chaffinches are excluded from the true habitat of the species by the resident population. The chaffinch has an advantage over the other finches of farmland in that its short legs and ability to walk (as distinct from hopping) enables it to search for small seeds on the ground more efficiently than the hoppers; but this prevents it from tree-feeding, except when a firm perch is available.

Many graminivorous species must for long have been influenced by man's activities, because the weeds and ruderals on which they feed have themselves adapted and changed in response to improved cultivation, better threshing and seed screening. Pollen analysis of deposits from Iron Age settlements at Glastonbury reveal not only cereal culture, but also attendant weeds like fat-hen, various Compositae, *Plantago*, *Rumex* and *Artemesia*. Not only were these weeds then, as now, associated with arable, but they may well have been positively cultivated; an Iron Age man found buried in a Danish bog at Tollund had in his stomach the seeds of barley, flax, *Polygonum convolvulus*, *Spergula arvensis* and *Chenopodium album*. Similarly Godwin records that a middle Bronze Age culture in Bedfordshire was apparently intentionally collecting the seeds of *Viola arvensis* for food. Today it is also the spoliation and loss of natural habitats which is causing the re-shuffle, enabling the species best adapted to modern farmland to emerge. Two possible examples may be considered.

Greenfinches are birds of open parkland with scattered trees and shrubs. They must initially have prospered as a consequence of agricultural development and the fragmentation of woodland, especially as they feed much more on arable farmland than the other finches, taking cereal seed from stubbles, as well as the larger weed seeds such as *Polygonum convolvulus* (see Table 15). It seems reasonable to suppose that in the case of such a ubiquitous species as the greenfinch, the number of ringed birds would reflect the observer's ability to find them, which would in turn reflect changes in population size. Comparison of the number of greenfinches ringed as nestlings with changing status of *P. convolvulus* suggests that the two have varied in parallel (Fig. 24). Such a correlation seems reasonable and to be anticipated on biological grounds, but one must remain open-minded as correlations can be notoriously misleading and depend on some other and quite unsuspected variable. Although farmland with large straggling hedgerows is ideally suited to the greenfinch, a decline seems to have occurred in recent years. To some extent the greenfinch appears to have been replaced by the linnet as the commonest farmland finch in summer. Again, evidence for this change is found in the relative numbers of the two species which have been marked in different years by contributors to the B.T.O. ringing scheme. 'Progress' in the form of hedge stripping may account for this change, as the linnet is better adapted to open country with only scattered bushes. The linnet's main diet on the farm, with comparative figures for other seed-eating species, is summarised in Table 15, and its dependence on the weed species of arable farmland is apparent.

In Finland the linnet is on the edge of its range. They were widely associated with southern farmland, building their nests in small conifers, at the end of the century, but decreased markedly in the thirties and forties to become a rarity. Tast (1968) points out that the decline was not caused by climate changes and instead blames farm modernisation for removing suitable seed food supplies. Supporting this view is the fact that in one area, where farming methods did not change, linnet numbers did not decrease. Since the forties the linnet has been prepared to change its nesting and other habitat preferences, and in the absence of conifers will even use wood piles as a nesting site. This change now enables the linnet to occupy urban areas, finding weed seeds on old industrial sites, suburban gardens and such like, and it has now expanded in this new habitat to occupy a range similar to its previous distribution.

The goldfinch, which specialises on seeds taken from the inflorescence of thistles and other large compositae, favours rough farmland, especially where suitable food plants are left to flourish on headlands and hedge and ditch verges. It also favours large isolated trees for nesting and often builds at considerable heights (80 ft.). A charm of goldfinches is once more a familiar sight, as the species has markedly increased during the last twenty years, a trend which has been in progress since the start of the century. For thirty years or so before this time the bird had become very rare, the reason often being attributed to persecution by bird catchers, while the recent increase is claimed to be the result of protection. Neither factor seems adequate to account fully for the fall and rise in numbers, and it is evident that the period of rarity coincided with peak efficiency of weed control by mechanical means at the end of the nineteenth century. Farm labour was then cheap and headlands were kept neat with the scythe, whereas today the fields alone are sprayed with herbicides.

A species which is ideally equipped to utilise a particular seed may be prevented from really establishing itself on farmland because it lacks a nesting site and is too inflexible to adapt to a new one. Under such circumstances a less efficient feeder could become established. Chaffinches ought to be prospering from cereal production, but they seem doomed by the absence of tall hedgerow trees. Low hedgerows possibly fail to provide suitable insect food to make breeding feasible, but the psychological need for a high singing post seems important. To complicate the picture, many species have modified their diets over the years to take advantage of the changing status of various weeds, and dietary preferences can also vary in different regions. Newton has compared his data for the diet of linnets near Oxford with those obtained by Eber (1956) in Holstein, Germany. At Holstein, the records show that 18% of the linnets fed on cereals and none on *Chenopodium*, whereas at Oxford no birds had taken cereals but 11% had eaten fat-hen. Similarly goldfinches at Holstein had eaten *Artemesia* seed but not at Oxford, and *Senecio vulgaris*, an important food at Oxford, was not taken in Holstein. Several finches fed extensively on corn-spurrey *Spergula arvensis* at the turn of the century, but do not do so now as it has become much rarer.

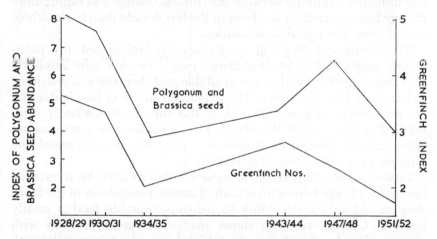

FIG. 24. Number of greenfinches ringed as nestlings as a percentage of all nestlings ringed under the B.T.O. scheme, assumed to be an index of population size (lower curve). The incidence of weed seeds favoured by greenfinches in previous autumns in samples of cereals examined by the official Seed Testing Station, an index of abundance of these weed seeds (upper curve). (Data on weed seed abundance from analysis by Broad, 1952).

Newton has also shown that the ecological isolation of finches in woodland is much greater than of those living on farmland, where considerable overlap in the food choice occurs as Table 15 shows. Furthermore, when the pigeons and partridges are also considered it is clear that a lot of farmland grain-eaters are all seeking the same foods. Newton points out that of the thirty commonest food-plants of farmland, thirty are eaten frequently by the greenfinch, at least twenty-five by the linnet, eighteen by the goldfinch and twenty-four by the chaffinch and bullfinch. He has also shown that on farmland all the foods eaten by the bullfinch are commonly taken by one or more other finch species, whereas only 10% of the bullfinches' food-plants in woodland are shared with other finches. Similar conclusions apply to the chaffinch. Here, then, we should expect dramatic changes in avian fortunes as man streamlines his monocultures and, with the help of selective weed-killers, wipes out the surviving common weeds, the chickweeds, *Rumex*, *Polygonum* and *Sinapis*, as he has already done with the corn-spurrey and poppy. Nor can we anticipate any immediate stability because agricultural change is so rapid; more change has occurred on the farm in the last decade than in the whole period since the agrarian revolution.

The progress of chemical weed control is highlighted in a particularly useful review by Woodford (1964). In 1911 only sulphuric acid and copper sulphate were available and their use was restricted to less than $\frac{1}{4}$ million acres. The expansion in use of herbicides and the availability of new agents since this time is conveniently summarised in Fig. 25 from Woodford. The significance for our farmland fauna can be imagined. Robinson (1964) has also reviewed the progress of weed control in horticulture.

Inter-specific competition in these conditions must be intensified because birds are born with a limited innate recognition of the foods they should eat; their ability to recognise suitable food is mostly learned. Current research shows that each species is born with characteristic hunting behaviour which has evolved in parallel with its physical adaptations. A species such as the stock dove will instinctively frequent open bare ground for feeding. What it picks up and learns to eat depends on such physical attributes as its bill size and its ability to walk over the ground and so on, and the choice of foods present. Stock doves quickly learn to eat *Polygonum* seeds because these are of the right size and occur commonly within its feeding habitat; given the choice the birds will avoid smaller seeds. In Russia buckwheat, which is commonly grown as a farm crop, provides an appropriate feeding stimulus and *Vicia hirsuta* is taken instead of *V. sativa* as in Britain. In both Britain and Russia, fumitory is the main food of the turtle dove, but whereas *Stellaria media* is also an important food in Britain it did not feature in Russian specimens which instead had eaten the cornflower *Centaurea cyanus* – a food

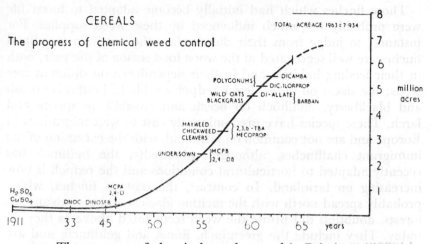

FIG. 25. The progress of chemical weed control in Britain as judged by the acreage of cereals treated with herbicides and the chronological sequence of introduction of new chemicals (from Woodford, 1964).

unrepresented in the British specimens examined. Various pigeons and game-birds have been experimentally trained to accept and even show a preference for foods of unusual colour, size and shape. It is evident that local populations of a species with unusual food preferences may quickly emerge, simply because they are exposed to these foods during life.

Proper understanding of the present state of flux among many of our seed-eating birds demands some knowledge of the origins of our weed flora. Basically this consists of two quite distinct elements which Bunting has defined, and which can be regarded as a long-established northern flora and a much more recently arrived southern component. The first comprises a large group of weeds which was established in full or late glacial times, possibly up to 57,000 years ago, and which is well represented in glacial pollen deposits; these weeds were naturally well established long before Neolithic agriculturalists reached these islands. In addition to most British perennials, nearly half of our thirty or so late-flowering or over-wintering annuals and biennials were present in at least late glacial times and these include *Atriplex patula*, *Stellaria media*, *Chenopodium album*, *Polygonum aviculare*, *Barbarea vulgaris*, *Cerastium vulgatum*, *Rumex* spp., various *Rununculus* spp. and *Viola tricolor*.

Those finches which had initially become adapted to forest life were probably not much influenced by these weed supplies. For instance, to judge from their diets today, the northern woodland finches are well segregated at the worst food season of the year, both in their feeding habitats and in their dependence on different tree seeds; the siskin on alder, lesser redpoll on birch, bullfinch on ash and blackberry, chaffinch on beech and crossbill on spruce and larch. These species have predominantly east to west migrations in Europe and are not common on farmland, with the exception of the immigrant chaffinches, although, admittedly, the bullfinch has recently adapted to horticultural conditions and the redpoll is now increasing on farmland. In contrast, the ecotone finches, which probably spread north with the melting glaciers and the advance of forests, doubtless did utilise the weed seeds listed above as they do today. They include the greenfinch, linnet and goldfinch, and are birds with north-south movements in Europe. They are common inhabitants of farmland, where they eat many of these seeds. All were established in Britain long ago, most being represented as late glacial fossils (see Fisher 1966), so we should expect that many were feeding on our familiar farmland weeds a good five thousand years before Neolithic man, in about 3000 BC, began the forest clearance which helped to spread these weeds. Hence, these ecotone finches are well differentiated species which must re-adjust their ecology to suit the results of man's impact on the environment; some, like the chaffinch and greenfinch, may have become too specialised in their habitat requirements to make this adjustment. But surprises may be in store. For example, greenfinches have learned to crack and eat the seed of *Daphne mezereum* while still soft in June. The habit seems to have originated between one and two centuries ago and to have been slowly spreading since, at a rate of 2–4 kilometres per year. It has now reached Ireland and Denmark, but apparently no other continental countries (Pettersson 1959, 1961). The change in behaviour in this case is interesting because it seemingly has evolved once and has spread from a single centre. In contrast, such new habits as birds opening milk bottles seem to have been discovered independently in many isolated centres (page 294).

Following this it is of interest, as Pettersson points out, to realise that neolithic agriculture reached Britain from its centre of origin at between $\frac{1}{2}$–1 km. per year, bronze-working at 2 km. per year, and iron-working at something like 5 km. a year. This contrasts with the speed of communication since the advent of radio, television and space exploration.

The buntings appear to be phylogenetically younger than the finches, as indicated by the complex of closely related forms many of which are polytypic and replace each other geographically. Examples are the yellowhammer and pine bunting and red-headed and black-headed buntings – these two species pairs interbreed when their ranges meet. Many buntings must have emerged in the inter- and post-glacial conditions created by the melting of the ice, when large, but local, expanses of moraine outwash, sand and gravel, richly supplied with mineral salts and with a good tilth from frost action, would have provided ideal conditions for weed growth. At present the ortolan bunting occurs in the boreal region alongside the yellowhammer and corn bunting and appears to have expanded its range northwards as a direct result of agriculture. It is more of an insect feeder than the yellowhammer and migrates to the savannas of Africa in winter (being caught and eaten by man as a delicacy as it passes through Europe), presumably avoiding inter-specific competition with the yellowhammer during the worst time of year. According to Durango, it will not tolerate areas where the rainfall exceeds 23 inches per annum. During the summer it is likely to compete for the same foods as the yellowhammer, especially in cultivated areas where original slight habitat differences are not maintained. It seems to favour more grassy areas than the yellow-hammer – presumably because it is here that insect food is most common. In Turkey and Greece a local race of the ortolan is established, known as Cretzschmar's bunting, which probably evolved as an isolated offshoot of the ortolan. In the Aegean islands, where both species occur, competition is evident and the ortolan is confined to the larger islands, while Cretzschmar's occurs only on small islands where its niche is unsaturated.

On English farmland today a readjustment is occurring in the relative status of the yellowhammer and reed bunting, which until now seemed to be well segregated. The reed bunting has an extensive Palaearctic range as an inhabitant of reed and sedge beds and other wet-land vegetation. During the 1940s the odd pair could be found in completely dry areas, and I well remember in 1950 being sur-prised when I flushed a female from a nest in heather about a mile from the nearest water in East Anglian breckland. In our Cambridge-shire study area (Fig. 15) the first pair inhabiting local arable land was recorded in 1957, since when it has increased and spread, in many cases nesting alongside corn buntings and yellowhammers. In 1963, Kent (1964) organised a survey in Nottinghamshire to examine the habitat preferences of these two species, and found that a substantial proportion of reed buntings was breeding in typical yellowhammer habitats. There seems little doubt that the reed bunting has changed its requirements and no longer instinctively requires a wet-land habitat which Lack (1933) considered to be the case in the early thirties; at the time this was the only point of difference from the yellowhammer which he could discern. We are left to speculate whether the encroachment of farmland into marshland led to a situation where reed buntings found themselves nesting in traditional areas now virtually devoid of water, or whether a sudden genetical mutation has altered the psychological habitat requirements of this species (cf. the curlew example on page 52). On one common bird census area reed buntings have been increasing coincident with a decrease of the yellowhammer. To summarise, the buntings were actively speciating in isolated areas during the post-glacial era, but have not evolved sufficient differences to keep them segregated as species, if they are forced to live in the same area. Advancing agriculture has broken through the boundaries between the various centres of evolution enabling spread and intermixing, a process which is also assisted by climatic changes.

The second group of weeds to be considered is a drought adapted southern element, which flowers early and is well able to withstand the dry conditions of south and east England. These weeds have their earliest records in Britain in Neolithic, Romano–British and later times, and they have arrived like many of our main crops from Mediterranean or Near Eastern sources. They include such species as *Sinapis arvensis*, *Galium aparine*, *Sonchus* spp., *Cirsium arvense* and the various kinds of fumitory *Fumaria* spp.; these last are still confined to artificial habitats in Britain. There are one or two seed-eating birds which subsist to a larger extent on these weeds and so may have first entered Britain with the arrival of this southern flora. The turtle dove is the best example, and, apart from cultivated cereals, feeds primarily on fumitory, with grass and weed seeds being of secondary importance. It is not represented as an Ice Age fossil and was first recorded in British literature in about 975 AD (Fisher 1966), though it was a bird well known to the biblical scholars. Until the early 1800s it was virtually confined to south of a line running from the

Wash to the River Severn. It spread into parts of Wales and northern England in the early nineteenth century, and has reached some of the south-eastern Scottish counties, in small numbers, since 1946. Its distribution in England corresponds with areas of light soils where its food plant occurs and where increased cereal farming has facilitated its spread. The linnet was included in the group of finches present in the late Ice Age times but stands out from the other common farmland species in taking much more *Brassica* and *Artemisia* seed, and may conceivably have prospered from the establishment of these plants in Britain. The serin is a small ground feeding finch occupying in southern Europe the type of country favoured by the goldfinch in England. It is of interest because it has been spreading north across Europe just as the turtle dove and other species must have done a thousand years ago. In 1550 it was confined to the Rhône Valley and Gascony, had reached the Loire in 1875, Paris in 1903, Deauville in 1921, Sweden in 1942 and is now nesting sporadically in southern England. Like the collared dove it has expanded suddenly after a long period of stability, and its success is certainly not explained by better weather conditions.

The British pigeons provide a good example of interaction between species complicated by changes in land usage. Like the turtle dove, the stock dove increased and spread in northern England and Scotland at the turn of the century, before which it was confined to south and east England. Nesting was first proved in Scotland in 1866 but by 1889 the bird had reached Sutherland. In Ireland, the stock dove first bred about 1875 but did not advance west of the River Shannon until 1896, and only after 1957 reached areas as far west as Kerry, Mayo and Donegal. The expansion of the stock dove in Britain can be attributed to the advance of arable farming, the development of farming having been much more restricted in Ireland. Side by side with the increase of the stock dove there was also a marked reduction in the numbers of the dovecote pigeon (see page 269) – these two events probably resulted from changing attitudes in agriculture rather than a more direct cause and effect. In contrast, the wild rock dove, which has the same food requirements as the stock dove, and also decreased over the same period as the stock dove increased, seems to have suffered from direct competition. The stock dove can live in a wider range of habitats and is not confined to cliffs for nesting. It has, therefore, a more fecund population, which in areas of overlap could swamp and replace the rock dove. Rock doves have declined much more slowly in Ireland in parallel with the slower advance of the stock dove.

Since 1957 the stock dove has declined drastically in eastern England but not, as far as can be judged, in western England. In 1963, only two out of 32 previously occupied sites near Chelmsford, Essex, were occupied and at both these, the eggs were infertile. At the same time it vanished from the central London parks where it had increased and spread between 1950 and 1957. The advent of toxic chemicals has been blamed and may indeed account for the initial decline. Stock doves are very prone to feeding on cereal sowings and more than wood-pigeons will visit the autumn plantings. But the wood-pigeon quickly recovered from the adverse effects of these chemicals in 1961 and there must be some other explanation to account for the slowness of the stock dove to do the same. Decreases in the availability of weed seed may provide the answer. Many stock doves pass through our Cambridgeshire study area on spring passage, but few are present in winter. Those that do over-winter feed on old stubbles and fallows, which are the only places providing weed seeds on the ground in adequate quantities. Improvements in farm mechanisation, leading to more autumn ploughing and the planting of winter corn, result in fewer and fewer fallows and old stubbles. There is evidence of some recovery of numbers in the late 1960s, this presumably representing a recovery from the effects of toxic chemicals.

Some kind of interaction may be taking place in the case of the grey and red-legged partridge. The red-legged (French) partridge replaces the grey (English) partridge in south-west Europe, while the Frenchman is replaced by an allopatric form, the chukor (rock partridge), west of a line starting in the French Riviera. Red-legs were successfully introduced into Suffolk in 1770 and since then have colonised south-east England, East Anglia, and some adjoining counties, doing particularly well on the dry heathlands of the area. Nevertheless, for many years red-legs and grey birds have occurred side by side in the same farmland habitats and both species reach their highest densities in the same eastern counties. However, even in those areas favoured by both species, the grey is always commoner and it tolerates conditions outside the red-leg's range, also occurring in much of Scotland and Wales. Bump (1958) considers that the red-legged partridge will not tolerate areas where mean January temperatures fall below 30° F (— 1° C) or where the annual precipitation is much below 10 or above 35 inches per year. In examining these climatic factors, Howells (1963) believes that temperature cannot be an inhibiting factor in Britain but that rainfall might be, as the distribution of the species conforms very closely to areas receiving an annual rainfall of less than 35 inches per annum.

According to Middleton and Chitty's early studies, both species have the same diet (see Table 15) and they also seem to have the same preferences for nesting sites, on agricultural land (see page 38). These food habits have recently been confirmed by Dr G. R. Potts in detail, who has shown that the main weed seeds eaten are of *Polygonum* species, particularly black bindweed *P. convolvulus*, and that these now form 44% of the total dry weight of dicotyledonous seeds eaten. In the 1930s *Polygonum* seeds constituted 88% of the weed component of the diet, at a time when a greater variety and abundance of seeds was available, and the lower percentage eaten today reflects a decreased availability consequent on agricultural improvements. Even so, *Polygonum* species have been the least affected of the wild weed seeds by the various herbicide sprays available, though this will not continue to be the case. Potts also reckoned that there are no major differences in the diet of the two partridges, although he considered that the larger red-leg preferred larger items. This is demonstrated by field studies in Cambridgeshire. At Carlton, of 377 partridges specifically identified during 1962 and 1963, 35% were red-legs. In experiments in which cereal baits treated with alpha-chloralose were laid in the area, 29% of 79 partridges caught were red-legs, which suggests that this species was being taken near enough in proportion to its true status. In contrast, when maple pea or tic bean baits were employed, 80% of 71 partridges caught were red-legs, which indicates that this species was selectively taken with large baits. Laboratory experiments also confirm the red-leg's propensity to select bigger items than the grey partridge.

Middleton and Huband (1966), using very comprehensive data collected by the Eley Game Advisory Service and the Game Research Association, have detailed the changes taking place in partridge populations on a representative sample of English estates outside East Anglia. They show that since 1961, grey partridges have decreased, whereas red-leg numbers stayed roughly stable until at least 1965. In East Anglia the decline in numbers of grey birds has been more marked because the 1961 population was proportionately

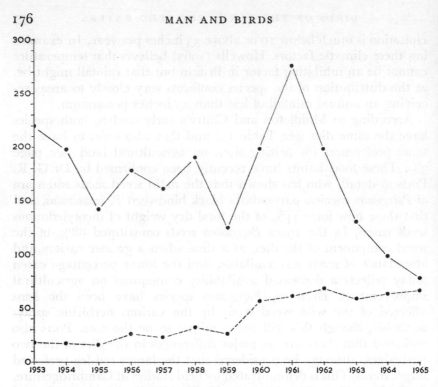

FIG. 26. Changes in number of pairs of grey partridges—and red-legged partridges - - - per 1,000 acres on three estates in Norfolk. (Data in Table 1, from Middleton & Huband 1966).

higher than elsewhere in the country. In addition, there has been a marked increase in red-leg numbers in this region, so that the relative proportions of the two species have shown a drastic change in favour of the red-leg. Fig. 26, derived from Middleton and Huband, sets out some figures for a Norfolk estate which has been particularly well studied since 1953. The authors have emphasised that while the two species differ in many respects, their exploitation and management for shooting is not unusually selective, so that the changes observed must be attributed to other, presumably natural, causes.

In Fig. 27a the percentage change in the size of the breeding population of the grey partridge in successive years is plotted against the corresponding percentage change occurring in the red-leg on the same estate. There is a small, but statistically significant, correlation which shows that those seasons which favoured an increase

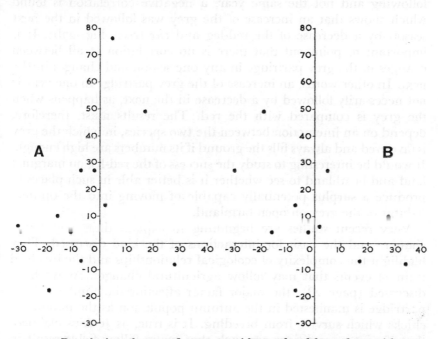

FIG. 27. Population change of grey partridge and red-legged partridge on three Norfolk estates as judged by the percentage difference in numbers between successive breeding seasons.

A. Percentage change of grey (horizontal scale) plotted against percentage change of red (ordinate) for the same season showing positive correlation $r_{11} = 0.580$.

B. Percentage change of grey (horizontal scale) plotted against percentage change of red in the following year (i e % change between breeding seasons of 1959 and 1960 in grey against % change for red between 1960 and 1961) showing inverse correlation with $r_{10} = -0.607$. (Original data in Table 1, from Middleton & Huband 1966).

in the grey partridge also favoured an increase in the red-leg. The spring population of the red-leg in this area appears to be determined by the number of birds moving in during the winter to take up territories (see page 30) and it is conceivable that such immigration would be easier in years when grey partridge numbers were low. It is therefore of interest that if the percentage change in the grey partridge is plotted against the change in the red-leg for the following and not the same year, a negative correlation is found which shows that an increase of the grey was followed in the next season by a decrease of the red-leg and *vice versa* (Fig. 27b). It is important to point out that there is no correlation at all between changes in the grey partridge in any one season and changes in the next. In other words, an increase of the grey partridge in one year is not necessarily followed by a decrease in the next, as happens when the grey is compared with the red. The results must, therefore, depend on an interaction between the two species, in which the grey is favoured and always fills the ground if its numbers are high enough. It would be interesting to study the success of the red-leg on marginal land and heathland to see whether it is better able in such places to produce a surplus potentially capable of moving into the optimal habitat of the grey on open farmland.

Very recent studies are beginning to explain these population changes and the basis for interactions of the kind discussed. They highlight the complexity of ecological relationships and the involved train of events that may follow agricultural changes. As we have discussed (page 28), the major factor affecting the numbers of the partridge is manifested in the autumn population as the number of chicks which survive from breeding. It is true, as Jenkins claimed, that if winter conditions are such that many fallow fields result in poor cover then there is much territorial interaction between adults, and this leads to a high mortality of chicks produced in the following summer. The reason seems to be that such winter conditions result in birds getting poor territories containing low food stocks and, in consequence, the females are unable to produce adequate yolk nutrients in their eggs. Thus eggs collected and incubated artificially were shown to be less fertile than normal if obtained from beats where large blocks of ploughed land provided little food or cover; in addition, the survival of any chicks that did hatch was below average (Southwood 1967). But these effects are not large enough to be important in the wild. Instead, Southwood and Cross show that the major reasons why chicks die is a combination of poor weather and food. These two factors interact in a complex manner, and together account for 92% of the annual variations in breeding success of the partridge, although the food supply is six times more influential than the weather (this last was reflected in the hours of sunshine recorded for June, the month when chicks hatch). It seems that bad weather is important only because it influences the abundance and activity of the insects needed by the chicks.

Southwood and Cross demonstrated that the relative abundance of the different insects eaten by the chicks, particularly sawfly larvae, Collembola and aphids, varied in different crops, being highest on downland, intermediate on grassland, and lowest among cereals. Moreover, barley fields treated with herbicides had a biomass of arthropods which was two-thirds lower than on untreated areas; in such places the chicks would need to search three to four times the area to obtain sufficient nutrient. It becomes clear that under these conditions the chicks would be much more prone to inclement weather. Accordingly, as Potts is continuing to demonstrate, the decline of the partridge can be attributed to a decline of its insect foods of which sawfly larvae (*Dolerus haematodes* and other species) are most important, followed by leaf-eating beetles. This decline has partly resulted from a decline in the amount of cereal crops which are undersown with clover, and also in the acreage of pure leys, because it is in these crops that the sawfly pupae over-winter. This has made the partridge more dependent on the other insects it can obtain in cereal crops, particularly such aphids as *Sitobion fragariae*. Actually, these aphids have increased since the 1950s, but they become available rather late in the season to be really useful foods for grey partridge chicks. Many other cereal insects have been affected by the herbicide treatments which gradually became important in the mid-1950s (see Fig. 25). So, with the need for partridge chicks to be more dependent on the herbicide affected and poorer food supply of cereal fields, their survival became nearly six times more sensitive to spring temperature in the mid-1950s. It is coincidental that summers have been on average cooler and damper since 1950 than in the previous twenty years, because fundamentally it is changes in the food supply that have made partridges more susceptible to cold wet summers.

The above account explains the population changes of the grey partridge apparent in the national records (and Fig. 26) because agricultural change has been mainly of the kind described. But there are areas where little agricultural change has occurred and where grey partridge numbers have correspondingly shown little or no signs of decline while other factors may be involved in causing decreases outside the main agricultural habitats. For example, on downland and marginal grassland ants are more important in the chick's diet.

In particular, the yellow mound building ant *Lasius flavus* has declined because grazing by other animals is no longer keeping grass short and the ground relatively open; this has been partly the consequence of a reduction in sheep farming, but it also depends on there being fewer rabbits since the advent of myxomatosis.

Red-legged partridge chicks hatch later than those of the grey partridge, and many birds have a second brood later in the summer. This enables red-leg chicks to feed more effectively on the cereal aphids, and *Sitobion fragariae* as well as grass seeds are utilised by the young birds. As mentioned, the availability of cereal aphids has actually increased in recent years, and this provides a very plausible explanation for the success of the red-leg. It becomes conceivable that in years when grey partridges survive particularly well they eat many of the aphids that would otherwise be available to red-legs, with the converse situation occurring. This could explain the relationship already discussed, but obviously much more work will be needed before final conclusions are made.

Mention must also be made of the pheasant. An introduced alien, its density may sometimes exceed that of any other species on lowland farms as a result of artificial propagation. The national average shooting bag of pheasants in the 1966/7 season (1 October–1 February) amounted to 34 birds per 100 acres (7th Annual Report, Game Research Association), of which just over a third were hand-reared birds, the remainder being wild. Normally only about one-third of pheasants which are released are shot, which emphasises that an even higher density exists at some seasons.

The procedure involved in rearing pheasants is roughly as follows: gamekeepers trap some of their pheasants in winter and pen between five and eight hens with a cock in the 'home coverts'. The eggs laid in spring (up to 30 per female) are collected and incubated by broody domestic fowls, and the chicks are either reared by the hens or in artificial brooders. The young are allowed to wander into the home woods during late July and August, and, although food is provided, the birds are encouraged to become more and more independent, so that they are reasonably dispersed and 'wild' by the start of the shooting season. While ranging in the coverts adjacent to the rearing pens, these young birds obviously constitute a highly attractive food supply for various predators, and it is understandable that keepers do their utmost to rid their beats of so-called vermin. This sometimes provokes ill feeling between conservationists, and for that matter other country men – for instance, between a Master of Foxhounds, who wants a few fox cubs left unmolested, and the keeper who sees a vixen removing his young pheasants. One of the concerns of enlightened game farming is to ensure a balanced attitude towards the conservation of predatory birds and mammals on the one hand, and productive game management on the other, but this is not always easy to achieve. Unfortunately, there are still many gamekeepers who set pole-traps and other illegal devices which kill indiscriminately.

When the pheasants are released in late summer the population is very high, but at this time of year there is plenty of food on the autumn stubbles and the birds usually do no harm to agriculture. Certainly, it is sensible to regard them as a farm crop in terms of the revenue to be obtained from shooting leases and the sale of carcases. From this viewpoint, concern is felt that a relatively low proportion of released birds is usually shot (usually a little over a third), because a high mortality occurs in early autumn before the shooting season begins. Current research is aimed at reducing this wastage, which tends to nullify much of the effort devoted to artificial propagation (Bray 1967).

Pheasants still alive in spring may constitute more of a problem to farmers at a season when they are not fed. Views are rather sharply divided on this point between shooting men and farmers not interested in game. The former tend to ignore birds eating the newly sown corn and peas, even though they may take as much as rooks or wood-pigeons. It is not fair to blame some species and excuse others. Growers are often more vocal and, although remedial action is possible (see page 208), the game laws have for long caused discontent. Marshall, writing in 1787, is quoted below (page 184) and he added that many shared his view that the game laws are a disgrace, 'neverthelefs they ftill remain an abfurdity in English jurifprudence'. The foot and mouth epidemic of 1968 prevented the holding of winter pheasant shoots and led to the suggestion that because too many birds would be alive in spring and might well damage crops, the shooting season should be specially extended. This raises an interesting point because, as in the case of the grouse (page 35) and partridge (page 32) which I have already discussed, it is clear that the number of pheasants alive in the spring, contrary to what is sometimes thought, is not determined by the amount of winter shooting. Bray has shown that artificially reared pheasants released on five estates invariably suffered a 70%–80% loss before the following February, with shooting accounting for less than half of the deaths. Moreover, similar high death-rates were also found in the case of wild juvenile pheasants on *unshot* areas. The adult death-rate of pheasants, about 70% per annum, is also high whether or not the population is shot. The productivity rate of pheasants is correspondingly high which means that this is a species with a very rapid turnover able to provide man with even greater enjoyment without interfering with his agriculture in the process. As in the case of certain other game species there may be some justification for re-examining the shooting seasons, which to a large extent have been fixed arbitrarily, but discussion of this interesting question is outside the scope of this book.

The wood-pigeon and house and tree sparrows are the grain-eaters which have the greatest economic impact in this country, but as the first two have been the subjects of special monographs, repetition is out of place here and only a few points need to be made. The wood-pigeon is considered again in the next chapter. I sympathise with the views of Summers-Smith that the house sparrow had probably evolved as a commensal of man and is consequently well-placed ecologically to make itself a nuisance. Summers-Smith envisages that an ancestral African sparrow spread to the Mediterranean region and to the east in the late Miocene or Pliocene and evolved by the Pleistocene to form *Passer pyrrhonotus* and *P. montanus* in Asia and the east, and *P. domesticus* and *P. hispaniolensis* in the west, while the Italian sparrow *P. italiae* arose between these last two as a stabilised hybrid. Speciation was possibly helped by the isolating effects of the last glaciation after which *P. domesticus* spread into Europe in close association with agricultural man. This expansion is still in progress with the steady improvements in communications and spread of cultivation. In addition, the house sparrow has been purposely introduced into other continents including North America, Australia and New Zealand, and chance transportation in the wake of man has enabled it to reach outlying islands like the Faroes. The tree sparrow occurs as a commensal of man in the east Palaearctic and Asia, living in his villages and on farms just as the house sparrow does in the west. Summers-Smith believes that it could have emerged with the separate evolution of agricultural man in south-east Asia, subsequently expanding north and west, parallel to the evolution of *domesticus* in the west. Throughout most of its range in Europe it is a bird of the countryside proper and not of buildings or villages. It does occupy these sites when the house sparrow for some reason is absent, as in parts of the Swiss Alps and southern Germany. When house sparrows and tree sparrows do occur together the slightly larger house sparrow is almost always dominant in man-made habitats. For instance, both species were introduced at the same time to eastern Australia, but whereas the house sparrow has become widespread in inhabited areas, the tree sparrow has been confined to a rural habitat and is nowhere common. A similar story applies in the United States and elsewhere.

Tree sparrows are fairly well distributed on farmland away from the buildings where house sparrows hold domain, but the two come together after the breeding season to form large flocks wandering around the grain fields. Locally the tree sparrow may be very common, as at Carlton (see Table 6), but in many other areas it is certainly overlooked. At Carlton many nest in the bottom of rooks' nests – as well as building untidy nests in thick hedgerows – and they spend much of their time high up among the rooks' nests foraging for old scraps of food dropped by their hosts. The high tree sparrow population in such places is easily overlooked by ground observers. Similarly, casual observers take little notice of the post-breeding flocks, and it came as a surprise to us while we were mist-netting sparrows that were damaging a cereal crop to find almost a 50:50 ratio of tree to house sparrows. There must be a considerable overlap in the diet of the two sparrows otherwise less competition would be expected when the two occur together in the same habitat. Although this is so, decided differences in food choice are found when the birds are segregated into their preferred habitats in Europe; this being well shown by a study in Denmark by Marie Hammer (1948). Considering the year as a whole, the house sparrow takes about two-thirds more cereal grain, presumably because it frequents places like barns and storage bins, where there is a fairly constant supply. To compensate, the tree sparrow feeds on twice as many insects and takes a very much higher proportion of weed seeds, especially in winter. Both species take most of their insect diet during the breeding season, and insects hardly feature in the winter diet of house sparrows, but are fairly prominent at this time in the tree sparrow. When one considers food choice within these groups there seems to be no obvious difference in cereal preference. In general both species take the same weed seeds, their order of importance for the tree sparrow being *Chenopodium album* (which exceeded in amount all the other seeds together), *Polygonum aviculare*, grass seed, *Stellaria media*, other *Polygonaceae*, *Spergula arvensis* and *Rumex acetosella*. The house sparrow had near enough the same preference but *Chenopodium* was not as predominant, with grass seed nearly as important in second place. As with many other grain-eating species, seeds of *Polygonaceae* assumed greater importance in the winter months. Turning to insect food, little difference was found between the species, except that the house sparrow took more dung beetles, probably because it lives in closer association with domestic animals, stable yards and cowsheds. The important insect foods were Coleoptera (mostly weevils), aphids, and larvae of Lepidoptera and Diptera in that order. From this account, it appears that the tree sparrow would be the most successful species away from man's immediate influence, as it is better able to live on weeds and insects. This is, indeed, the pattern of distribution found.

House sparrows are giving rise to an increasing volume of complaint from farmers and people concerned with food storage. There is little evidence to show that the problem is increasing, as is often suggested, but rather it seems that man's ability to deal with many of his other farming problems enables him to focus attention on this one. Early references make it clear that the sparrow has always been considered a pest on the farm. William Marshall (1787) in *The rural economy of Norfolk* says, 'I confefs, that having preconceived fome idea of the mifchiefs that muft neceffarily arife from an inordinate quantity of game, the clouds of fparrows which are fuffered to prey upon the produce of this country, were to me the greater caufe of furprife.' Bloomfield (1799) in 'Farmer's Boy' describes a familiar picture:

> Whilst thousands in a flock for ever gay
> Loud chirping sparrows welcome on the day,
> And from the mazes of the leafy thorn
> Drop one by one upon the bending corn

At the beginning of the nineteenth century, the destruction of sparrows was charged to parish and church rates, but when the compulsory payment of church rates was abolished sparrow clubs were formed in the principal corn-growing parishes, and bounties were paid for birds and their eggs. In one Suffolk village between 1819 and 1835, 2,587 dozen sparrows and 34 dozen eggs were rewarded with a bounty of 1½d. per dozen eggs and 2d. per dozen birds. Writing in the early 1860s Stevenson quotes the following from the *Sussex Express*. 'The thirteenth anniversary of the Sparrow Club, Rudgwick, was celebrated with a dinner at the Cricketers' Inn, on Tuesday last. On reference to the books, it was ascertained that 5,313 birds' heads had been sent in by members during the year, 1,363 being contributed by Mr. W. Wooberry, to whom was awarded the first prize. Mr. W. Botting, with 912, claimed second honours.' These clubs fulfilled some of the functions of the present day Dart Clubs and were preferable to cock fights, but it is difficult to conceive of a duller excuse for conviviality.

As early as 1600 in Holland, Delftware pots with a narrow entrance hole were fixed to the walls of houses to encourage sparrows to nest in them. Meise (1953) points out that Delft was a centre for brewing where sparrows were a nuisance and the pots formed useful nesting places where the birds could easily be caught and killed. These pots were probably introduced into England by Dutch engineers employed on draining the fens in the 1630s as Buxton (1953) quotes a reference to them made by the Poet Thomas Randolf writing in 1640:

> Another story make wast chinne
> With breasts like Pots to nest young Sparrowes in

Such pots were still in common use in Kent and Sussex during the late nineteenth century and Ingram (1953) records their widespread use in France. It was the practice to remove the nestlings when well grown to eat, and this source of food has always been a large, if not the main, incentive to erecting these early nestboxes. According to Meiklejohn, starlings were attracted to nest in similar pots; he refers to Brueghel's picture *Dulle Griet* (c. 1560) which depicts these pots in the background with birds resembling starlings nearby.

Today, attention is being focused on the large post-breeding flocks containing a high proportion of juveniles, which resort, like tropical weaver birds, to crops of standing corn. Sparrows are able to pick the grains from the ears of the standing crop which causes the farmer a direct loss just before harvest. The importance of this problem has not been properly investigated, although small-scale surveys suggest that few fields (under 5%) are affected, and then only a very low proportion of the crop suffers; damage, as Summers-Smith showed, tends to be highest when the fields are very near a village or farm.

The edge of a field, especially if this adjoins a convenient hedgerow, is most open to attack and, as this is the part most easily seen by the farmer, it is all too easy to exaggerate the amount of damage. Hammer in Denmark undertook some feeding experiments with house sparrows and helped by a knowledge of the normal stomach contents, considered that in one year a single bird would consume 4.7 kg of oats or 3.90 kg of barley, and in addition, about 23,000 insects during the period from April–August alone. What this means in terms of actual crop damage depends very much on the source of these food items, and it can be misleading to extrapolate from such figures. J. M. Gurney (in Watson 1893) quotes a Cheshire farmer who made such a calculation and reckoned that sparrows caused £770,094 worth of damage a year, though what the odd £4 means is anybody's guess!

A special case of damage to ripening cereals has occurred at certain research stations where small plots are grown under experimental conditions to investigate the yields and genetical properties of new varieties. The cost of this ruined agricultural research may be enormous in relation to the amount of corn eaten. In most cases the cheapest and most sensible long-term answer seems to be to place protective netting round the crop, expensive though the initial erection may be, and certainly not to try to control the sparrow population, which would be a lasting commitment. Another cause for concern arises in farm and urban grain stores where sparrows concentrate their feeding and do additional damage by fouling the stored product. As with so many things, the inefficient man who keeps his grain in open bins inside unproofed buildings suffers the most, and attention to hygiene and elementary proofing of buildings can go a long way towards combating the problem.

Figs. 28 and 29 depict the breeding seasons of some farmland seed-eaters. Those like the chaffinch, which are dependent on animal food for rearing their young are restricted to nesting in spring and early summer, when defoliating caterpillars or other invertebrates are most readily obtained. Species such as the chaffinch behave more like the animal feeders already discussed, and any clutches laid late in the season are smaller than those laid at the beginning or during the main breeding season. In Britain both sparrows have virtually identical breeding seasons, as shown by B.T.O. nest records analysed by Cramp (in Summers-Smith 1963) for the house sparrow and by Seel for the tree sparrow (see Fig. 28). The availability of grain in abundance over a long period does not favour autumn or winter breeding in either species, because both depend on the same insects to rear their young. These consist of aphids and invertebrates living on the ground among tangled vegetation (nettle patches near hedge-rows or ditches) and are available over a longer period than the defoliating caterpillars favoured by the chaffinch. During the first three days, nestling sparrows are fed on over 80% animal food, and this still forms over 30% of the diet at fledging. Judged by their respective diets, the tree sparrow is probably slightly more adept at collecting insects than the house sparrow, and this may account for its average clutch size being slightly, but significantly, higher (4.7) than that of the house sparrow (4.1). Success in rearing nestlings declines throughout the season in the case of the house sparrow, but stays more or less constant with the tree sparrow. The hatching success of tree sparrow eggs is considerably higher than that of house sparrow (88% against 71%), possibly because the tree sparrow is able to incubate more assiduously as a result of being able to find nutritive food for itself more readily, but this is speculative. For the most up-to-date breeding studies of the house and tree sparrow the reader is recommended to the work of Seel (1970 for references).

The bullfinch has two gular pouches in which it can store seeds and so reduce the number of sorties from the nest. Nevertheless, it still needs to supply its young with animal food during the early stages of their growth, but to a lesser extent than the sparrows, with which it otherwise shows similarities in its breeding biology. D. D. B. Summers showed how the proportion of items of animal food in the chick's diet fell from 30% at hatching to about 2% near the time of fledging, spiders being overwhelmingly the most important com-ponent. Spiders which live in damp places, in nettle beds and thickets, are available for much longer than defoliating caterpillars. Thus it is noticeable that of four warblers which inhabit bramble-covered downs and heathland, the willow warbler and whitethroat specialise on defoliating caterpillars and have short breeding seasons, whereas the Dartford warbler and grasshopper warbler forage low down in damp herbage and collect many arachnids for their young.

The buntings, greenfinch, goldfinch and linnet show an increasing independence of animal food, in fact the linnet rarely gives animal material to its young. These species have very long breeding seasons and many still have young in the nest in October in dry and favour-

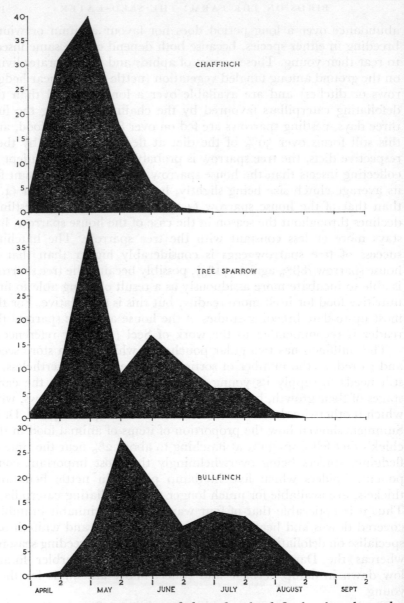

FIG. 28. The breeding seasons of three farmland finches based on the percentage of clutches laid per half-month period. (Data for chaffinch from Newton 1964; data for tree sparrow from Seel 1964; data for bullfinch from Summers & Wright unpubl.).

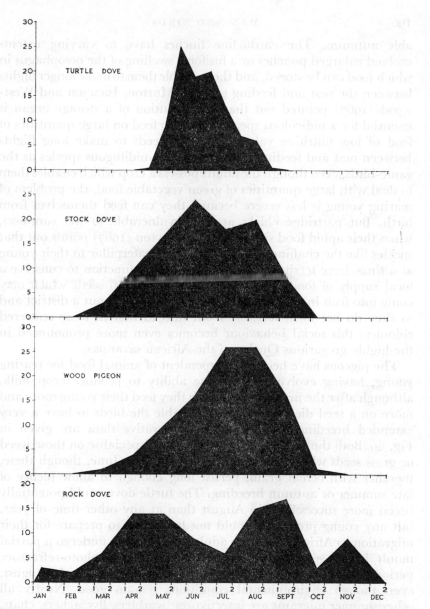

FIG. 29. The breeding seasons of four British pigeons based on the percentage of clutches laid per half-month period. (Turtle dove from Murton 1968; Stock dove from Murton 1966; Wood-pigeon from Murton 1958; Rock dove from Murton & Clark 1968).

able autumns. The cardueline finches have to varying extents evolved enlarged pouches or a fusiform swelling of the oesophagus in which food can be stored, and these enable them to make longer flights between the nest and feeding ground. Murton, Isaacson and West-wood (1963) pointed out that the evolution of a storage organ is essential for a nidicolous species forced to feed on large quantities of food of low nutritive value, or which needs to make long flights between nest and feeding ground. In such nidifugous species as the game-birds, even though the adults possess a crop which enables them to deal with large quantities of green vegetable food, the problem of rearing young is less severe because they can feed themselves from birth. But partridge chicks are very vulnerable to wet summers, when their aphid food supply suffers. Newton (1967) points out that species like the chaffinch, which bring one caterpillar to their young at a time, have territories, and these possibly function to conserve a local supply of food. The carduelines depend on seeds which may come into fruit in widely scattered patches throughout a district and so they do not form territories but instead nest in loose scattered colonies; this social behaviour becomes even more pronounced in the highly gregarious Quelea of the African savannas.

The pigeons have become independent of animal food for rearing young, having evolved the unique ability to produce crop milk, although after the first few days of life they feed their young more and more on a seed diet. These factors enable the birds to have a very extended breeding season; some comparative data are given in Fig. 29. Both the stock dove and turtle dove specialise on those weed or grass seeds which become most abundant in June, though these, together with cereal grain, persist long enough to allow plenty of late summer or autumn breeding. The turtle dove could potentially breed more successfully in August than at any other time of year, but any young produced would not have long to prepare for their migration to Africa, while the adults need time to undergo a partial moult before setting off south. The onset of a photo-refractory period causes the gonads to regress in late July and early August, even though environmental conditions remain good. Nearly all other summer migrants are insectivores (warblers, flycatchers, chats, nightjars), and breed in late spring or early summer which gives the adults time to moult before migrating. But the seed-eating turtle dove would hardly have a chance to breed if it began moulting too soon, and it must therefore compromise. Some wing moult is of obvious advantage to a long-distance migrant, and so the turtle dove undergoes a partial moult in late summer which is then arrested, and will end when the bird arrives in Africa. A similar pattern of arrested moult is found in certain other migrants which must have late breeding seasons (honey buzzard, juvenile quail).

The wood-pigeon is not a specialist on weed seeds of arable land, like the stock or turtle doves, but instead feeds on pasture weeds and the larger grass seeds which tend to ripen later in the year (buttercup seed is mostly available in July) and on tree fruits. None the less, its breeding season in Britain today is almost entirely dictated by cereal availability and it can breed less in June than the other two doves already mentioned. In June most wood-pigeons are still collecting clover and weed leaves from pastures and finding rather few weed seeds, so although the adults are physiologically capable of breeding from March until September, most individuals must wait for the cereals to ripen in July before attempting to lay their eggs. The rock dove's food is intermediate between the wood-pigeon's predominantly cereal diet and the arable weed seed diet of the stock dove, and its breeding season accordingly shows the features of both these species combined. In the area where the rock doves represented in Fig. 28 were studied, many grain stubbles are left throughout the winter. This enables a small proportion of the population to breed throughout the year – an extended breeding season is even more apparent in town populations of the feral pigeon where winter food supplies are abundant. An appropriate physiological breeding season can be maintained in the British Columbids by a direct response to appropriate daylengths; the rock dove is sensitive to comparatively short days and has the longest potential breeding season, and the wood-pigeon, which needs the equivalent of March days to respond, has the shortest. Within the potential breeding season eggs are actually laid according to the food supplies available, so the actual breeding season can be adaptively controlled without the need for a photo-refractory period (cf. the rook). As I have said, this is not so in the case of the turtle dove, which would attempt breeding for too long if this safety mechanism did not intervene. An obligatory refractory period would also be a disadvantage for birds like the greenfinch and linnet, which in favourable years continue breeding later than usual. Experimental evidence suggests that the greenfinch does not undergo a refractory period, or at least if it does it is very short and easily dispersed under regimes of comparatively long days.

The typical pattern of seasonal mortality for a graminivorous bird has already been well detailed elsewhere in this series for the house sparrow and wood-pigeon; the bullfinch provides yet another example and is discussed more fully in Chapter 9.

CHAPTER 8

BIRDS ON THE FARM: THE GRAZERS

BIRDS which are able to feed on green vegetation have a potentially enormous supply available on farmland. But to extract sufficient food energy from green leaves, very large quantities must be consumed during the course of a feeding day and under such conditions slight variations in nutrient, particularly protein, content may have profound consequences for the species concerned. The grey partridge occupies the place for a grazing bird on English downland (see page 175) and subsists to a large extent on grass leaves during the winter months (compare the grazing habits of the northern tetronids discussed in Chapter 4, page 97). On farmland, it prefers growing wheat as this usually has a higher protein content than grass with rye intermediate. It is remarkable how few farmers complain of partridges causing damage to winter cereals; the incidental feeding on winter wheat by wood-pigeons often provokes strong words but partridges, which go in for this sort of feeding most of the winter, are excused. Herbivorous feeding is greatly helped by the development of a storage organ and the crop, a sac-like outgrowth from the oesophagus, enables the birds to take in and store food more quickly than the digestive system would otherwise allow.

From spring onwards partridges feed primarily on weed and cereal seeds (page 331) with a predominance of cereal grain when it is available after harvest. Young partridges are dependent on insect food during their early life and mainly have to feed themselves from hatching, although they are accompanied and guided towards food by the parents. The breeding season has to be restricted to the period when suitable insect food is available, and eggs are laid in late May to produce peak hatching in June. Wood-pigeons have an advantage in that the production of crop milk gives them a much longer breeding season independent of animal food supplies (page 190), and allow them to care for their young in a nest. The wood-pigeon was originally a woodland species but its ability to graze off tree as well as ground vegetation, its greater flexibility in breeding and its

ability to live in a wider range of habitats than the partridge have
made it the most successful and common grazing bird on English
farmland. In winter it specialises on clover and weed leaves and
much less often takes the leaves of winter corn. During periods of
hard weather when the ground is covered with snow or frost it turns
to winter brassicae. Cabbage leaves do not contain sufficient nutrient
in relation to water content to sustain a pigeon during the period of
shortest winter days, and at this time birds forced to use such food
sources lose weight but do considerable damage in the meanwhile.
The adaptation of the wood-pigeon to the grazing niche is particularly important since this is the bird which has the greatest economic
impact in Britain. Because I have dealt with the bird in a monograph
of its own I shall make only a passing reference to it below, and then
only for comparative purposes, but the reader should appreciate the
gap which occurs at this point.

WILDFOWL AND AGRICULTURE

Wet fields, estuarine flats and the more open farms of northern
Scotland are not ideal habitats for pigeon or partridge, and here
the niche for a herviborous bird is occupied by geese and grazing
ducks. These do not possess storage crops but do have the advantage
of long necks and highly efficient shearing bills which enable them
to graze off large quantities of vegetation. They probably move to
sub-arctic regions to breed in order to take advantage of the long
feeding day at a time when extra reserves are needed for egg-laying.
The protein content of grass reaches a peak in April and May in
Britain, but not until July and August in Iceland. Furthermore, as
Kear has emphasised, the cooler conditions in Iceland and the long
hours of daylight ensure that the nutritive content stays higher for
longer than in southern areas of Europe, where summer droughts
occur. Young geese and ducks, like partridge chicks, must have
access to a rich supply of animal food during their early life and the
mosquito and other insect ridden wetlands of the far north provide
suitable feeding conditions.

Of course, wildfowl are well enough represented in Britain during
the breeding season, but in comparatively small numbers. They are
widely dispersed at this time and, apart from the mute swan and the
introduced Canada goose, have no impact on agriculture. Britain
could never be described as a 'factory' for wildfowl production, an

expression coined by American ornithologists and since borrowed by European workers to describe the northern muskegs and tundra which support an enormous breeding population of ducks and geese. But Britain is an important wintering ground for very large numbers of wildfowl and many, particularly certain of the geese, winter on farmland, where they inevitably give rise to complaints of damage. To put the matter into perspective, we are still fortunate enough in Britain to have wintering with us between 45–60,000 pink-footed geese from Iceland and Greenland, about 26,000 greylag geese from Iceland, between 6–8,000 white-fronted geese of the Russian sub-species (*Anser a. albifrons*) and 12–15,000 of the Greenland race (*Anser albifrons flavirostris*), and 2–400 bean geese. Of the black geese the total population of barnacle geese in the British Isles, including Ireland, is rather less than 20,000, of which 10,000 winter in the Hebrides and come from Greenland, and 3,000 winter in the Solway originating in Spitzbergen. Dark-bellied brent geese, which once provided a wildfowler's paradise on the east and south coasts of Britain, total nearly 15,000 birds (said to be about two-thirds of the world population of this subspecies), while between 1–2,000 light-bellied brents arrive in north-east England and Scotland. For most of these species the present picture is still rosy, but there is no room for complacency if future generations are to enjoy the magnificent spectacle of wild geese at liberty. We can boast of nothing like the 3–5 million wildfowl that may be present on only a few hundred acres in the Sacramento and San Joaquin Valleys of California, to give but one example in the United States. Nevertheless, numerous conservation bodies, at both local and national level, and the Wild-fowlers' Association of Great Britain and Ireland are making every effort to maintain the *status quo* at least, and it is against this background of active public interest that we must view the incidence of wildfowl damage.

Dr Janet Kear has made a special study of the problems raised by wildfowl, and this section, unless otherwise stated, derives from her observations and various published papers. The grazing habits of the various geese make them particularly suspect, and complaints have been levelled at all the regular British species except the bean and brent geese. In particular, they have been accused of damaging pastures, growing cereals and various root and fodder crops. The same charge has been made against the mute and whooper swans, and against the wigeon among the ducks, while three other ducks, mallard, pintail and teal, have caused sporadic damage by taking grain.

Both the greylag and pinkfoot nowadays depend very much on arable farmland for food during the months when they are resident in Britain. Migrant greylags arrive in October and leave again in March or April; pinkfeet arrive earlier, sometimes in mid-September, and depart rather later, some not leaving until early May. Although both species prefer to feed on grain from the autumn stubbles, later turning to ley or pasture grass, the pinkfoot is more fastidious in its preference for old barley fields, and it will fly up to 30 miles from its roost to find suitable fields. The greylag is content with smaller, rougher fields, often at higher elevations, and so usually feeds nearer its roosting grounds, frequenting oat fields as well as barley stubbles and pastures. Wintering greylags are virtually confined to Scotland, and similarly most pinkfeet are to be found north of the border, except for roosting concentrations round the Wash Estuary and on the Southport sands in Lancashire (Fig. 30). On northern farmland, these immigrant geese occupy a position very similar to that of the wood-pigeon in England, and show many parallels in feeding habits in first taking the stubble grain, then becoming herbivorous – although in this case they specialise in grass, or growing wheat, instead of clover, and sometimes turning to the leaves of root crops such as swedes or turnips.

While the acreage of all cereals grown in Scotland has fluctuated during the present century and currently shows a 9% increase since the beginning of the last war, the acreage of barley has risen considerably and this seems to have affected the total population of wintering pinkfeet. Kear has analysed the total barley acreage for seventeen Scottish counties from Aberdeenshire to Wigtownshire, which hold virtually all the feeding flocks of pinkfeet in November. In 1957, there were 175,251 acres of barley in these counties and 31,180 pinkfeet (21,000 greylags) in November, whereas by 1964 the acreage had steadily risen to 385,367 and the pinkfoot population to 56,230 (there were then 42,790 greylags). Fig. 31 is based on Kear's work and shows these changes graphically by expressing the pinkfoot population in the seventeen counties as a percentage of the total population in Britain. These results partly reflect an absolute increase in the total population of pinkfeet in Britain, which, together with the increase in the numbers of wintering greylags, is to some extent consequent on broad improvements in climate and food

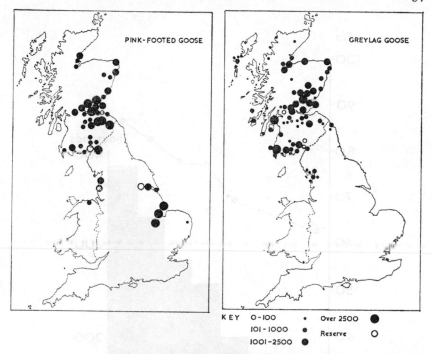

FIG. 30. Principal wintering areas of the pink-footed goose and greylag goose in Britain. (After Atkinson-Willes 1963).

supplies at the breeding grounds. But Fig. 30 mainly reflects a tendency of the Icelandic and Greenland populations of pinkfeet to stay longer in Scotland before some individuals are forced to move to new feeding grounds further south.

The barley harvest takes place up to six weeks later in Scotland than in England, and bad weather in the north causes a greater amount of grain spillage. In addition, more barley fields in Scotland are undersown with grass and clover, partly because stubbles are not so readily ploughed in the autumn as in the drier south. As a result there is more stubble grain in Scotland than in England, and it lasts for much longer. Using the national average figure for the spillage rate of barley (5% of the yield), Kear has estimated that one acre of actual cereal provides a maximum of 800 goose feeding days. In the south of England, one acre of barley stubble provides a potential of 1,099 wood-pigeon feeding days, but the number of pigeons which

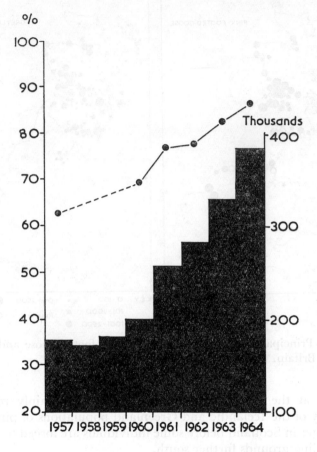

J 1761

FIG. 31. Relationship between the percentage of the total population of pink-footed geese wintering in Britain to be found in mid-November in 17 Scottish counties and the acreage of barley. More geese have remained in Scotland as the acreage of barley stubble has risen. (After Kear 1965).

have to feed on the stubbles is higher than one bird per acre. It works out that on average the stubble grain supply of both wheat and barley combined provides a potential food supply which could last the average pigeon population 26 weeks, provided no ploughing takes place and nothing else eats the grain. Clearly geese, like pigeons, must make severe demands on the grain stocks and when these are depleted must turn to other foods. When grain is exhausted, pink-feet and greylags turn to grass feeding, although in some areas they may find potatoes. No harm is done when geese feed on harvested fields of potatoes, where it is usual for 15% of the crop to be wasted through the tubers being either broken or diseased. A good potential food supply rich in carbohydrate is found on these fields, as there is an average of 24 cwt. of wasted potatoes per acre, which could last one goose for 600 days. Unfortunately this food source usually only lasts until November, because three-quarters of the potato fields are then planted with winter wheat, and only a few survive until March when spring barley may be planted. This feeding behaviour of the geese compares with the wood-pigeon's habit of resorting in Decem-ber to fields where a sugar beet crop has been lifted and many broken fragments remain.

Kear considers that pasture grazing in winter does not harm established grass, and may in fact improve the sward by encouraging tillering and the spread of white clover. The nutrient composition of grass in winter is also improved under close-cropping even though the total dry matter may be reduced. It should also be remembered that a tall sward with much red clover and long grass is particularly vulnerable to frost damage, and that in grazing down such sites geese may be eating what would in any case be lost. But over-grazing occasionally occurs, for instance when geese feed too intensively on a new ley soon after harvest, although generally their feeding at this time is beneficial because it firms the roots, encourages tillering and removes rogue self-grown grain and wild oats. Over-grazing some times occurs in wet areas too, when much of the damage is caused by paddling. The most important damage, however, occurs after the beginning of the spring growing season. In particular, those fields of fresh green grass specially rested and prepared with nitrogenous fertiliser to provide early 'spring bite' for lambing sheep flocks attract geese. Grazing in such sites certainly reduces the yield, weakens the plant and deprives the grazing stock. Kear recommends such fields to be sited when possible near roads or buildings where geese are less likely to feed.

As an alternative to grass, geese sometimes graze winter wheat, and this causes the farmer much more consternation. Actually winter grazing does more good than harm by increasing tillering and

firming roots and by preventing the development of too much top-
growth in mild winters. The practice of allowing sheep to graze off
winter cereals developed for just these reasons. Occasionally geese
cause damage by uprooting plants or by excessive trampling and
caking in wet fields. Kear carried out some valuable trials in which
geese were prevented from feeding by enclosures erected on winter
cereal and clover fields. No differences in yield between protected and
unprotected areas could be discerned at the end of the experiment.
Similarly the simulation of damage by artificially clipping silage
grass or winter wheat suggested that a loss of foliage was not necessarily detrimental to final yields. She followed up this work with an
interesting experiment in which three replicates of 8½ ft. × 30 ft.
plots were sited on winter cereals, where grazing treatments in four
different months were performed, and on spring barley where there
were two periods tested for grazing. In these plots seven greylags
and three pinkfeet were penned for 6½ hours at some stage in the
appropriate month, such grazing being equivalent in intensity to
11,000 goose-hours per acre. This is a high level because Kear
calculated that on the Slimbridge Marshes 9,000 goose-hours per
acre is the maximum. Again at harvest-time no statistically valid
differences in crop yield could be found between ungrazed control
plots and plots of winter oats or wheat heavily grazed in either
December, March or April, or of spring barley grazed in May.
These results agree with similar studies made by Murton, Isaacson
and Westwood (1966) who artificially removed up to 89% of clover
from leys and pastures in January or February to simulate very
severe pigeon damage and found that plant recovery was complete
after only two months. Similarly, Kinsey (1959) found that grazing
sheep made no difference to grain yield, provided that grazing
ceased by mid-April.

   During bad weather in winter, geese may be forced to leave the
pastures or winter cereal fields. Pinkfeet usually move further south
to find better feeding conditions, whereas the greylag may turn to
eating turnip leaves, rape, kale or brassicae. In Aberdeenshire and
Bute, swede turnips are regularly eaten as the mild climate of these
two areas allows the crops to be left in the fields throughout the
winter until they are needed for feeding stock. In Bute, the numbers
of wintering greylags have increased from about 2,000 in 1940 to
about 10,000 at the present time. These changes were partly the
result of the overall increase of the species, but they also depend on

a growing tendency for the birds to favour regions of less severe winters than are generally found on the Scottish mainland. Complaints of damage have increased, and this is now said to involve a tenth of the crop which represents a serious financial loss to the farmer. The obvious remedy would be to lift the vegetables before the onset of hard weather, but this is not realistic: because the roots continue to grow until the end of the year, because they seem to be relished more by cattle if taken direct from the field, and because labour is difficult. The possibility of scaring the geese from the area by using rocket fireworks has also been considered but not yet attempted.

The value of droppings as manure may to some extent offset the limited damage caused by geese. The total quantity deposited is certainly low in relation to the farmer's usual needs, but nevertheless the birds may sometimes introduce trace elements to a deficient area, and are certainly efficient at converting plant remains into a useful soil constituent.

The large whooper swan is giving rise to an increasing volume of complaint of damage. Although it normally prefers semi-aquatic feeding grounds such as wet meadows and estuaries, the whooper will feed on dry land far more than the mute swan, and often flights to arable land. Damage to swede-turnips in Aberdeenshire seems to be the most serious cause for complaint, and in many ways resembles that caused by greylags in Bute. Whoopers have also fed on both unharvested and harvested fields of potatoes, particularly in Perthshire and Angus although, according to Pilcher and Kear (1966), the habit has only become established since the severe winters of the 1940s, and is now spreading to England, where until now the pinkfoot has normally eaten only the old potatoes. There have been suggestions that the whooper swan has increased in recent years, and evidence presented by Boyd and Eltringham (1962) shows that the wintering stock may have grown considerably from 1948–1952, since then remaining very constant until at least 1960. A general increase in wintering whoopers may have occurred over the last 50 years. In 1960 the British population in November was about 2,200 birds, with 1,840 reported for Scotland, 320 for England and 70 for Wales. As with the geese already considered, whooper numbers decline during the winter as food supplies become depleted. The rate of loss is too great to be caused by death alone, and it is very likely that some birds pass on to other wintering grounds outside

Britain. The origin of the British stock is by no means certainly established and although most immigrant birds probably come from Iceland, some may well come from Eurasia.

It has often been argued that the mute swan in Britain derives entirely from domesticated stock originally brought to Britain in a captive state, but Ticehurst (1957) has produced strong evidence for its being an indigenous animal. It probably became a Royal bird before 1186 and since then any individual which is not privately owned has belonged to the reigning monarch. Continuous interference and the removal of cygnets for hand-rearing and subsequent release on the captor's land transformed the mute swan into a semi-domestic species, a state which has persisted until the present time. Ticehurst has suggested that this intensive semi-wild culture brought the owner distinction, profit and food, while the bird's Royal status made it a very respected gift. Thus in 1274 swans were fetching three shillings as against 5d. for a goose, 2½d. for a capon and 4d. for a pheasant.

Ticehurst has noted that in one small part of the Fens in 1553, upping figures referring to 29 different owners indicate a total of 35 broods with 183 cygnets. At this time there were over 800 registered owners of swans and, if one attributes to them the same level of stocking, a swan population emerges of at least 24,000 in Fenland alone. Earlier at a Christmas feast at York in 1251 Henry III had provided 125: if this scale of eating was at all frequent a high swan population would be needed to satisfy the privileged classes. This was probably the case, since after Capello, the Venetian Ambassador, visited London in the winter of 1496–7, he reported 'it is truly a beautiful thing to behold one or two thousand tame swans upon the river Thames' and remarked that the English seemed to eat them as frequently as the Italians ate ducks and geese.

A B.T.O. census in the breeding season of 1955 revealed 2,595 nesting pairs in England and 8,014 non-breeding birds. In Wales there were 115 breeding pairs and 242 non-breeders. Scotland produced 463 nests and 2,121 non-breeding birds (Rawcliffe 1958, Campbell 1960). Accordingly the British mute swan population in 1955 numbered about 20,000 birds, with the highest densities in S.E. England, the Thames valley, Norfolk, Somerset and Wiltshire, and Cheshire – the districts providing the largest areas of riparian habitat. It seems likely that numbers have been increasing, although it is difficult to measure any changes. Campbell quotes some swan-upping figures given by the Royal Swankeeper for the upper Thames which show an increase from 412 birds in 1948 to 1,311 in 1956. The records for earlier periods are less satisfactory. Ticehurst (1957) has given upping figures for the Thames from London to Henley with totals of 437 in 1841, 330 in 1884, 392 in 1887, 343 in 1888, 457 in 1893, 455 in 1894, 411 in 1895 and 559 in 1941. The figures support the view that there was a period of relative stability until the 'forties followed by a marked increase. A further partial census was taken in 1961, organised on behalf of the B.T.O. by Eltringham (1963). This included detailed aerial censuses and provided a much better coverage of the areas selected for sampling. In comparable areas there appeared to be no change in the total population of swans between 1955 and 1961, nor in the ratio of breeding to non-breeding individuals. However, data obtained from winter wildfowl counts, which are regularly made in a standard way by voluntary watchers, suggest that mute swans increased at a rapid rate from about 1955 to reach a peak in 1961, since when a decrease has brought the population back to the 1955 level. In continental Europe, swans have also increased, particularly in Holland, Denmark, Sweden and the Baltic, while the bird is now regarded as a pest in Germany.

Mute swans prefer to feed in wet situations where they pull up aquatic vegetation. Flooded meadows often attract birds from nearby rivers and lakes and it is here that damage sometimes occurs. On two estuaries in south Devon, Dr Mary Gillham (1956) studied the feeding habits of the birds, with the help of swan-proof enclosures, and found that they had a considerable effect on the nature of the vegetation. During April, May and June the birds grazed salt marsh turf where succulents like sea arrow grass *Triglochin maritima* and sea plantain *Plantago maritima* were eaten as well as the salt marsh grass *Puccinellia maritima*. Late in summer when the land vegetation became coarser the birds moved to feed on the *Zostera* beds and some individuals then took the green alga *Enteromorpha intestinalis*. In winter the swans moved to fresh water stretches of the rivers, leaving the river when the water level was high to feed on the surrounding meadows.

Unlike the geese, which truly graze grass and corn crops, mute swans frequently pull up the roots as well, leaving bare patches which may take a long time to recover. Also, they are wasteful feeders leaving much torn and uneaten vegetation. Damage is frequently aggravated by excessive trampling, especially in flooded fields, which together with the birds' droppings effectively spoils the grazing for domestic stock. In many cases flocks of non-breeding and immature birds are responsible for this kind of damage, conceivably because they are excluded from more suitable feeding grounds by established territory owners. This appeared to be the case in 1964 on the Romney grazing marshes in Kent, where of a flock of 21 birds, 17 were in their first year of life. These birds spent two months fouling and grazing 12 acres of a three-year ley intended for sheep grazing. Similar reports have come from Ayrshire, Dorset, Oxfordshire, Somerset and Wiltshire, and in one instance reported by Eltringham damage to the farmer was assessed at £75. Although serious enough to the individual farmers, swan damage is very local and is probably best dealt with by shooting the offending birds; this is legal if damage can be proved. The erection of a wire fence, especially if it is electrified, will often deter birds from walking on to farmland from adjacent rivers.

Anglers sometimes complain that swans directly disturb their fishing, and more important, cause long term damage by destroying water vegetation. An unusual incident occurred at Gosport where a flock of 50 swans moved on to a small boating lake reserved for model boat racing and disrupted proceedings. A pair of swans will also disturb other waterfowl; I have a record of a dabchick's nest destroyed by the feeding actions of a pair of swans on a drainage ditch. Similarly swans may interfere with breeding waterfowl on gravel pits. According to Eltringham, the Central Electricity Generating Board reports that electricity failures due to the collision of flying swans with overhead lines are increasing faster than the increase in mileage of these cables, but that they consider this damage as very slight compared with other causes of power failure. Even so, of 400 ringed swans recovered dead, 95 had died through colliding with overhead wires. Perrins and Reynolds (1967) have shown that accidents of this sort reach a peak in March and again in October, presumably because the birds move around to a greater extent at these times. Against local incidents of swan damage must be set the considerable public regard and sympathy towards the bird, and there is no doubt that in many places resident swans provide great amenity value. Probably no species reaches the headlines more frequently, as when some local R.S.P.C.A. officer is called in to deal with a swan grounded in some unlikely place after a

PLATE 21. *Above*, mute swans at times damage grazing meadows near waterways by eating, trampling and fouling the grass. *Below*, kingfisher – sometimes badly maligned by anglers who begrudge its fishing skills. In fact, these birds very rarely harm angling interests.

PLATE 22. *Above*, black-headed gulls in Perthshire waiting in lay-by for scraps from motorists: one factor helping the increase of this species. Because the black-headed gull population has been expanding, there has probably been less selection in favour of deferring the age of first breeding. *Below left*, adult in nuptial plumage. *Right*, first-year bird breeding.

collision. There are a few places where very large swan flocks occur, apart from the famous Abbotsbury herd, and these provide something of a spectacle. Herds of over 300 birds may be seen on the River Stour at Mistley, Essex, where waste from the maltings provides a big attraction, on Michling Broad in Norfolk and on Loch Leven in Kinross.

Canada geese were first introduced into Britain at about the time of the Restoration – the period that saw the reinstatement of the sporting upper classes and the blossoming of large estates and gardens equipped with their various prestige symbols. We do not know whether Charles II was mindful of their potential sporting value or whether they reflected his extensive aesthetic tastes, but he had Canada geese on his lake in St James's Park and these birds are the first recorded. Since then other introductions have been made, always apparently of the race which breeds in the extreme east of North America (*Branta c. canadensis*), although a few from a little further west belonging to the slightly smaller and darker race *B. c. interior* may also have been imported. (The racial status of the Canada goose is still not fully established through lack of information from breeding grounds in the unpopulated wilds of Canada.) By the late eighteenth century the bird appears to have become well established on suitable waters.

At first consideration the Canada goose seems to be occupying a vacant niche for a grazing bird living close to large areas of water, which in this case are required for roosting and breeding. There is no natural habitat in Britain quite like the forested muskeg of the Hudson Bay lowlands and similar habitats in the eastern United States and Canada. The native areas preferred contain many small deep ponds with islands and peninsulas which have clean shorelines uncluttered with sedge or sphagnum. Here, the birds can gain easy access to the banks, where grass and sedge flats provide ideal grazing conditions and islands make safe nesting refuges. The Canada goose in Britain still lives a semi-artificial life and shows no tendency to colonise new areas unless deliberately aided by man. In consequence, there are many small local populations with very little interchange between them, possibly, as Blurton Jones has suggested, because these feral birds have no migratory movements, in complete contrast to their wild relatives in North America and Canada. This suggests that the British environment is not entirely satisfactory.

In July 1953, when a B.T.O. census was organised by Blurton

Jones (1956), there were between 2,200 and 4,000 birds in Britain including adults, non-breeding birds, and independent juveniles of the year. Most of this population was living in the Midlands extending north to Yorkshire, south to Berkshire, west to Shropshire, and with outposts in north Norfolk. Elsewhere, as in Surrey and S.W. England, only isolated colonies existed. Complaints of damage to grazing, growing cereals and other farm crops have been so frequent that since the inquiry many large flocks have been culled and some of the birds have been taken to new localities and released, especially by wildfowling clubs, so that their present status and distribution is no longer accurately known. There is no doubt that the bird can be a nuisance to farmers, as at Combermere in Cheshire where in 1960 and 1961 a flock ranging between 150 and 200 birds caused severe damage to winter wheat sown near the edge of the lake where the birds live. Mostly, damage only occurs in cases where farming is carried out close to the birds' quarters, and it can be controlled by shooting the birds during the season lasting from September–January. Under the 1954 Protection of Birds Act, the birds may also be shot in the close season, if it can be proved that the action 'was necessary for the purpose of preventing serious damage to crops, vegetables, fruits, growing timber or any other form of property or to fisheries'. Shooting is likely to be more efficient than any form of egg-destruction even though this is widely practised to prevent recruitment (the actual taking of eggs is illegal under the 1954 Act).

Most other incidents of wildfowl damage to agriculture are on a very local and minor scale, especially those involving the ducks. A typical incident in Cumberland in the summer of 1962 involved about one hundred mallard which were flighting from a river adjacent to a field of barley to feed on the ripening grain; the birds obtained this by pulling down the heads. A special problem sometimes occurs on watercress beds, especially in Hampshire, where about one-third of the national crop is grown, and where wintering flocks of mallard may do damage out of all proportion to their numbers by pulling up and eating the plants. Moorhens also pull up the vegetation when searching for food and this, together with the movements of the birds, opens up new channels where weeds can become established. The problem may be particularly acute owing to the concentrated nature of the crop and the high standards of maintenance and hygiene necessary for successful culture. Various scaring devices have been used to remove the waterfowl, including acetylene bangers, as well as direct shooting. Many other birds visit watercress beds to feed and drink, especially as the beds usually remain open when other ponds and sites are frozen. Such passerines as the blackbird can be particularly troublesome in feeding among and uprooting the plants in their search for molluscs and other invertebrates.

OTHER GRAZERS

Occasionally moorhens can be a nuisance by grazing and eating other crops especially when these are planted close to a pond or river supporting a high density of moorhens – on some farms up to 60 adult moorhens per 100 acres have been recorded. On Tresco, Scilly Islands, moorhens were seen digging up and eating potatoes grown in a field adjoining a large lake; the birds attacked seed potatoes in February, as well as the main standing crop through until June. Admittedly this was a very local incident but up to £50 worth of damage may have been caused. Damage to winter wheat and even growing peas is occasionally recorded, and is more of a problem than duck grazing because moorhens tend to uproot the plants. At one site in Hertfordshire about half an acre of wheat was eaten down by moorhens during the winter. Similarly a pasture was severely grazed in Hampshire by up to 100 birds, which were thought to have completely spoiled half an acre of a young ley by their intensive feeding and soiling with droppings. As mentioned, most troubles arise when crops are sited in particularly vulnerable positions, as was the case when peas were grown between a river and an old disused canal, inducing moorhens to graze some of the young shoots during the spring. In the Netherlands, where crops are perforce often planted near water, moorhens have caused expensive damage by grazing violet plantations and by pecking at other sprouting bulbs from November to March (van Koersveld 1955). In the Holland division of Lincolnshire, bulb growers have only occasionally been troubled by moorhens. Instead, greater concern has been caused by pheasants attacking tulip bulbs under the ground. The tulips are grown on a large acreage with here and there a small plot of a particularly valuable variety. Pheasants have learned to dig down to the bulb and peck out lumps *in situ*. A few birds may become used to this food and as the bulbs remain in the ground

until autumn, there is a long period over which expensive damage
may occur.

This gives a good illustration of the kind of very local but important problem that can arise with game-birds. In this case the
answer is to shoot the animals causing damage, which can legally be
done during the shooting season from 1 October–1 February, provided the person concerned owns the shooting rights. Additionally
the Minister of Agriculture has power, which he has delegated to
the Agricultural Executive Committees (under section 98 of the
1947 Agriculture Act) to order the destruction of certain birds or
their eggs, even during the close season, if this appears necessary to
prevent damage to crops, pasture, animal or human foodstuffs,
livestock, trees, hedges, banks or any works on land. Paradoxically,
this may mean that an owner will actually request that an order be
made against him if he is suffering damage and requires to kill
birds for which he owns the shooting rights. In the same way, an
order may be served on the owner of the shooting rights, even though
he himself is not suffering damage. This requires him to destroy a
specified number of birds, or where this is not possible, to state
precisely the extent of destruction necessary to prevent the birds
causing damage to neighbouring farms, to the satisfaction of the
Committee. Thus remedial action to prevent this kind of damage is
possible, although situations may well arise where hard feelings are
roused in small communities. The local members of Committees
obviously have to be alert to these problems in human relations.

Skylarks frequently graze young seedling crops. High skylark
densities are encountered on low flat grassland, and this is especially
the case on the drained marshland of the East Anglian fens, on the
Lancashire mosses, the north Kent and north Thames marshes; on
the Isle of Thanet it becomes the dominant bird. It is not surprising
that Essex farmers working rich reclaimed arable land just north
of the Thames experience trouble with skylarks. Many growers in
the area specialise in early cash crops and grow small strips of
market vegetables, such as spring cabbages, lettuce and peas, aiming
to benefit from the early growth of the plants on the warm south-
facing slopes. Skylarks have caused havoc among the seedlings and
in particular have ruined lettuces by pecking the young plants. In
the cases examined, the plants were more severely attacked after
they had been thinned and it was too late to remove the damaged
ones – presumably because the larks prefer to feed in the more open

patches. In the same way, the pecking of young pea seedlings has severely retarded their growth, an important consideration when one remembers that the grower's economy is geared to producing an early crop which will bring a high cash return on small acreages. One grower estimated that larks were causing the loss of one-fifth of his potential pea crop and, although this was not checked by a proper study and is likely to be an over-estimate, it remains a fact that in special circumstances like these the level of damage is higher than can be tolerated. Feeding on winter wheat at the chitting stage has aroused comment in Warwickshire, Lincolnshire and East Anglia and is doubtless a widespread and regular habit. Considering the negligible consequences of most wildfowl damage it is unlikely that the final yield is ever affected. The defoliation of sugar-beet seedlings after the crop has been singled is far more significant, but again no objective assessment has been made of the effects on final yield. Most skylark damage seems to be recorded in those favourable localities where breeding densities exceed one bird per acre. These areas probably support even higher post-breeding and winter populations due partly to the presence of winter immigrants; these migrants may indeed play a large part in incidents between November and March.

Many other species, incidentally, eat leaves and have been blamed for damaging root crop seedlings, but apart from the wood-pigeon, only pheasants and the two partridges can be regularly incriminated. In most cases it is impossible to demonstrate lasting detrimental effects, because plants will withstand a very high degree of defoliation before final crop yields are reduced.

CHAPTER 9

BIRD PROBLEMS IN HORTICULTURE

SURPRISINGLY few birds live their full annual cycle in orchards but instead resort to them temporarily to breed or to feed from a locally good food source. Of course, most large orchards have their resident blackbirds and song thrushes, a few pairs of blue and great tits and the odd greenfinch, linnet or redpoll. But there is no species which has really adapted to living in orchards in the same way that the wood-pigeon has become associated with the cereal/clover ley rotation of arable farming, or the rook and starling with pasture/arable farming. The reasons for this are various. Many species typical of deciduous woodland have evolved a feeding dependence on the insect food of natural forest, but these insects are not found in well-kept stands of cultivated fruit; furthermore, the intensive use of insecticidal sprays ensures that fewer other insects emerge to replace this lost forest fauna. In addition, secondary and old growth is carefully cleared and generally only young healthy trees are kept. All in all, tidy orchards make impoverished habitats for birds, and it is not surprising that they are visited rather than lived in. Even so, a really old, neglected orchard may become a most attractive place and one of our most fascinating birds, the wryneck, now rapidly disappearing as a result of our wetter summers (see page 39), still favours the old orchards of Kent apparently in preference to natural woodland.

Disregarding the depleted invertebrate fauna, orchards offer two main food sources for birds; buds in late winter and spring and ripe fruit from summer until harvest. It is somewhat surprising that the bullfinch, which specialises on buds to the extent of being a serious pest to the grower, takes these only as a last resort when its preferred seed crop fails.

THE BULLFINCH

Throughout most of its range in Europe and western Siberia, the bullfinch inhabits coniferous forest with a fairly dense undergrowth. Spruce taiga is much frequented, but mixed conifer and birch woodland, and further south, beech, also satisfy its needs. In such places the buds of conifer trees, particularly those of larch and spruce but also birch and willow, comprise an important part of the diet, together with various weed seeds. At the western and eastern extremes of its range, in Britain and in Japan, bullfinches are essentially birds of deciduous woodland, where they live on the seeds and buds of various herbaceous plants and trees. It is only in these areas that they have become a pest of cultivated fruit.

Improvements in horticultural practice over the last two decades focused attention on the harm done by the bullfinch, and in 1953 increasing complaints from growers led the Ministry of Agriculture to authorise an intensive investigation into the biology of the species by my colleagues E. N. Wright and D. D. B. Summers. Their studies paved the way for a more recent investigation into the population dynamics of bullfinches living in natural woodland at Wytham, Oxford, by Dr Ian Newton, formerly of the Edward Grey Institute of Field Ornithology. This account then is primarily a synthesis of their findings.

As with so many bird problems which we tend to imagine are recent in origin, our forefathers were well acquainted with the bud-eating habits of the bullfinch. This was well shown by F. A. Roach who has quoted an old statement by William Lawson made in 1618 in *A new Orchard and Garden*: 'Your cherries when they bee ripe, wil draw all the blacke-birds, Thrushes and May-pyes to your Orchard. The Bull-Finch is a devourer of your fruit in the budde, I have had whole trees shald out with them in Wintertime.' Earlier still an Act of Parliament had been made in the reign of Elizabeth I (1566) whereby a sum of one penny was offered in reward for 'everie Bulfynche or other Byrde that devoureth the blowth of Fruite'. The churchwarden's records from Tenterden in Kent show that many such payments were made in 1628–9 and again in 1678–80 indicating that the bird was regarded as a pest even then.

However, there is good evidence that the bullfinch underwent a marked expansion, beginning in the mid-1950s, which led to the occupation of new habitats, particularly parks and gardens, and in Ireland the species increased tremendously (Parslow, 1968). The expansion has coincided with increased reports of bud damage in orchards and is reflected in ringing recoveries by a marked increase since 1960 in the number of bullfinches recovered more than five miles from the place of ringing (Summers *in litt.*). It is conceivable that the bullfinch has undergone a change in its psychological tolerances enabling it to spread to new habitats in a way comparable with the reed bunting (see page 172).

Like many other seed-eating birds the bullfinch has an extended breeding season and eggs may be laid from April until August, and sometimes even September (Fig. 28). The first peak of egg-laying takes place in late May so that the first young are being fed in early June (incubation period averages 13 days) when weed seeds first become freely available. Important seeds collected by the adults in woodland and also fed to the nestlings during the breeding season include dog's mercury *Mercurialis perennis*, jack-by-the-hedge *Alliaria petiolata*, wych elm *Ulmus glabra* and in July birch *Betula alba* (data from Newton). On farmland both Summers and Newton found that different seeds were important: in particular the chickweed *Stellaria media*, various compositae including dandelion *Taraxacum officinale*, groundsel *Senecio vulgaris*, sowthistle *Sonchus oleraceus*, and also shepherd's purse *Capsella bursa-pastoris*, charlock *Sinapis arvensis* and in August fat-hen *Chenopodium album*. Many of these field seeds are eaten by the turtle dove, which also collects them from the plant. It has a very similar breeding season as comparison of Figs. 28 and 29 shows. The female bullfinch does virtually all the incubation of eggs and is fed on the nest by the cock. This also applies when small young are being brooded, the male and sometimes the female now passing some of the food to the nestlings. As the young grow and can be left unattended, both sexes collect food and bring it back to the nest about every thirty minutes, so that altogether there are about four feeds in every hour (in 224 feeds observed by Summers throughout the day, half were given by the female). However, usually the male and female forage and return to the nest together, so that the young are visited only once in every 30 minutes. This kind of feeding behaviour is typical of many seed-eating finches, particularly the linnet, greenfinch and goldfinch and arises as the compromise of various selective influences.

The marked tendency for the male and female bullfinch to visit the nest together is probably an anti-predator device reducing the number of dangerous visits to the nest, especially necessary because the male is so conspicuous. It is noticeable that bullfinches approach their nests very cautiously by a circuitous route – as do many other birds – but they leave by flying out again by the most direct route. Presumably predators are not able to refer back and calculate where a bird might have been, but they can and often do follow a bird which could by chance lead them to a good meal. A very good example is provided by the long-tailed tit, which has been well studied by D. and E. Lack. These birds are very conspicuous when nest-building and later when feeding their young. This leads jays to watch them and to find and prey on their nests very frequently. The Lacks showed that in many cases the tits' nests were ragged by jays before any eggs had been laid, which means that the jays responded to visual cues from the parents, and not to the sound or even smell of the nestlings. As a result, abortive attacks were often made. If there was a way of knowing the best time to visit a nest, it would clearly repay a jay to wait until a plump brood of young was ready to eat. But again a compromise is necessary, because by waiting too long another jay might get there first. The risks of predation for adults or their young is a very important factor which affects much of bird behaviour and other adaptations. For instance, it has long been established that most hole-nesting species hatch more of their eggs and rear a higher proportion of young than comparable species building open nests; those building domed or covered nests are inter-mediate in this respect. Relationships can also be traced within this overall pattern, so that birds which make frequent visits to their nests have a lower rearing success than species breeding in compar-able sites which reduce the number of nest visits.

Bullfinches hatch about 72% of all their eggs, if losses caused by the complete predation of a nest of eggs are included. They rear about 55% of the young they hatch and so the overall success from eggs to flying young is around 39%. Wright and Summers, in a 350-acre study area in the Weald of Kent, estimated that 34 bull-finches (17 pairs) produced about 46 fledged young (the average clutch size is 5.7 and the mean brood size immediately after hatching is 4.1 young). Hence, the mean number of young fledged at each breeding attempt, which is about three, is more than enough to provide for the replacement of adult losses, bearing in mind that two or three broods are produced a year. The ratio of young caught in woodland in autumn by mist-nets at Oxford (by Newton), and by baited Chardonneret traps in Sussex and Kent orchards (by Summers), ranges between 2 and 3 young to each adult, and these figures are in keeping with the production rate mentioned above. As a result of breeding, the bullfinch population may be almost trebled in size.

In autumn, seeds of various herbaceous plants still comprise the main diet, particularly sowthistle, various docks *Rumex* spp., fathen on farmland and bramble seed *Rubus fruticosus*, meadow sweet *Filipendula ulmaria* and elder in woodland. In addition, tree seed from the birch *Betula alba* and ash *Fraxinus excelsior* becomes increasingly more important. The birds now form small flocks which may grow to large numbers as dwindling stocks force them to congregate on local patches of suitable feed. Ash, like many other trees, does not fruit equally in all years and a good seed year is usually followed by a poor one. Hence, in some years bullfinches enjoy a good tree seed crop when the herbaceous weed seeds are finished, while in other years quite the reverse applies. In either event, when tree seeds become exhausted the birds turn to eating buds, just as wood-pigeons and geese start eating clover when stubble grain is exhausted. Fig. 32 based on Newton (1967), shows this very clearly. In a year when weed and tree seeds failed the bullfinches began feeding on buds earlier, and to a much greater extent, than in the 1962–3 winter when ash and other seeds were abundant.

Buds are a poor substitute for highly nutritive weed seeds and the birds need to eat large quantities and spend long periods in feeding in order to obtain sufficient nourishment. Even so, they may take hawthorn and gooseberry buds at an average rate of 30 per minute and can maintain an intake rate of 25 per minute when feeding on pear buds. Originally the bullfinch probably fed mainly on such buds as hawthorn, which Summers and Newton found in their crops from November to February. Summers recorded them eating larch buds from December to March, but blackthorn buds were not found until March. It seems probable that some wild buds have a higher nutritive value than others and that these are definitely preferred when available. It is now well established that the buds of cultivated fruit trees are preferred to those of wild species, almost certainly because they are larger and contain more nutrients. During feeding experiments on captive bullfinches, in which prunings of different trees were placed in the cages, Newton was able to demonstrate that the birds suffered a severe decrease in weight if fed entirely on a diet of hawthorn buds, unsupplemented by seeds; indeed he was kept extremely busy cutting branches and putting them into aviaries where his birds were housed. In January, birds fed on a diet of only hawthorn buds lost around 27% of their body weight over three days; those fed on Comice pear buds lost 16%, whereas those

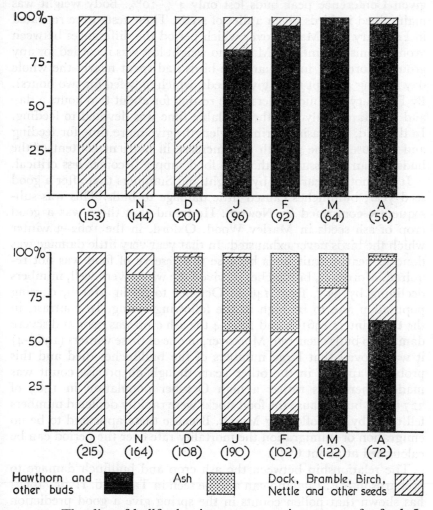

Hawthorn and other buds ■   Ash ▦   Dock, Bramble, Birch, Nettle and other seeds ▧

FIG. 32. The diet of bullfinches in two contrasting seasons for food. In the winter of 1961-2 (*above*) ash seed was not available after other weed seed supplies were exhausted and the birds transferred to feeding on various buds. In 1962-3 (*below*) ash seed was plentiful and buds featured only slightly in the winter diet. (After Newton 1967).

given Conference pear buds lost only 4%–10%. Body weight was maintained in birds given a diet of seeds. These tests were repeated in February and March, over which period the differences between groups vanished until by March no weight loss was recorded for any group. Moreover, in January the birds had spent nearly the whole day feeding (except those given seeds, which only fed for two hours). By February the bud feeders were resting for about two hours a day and by March only half the available time was devoted to feeding. In the wild, increasing spring daylengths give more time for feeding and because of the growth and increase in nutrient content of the buds, it can be assumed that the food supply becomes less critical.

It was noticed early on by Wright and Summers that after a good seed year, bullfinches caused little damage to buds. This was subsequently confirmed by Newton. He found that there was a good crop of ash seeds in Marley Wood, Oxford, in the 1962–3 winter which the birds never exhausted. In that year very little damage was done to nearby fruit buds because this reserve of food was not required. Moreover, bullfinches survived the winter very well, numbers declining by 33% from 146 in October to 98 in March, causing population size to be high in the following spring. In contrast, in the two winters 1961–2 and 1963–4 the ash crop was poor and severe damage to buds occurred. Moreover, in one of these winters (1963–4) it was proved that large numbers of the bullfinches died and this probably applied in the other year, though no precise count was made. There was rather a high October population in 1963 of 227 birds, but because the food stocks were rapidly depleted numbers fell to 74 by the following March. Because there appeared to be no emigration or immigration the mortality rate over the period can be calculated at about 67%.

The relationship between the ash crop and bullfinch damage to orchards in S.E. England can also be seen in Table 16. Hyde (1963) has shown that pollen counts in the spring give a good prediction of the state of the ash harvest, and the up and down fluctuation in bullfinch damage in parallel with the ash crop is apparent.

Again it is worthwhile making a comparison with the woodpigeon. In years when the grain supply on stubbles is exhausted early in the autumn, the pigeons transfer to clover feeding earlier than in good grain years, and the level of damage to clover is correspondingly increased. This raises an important point, because the highest level of crop damage may not occur when the highest bird-pest populations are found. In this case, control techniques such as shooting and trapping, which may only produce good results at high population densities, are not the best solution to the problem. There is the additional risk that the killing of birds while still feeding on grain or weed seeds may result in less competition for the remaining food stocks, allowing larger numbers to survive and eventually cause damage; unless, that is, it is possible to reduce numbers sufficiently to ensure that the wild food supply is never depleted. Newton also considers, and I very much agree, that it is a dangerous policy to put out surplus weed seeds in orchards, as some growers do, in the hope of decoying birds from the buds. It introduces a grave risk that the artificial food source may attract and hold an even bigger population, potentially liable to cause damage if the seed crop eventually does fail.

In a later study Newton noted that the gizzards of birds from raspberry growing areas often contained the seeds of these fruits. In some orchards these formed up to 80% of diet whereas in other areas no such feeding seemed to occur. This could be correlated with the amount of weeds present in the orchards, as in those where large numbers of weed seeds were present the birds left the raspberries alone; but this was at a season when food stocks were not limiting (see above).

Severe outbreaks of bud damage may occur rather rapidly, often taking the grower by surprise. The high feeding rate means that the birds can strip two gooseberry bushes in an hour, so that spectacular damage may occur suddenly once a flock moves into an orchard. In spite of such devastation it has not proved easy to demonstrate significant reductions in crop yields, primarily because so many other factors affect the plant between the time flower-buds open and the fruit is ready for picking. In the case of apples and pears, not every fruit that sets can be nurtured by the tree and continual losses occur as the tree sheds surplus fruit. Furthermore, wind and other agencies such as insect attack result in a proportion of the developing fruits being lost. A tree cannot lose the same fruit more than once and a bud eaten by a bullfinch cannot become a young apple harbouring some insect pest. Moreover, there is usually scope for compensatory changes in that, as the tree cannot carry more than an optimum quantity of fruit, less fruit may be shed during the growing season if much bud loss has been suffered. To complicate the matter even more, many growers do not want their trees to bear a bumper crop, since a smaller yield of larger, better quality fruit may be worth more. Indeed, the grower may himself remove surplus fruit. It is these complications that make it so difficult to estimate damage.

In one experiment Wright and Summers measured the amount of bud loss caused by bullfinches on individual trees of Conference pear, by counting samples of 100 buds on branches selected at random. The trees were all in a very uniform plantation. Their results are plotted in Fig. 33, which shows that there was no relationship between the percentage of buds damaged on the different trees in March and the final yield of fruit from these trees at harvest, despite a very wide range of bud damage. Indeed, significant reductions in final yield could not be attributed to the degree of bud damage unless this was more than 70% of all buds present. Nevertheless, it is extremely hard to convince a grower that there are circumstances in which at least half the buds may be removed from a pear tree without depressing yields.

Another complication is shown in the case of bullfinch attacks on gooseberry bushes. Wright and Summers have shown how the birds alight on the end of a branch and then feed inwards, stripping buds as they go and then moving to a new branch. In this way the terminal bud does not get eaten and it is the buds on the outside of a plant which are most severely attacked. But following such bud damage, late and intense spring frost may kill many flower-buds, although frost tends to affect the outermost unprotected branches more than the centre of the plant. Consequently, the subsequent action of frost and other agencies may cause little or no difference in yield between badly damaged and unattacked plants. The story is still not complete because, although yields in the first season may be unaffected, selective bud removal may so artificially prune the plant that a tangle of middle growth develops and the shape and value of the plant is prematurely lost.

Much bud damage can, therefore, be ignored and although an orchard can appear to be sadly devastated in spring this need not imply a reduction in crop yield. Admittedly growers may become despondent at such times and alarmist attitudes may lead to pressures for remedial action to be taken, and against such a background it is difficult to remain objective.

However, there *are* plenty of cases where damage is important. Fruit trees or bushes growing near the edge of an orchard adjacent to natural shelter belts or hedgerows are particularly prone to

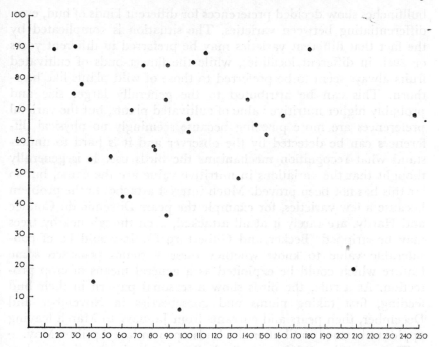

FIG. 33. Percentage of Conference pear buds eaten by bullfinches by March on different trees in a uniform orchard stand and the weight of fruit eventually harvested per tree. There is no correlation between bud damage and fruit yield $r_{29} = -0.137$. (Data supplied by Wright and Summers).

attack, partly because bullfinches are shy birds and like to sally forth from the comparative shelter of their more natural habitat. In one experiment Wright and Summers compared a plot of Leveller gooseberries growing near the edge of a plantation which had suffered damage over a period of five years, with another plot in the centre of the orchard where damage was markedly less. This variety of gooseberry does not regenerate new buds and the experiment was therefore comparing the effects of cumulative damage. The total fruit yield in the centre plot was 672 lb. compared with 197 lb. in the badly attacked area. Though the fruit quality was better in the plot which produced less, it by no means compensated for the reduced yield.

Quite apart from showing a preference for the edge of the orchard, bullfinches show decided preferences for different kinds of bud, even differentiating between varieties. The situation is complicated by the fact that different varieties may be preferred in different years or even in different localities, while the flower-buds of cultivated fruits always seem to be preferred to those of wild plants like hawthorn. This can be attributed to the generally larger size and probably higher nutritive value of cultivated plants, but the varietal preferences are more puzzling because seemingly no physical differences can be detected by the observer and it is hard to understand what recognition mechanisms the birds use. It is generally thought that the variations in nutritive value are the cause, but so far this has not been proved. Much interest attaches to the problem because a few varieties, for example the pears Doyenne du Comice and Hardy, are rarely if at all attacked, even though nearby trees may be stripped (Becker and Gilbert 1958). It would be of considerable value to know whether these varieties possessed some feature which could be exploited as a general means of crop protection. As a rule, the birds show a seasonal pattern in their bud feeding, first taking plums and gooseberries in November and December, then pears and currants from January to March leaving apples unharmed until after the buds open in late April or May.

The worst time of the year for bullfinches is clearly winter, when weed seeds are at their lowest ebb, and bud feeding becomes necessary and many birds die. This being the case, it seems highly unlikely that Britain could support an immigrant population of bullfinches from Europe. Rather it would be expected that some British birds might be better off if they left Britain during the bad season. All the same, growers were convinced that much of their winter damage was caused by immigrants – the attitude that things are somehow better if you can blame a foreigner seems deeply ingrained in our psychological make-up. However, all the evidence shows that no such immigration occurs, and the British population seems to be strictly resident. Of 336 recoveries of British ringed birds, 93% had moved less than 5 miles (87% less than 3 miles) while only 4% had travelled more than 16 miles (Summers unpubl.). The European subspecies *Pyrrhula p. coccinea* can be distinguished from the British race by wing measurements and by the density and distribution of the breast colour. Six hundred birds shot in south-east England and examined by Dr J. M. Harrison were all of the typical British form – further, if negative, evidence against an influx of continental birds.

PLATE 23. The herring gull, *above*, has increased as a scavenger of rubbish tips and human waste. The very closely related lesser black-back gull, *below*, has increased less dramatically. It avoids competition with the herring gull in winter by emigrating, but recently more individuals have been able to over-winter in Britain.

PLATE 24. The auks are very vulnerable to oiling because, on sighting a slick, they dive and are liable to surface in the middle if it is at all extensive. Puffins, *above*, razorbills, *below*, have declined in the south of their range, partly in consequence of climatic changes affecting the distribution of fish stocks, but seriously aggravated by unnecessary mortality through oil pollution.

Wright and Summers have developed a trapping technique for bullfinches using a modified Chardonneret trap baited with the seed heads of the sharp dock *Rumex conglomeratus* or of the red or bloody-veined dock *R. sanguineus*. The method is highly selective from December until March when over 85%, and usually over 90%, of the captures are bullfinches. It is debatable whether trapping on the scale realised in practice does more than crop the population and allow infiltration from nearby areas. Growers often catch more birds in a season than can ever be present at any one time, and so must be 'milking' the population from a much wider area. If such trapping were curtailed it would not necessarily cause the number of birds in an area to increase. Growers frequently use modified Chardonneret traps baited with decoy birds, and these are highly selective towards juveniles. Thus Summers found in orchards that the ratio of young to old bullfinches caught between December and March was 1.4:1 with normal traps, while over exactly the same period and in the same areas, decoys caught a ratio of 12.0:1. Similarly, when decoys were used by growers, Newton found that for every one adult there were 38 young caught between October and December, 4 between January and February and 21 from March to April, but the ratio in a mist-netted sample declined from 3:1 to 2:1 over the same period. Only during the period of hard weather and shortest food supplies from January to February did the proportion of old birds caught approach a level which represented their true ratio. Such a persistently biased capture of young makes it extremely unlikely that the growers were in fact managing to control the population – otherwise all young must eventually have been removed causing their ratio in the population to fall as only adults were left to be caught.

In Britain, several other birds may occasionally cause trouble in orchards by destroying buds, though often they are only seeking insects living in the bud. Titmice, goldfinch and greenfinch have all been incriminated, but the house sparrow is the only other species which regularly causes damage in orchards on a scale to warrant concern, especially near habitations. A particularly irritating feeding habit of both bullfinches and house sparrows is taking the buds of ornamental plants, particularly forsythia, and the cultivated *Crataegus*, *Malus* and *Prunus* species; and countless gardeners have long deplored the sparrow's liking for the flower-buds of *Polyanthus*.

In New Zealand, in the absence of the bullfinch the introduced

European redpoll has taken to eating the opening flower-buds of fruit trees in the spring, particularly in the orchard districts of central Otago. The birds alight on a lateral branch and hop along taking each bud in turn in the same manner as the bullfinch (Stenhouse 1962, Hawkins and Bull, 1962). Apricot trees have suffered the most damage. In Britain, redpolls normally take a few birch buds in winter, though their main diet consists of birch seeds, as well as other small seeds (Newton 1967). Bud-feeding becomes much more marked in spring from March to May, and although a few buds are actually eaten, Newton has shown that the birds are primarily concerned with finding the small invertebrates that live among the opening flower petals. It seems highly probable that the bud-eating habit in New Zealand originally developed from this search for invertebrate food, a view strengthened by the fact that the birds do not interfere much with the buds until they are well open, when the petals can harbour various insects. This does not alter the fact that the birds do pull off and destroy many of the buds. In April 1965, similar behaviour was noted in England on a large fruit farm near Canterbury, Kent. According to Newton about 1,000 redpolls were involved in damage to pear trees, some of which had nearly half their buds destroyed. The redpolls left the orchard when the ground was ploughed and the fat-hen on which they had been mainly feeding was removed.

In New Zealand, it was noticed that redpolls were attracted to heaps of seed cleanings which had been dumped in the orchard; and tests soon established that the birds had a marked preference for fat-hen and timothy grass *Phleum pratense* seeds. Piles of waste seed were accordingly used to pre-bait the birds in early winter. When large numbers were feeding, timothy seed poisoned with H.E.T.P. (hexa-ethyl-tetra-phosphate) was laid and resulted in a high catch. Later in the season when food became generally more abundant such poisoning was less successful. Instead of poisoning the birds, clap-nets were successfully placed near the seed tips and in some instances over 90% of the birds at risk were captured. At one research orchard 475 redpolls were netted, 222 poisoned and 72 shot between July and October, and this scale of destruction is said to have reduced damage to negligible proportions. The trapping technique seems to have been fairly selective and of 2,500 birds so taken in the district only 12 were not redpolls.

BIRD DAMAGE TO RIPE FRUIT

Bird damage to ripe, hard fruit is often annoying to the grower, for in most cases there is no question of the plant making good any losses, especially if damage occurs close to harvest, after other agencies like wind and wasps have already taken their toll of the fruit. Many species, including rook, magpie, jay and mistle thrush may occasionally and casually peck at ripe fruit. Generally the main offenders are starling, blackbird, song thrush, house sparrow and blue tit. Tits, especially the blue tit and coal tit, naturally obtain some of their food by hammering at buds and tree galls, and their predation of *Ernamonia* larvae living in pine cones has already been mentioned. Pecking at ripe fruit seems to be an extension of this behaviour. Of the thrushes, it is notable that Hartley in a widescale inquiry found that only blackbird and fieldfare were regular feeders on wild crab apples during times of shortage of their preferred invertebrate foods, and both these species are regular feeders on the heaps of waste apples in orchards. Occasionally, too, comparative rarities like the crossbill will plague the horticulturist. Matthew Paris, the Monk of St Albans, records how during an irruption of the species in 1251, flocks did immense damage to apple orchards in the west country, already famous for their cider production. The birds lacerated the apples to get at the kernels.

A small hole in an apple or pear can provide a site where a wasp can begin feeding or where disease can later become established. In spite of these secondary consequences of bird attack, bird damage to hard fruits is not generally important and only exceptionally does damage reach a level where remedial action is necessary. Occasionally, small clumps of trees grown in isolation or near natural cover attract more attention and Wright and Brough, who have studied the problem, recorded cases where 19% of the fruit had been pecked by birds and its market value considerably reduced. The authors consider that bird damage to buds is much more important than damage to the ripe hard fruit.

Wright and Brough (1966) counted the number of apples and pears that had already been pecked by birds by the time the fruit was harvested in the 1961–63 picking seasons. Their results are given in Table 17 and refer to thirteen orchards distributed throughout Kent, Sussex, Hampshire, Berkshire and Oxfordshire. Actually these figures exaggerate the amount of damage because if there was any doubt about the origin of a hole it was attributed to birds. In this way some damage due to wind and insects has been included. During this study the varieties Cox and Bowden's Seedling were more prone to attack from blue tits than from other bird species, the blue tits being more adept at perching on the somewhat inaccessible fruit. Apples and pears attacked by tits are characterised by a small hole and in 1961 2.6% of the apples examined (17,675 apples) had such damage as against 0.3% (40,050 apples sampled) in 1962. Over 80% of the damage to Conference pears could also be attributed to tits, whereas large birds were mainly the cause of damage to Worcester Permain, Laxton's Fortune and Lord Lambourne apples. The drooping branches of these varieties provide better perches for less agile species such as the starling and blackbird, and those of Lord Lambourne make it particularly prone to bird attack. In one plot of this variety which was sampled, 60% of the holes could be attributed to 'large' birds as against only 18% in comparable plots of Cox's orange pipin where blue tits caused most damage.

In 1957, Wright records that damage to ripe fruit was particularly severe, and noted individual trees with up to 25% of their fruits pecked. The outbreak was correlated with an unusual irruption of tits, particularly blue and great tits, following the 1957 breeding season, which in turn resulted from a particularly high survival of birds over the previous winter. The irruption has been very thoroughly detailed by Cramp, Pettet and Sharrock, who showed that a similar population explosion also occurred in north-west Europe leading to a big immigration of continental birds into Britain in the autumn. The invasion started in September and reached a peak in October, with a return passage lasting from January to mid-May 1958. In addition, there was a marked increase in the movements of British birds, judging from ringing recoveries: the number which moved more than 10 miles doubled, while there was a threefold increase in the number of birds travelling more than 30 miles. At Oxford, where Lack and his colleagues have studied the blue and great tit for many years, there was a marked increase in the breeding population in 1957, the result of a low mortality the previous winter.

The complex ecological background which may underlie bird damage is well illustrated in this case. Blue and great tits fluctuate in parallel with each other and both fluctuate synchronously over a wide area of north-west Europe. These fluctuations depend on the mortality of juveniles between leaving the nest and the beginning of winter and this mortality appears to anticipate the forthcoming beech mast crop which the birds will only later feed upon. This, as Lack suggests, is presumably because both birds and beech mast are initially affected by the same, probably climatic, conditions. Conditions in one year may give rise to high breeding populations in the next season which can then be followed by very high post-breeding numbers. Before this surplus dies circumstances exist for outbreaks of damage, apparently caused by general food shortage and the birds' need to find new food sources. Lack also recorded a high breeding population in 1960 followed by an unusually high density in 1961, numbers dropping to a more normal level in 1962. It is interesting to note that the general incidence of bird damage to ripe fruit in the years closely studied by Brough followed the same pattern, although from the data available a causal relationship cannot be proved.

To put bird damage to hard fruit into proper perspective it should be noted that of 8,828 apples harvested at East Malling in 1965, 429 had to be rejected and birds could only be blamed for harming 27 of these. Insects accounted for the loss of 6 of the apples, a small rodent for one, and the remainder (395) were rejected because they were cracked or bruised. In relation to total losses, bird damage was very slight.

Apples and pears ripen late in the season when there is plenty of natural food on which the various birds prefer to feed. This is not the case earlier in the year and certain soft fruits such as the currants and cherries may become important sources of food for several bird species. These fruits ripen in June and July when summer droughts seriously reduce the ground living and soil invertebrates on which the thrushes and starlings depend. Further, it is at this time that the population is swollen with large numbers of young birds eagerly seeking food. Most of these are doomed to die during the summer months but this mortality may be delayed as long as the soft fruits last. Attempts to effect a lasting reduction in population size by killing those birds which cause damage will be unsuccessful because numbers are not ultimately determined by fruit stocks. Nevertheless, provided the killing is limited to the site and season of damage it may do some good in removing individuals that could cause considerable losses before dying from natural causes. The need to confine such

artificial killing to the place of damage is also rendered more imperative by the fact that damage is usually related to the season and
availability of natural food, and not to population size *per se* (as in
the case of bullfinch attack on raspberry seeds, see page 217). In
Europe, starlings can be particularly troublesome in vineyards, and
the introduced starlings of Australia have taken these 'bad habits'
with them and some growers in the Sunraysia district of the Murray
River basin estimate losses of two tons per season.

Just as birds seem to favour particular varieties of buds, so they
are sometimes prone to eat certain fruit varieties more than others.
It is not simply a matter of the birds having preferences for these
varieties because there is evidence that the choice of foods available
in an area helps determine the birds' tendency to concentrate on any
one kind: in other words, availability and the choice situation helps
determine the development of the bird's food image. Brown (1969)
mentions that he has evidence that the damage done by starlings to
cherry orchards in N. America depends on the combination of fruit
varieties planted.

Some people are fortunate enough to have their cherries eaten by
the hawfinch! This bird is highly specialised to feeding on the kernels
of fruit stones and other hard seeds which occur in the natural oak-
hornbeam forests it frequents. Its diet comprises a high proportion
of hornbeam seeds, acorns, wych-elm seed, beech mast and also
stones of the wild cherries *Prunus cerasus*, *P. avium* (Gean) and *P.
padus* (Bird Cherry), as well as tree buds and invertebrates. Cherry
orchards provide a big attraction, though Mountfort, who has
described the biology of this species, states that the bird normally
waits until the cherries have fallen to the ground and relies on the
stones as a winter food source. When seen in isolation it is difficult
to imagine how such a bright bird can so easily escape attention. Its
colouring is similar to that of the jay, another oak-canopy inhabitant.
Oak woodland has a distinctly red caste and it is possible that by
convergence both species have acquired the same cryptic colouring.
A book entitled *Fruiterers Secrets* published in 1604, refers to bird
damage to cherries, and after mentioning the jay says, 'The other
which is called a Bullfinch, will eat stones and all day you shall heare
her chirpe before she lights upon the tree'. This could not have meant
the bullfinch and was certainly a reference to the hawfinch, the
suggestion of wariness being particularly apt. In those days there
was much overlap in the names applied to birds. Mountfort refers to

a statement by Sir Thomas Browne (1605–82) that the hawfinch in Norfolk 'is chiefly seen in summer about cherrietime'.

In the Tiptree district of Essex strawberries are intensively grown in a small area of about four square miles which was once heathland and adjoins a nearby common. Linnets, which of course frequent this kind of habitat, were first reported taking the seeds from the ripe fruits in 1950, since when the number of attacks seems to have increased somewhat, while the birds even nest among the growing strawberry plants as well as in gorse bushes on the nearby common. W. H. Edgar spent some time investigating the problem and noted that at dawn blackbirds were the first species to visit the crops, followed by linnets which then spent the day flying backwards and forwards in ones and twos to feed on the strawberries. In addition, turtle doves, song thrushes and house sparrows also did some damage. Half the smallholders in the district had suffered linnet damage and it proved particularly difficult to scare the birds as they had grown used to the fruit-pickers and would feed only 25 yards away from them. Black cotton was shown to give protection from the birds, but hindered the fruit-pickers. Once the seed is picked out of the fruit the rest is liable to rot and in any case is ruined for marketing. Brown (1961) in discussing this problem has pointed out that the strawberry seed beetle *Harpalus rufipes* causes very similar damage and that the wrong culprit can be and often is blamed in retrospect. Beetle damage is usually confined to fruit growing near the ground and frequently the insects tear the fruit apart in extracting the seed. Linnets take seeds from the exposed surfaces of the fruit on any part of the plant, but they prefer to tackle the varieties which have very prominent pips, such as Talisman and Cambridge Favourite. In the same district, linnets are also a nuisance on crops grown for seed – a paradise for the birds but a nightmare for the grower. In particular the seed heads of savoy, candy-tuft and forget-me-nots may be visited by flocks of up to 500 birds.

Pied wagtails sometimes raise an unusual horticultural problem by resorting in large numbers to roost in greenhouses. Conditions in the stable yard and other places where manure is accumulated give rise to a high concentration of invertebrate food especially in the form of the hovering flies. In the absence of perches, a bird must catch the flies by making short sallies from the ground and for this method of feeding the pied wagtail is well adapted. It is the existence of a similar food source that attracts a high density of pied wagtails at many sewage farms. Good feeding conditions may attract the wagtails to greenhouses in the first place but their use of such places for roosting seems to reflect a more general tendency among several species to resort to urban areas to roost. Safety from predators and greater protection from cold may be important reasons and this subject will be dealt with again in Chapter 11. Boswall has studied the problem in some detail and notes that greenhouse roosting was first documented by Bunyard in 1936 for a site at Canterbury, Kent. In response to a request for information, which he published in *The Grower and Prepacker* and *The Commercial Grower* in 1965, records of roosts inside greenhouses at 18 sites were received, to which another four known records could be added. These embraced counties as far apart as Co. Dublin and Essex, Yorkshire and Dorset. At one site in Middlesex up to 500 birds had roosted annually in autumn over a period of about thirty years.

Minton (1960) has described a large roost of between 600 and 800 birds in greenhouses at Milton, Cambridge. The habit apparently developed in the early 1850s and the roost was mainly occupied from July to November, with smaller numbers present in the spring. As in many other cases, the houses were used for tomato growing and the birds roosted on both the plants and their supporting wires, causing considerable damage by fouling the small plants in spring and the ripe fruits in late summer. At this roost 453 birds were caught and ringed in September and October 1959, of which about half proved to be first-winter birds. It was evident that the roost drew birds from a wide area because one ringed bird was caught seven miles away the day after it was ringed, and ringed birds were also seen following the plough on farms up to nine miles from Milton. This large roost dispersed to several more typical small reed-bed roosts when the greenhouses were closed at the end of the growing season in late October. Some of the birds evidently came originally from such local roosts, because a few birds marked at these places in previous years turned up at the greenhouse site. Passage birds were also involved for one bird ringed in September 1959 was recovered in southern Spain in October.

Another wagtail roost, reported by Cohen (1960), was established at Sway in Hampshire, where this time the greenhouses were used for growing carnations. The roosting habit began originally in the early fifties when small numbers of birds nested among the growing plants. Their numbers gradually increased to such an extent that the birds were breaking many blossoms, and fouling was so extensive that the staff refused to pick the blooms. In this case the owner had to close all but one of his fourteen greenhouses, forcing the birds to use the only open one. This was left closed one morning when the birds were inside. It was estimated that up to 600 birds were killed in this way. This was done in 1958 and there was no more trouble from the birds in 1959, though numbers subsequently began to build up again. It is easy to deplore this scale of killing but the man concerned was certainly suffering very severe damage and his livelihood was being threatened; and this might enable him to defend himself successfully under Section 4(2)d of the 1954 Protection of Birds Act. An obvious answer might have been to use some kind of proofing, but in fact this is not at all easy. Ventilation for growing carnations is extremely critical and is impaired by protective nets, which accumulate dirt. In any case the birds are not casually trying to gain access to the greenhouses, they enter very purposefully and are not easily deterred by obstructions.

On two occasions owls (a little owl was specifically identified at one site), and on one occasion a cat, gained access to pied wagtails roosting in a greenhouse and slaughtered virtually all the occupants, which seems to oppose the view that these places provide safety from predators. At many sites man also actively kills the birds. Minton noted wagtails returning to a greenhouse in severe February weather, the same occurred in Essex, and Bunyard noted the birds actually sitting in close rows on the hot water pipes of a greenhouse. This summary from Boswall suggests that shelter from the elements is the main reason for the greenhouse roosting habit.

CHAPTER 10

BIRDS AND THE FISHERMAN

THE GULLS

IT may seem incongruous that the niches for scavenging birds which exploit the countless rubbish tips throughout the country have been filled by seabirds. Yet the opportunism displayed by herring, black-headed and common gulls has been rewarded by the absence of competition from a better adapted scavenging land bird. When Capello visited London in 1496–7 he marvelled at the large numbers of ravens and kites which were suffered to help clean up the city garbage. The kites were then so bold that they would sometimes snatch a man's cap for nesting material and housewives had to stand guard over their washing – Autolycus exclaims in the *Winter's Tale* 'When the kite builds, look to lesser linen'. Capello reported 'they often take out of the hands of little children, the bread smeared with butter, in the Flemish fashion, given to them by their mothers'. Improvements in hygiene and the persecution of both these species during the nineteenth century caused them to disappear from most parts of the country leaving no land species to prosper from the increased waste of the twentieth century. The gulls have proved ideal replacements for the kite, as they have the same ability to watch out for likely food sources from aloft and then to hover and plunge when they notice suitable foods – today they can be seen snatching bread from the hands of people along the Embankment, as the kites did before them. The gull's opportunism and adaptability is constantly displayed; following the plough on farmland, hovering over tree-tops to collect insects, and even waiting in lay-bys in Scotland to collect the scraps from picnicking motorists.

The enormous increases and range expansion of the gulls in recent years are without doubt primarily a result of man's activities, but these cannot always be readily distinguished from the more profound influences of climatic change and long-term ecological interactions. The recent climate amelioration may well have helped the

great black-backed gull to spread further north to Spitsbergen and
Greenland to replace the resident glaucous gull. In the same way
the herring gull spread to Iceland in 1927, Bear Island in 1932
and Spitsbergen in 1950 and the common gull first reached Iceland in 1955. The black-headed gull too has expanded throughout
Europe.

The herring and lesser black-backed gulls provide an interesting
illustration of the complex changes in progress. These so-called
'ring-species', which provide one of the textbook examples of speciation in progress, have arisen from a common ancestor whose initial
range cannot now be determined (possibly it was in the Bering
Straits), but which expanded to the east and west gradually evolving
slight differences in the process. The ends of the chain meet in
Britain where morphological and behavioural differences are
sufficient to prevent interbreeding, although there exists a circumpolar chain of ten recognisable subspecies linking these two extremes.
Both species are adapted to collecting various intertidal and littoral
invertebrates, and the smaller fish by plunge-diving. Records
collected and collated by Harris (1965) suggest that such molluscs
as species of *Patella* (Limpet), *Mytilus* (mussel), *Cardium* (cockle),
Tellina, *Sepia* (cuttlefish), crabs of the genera *Cancer* and *Carcinus* and
the star-fish *Asterias*, are the most important of the natural foods.
Apart from their coastal feeding, these gulls frequent arable land,
particularly in the autumn and spring when earthworms are abundant. The herring gull seems to be a more efficient scavenger of
human fishing and other waste, so that even today the lesser black-
backed gull, according to Harris, does not visit the fish market at
Milford Haven, beloved of the herring gulls. The herring gull has
been increasing, but although the lesser black-backed gull is changing
some of its habits, its numbers seem to have remained more constant.

At the breeding colonies ecological separation is evident from the
fact that the herring gull prefers cliffs and steep sides of dunes and
islands, whereas the black-back favours the flat tops of the islands.
The lesser black-back seems more aggressive than the herring gull
and takes a higher proportion of animal food in the form of nestlings
of other seabirds such as puffins and shearwaters, young rabbits,
small mammals and ground-living invertebrates. That interspecific
competition between these two gulls is important during the winter
is shown by the fact that the herring gull manages to remain a com-

plete resident, whereas virtually all lesser black-backs move south to winter on the Iberian coast. In contrast, Harris (1964) has shown from ringing recoveries that the major herring gull colonies are surrounded by well defined areas, usually not extending more than 70 miles, in which the bulk of ringing recoveries occur. These winter grounds have been called local dispersion zones by Poulding, and include areas densely populated by man. For example, the South Wales industrial complex is mostly frequented by birds from Lundy, Skokholm or Skomer, and the Liverpool conurbation serves as a wintering area for herring gulls from Puffin Island, Anglesey. In these urban areas, garbage dumps appear to provide the chief attraction. A further complication in the ecology of these two species is that the juvenile and immature birds favour rather different feeding grounds from the adults and, in particular, are far more attracted to the intertidal zone. Phillips (1962) showed that plumage differences between the age groups are adaptive in that the white plumage of the adults facilitates a close approach to fish when plunge-diving, whereas the inexperienced immatures do not at first adopt this method of feeding; their brown mottled plumage is cryptic in the intertidal zone where predatory attacks from skuas and the white-tailed eagle may once have provided the predation pressure. Contrasting with the *Larus* gulls, the kittiwake is at all times an oceanic feeder, or at least it was until recently (see below), where immatures could not afford to be very differently coloured from the adults; accordingly, kittiwakes have white underparts and heads from their first juvenile plumage.

Today it is far from easy to define the ecological differences which enable the herring and lesser black-backed gulls to co-exist, because each has modified its feeding habits, and the lesser black-back, to a small extent, its migratory habits also. Barnes conducted two national investigations into the wintering status of the lesser black-back in Britain. Between 1949–52 a small but apparently increasing number of these gulls, principally adults, wintered in Britain. The main concentrations were in Morecambe Bay, near Leeds and in the London, Bristol and Cardiff districts, and just over 300 birds were involved. By 1959–60 the total had risen to 2,800, the increase being especially noticeable in the London area and West Midlands. Moreover, at least three-quarters of the wintering birds were adults, or at least fourth-years, of the British subspecies (*Larus fuscus graellsii*). The commonest habitat for over-wintering black-backs seems to be on refuse tips, but many birds collect natural food, chiefly earthworms, from fields (often playing fields) and sewage farms. Shore-feeding is rarely seen and Barnes has suggested that in winter the short days may restrict accessibility to the mollusc *Tellina*. This mostly frequents the lower shore, so that during winter maximum availability would be along coasts where low water of spring tides occurs at midday. In addition, the shore crab *Carcinus maenas* may also be less likely to move on to the shore in winter (Naylor 1962).

By 1962, when Hickling (1967) organised yet another survey, 7,000 lesser blackbacks were wintering in England. To a large extent this increase seems to depend on the change in migratory habits, because many more sub-adults are spending the late summer months on inland reservoirs and are then staying to winter instead of moving south.

All local bird reports testify to the enormous increase of the herring gull this century, and Parslow believes that it may have doubled its numbers in the last twenty years. One of the biggest colonies today, at Walney Island, Lancashire, had 35 pairs in 1934, 700 pairs in 1950, 12,000 in 1957, and 18–19,000 pairs by 1966. Brown (1967) has demonstrated that the fecundity of this local population cannot account for the rate of increase and that immigration from other colonies – possibly Puffin Island in Anglesey – has been partly responsible for the increase. In Holland, the herring gull increased from about 10,000 pairs during the period 1925–30 to 26,000 in 1938 after which poisoning at the colonies was undertaken (using bread or eggs treated with strychnine nitrate) and about 10,000 adults were killed annually. Following the war, numbers averaged 19–20,000 between 1949 and 1955, and large numbers of eggs, young and adults, were destroyed each year. Thus 12,000 were killed in 1954, 10,000 in 1955 and 7,300 in 1956. Bruyns (1958) reckons that in the absence of control, 8,000 immatures would survive until 3–4 years old to arrive at the breeding colonies and replace a total adult loss of only 6,000 (based on a 15% adult mortality). This means that the intensive killing, with up to a quarter of the breeding population removed each year, may have prevented a population increase between 1946 and 1954. The extra effort made in 1954 and 1955 seems to have brought about an actual decrease, but this was not continued in 1956 so that numbers increased again in 1957. The immigration of birds from outside Holland was presumably involved.

These data illustrate the enormous amount of slaughter needed to deal with a relatively small bird population under the easiest of conditions, in other words with a colonial nester with a fairly low fecundity.

In the United States the situation is similar. In New England the herring gull was rare in the latter half of the nineteenth century as people cropped the eggs and young for food and sold skins to the plumage trade. There followed protection measures in the 1890s, coincident with a decrease of human pressure as the old fishing economy changed. These later changes have allowed the breeding gull population to increase from around 4–8,000 pairs in 1900 to 115,000 pairs in 1966, numbers having doubled roughly every 12–15 years (Drury 1965, Kadlec and Drury 1968). Earlier, estimates of the death rate of these gulls based on ringing recoveries over-estimated the true value because it was not realised that many gulls lost their rings, particularly after the age of four years. A low rate of natural loss in the first autumn and winter necessarily had to be postulated to reconcile the known productivity with the number needed to replace adult losses. In consequence, people concluded that attempts at inhibiting reproduction would result in a population decline, and various attempts were made to treat eggs so that they would not hatch.

Between 1938 and 1952, following complaints about gulls, the U.S. Fish and Wildlife Service contracted A. O. Gross to attempt the inhibition of reproduction, and this he did by spraying eggs with a mixture of high grade oil and formaldehyde. On thirteen islands in Maine, where Gross personally supervised the programme, the breeding population began to decrease after a 4–5-year delay, but after 10 years the decline ceased. It seems that the disturbance associated with spraying in Maine caused many gulls to move elsewhere, in particular to Massachusetts, and that after a delay of one or two years they began breeding again at new sites. There is therefore no evidence that the inhibition of reproduction *per se* has resulted in artificial regulation of numbers. Indeed, it is now realised that a programme of egg sterilisation carried on for 10 years with an 80–90% efficiency (a very high level) would prevent further population increase, but would not reduce the present winter gull population. Similarly, killing 100,000 gulls on the coast would have insufficient effect to be detected by the public in nearby metropolitan areas. As in Britain, the New England herring gulls appear to be chiefly resident in winter, and they depend heavily on man-made food resources in the form of local refuse dumps, pig farms, fish piers, and so on.

In Britain various people and organisations have attempted to control gulls by taking their eggs. The decline of black-headed gulls from 5–6,000 pairs down to 500–1,000 in the R.S.P.B. reserve at Havergate has been claimed to result from egg pricking, but is more likely to have resulted from the birds moving elsewhere. Indeed, plate 22 was obtained at a site to which some of these birds were probably displaced on the opposite shores of the Butley river from Havergate. As the adult death rate of gulls is only 5–10% per annum, only 5–10 young per 100 adults need survive to maintain stability. The adults live for ten years so only need rear two young over such a period, and it would require very diligent interference to prevent them achieving this low level of production.

The much larger great black-backed gull seems to be well separated ecologically from the lesser black-backed and herring gulls. Its winter diet needs more study although it is known to take much carrion and fish offal. In summer it preys on the young of other gulls and the adults of other seabirds, particularly shearwaters and puffins; mammals including young rabbits are also a favoured food. On Skokholm, between 633 and 1,426 shearwater corpses were found per annum in the breeding seasons of 1960–3. As there were only 10–12 pairs of breeding gulls, Harris reckoned that many of these deaths were caused by a flock of non-breeding individuals. On Skomer, Buxton and Lockley (1950) estimated that 60 pairs of great black-backs killed 2,500 adult and young shearwaters in one season, while Mylne (1960) put the figure as high as 8–10,000 per year. It is extremely difficult to calculate the true figure, but it is apparent that these gulls remove a substantial proportion of the total breeding population of shearwaters which numbers about 35,000 pairs on Skokholm. Davis (1958) has estimated the summer population to be between 4,000 and 5,000 great black-backs in England and Wales of which about 3,600 are breeding adults, but the situation in Scotland is unknown. Rocky coasts in the west are preferred, nesting records being sparse between Hampshire and Cornwall. The highest breeding numbers occur in Pembrokeshire and in adjoining areas of Wales and the Bristol Channel. Areas which were compared directly in 1930 and 1956 in Davis's survey indicate that there has been a three-fold increase in population size. The species is mostly sedentary, as the adults remain near their nesting colonies and the juveniles do not often move more than 50 miles.

The most numerous gulls in winter, and those most impinging on man, are the black-headed and common gulls. Hickling (1960) received details from 98 coastal roosts in England and Wales in 1955–6 involving about 441,000 gulls. Of these 43% were black-heads, 40% commons, 14% herrings and 3% great black-backs; common gulls were found in large numbers at only a few roosts and in most they formed no more than one-third of the total. Similarly there were only a few roosts with more than 200 great black-backs. In another survey a few years earlier (1952–3) Hickling had records of about 330,000 gulls which roosted inland in England and Wales, and of these 70% were black-heads, 14% common gulls, 10% herring gulls, the remainder comprising a few great and lesser black-backs. The majority of these inland roosting gulls were concentrated in East Anglia and on the London reservoirs. According to Mrs Radford (1960), the British breeding stock of common gulls (nearly all breed in Scotland) is mostly sedentary while the young individuals disperse south to south-west, and none appears to go abroad. Most of the winter visitors to East Anglia and the south came from Scandinavia, Denmark and north Germany. Mrs Radford (1962) has shown that roughly the same applies to the black-headed gull, except that more young birds disperse to coastal France and Portugal, and some seem to winter inland in Spain. Winter visitors in south-east England originate in Denmark, and those in northern England from Scandinavia.

When this survey of inland roosting was repeated in the winter of 1962–3 evidence of a 50% increase was obtained with around 504,000 gulls being recorded. Now, 62% were black heads, 25% common gulls, 11% herring gulls, with lesser and great black backs 1% each. Hickling (1967) who was again responsible for the survey, makes the important point that changes in methods of disposing of refuse may be important in providing food sources for the gulls. Quite apart from a general increase in the amount of refuse from an expanding and more affluent human population, more rubbish is disposed in open controlled tipping rather than by being burnt in destructors; in Leicester alone 20% of the refuse was tipped in 1936, 51% in 1939 and 80% in 1955.

Some of the best evidence for the increase of gulls in Britain comes from the 1958 census of the black-head in England and Scotland

PLATE 25. Two seabirds which have increased, apparently in consequence of the extra food made available as waste from the trawler industry. *Above*, fulmar, *below*, kittiwake.

PLATE 26. *Above left*, gannets have increased since persecution by man in the nineteenth century reduced the world population by two-thirds. *Right*, sea-birds like the sandwich tern which nest in large colonies are much more amenable to protection than those like the little tern, *below*, which nests in small scattered colonies round our coasts. The latter has suffered through the increased demands being made on our beaches for leisure.

organised by Gribble and Hamilton respectively. In England and Wales, 185 colonies held between 46,000 and 52,000 pairs, an increase of 25% since 1938 when Hollom conducted a similar inquiry. Most of the change resulted from increases in south-east England, at inland colonies. Similar increases also occurred during the first decennia of this century in Denmark, Norway, Sweden, Finland and France and by 1961 there were between 65,000 and 95,000 breeding pairs of black-heads in Holland and another 15,000 to 22,000 in Belgium (Higler 1961). In Britain, much of the increase has occurred at man-made sites; sugar beet factories, flooded clay and gravel pits. That a man-made, rather than climatic, causation is involved is suggested by the fact that numbers have mostly increased in the populous south-east of England. In Scotland, complete coverage was not possible. However, of ten colonies studied accurately in both years, only one showed an increase. In an expanding population, one way for the black-headed gull to increase its productivity would be for it to begin breeding before reaching the usual two years of age, and this may be happening to a greater extent. With a reduced natural mortality the selective disadvantages attached to early breeding would assume less importance.

For most of the time the gulls are only harmless commensals of man. Sometimes they pose local problems, as in Hertfordshire where they carried small tins and pieces of plastic to fields adjoining rubbish tips, causing farmers concern for the safety of their cattle. When roosting or feeding on or near aerodromes they constitute a potential air-strike hazard. Otherwise their major offence is the fouling of man's buildings and structures. For instance, herring gulls have taken to nesting on buildings in some towns, and their tenacity to these new colonies causes some residents much disturbance from their calls and the expense of unblocking gutters of surplus nesting material. War-time restrictions made many seaside towns acceptable as nesting areas, and a herring gull colony with twenty nests was established on Brighton West Pier where the birds made use of 'army surplus' kapok for building their nests (Boswall 1947). Nests on buildings were also established at other places as far apart as Newquay, Cornwall, and Bridlington, Yorkshire. According to Took one or two pairs of herring gulls were nesting on a roof-top near the entrance to the eastern harbour at Dover before 1939. Extensive war damage encouraged the birds to move into the town itself and by 1954 no less than 200 pairs were nesting on rebuilt buildings, fouling the roofs and blocking drains and gutters. Other examples could also be given and the habit seems to be increasing. A slightly unusual complaint against gulls has been occasioned by a large colony of lesser black-backs which nest on a Lancashire moor and allegedly interfere with the owner's grouse-rearing programme. The importance of gulls in disease dissemination requires more investigation, and they are known to be intermediate hosts in the life cycles of certain cestodes and trematodes which infest fish.

Man has also praised the Laridae. It was seriously suggested during the First World War, both in Britain and America, that gulls be trained as submarine spotters. Eminent sailors believed that the gulls might be trained at first by tying fish to submarines. The Mormons of Salt Lake City, Utah, erected a monument in their Temple Grounds to the Californian gull, as it was supposed to have saved the crops of the early pioneers from a plague of crickets. Gradually a social taboo developed which restrained the bird's destruction, but caused embarrassment and a change of attitude when the gulls more recently started taking cultivated cherries in Davis County; even the saints may sin.

The kittiwake has been increasing geometrically at a rate of 3% per annum since the turn of the century, at first expanding within existing colonies and later creating new ones. Coulson (1963) reckons that neither climatic amelioration – the bird is a northern species at the southern limit of its range in Britain – nor changes in food supply explain the increase. He and White have pointed out that the colony at Flamborough Head, probably the biggest in Britain for several hundred years, was drastically reduced in the nineteenth century after being over-exploited by commercial egg collectors – the same was true of other colonies. Any slow breeding seabird with a low recruitment rate must have been particularly vulnerable to intensive predation by man; as the adult death-rate of the kittiwake is only 12%, it would not need many extra deaths to necessitate a compensatory increase in recruitment rate by young. However, the bird does not breed until its third or fourth year and 21% of the young die in their first year. In addition, as only 1.16 young are produced per pair, it is evident that the species is far more likely to be too heavily preyed upon than, for example, fast breeding species like the wood-pigeon (which produces 2.1 young per pair, breeds in its first year and has an adult death-rate of 36%). Hence, much of the recent increase represents a recovery from a previously high level.

The kittiwake has, however, now increased to a higher level than in the nineteenth century. Whether this has depended on some improvement in food supply, as an indirect result of human fishing, is not clear, because the bird feeds much on plankton, although it certainly feeds extensively on waste from trawlers, such as fish guts (H. A. Cole, *personal comm.*). Coulson does not think that food was ever a factor limiting numbers and instead ascribes a major role to natural predators, considering that the decline of these, as well as the stopping of human persecution, accounts for the present continuing increase. Since about 1920 the bird has expanded by creating new colonies and as these contain a much higher proportion of birds breeding for the first time the implication is that juvenile survival has increased. These are conditions under which genetic variability would also be expected to increase and new traits to be established. It is therefore of interest that following the increase, kittiwakes have been prepared to nest on lower cliffs and, in consequence, to use man-made imitations. They first tried nesting on the harbour wall at Granton, Midlothian, in 1931–3, then moved to the window-sills of a building at Dunbar, East Lothian where they have nested ever since. They also started nesting on the window-sills of a riverside warehouse at North Shields on the River Tyne in 1949, and the colony thrives today. Attempts to nest on buildings have also been made at West Hartlepool and on the side of the Pier Pavilion at Lowestoft in 1959. At Gateshead in 1962, two pairs built nests and one pair reared a chick nine miles from the sea. Quite remarkably, a pair nested among the marram dunes in the terneries at Scolt Head in 1948, and two pairs at Blakeney in 1958. Since 1940 kittiwakes have nested on the ground on the small island of Hirshølmene in Denmark. It is well established from the studies of Dr Esther Cullen that the kittiwake has evolved various special adaptations to fit it for cliff-nesting, where it is relatively safe from predators. Its eggs are far less well camouflaged than those of other gulls because they are at less risk from predators. That the bird is able to make such a break with tradition suggests that some genetic change has taken place and that the species is nowadays being subjected to less predation pressure.

Kittiwakes have also shown some other surprising changes in behaviour which Coulson and Macdonald (1962) have listed. These include flighting and resting far up the River Tyne into Newcastle, where they feed on sewage waste and higher up the river on fresh-water fish. They have also started taking bread from humans at the Dunbar colony and at South Shields. It is not absolutely certain whether movements upstream represent a return to behaviour apparent during earlier times of abundance, although Bucknill in his *Birds of Surrey* (1900) reckons that kittiwakes were regular on the Thames and were shot on some of the Surrey waters fairly frequently. After the turn of the century inland records seem to have declined markedly and have only started to increase since the mid-1950s. Various other county recorders, including C. Ticehurst in Suffolk and his brother N. F. Ticehurst in Kent, give evidence of more inland records at the close of the century.

OTHER SEABIRD CHANGES

The fulmar has achieved an even more spectacular expansion since the turn of the century. It has been accorded a specially large mono-graph in this series by J. Fisher as befits a subject whose life history and increase have been so well documented. Fisher (1966) recently conducted another national census, the sixth, supported by about 600 voluntary observers – a tribute to the massive support amateur bird-watchers give to a sound and valuable investigation. Originally the only British fulmar colony was on St Kilda with 20,000 to 25,000 occupied nest sites. Prospecting birds started visiting one site at Foula in Shetland shortly before 1878 in which year 12 pairs bred. Since then their numbers increased geometrically at a rate of 7% per annum, the rate subsequently slowing down after the 1950s; the slow down at first became noticeable in the more densely colonised parts of the range in northern Britain. The average rate of compound increase today is 3%, and in 1959 there were 486 nesting colonies in Britain, with 100,000 nest sites and a further 222 sites being pros-pected. This increase implies various possibilities. For instance, a genetic change could have occurred enabling a new and vacant feed-ing niche to be exploited, as seems to have happened in the case of the collared dove and has been suggested for the kittiwake. Alternatively the species may be responding to the sudden appearance of a vast new food supply to which the population is readjusting as quickly as possible. Normally one would expect any environmental change to be gradual with the animal slowly increasing in parallel with the new resources – but not necessarily geometrically. In the present case it seems that fortuitously the amount of offal, at first from whaling and later from an expanding trawler industry, has also risen geometrically, allowing the fulmar to expand at about the highest rate possible for this slow-breeding bird. The species does not begin breeding until 7 years old; each pair then produces on average less than half a fledged young (0.44 young per pair) and the adults have a very low annual mortality of only 6%. In fact, Fisher has demonstrated that the increases have been too rapid to be feasible from the local breeding output. For instance, a 7% annual increase in the population would necessitate the fledged young having a lower mortality (4%) than the adults which would be a unique situation among birds and extremely unlikely. It is much more probable that some of the increase has depended on the immigration of young fulmars from outside the British Isles, and this would be in keeping with Fisher's view that the prospecting of new sites is performed by immature birds.

Fig. 34 is a graphic presentation of some of Fisher's data and to my mind provides very strong evidence that increased food stocks account for the fulmar's increase, while there is no need to invoke more esoteric, but less factually justified, explanations as some of Fisher's critics have done.

The gannet too has increased under protection after excessive slaughter by the nineteenth-century bird-fowlers had reduced the world population by about two-thirds, as Fisher and Lockley showed in their book on *Seabirds* (present series). To what extent improvements in food supplies have been influential is difficult to decide; for example, the increase at the Grassholm gannetry, which now numbers around 16,000 pairs, has coincided with an increase in mackerel in the Irish Sea – a preferred food along with saithe (coal fish). Boswall (1960) observed the use made by seabirds of human fishing activities from a boat which was seine-fishing in August off North Rona and Sula Sgeir. Day and night up to 300 birds were in attendance – fulmar, gannet, great and lesser black-backed gulls, herring gull and kittiwake. Gut from saleable fish and all unsaleable fish were thrown overboard as each was dealt with; about two hundredweight of gut was thrown overboard in about 24 hours of fishing. When the boat was stationary and the net was being hauled in, fulmars swam close alongside and obtained almost all the gut. When the boat was moving, however, the gulls and gannets were at an advantage because they could hover, dive and then rise quickly from the water, whereas the fulmars had to half-paddle and half-fly from the surface. The gulls had an additional advantage in being able to perch on the ship's gunwale. When the unsaleable fish (mostly gurnet *Trigla* sp. 7–9 in. long) was thrown overboard (about 56 stone against 833 stone of saleable fish caught) most of it was eaten by great black-backed gulls and gannets.

Man is also responsible for the decline of many seabirds today. Those which rely on flat coastal dunes for breeding have been hard hit by the increased pressures from seaside visitors, especially if they do not nest in traditional colonies which can be protected. The little tern, which nests in small scattered colonies, is one of the chief sufferers and has declined drastically since the war. Not more than 1,600 now seem to be nesting in Great Britain and Ireland, most (around 1,000 pairs) being concentrated in south-east England (Norman and Saunders 1969). The ringed plover is also likely to be suffering increased disturbance. Its close relative, the Kentish plover, always on the edge of its range in Britain and confined to the south coast, had its fate sealed when ribbon bungalow development at Dungeness isolated its feeding and breeding grounds. It bred sporadically in East Sussex in the early 1950s and at Walberswick, Suffolk, in 1952. Concern is also felt for birds such as the guillemot, razorbill and puffin, which may be suffering from the increased pollution of our seas by oiling (see page 17).

The colonial nesting of many seabirds is an anti-predator device, and it is ironic that this should make many of the species more vulnerable to interference and predation by man: as an egg- or young-stealer or through thoughtless disturbance. In undisturbed conditions, gregarious nesting and a high degree of synchrony in egg-laying are advantageous so far as natural predators are concerned, in that a swamping effect is achieved. Any particular pair will run less risk of losing their eggs or young if surrounded by numerous others which may be taken instead. The advantages, of course, only apply so long as the whole colony is not killed and so the colony habit should be thought of as an insurance for the individual rather than a way of preventing predation on the colony as a whole. Over a period of years one would expect local predators to anticipate the good feeding conditions at a colony and to settle in greater numbers and become a nuisance. Figures are not available, but the level of predation at a colony, particularly by mammals,

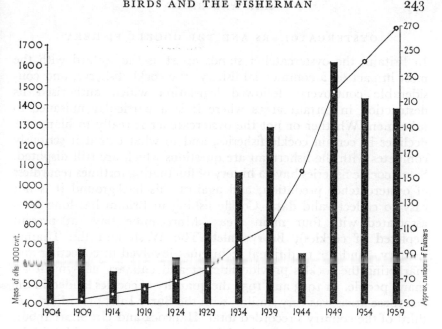

FIG. 34. Increase in the approximate number in thousands of adult fulmars (line) occupying sites at breeding colonies in St. Kilda, Britain and Ireland and approximate mass of offal discharged from trawlers as a tenth of mass of fish trawled in thousands of cwt. (columns). (Data from Fisher 1966).

might well increase over the years although each individual bird would ensure (albeit not consciously) that it did no worse than its neighbours. This probably explains why those seabirds nesting on flat shores which face this risk move their colonies from time to time as the terns do. The great auk, solitaire and dodo had all evolved adequate defences against natural predators by nesting on cliffs of inaccessible islands but could not withstand the toll taken when man invaded their stronghold. On Ascension Island, the wide-awake tern had nested in the relative safety of an island free from land enemies, and had evolved defences against its chief predator, the frigate bird. One of these is to come to land at night. But in 1815 wild cats were established on the island, and as their predations more than decimate the colonies, less than 2% of the eggs laid nowadays give rise to fledged young (Ashmole 1963).

OYSTERCATCHERS AND THE COCKLE FISHERY

In Britain, the oystercatcher stands apart as the seabird with the most impact on a commercial fishery (the cockle fishery), and considerable controversy followed legislation which authorised its destruction in certain areas where it is a particular nuisance to fishermen. Whether or not the oystercatcher is really to blame for declines in certain cockle fisheries, and to what extent it seriously competes with the fisherman are questions which are still disputed. Some cockle fisheries have a history of fluctuating fortunes regardless of oystercatcher predation, and against this background it is not easy to collect valid data. Cockle fishing in Britain has long been associated with four main areas – Morecambe Bay (at present depleted of cockles), Burry Inlet, The Wash and the Thames Estuary – and the traditional techniques involved in collecting and marketing the cockles provide interest and culinary enjoyment for many people. In 1953 and 1954 the quantity of cockles landed in the last three areas was very similar, with the Burry Inlet providing one-third of the country's recorded total (Hancock and Urquhart 1966). At Burry the industry has existed for at least 100 years and has in the past given part-time employment to over 200 women. Since 1954, however, the landings at Burry have declined and by 1965 usually only 40–50 cockle gatherers took part in the industry each taking 2–3 cwt. of cockles per tide during the Monday to Thursday period when most fishing is done.

The declining status of the Burry industry led to an official scientific investigation by the Government which was started in 1957. Inevitably attention was focused on the significance of the oystercatcher, especially as it eats large quantities of commercial cockles. Davidson (1967) has calculated that in three winters oystercatchers removed between 557 and 1,237 million second winter and older cockles compared with fishing catches of 46–128 million and the total stocks of 1,001–3,232 million of the same age groups in November.

The oystercatcher belongs to a distinct and highly specialised cosmopolitan monogeneric family with a long stout chisel-shaped bill adapted for feeding on lamellibranchiate and gastropod molluscs. Many other waders and diving ducks feed on molluscs but not on those of commercial importance. The eider duck is a specialist in mussels but it dives for those on submerged reefs, mostly in the sub-littoral zone where they are not cropped by fishermen, and it is only the oystercatcher which feeds extensively on mussels in the intertidal zone (contrary to its name the bird does not normally eat oysters although these have been recorded in its diet in the United States).

The oystercatcher can take a fairly wide variety of shore-dwelling molluscs, crustacea and annelid worms, but during the winter months it depends primarily on the edible mussel *Mytilus edulis* and cockle *Cardium edule*, taking the smaller *Macoma balthica* when cockles are scarce. Not surprisingly, the large sandy bays and inlets of Britain, which support large shell-fish populations, are the important wintering grounds of the oystercatcher, notably the Solway Firth, Morecambe Bay, the Burry Inlet in South Wales and the Wash. Dr P. J. Dare has studied the breeding and winter distribution in considerable detail, and his winter and summer distribution maps are reproduced in Figs. 35 and 36. He estimates that the combined breeding population of England, Scotland and Wales exceeds 19,000 pairs and that it could be as high as 30–40,000 with Scotland providing the most important breeding areas; indeed Scotland is one of the most important breeding areas in north Europe, with the Faroe Islands and Iceland coming next. The breeding population of England and Wales is known in better detail and currently lies between 2,000 and 3,000 pairs.

Dare shows that at the beginning of the nineteenth century the oystercatcher was commonly distributed round the entire coast of England, but that a big decrease occurred late in the century. This has been attributed to the collection of adults, eggs and young for food (*cf.* other seabirds), industrialisation and urban development on the coast, and a general increase in human disturbance. However, the species is again expanding today, which is true of the European population as a whole, and the spread may be partly attributed to climatic amelioration. In Britain, populations in various parts of Scotland have increased, former coastal areas in south and east England have been recolonised and there has been a marked development of inland breeding which was previously unknown. The re-occupation of previously deserted areas is quite possibly the result of current protection measures and it is notable that much of this return occurred during the war years, when the shingle beaches which the bird prefers for nesting were undisturbed. This was particularly true in Essex, Sussex and parts of Suffolk.

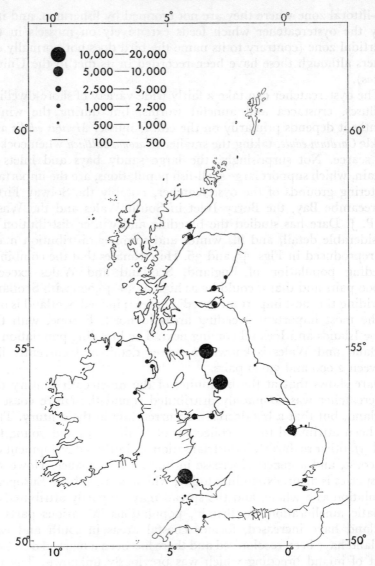

FIG. 35. Major wintering areas of oystercatchers in the British Isles, 1963-65, in December and January. (After Dare 1966).

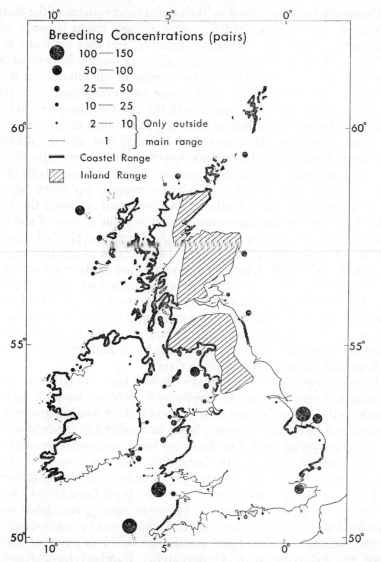

Breeding Concentrations (pairs)

100 — 150
50 — 100
25 — 50
10 — 25
2 — 10 ⎤ Only outside
1 ⎦ main range
—— Coastal Range
▨ Inland Range

FIG. 36. The breeding distribution of oystercatchers in the British Isles, 1960-65. The thickened coastline and shaded area inland indicate the main breeding range where scattered pairs occur frequently. Symbols represent large breeding concentrations except that full information for he west and north of Scotland and Ireland is lacking. (After Dare 1966).

Oystercatchers have bred on the inland river systems of the eastern Highlands of Scotland, utilising large shingle banks in wide river beds, since at least the eighteenth century, and they continue to do so. There is also a large inland breeding population in central Asia which is usually considered to be a relic of an inland sea which existed in the Pleistocene. With these two exceptions the oyster-catcher was markedly associated with the coast of Europe until there was a sudden spread of inland breeding at the turn of the century in Holland, Germany, Denmark and Sweden and also in northern England. Buxton (1961) has documented this range expansion in England, showing how the bird spread along the shingle beds of the Solway river system from 1880–1910 moving up river until it crossed into Northumberland and Durham, and occupied the York-shire Dales in the late 1940s and 50s. The same is true of the river systems of the Southern Uplands of Scotland, the rivers Lune and Ribble of Lancashire, and others. In all cases rivers flowing east have been colonised from over the watershed in the west – perhaps because the coastal areas of the west originally had bigger breeding and wintering populations. Not only has the bird spread inland in northern England, but here, in Scotland and in other parts of Europe it has moved into new breeding habitats, nesting on arable fields, heather moorland and even in young birch and larch plantations in Scotland, miles from any large river.

It is not clear whether climatic factors have contributed to the change in feeding habits. Certainly oystercatchers may die in large numbers during prolonged cold winters if their feeding grounds are frozen, and Dare records heavy losses in Scotland in the cold winters of 1947, 1955 and 1963. On the other hand, oystercatchers did very well at Morecambe Bay in the hard 1962–3 winter, where they could still find their food, even though many died in other places. However, at Morecambe, oystercatcher numbers declined from about 120,000 in the 1960–1 winter to 10,000 to 12,000 in 1964–5, associated with a parallel fall in cockle stocks; this food source was virtually destroyed by the prolonged frost of 1962–3, although the birds were not affected until the following year. Oystercatcher numbers have remained low in the Morecambe district ever since, as there has not been a good spat-fall to replace the lost cockle stocks, although numbers had risen to about 30,000 by the 1967–8 winter. The present situation, therefore, contrasts very markedly with the enormous numbers of wintering oystercatchers recorded by Macpherson in 1892 which seem to have been maintained until the 1950s; the decline at More-cambe also contrasts with the general increases elsewhere. In the two seasons following the 1962–3 winter many hundreds of oyster-catchers were seen feeding up to four miles inland from Morecambe Bay, mostly obtaining earthworms. So it could be that the enforced need to take foods other than shellfish has led various local popula-tions to learn new feeding habits.

Most wintering oystercatchers feed on shellfish, but several small groups exist locally in Britain specialising in other foods and demon-strating the broad feeding habits this bird can adopt. According to Dare, on the Cardigan and south Devon coasts the birds take limpets and periwinkles; in the bays of Pembrokeshire, North Corn-wall and Aberdeenshire and the estuaries of East Anglia polychaete worms are an important food; while small flocks now winter on coastal fields in North Wales, Cheshire and north west England and live almost entirely on earthworms. Dare (1966) has shown that the average size of a flock varies according to the source of food, with the bivalve feeders on the wide sandy mud beaches comprising the largest flocks. The size and shape of the bill varies considerably in different parts of the oystercatcher's range and even between members of the same pair. It is not clear how far these variations reflect adaptations to the different foods preferred.

The bird's techniques for dealing with bivalves are extremely complex. Exposed and therefore closed mussels are hammered open by repeated blows, which the bird delivers with down-pointed head pivoting itself from the pelvis. Dewar (1908), Drinnan (1957, 1958) and Norton-Griffiths (1967) have described the method in detail, and all found that the great majority of shells are attacked from the ventral surface. Using an ingenious machine to simulate the feeding actions of an oystercatcher, Norton-Griffiths demonstrated that the ventral shell surface is much easier to break especially in the larger mussels. The birds take care to orientate the mussel correctly before starting to hammer, and this behaviour has a clear functional signi-ficance. Another method of feeding involves the careful stalking of submerged mussels in rock pools. With a single rapid stab between the valves, the bird severs the adductor muscle causing the valves to gape. Tinbergen and Norton-Griffiths have shown how the bird then makes repeated chiselling movements to sever the mantle from the shell, finally inserting its bill to prise the two valves apart. The force needed to detach mussels from their substrate varies with their size but it also depends on local conditions; mussels subject to strong wave or tide influences are more firmly attached than usual. These considerations may be important as, unless the mussel is attached to a firm substrate, it must be carried to a suitable place by the bird. In the same way cockles are carried from areas of soft sand to firm patches which can serve as anvils. The birds return to these same firm patches time and again so that piles of broken shells accumulate (Plate 27). The birds have other feeding movements when dealing with such foods as crabs or when they probe for worms, so the range of feeding behaviour is remarkably wide. To become proficient probably requires a long training, which may partly explain the long period of immaturity before breeding status is reached; this can be in the third year but is more usually in the fourth. Immature birds remain on the winter feeding ground throughout the summer when the adults depart for the breeding areas.

Harris (1967) has made a detailed study of the breeding habits of oystercatchers on Skokholm Island, Pembrokeshire. Oystercatchers lay between one and four eggs, and on Skokholm the average clutch size varied from 2.5 to 3.3 in different years. In some years many more females produce four eggs, nearly a quarter of the females doing so in 1963 but only 5% in 1965. Variations in local feeding conditions are likely to influence the ability of the females to accumulate sufficient food reserves (see below). Clutch size decreases during the season from a peak in late April and early May, and again this probably represents an adaptive response to declining food stocks. The proportion of young fledged also declines after an initial peak in late May, which is when chicks from the first-laid eggs begin to become independent of their parents. On Skokholm, about 61% of the eggs laid are hatched and 47% of the young fledged. Losses of both eggs and chicks are largely caused by predation, particularly by lesser black-backed gulls. Harris found that an average of 50 pairs produce 45 young until fledging. Between 11 and 15 adults out of every 100 die per annum, so it is evident that in a stable population only the same number of young can survive to replace the adults lost. During their years of immaturity over three-quarters must therefore perish. It is unlikely that this loss is evenly distributed over the three years, and the indications are that something like 50%–60% of British oystercatchers die in their first year of life and about 30% in their second year. Third year mortality must be close to that of the adults and could conceivably be lower for these individuals which spend the whole summer and winter on the same feeding-grounds without exposing themselves to the dangers of migration and breeding.

Birds which nest near coastal feeding-grounds and which feed their young on shellfish and marine invertebrates, lay eggs about a fortnight to a month later (early mid-May in Anglesey, Scolt Head and Skokholm) than inland breeders, even if these last are breeding farther north in such areas as Aberdeenshire. The inland breeders lay from early to mid-April and their season is clearly adjusted to take advantage of the peak season for earthworms, leatherjackets and other soil invertebrates (see page 134). All the same, cockles, mussels and polychaete worms are abundant in early May, and it is not clear why coastal dwellers should breed later. It is possible that the day-length in relation to tide cycle is important as only one period of low tides in daylight will be available when days are short. Adults feed by day or night, but they only feed their young in daylight. Uriel Safriel working on Skokholm found that oystercatchers feeding on earth-worms raised 0.95 young per pair whereas limpet feeders could only achieve an output of 0.16 young per pair. This perhaps suggests that breeding is much more difficult on a shellfish diet and could explain why extremely few oystercatchers remain to breed on the winter feeding-grounds, which at first thought would seem to provide very attractive conditions.

Norton-Griffiths (1969) has data which help explain some of the apparent anomalies. It seems likely that the parents' highly special-ised method of feeding on bi-valve molluscs does not help them when feeding small young, because these are unable to gain immediate access to the intertidal zone where such foods occur. In any case, the chicks have to grow suitable bills and learn the complex feeding movements involved. Accordingly, the oystercatcher must compro-mise by rearing its young on a diet which can be easily obtained and given to the small chicks without leaving them exposed to the risks of predation. In short, they must resort to the more usual wader methods of probing for invertebrates in soft mud or soil or else find foods which can be readily transported back to the chicks in sufficient quantities. It is for this reason that when Safriel studied oyster-catchers on Skokholm Island he found that the young of those birds with territories on top of the island, and which carried marine molluscs from the shore to their young, grew more slowly than those of parents feeding on nearby terrestrial invertebrates. It is clear why selection has favoured the spread of inland breeding whereby oyster-catchers can profit from the earthworms on upland pastures. A behavioural change allowing the oystercatcher to probe in inland terrestrial habitats as distinct from coastal sand and mud-flats seems to be the chief reason for the spread of inland breeding.

Dare finds that adult male and female oystercatchers living in Morecambe Bay start to accumulate fat reserves in November, and leave their wintering grounds from February onwards. The mean weight of adults increases over this period, but the scatter of individual weights becomes very much greater than in autumn; some birds are now found with very low weights but others become very heavy. I provisionally interpret these data as indicating that some birds suffer from food shortage at this season, and it needs to be established whether there is some form of social hierarchy giving the birds unequal shares in the food reserves available. At this time of the year cockles and mussels decline in numbers. Furthermore, Hancock and Urquhart (1965) have shown that cockles make very little shell growth between mid-October and mid-May and that during this period their meat content declines, presumably because this is when cockles experience their worst feeding conditions. The mean weight of first-year oystercatchers declines steadily between December and March, which further suggests that feeding prospects become critical over this period. In spite of this apparent decline in food supplies, oystercatchers do not feed as long as appears to be possible. This again argues against the food supply being critical, except that it is possible that, if social behaviour is at all important, subordinate birds may possibly be forced to leave the feeding-grounds before they have eaten enough, assuming that the need to remain in the flock is more advantageous.

The familiar 'piping-parties' which can often be seen on the winter feeding-grounds appear to be aggressive displays and add weight to the view that social interaction may be important. The piping display is also employed by breeding pairs to drive intruders from the breeding area. In this connection Buxton considers that the white collar of non-breeding birds serves to inhibit sexual approaches and is not in itself a sign of immaturity. Adults have a white collar in autumn but acquire black necks later in the winter when piping displays become more frequent. Adults arrive singly on their breeding areas, so pair formation is probably deferred until this stage.

PLATE 27. *Above*, oystercatchers, despite their name, are a problem in areas of commercial cockle production. The birds carry the cockles they retrieve from soft sand to firmer patches of sand where the shells are more easily smashed. *Below*, piles of empty shells accumulate in these places.

PLATE 28. Herons, except when they take to visiting ornamental goldfinch ponds, do not impinge on fishing interests, being restricted to pouncing on fish that can be found in shallow water. Prof. D. F. Owen found that eels taken from a pond in Kent averaged 25–45 cm. in length, which was less than the most frequent length class in the pond – 55 cm. The birds take relatively few fish of commercial size.

As suggested above, food supplies could be important in determining the female's ability to lay down body reserves in preparation for egg-laying. As body weight declines in some birds just before their departure for the breeding grounds it seems reasonable to suppose that at least in some years preparation for breeding may be difficult. This may explain why some birds seem to miss a year of breeding and fail to put in an appearance at the breeding places (Harris 1967; Mercer *in litt.*). If adults are faced with such difficulties it is evident that the younger age groups may be even more hard pressed, which partly accounts for the long period of immaturity and the fact that birds sometimes breed first at three years of age but more often at four. At present the indications are that adults suffer their highest mortality on their journeys to and from the breeding grounds and while they are on these rather than on their wintering grounds, but that this accidental mortality is slight. Most population fluctuations must be caused by the changing fortunes of the juvenile and immature age groups, and the worst season for these appears to be in late winter and early spring. Unfortunately, as will be shown, many immature birds winter away from the main winter study localities in Lancashire and Wales and no satisfactory figures exist to show whether the proportion of young in the studied populations varies in relation to food stocks.

Dare has shown that first-year oystercatchers start moving to the winter grounds in late July and August; while many individuals reared in Britain move south to winter on the Biscay coast of France and Iberia during the first winter. Consequently, in places such as Morecambe Bay and the Burry Inlet there is at first a passage of young birds which do not stay. These are followed from August until mid-October by adults and by November first-winter birds comprise only about a twentieth of the flocks.

The main European wintering grounds are the Waddensee and Delta area in Holland, the Solway, the Morecambe Bay/north Wales area, the Burry Inlet complex, the Wash and the Biscay coast of France. Birds from the Faroes, Iceland, Scotland or England may occur at any of these places and there is no evidence that they have defined wintering areas, except that Baltic, German and Dutch oystercatchers seem to winter only on the Waddensee or French coast and very seldom in Britain. In some places, the Burry Inlet for example, the adults show marked attachment to their site, returning to and remaining in the same area for successive winters. Elsewhere, as on the Welsh Dee Estuary, the flocks seem to disperse much more in winter, marked birds having been recovered from the Devon Exe and the Solway Firth, but this may be caused by low cockle stocks.

Davidson (1967) has studied the wintering population of the Burry Inlet in considerable detail. These birds subsist primarily on the edible cockle which they can find buried in the sand with an extremely high degree of efficiency. On bare dry sand they were locating cockles with every second or third probe in spite of the fact that to the human observer there were no surface indications of the cockle's presence, while 300 random probes by Davidson produced only 10 cockles. Presumably the birds must rely on some visual or auditory cue, but its nature remains unresolved. The feeding rate maintained by the birds can be very high; an average intake of 1.2 cockles per minute is achieved when the birds feed on second winter cockles (Davidson 1967). As the birds feed for over half the $8\frac{1}{2}$ hours when the cockle beds are exposed during daylight tides, they can achieve an average intake of about 336 cockles per daylight tide. But oystercatchers also feed during low water at night, and although Drinnan (1957) estimated that they fed with about half the intake rate of daytime, Davidson and others have evidence that the rate of feeding at night can be close to that of the day. Assuming a figure of only half for night feeding, the birds still consume 504 cockles per twenty-four hours, equivalent to 327 g net weight of actual cockle meat (shell excluded). The curve for feeding activity, as with many other species which have been studied, has a bimodal form, peaks occurring in the proportion of individuals feeding and in their intake rate just after the beds are uncovered by the tide and just before they become covered again. The birds' intake rate when feeding on the mussel beds of the River Conway in Caernarvonshire, was calculated by Drinnan (1958) to average 1.6 mussels per minute which indicated a total weight intake of wet meat of 200–250 gms per daylight tide (which compares with a wet meat weight of 149–202 gms when feeding on cockles).

Oystercatchers prefer cockles which are in their second winter, but when these preferred sizes are in short supply, they will take the newly settled spat, as they did in the 1963–4 winter at Burry. Second-year cockles normally form the bulk of the commercial fishery stocks; at this age the cockles attain the legal size for commercial fishing (about 23 mm in length in south Wales). As a large number of second-year cockles die and the fishing of older animals is selective, few cockles reach the size of 30–35 mm, at which point their shell is too tough to be broken properly by the birds. In one set of samples there were 6,070 first winter, 29 second winter and 40 older cockles per square metre in the beds, a ratio of 4:3 old to second-winter cockles. Yet the birds were selecting the second-year category in the ratio of 24:1 older cockle. Normally old cockles are only obtained occasionally, when the birds can find them partly covered by the tide and half-open. At Morecambe Bay in 1954–5, Drinnan judged the rate of predation by birds from their calculated intake rate and knowledge of the total cockle population. Of all age groups of cockles, 74% were lost between September and March, although oystercatchers were responsible for only 30% of this loss. Of the two-year age group which suffered an 80% mortality, oystercatchers were responsible for 41%.

Hancock and Urquhart (1965) have examined the rate of predation in another way as part of a general study of the causes of death of cockles on the Llanrhidian sands of the Burry Inlet. They sampled cockle numbers in enclosures from which either fishermen alone or both fishermen and oystercatchers were excluded, and compared the results with those from other areas which were not controlled in any way. In the three-month period from mid-November to mid-February, mortality in unprotected areas was 48% for first winter animals, 91% for those in their second winter and less than 20% for older animals. The extremely high rate of loss of the second winter cockles was prevented where oystercatchers were excluded from feeding; a small residual number of deaths could be attributed to other predators and unfavourable environmental conditions; for instance, flounders *Platichthys flesus* were known to inflict heavy losses on brood cockles during the summer months. In this and Drinnan's studies a high natural wastage of cockles was found irrespective of oystercatcher feeding, and it is important to know how much higher cockle stocks would be at the end of the season in the absence of birds. The authors were careful not to assume that all cockles eaten by birds would have otherwise survived because (as explained on page 31) different causes of death replace each other and are not usually combined in their effects.

The simplified data set out in Table 18, which are derived from detailed and statistically valid figures collected and published by Hancock and Urquhart, emphasise that second-year cockles were selectively removed when oystercatchers, or both oystercatchers and fishermen were allowed access to experimental plots. The problem is complicated by the fact – which is demonstrated by Hancock and his colleagues – that viable settlement decreases above a certain density because of competition between cockles. It is also possible, as in the 1963–4 winter when there was a very high density of first-winter cockles but few second-winter and older individuals, for predators to cream off the excess of spat leaving better prospects for the remainder. The main effect of oystercatchers seems to be to alter the age composition of the cockle population, and it would be interesting to know what the long-term effect would be. In the absence of man, one would not expect a predator like the oyster-catcher to cause lasting harm to its prey, otherwise it would have brought about its own extinction by now. Each year, therefore, in the conditions which lasted until the hard winter of 1962–3, the cockle fishery was reduced to uneconomical densities by early summer because the oystercatcher, in the absence of its preferred food (second-year cockles), could turn to other age groups, or other species such as *Macoma* (Hulscher 1964). In contrast, the fishermen could only rely on the first-year cockles when these matured to market size.

Two rather distinctive attitudes towards the problem arise from the question of whether the need is (a) to maintain a traditional local industry and safeguard the fishing prospects of relatively few families or (b) expand the industry as efficiently as possible, without upsetting the livelihood of local fishermen, in order to take advantage of a growing market for cockles. In the first place, the fishermen are evidently in direct competition with the birds during the winter season and the crucial question is whether, as the fishermen maintain, this reduces their own fishing rate. It is not fair to argue that in the absence of birds appreciably more cockles would be available, as it is apparent that by the end of summer stocks are largely depleted in any case, though not as much in the absence of birds. One must compare the effects of the birds and men at the same time in relation to the factors actually present and not those which might or might not be present later, because on balance both birds and men are fishing a steadily declining resource, which is good for both at first but finishes with the fishermen at a disadvantage. The situation is not fairly represented by a profit and loss account which examines only the beginning and end of the season.

In the second situation (b) the number of cockles left at the end of the winter season assumes greater significance, as this stock will produce the next generation of spat, and the efficient exploitation of the fishery makes it undesirable to rely on a single-year class. At one time the fishermen of the Burry Inlet limited their catch to two bags (2 cwt.) per day in order to conserve stocks, and because they needed to maintain a regular catch for fresh markets thereby ensuring stability in sales and prices. The alternative was to collect as many cockles as possible at the beginning of the winter, before oyster-catchers or other agents could take their toll. But for this approach the whole structure of the industry, its fishing methods, means of storage, and presentation of the final product would have to be radically changed. Against this possibility must be weighed the fact that before their second winter cockles in the Burry Inlet have not reached optimum commercial size, and many of them are still smaller than the legal minimum. Any marked reduction of this age group before the winter is also likely to intensify predation pressure on the younger cockles and perhaps on other areas. A limited bag of 2 cwt. per day was not enough for the fishermen to live on, whereas a take of 3 cwt. would have left no stocks in May. At the same time the oystercatchers took what they wanted and left a little for May; the amount was not large enough, but was more than if the fisher-men had taken 3 cwt. a day.

The hard winter of 1962–3 drastically reduced cockles throughout Britain, and the Morecambe Bay and Dee Estuary fisheries have been ruined, at least for the time being, as there has been no appre-ciable spat settlement since. But in Burry Inlet there was an enormous settlement in the summer of 1963 which caused such a glut of cockles in 1964 that the market was unable to take immediate advantage of the extra yield and the birds were also unable to make much impres-sion on the surplus. Since then, Davidson (1968) states that a pro-cessing plant was reopened in 1966 and that a deep-freezing plant also took cockles in 1967, providing an outlet for 6,000 cwt. of cockles per month, with the result that potential markets have expanded considerably. This is an important consideration as im-ported cockles (mostly from Holland) valued at more than £100,000 per annum form about 40% of the total cockle industry in Britain. While cockling remained a local tradition, the wholesale slaughter of oystercatchers could hardly be justified. In the light of recent developments in the industry the question needs to be reassessed and so do methods for the more efficient exploitation of cockles, especially as the abnormal effects of a high spat-fall after the 1962–3 winter decrease in significance and the situation returns to that of 1959.

FISH-EATING BIRDS

Many other fish-eating birds arouse the suspicion, if not the enmity of fishermen, whether on inland waters or the open sea. It is known that the birds often eat fish below the size normally taken by the angler, but the belief remains prevalent that they depress fish numbers in the older age groups. Herons and kingfishers are pilloried when they take to visiting fish hatcheries and ornamental goldfish ponds: in Hungary some people have even employed tame goshawks to scare herons away from fishponds to nearby streams. In Scotland, but not in England, both the red-breasted merganser and the closely related goosander can be legally killed by authorised persons in the supposed interest of the fisherman. In fact, certain district fishery boards and angling clubs pay rewards for their slaughter and the same attitudes are held in North America and Canada. The contrariness of human nature is such that on the Indal River in north Sweden, where natural nesting places are in short supply because of an absence of trees, the red-breasted merganser is allowed to nest under fishermen's huts. Further north, on the Ångerman River, Holmer reports that the local inhabitants actively encourage this bird by making holes for it to enter their attics; four birds nested in one particular roof.

When Mills analysed the food remains in gizzards of 147 goosanders, mostly from the rivers Dee (Aberdeenshire), Ness, Brain and Tweed, and of 148 mergansers, mostly from the rivers Conon, Ness, Tay and Dee he found that both species rely on salmon, mostly parr, in Scottish waters. Food items other than fish seem to be of little importance; occasional water shrew remains were identified in goosanders and both species seem to feed a little on aquatic insects, which with crustacea are also the main food of small ducklings. Some degree of ecological competition is apparent in the choice of food items, but is presumably avoided as the two species prefer rather different habitats. The goosander mostly frequents the upper reaches of rivers and inland lochs, while the merganser favours more estuarine conditions, sea-lochs and the coast, and in winter is almost completely marine. The merganser is a rare passage visitor to the London reservoirs sometimes appearing in February or March, whereas these are among the principal wintering places for the goosander in the British Isles. Differences in food choice would be expected in winter and it seems that various mysids, shrimps, flounders, gobies, butter fish and coal fish feature much more in the diet of the merganser.

In spite of fairly intensive persecution both species have increased in this century. The merganser started increasing in Scotland after about 1885. It first bred in Cumberland in 1950, nesting in the marram dunes of Ravenglass, since when it has spread to Westmorland, north Lancashire and north Wales. The goosander first nested in Scotland in 1871, spread during the late nineteenth century, and reached the Borders in the 1940s and Cumberland in 1950, where it has since increased. Reasons for the increase are not known, but it is certainly true that since the late 1940s there has been a tremendous increase in angling which, in north Wales for instance, has led to more game-fish being reared in and released from nursery waters. Both these sawbills probably have the most serious economic impact when they concentrate their feeding on fish reared in hatcheries. Mills records that two goosanders shot on the River Bran, Ross-shire, respectively contained 30 and 32 tags from salmon which were part of a consignment of 250 marked smolts released only three days before.

The significance for commercial fisheries is also demonstrated by studies in Canada particularly by White and by Elson. On a ten-mile stretch of the River Pollett in New Brunswick, Elson released known numbers of salmon under-yearlings reared in hatcheries and, by very careful and intensive methods of recapture, recorded how many survived, depending on whether or not goosanders (the American merganser *Mergus merganser* is the same species as the European goosander) and belted kingfishers *Mergaceryle alcyon* were killed. The simplified results are summarised in Table 19. In undisturbed conditions very large plantings evidently did not bring proportional increases in smolt production and the optimum planting necessary is estimated by Elson to be between 40,000 to 80,000 under-yearlings. This being so, it is a pity that very large plantings were made in the four years when bird control was exercised. In spite of very intensive efforts, only about one quarter of the total number of goosanders which were sighted were killed. This amounted to an average of 50 adults a year for the 10-mile stretch of river. In addition, virtually no birds were allowed to rear broods on the river, otherwise there would have been about 40 young birds. The average goosander density in Elson's study area was one bird per 6–8 acres, but the benefits of control were slight until a bird density of only one per 18 acres was achieved – there was no advantage in reducing bird numbers below one per 55 acres. The density of goosanders on the Ross-shire rivers studied by Mills was one per 24 acres.

Goosander predation on salmon appeared to be of the kind which removed all individuals above a minimum number. This minimum was equivalent to one smolt per 100 square yards, but it could be increased to five smolt per 100 square yards by bird control (a 5-fold increase at the smolt stage but a 10-fold increase of parr). Although they were killed, kingfishers appeared to make little difference to salmon numbers as they concentrated on other species of fish. These results raise the crucial question of whether the number of mature salmon which would return to the river two or even ten years later could possibly be affected by this level of bird predation on immature fish. Would salmon deaths at sea be proportionately or directly related to the number of smolts leaving a river? Would, in any case the total loss be so high as to cancel the effort involved in increasing the output of smolt? Huntsman (1941) concluded that there is a positive relationship between smolt output and increase in the resulting commercial fishery, but more detailed studies are required. Meanwhile doubts exist regarding the value of bird control. It should be mentioned in passing that stocks of various other coarse fish were roughly doubled by bird control, and eels benefited nearly as much as the salmon.

Whatever the long-term effects of goosanders and kingfishers on fish stocks, an immediate reciprocal relationship between the number of birds killed and fish stocks is apparent from Fig. 37. The more numerous the salmon parr the more goosanders moved in to feed on them, but their numbers, unlike those of the kingfishers, did not appear to depend on variations in stocks of minnows *Fundulus* and suckers *Catostomus*, whereas kingfisher numbers did not vary causally with salmon stocks. As Elson points out, any improvement of fish stocks brings the attendant risk of attracting more goosanders. If control operations destined to reduce predation are relaxed most of the benefits must immediately be lost. This means that once it is decided to attempt bird control, and if this is at all successful, there

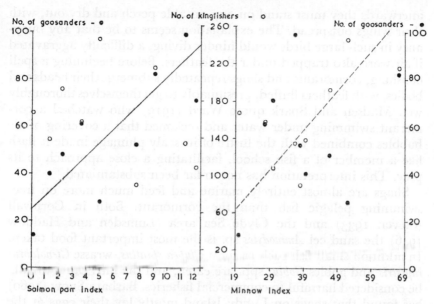

FIG. 37. Relationship between number of goosanders or belted kingfishers killed annually on a ten-mile section of the Pollett River, Canada, in relation to fish stocks.

Left. More goosanders (closed circles) were killed when salmon parr were common (expressed as no. per 100 sq. yd. of river) whereas kingfisher (open circles) numbers were unrelated to salmon stocks.

Right. In contrast, more kingfishers were caught when minnows were abundant, whereas goosander numbers were unrelated to this food supply. (Figures from Elson 1962).

is considerable danger in then ceasing operations. This is because any increase achieved in the number of salmon parr as a result would increase the risk of a heavy density-adjusted predation by birds.

In Britain, the congeneric shag and cormorant are often accused of depleting fishery stocks. They are very similar in morphology and habits, but are well separated ecologically by differences in food choice, breeding habits and movements. At first consideration, it is peculiar that the plumage of the cormorant and shag, which are completely dependent on fish for food, have almost no water repelling property so the birds get saturated every time they enter the water;

afterwards they must stand on any suitable perch and dry out, with their wings outspread. The explanation seems to be that any buoyancy in such large birds would hinder diving, a difficulty aggravated if air were also trapped under the feathers. Before beginning a spell of fishing, cormorants and shags repeatedly submerge their heads and bodies, with feathers fluffed, presumably to get themselves thoroughly wet. Madsen and Spark quote Ward (1919) who watched a cormorant swimming under water and reckoned that a covering of air bubbles combined with the lustre of its scaly plumage made it flash like a member of a fish school, facilitating a close approach to its prey. This interpretation has not so far been substantiated.

Shags are almost entirely marine and feed much more on free-swimming pelagic fish than the cormorant. Both in Cornwall (Steven 1933) and the Clyde Sea area (Lumsden and Haddow 1946) the sand eel *Ammodytes* sp. is the most important food taken. In addition small fish such as sprat *Clupea sprattus*, wrasse *Ctenolabrus rupestris* and gobies *Gobius* spp. are eaten, and the bird cannot really be considered harmful to commercial fisheries. Barbara Snow (1960) has found that shags on Lundy Island mostly lay their eggs at the end of April, the young hatching in early June. At this time sand eels, particularly the common species *A. tobianus* L., are very common as the young, from spawning made in fairly deep water about a mile offshore in December and January, now migrate to the surface waters and grow rapidly. The adult fish also move to shallow water for a second spawning in May and June which must make them easier to catch, and this enables the terns to catch them and breed.

Unlike the shag, the cormorant obtains much of its food in estuaries, and in many parts of its circumpolar range it penetrates inland to feed and breed on freshwater lakes and rivers. Rather surprisingly in North America the cormorant is ecologically replaced by the double-crested cormorant *Phalacrocorax auritis* which is a species more closely related to the Old World shag. However, factors segregating the various Phalacrocoracidae are evidently more complicated than a simple difference in choice of food. Stonehouse (1967) has shown how two species in New Zealand, the white-throated shag *P. melanoleucos brevirostris* and pied shag *P. varius* each have different physiological abilities which affects how long each must rest between spells of diving. As this determines the depth at which each species is most efficient, it also determines whether or not it feeds close inshore.

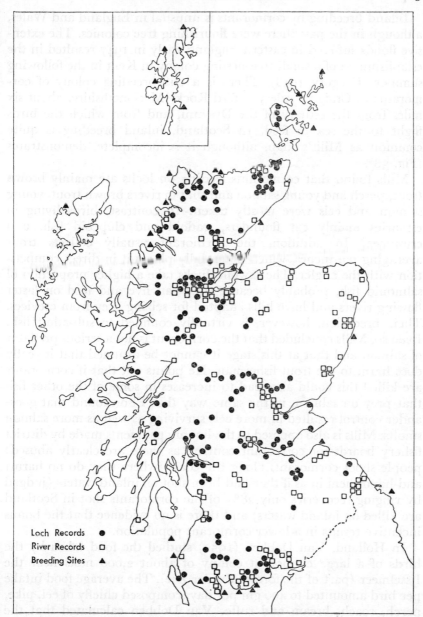

FIG. 38. Inland records of cormorants in Scotland and distribution of breeding colonies. (After Mills 1965).

Inland breeding by cormorants is unusual in England and Wales, although in the past there were flourishing tree colonies. The extensive floods suffered in eastern England early in 1947 resulted in the establishment of a small tree-nesting colony in Kent in the following summer (Gregory 1948). There is a cliff-breeding colony of cormorants at Craig yr Aderyn (Bird Rock) Merionethshire, about six miles from the estuary of the Dysynni, and from which the birds flight to the sea to feed. In Scotland, inland breeding is quite common as Mills's map, although it is incomplete, demonstrates (Fig. 38).

Mills found that cormorants feeding on lochs ate mainly brown trout, perch and young salmon and that in rivers brown trout, young salmon and eels were mostly taken. In contrast, birds living in estuaries mainly eat flounders, gadoid and clupeoid fish, and crustacea. In addition, the cormorant usually collects trout averaging ten inches, which potentially places it in direct competition with the angler. The sawbill ducks take a higher proportion of salmonid fish, probably because they can live and feed on faster flowing rivers and have bills adapted for seizing prey from crevices. Their predation, however, is virtually confined to sub-adult fish. Even so, Mills concluded that the cormorant is not a serious predator of salmon and that at this stage it cannot be assumed that it really does harm to the trout fisherman. He points out that if cormorants are killed this could also lead to increases in some of the other fish that prey on salmon, in the same way that Elson found that goosander control resulted in more eels surviving as well as more salmon smolts. Mills is also opposed to the bounty payments made by district fishery boards for cormorant control, as these are clearly abused: people shoot cormorants along the coast (where they do no harm) and hand them in as if they had been shot on inland waters (judged by ringing recoveries only 28% of the cormorants shot in Scotland are killed on inland waters) and there is no evidence that the bonus incentive results in a lower cormorant population.

In Holland, Van Dobben (1952) studied the food taken by the birds of a large cormorant colony of about 2,000 nests near the Ijsselmeer (part of the former Zuider Zee). The average food intake per bird amounted to 400 gm per day, composed chiefly of eel, pike, perch, roach, bream and ruffe. Van Dobben calculated that the colony removed 7½ million eels from the lake and that fishermen landed 55 million. The birds favoured eels 21–23 cm in length, while the legal size for fishing was 28 cm. If it is assumed that every fish eaten by the cormorants would have survived to be fished – a most unlikely assumption – then the birds were removing a tenth of the fishery stocks. Similarly, it was calculated that the birds depleted a tenth of the pike-perch fishery, again no allowance being made for differences in size of the fish caught. Once fish exceed about 40 cm in length they are too big to be taken regularly by the cormorant. Again emphasising the tendency for predators to select weak or ailing prey, Van Dobben found that 30% of the roach eaten by the cormorants were infected with an intestinal parasite *Ligula intestinalis* against only 6.5% of those fish which were left in the lake.

In Denmark Madsen and Spark studied the feeding habits of the southern cormorant (*P. c. sinensis*) which recolonised the eastern coast of the country from the Baltic during the 1940s, following earlier extermination. Outside the breeding season this subspecies is indistinguishable by field characters from the type species, though over most of its range it is more a bird of inland waters. In the lower Kattegat most of its food comprises eels, the viviparous blenny *Zoarces viviparus*, herring *Clupea larengus* and cod *Gadus morrhua*. The total Danish population of about 300 pairs could potentially eat only 1% of the total yield of the Danish eel fishery inside the Skaw, and again it is most unlikely that if the birds did not eat the eels the fishermen would gain any advantage. The same reservations apply to Sushkina's (1932) estimate that cormorants in the North Caspian Sea eat 5,000 metric tons of fish annually, representing 1.5% of the total commercial catch.

Like most of the other seabirds considered here, both the cormorant and shag have a low adult death-rate; in the former it is 9% for adult males and 11% for adult females in Holland (Kortlandt 1942), while in Britain about 14% of adult shags die each year (Coulson and White 1957, Snow 1960). The reproductive output of shags is fairly high at about 1.9 young fledged per pair.

CHAPTER 11

BIRDS AND INDUSTRIAL MAN

THIS chapter is something of a miscellany, in order to cope with the wide array of situations where birds raise problems for man other than those caused by their feeding habits. These problems include the fouling caused by roosting birds, the risks of disease transmission from the close proximity of man or his livestock to wild birds and actual collisions between birds and aircraft or other man-made structures. Many of these inter-relationships between man and birds can be seen most clearly in town and cities. Here man outnumbers the birds, while in the rest of the country there are still over two landbirds to every human being, regardless of the seabird population.

It is not my aim here to list the amazing variety of wild birds that exist, for example, within twenty miles of St Paul's Cathedral, as this topic has been ably covered by other writers in this series (Fitter 1945, Homes 1957), but instead to single out the special problems created when wild birds live in close proximity to man. But it is worth mentioning that 35 species breed or attempt to breed each year in the 40 square miles of Inner London and between 0.9–1.75 breeding pairs of birds exist per acre, feral pigeons and house sparrows accounting for about 88% of the total. Of the thousands of visitors to Alexandra Palace in the spring of 1967 who marvelled at our heritage of wild life during the second Observer Wild Life Exhibition, few glanced upward from the open courtyard to watch a pair of kestrels indulging in superb courtship displays around the roof and aerial. Kestrels have nested on the Imperial Institute, Savoy Hotel, St Paul's school and the B.B.C. building. In London they feed mostly on house sparrows and are one of the few species to have declined since 1950. A clean-up of war-time bombed sites, resulting in a loss of invertebrate and rodent food supplies, and a decrease in the numbers of the house sparrows, seem to be factors involved. The overall improvement in London's bird life seems attributable to a richer insect fauna following smoke abatement and other measures taken to reduce atmospheric pollution, and also to increased supplies of bread given by a benevolent public.

In the outer suburbs of London and in other built-up areas, there may be an average of five breeding birds per acre which compares well with mixed woodland (five birds per acre) and deciduous woodland (four per acre), while it exceeds the level on permanent grass (two birds per acre) and rough grazing (0.7 birds per acre).

Given adequate and suitable food in the absence of a typical habitat it is conceivable that all kinds of unlikely birds could adjust to urban conditions. In Michigan and also on the campus of Kent State University, the eastern nighthawk *Chordeiles minor* has nested on the flat roofs of buildings (Sutton and Spencer 1949, Dexter 1952) and E. M. Nicholson has also mentioned that numbers of this species roost in the town square at Villavicencio in Columbia. In several American and Canadian cities the peregrine has found a place, preying on small birds and nesting on the ledges of skyscrapers.

Apart from the special cases provided by parks, gardens and ponds, the number of birds which have really adapted to urban conditions is small, and the same genera are mostly represented throughout the world. In Britain, two species, the feral pigeon and house sparrow have adapted to a complete town life, living commensally with man, while a third, the starling, though dependent on man the farmer, has only exploited his densely urban areas as a dormitory. A paucity of niches usually prevents more than one species in any genus being present. There usually seems to be a place for a pigeon, one for a small grain-eating sparrow-type bird and sometimes one for a corvid. Moreover, it seems generally true that the Palaearctic species are better adapted to occupy the urban niche in diverse parts of the world than members of the local avifaunas and this could be the result of a longer association with and adaptation to the special conditions created by urban man. In towns where public hygiene is such that offal and appropriate garbage is available, the corvids profit, and kites may still occupy the place of a scavenging bird as the kites once did in England. Thus the house crow and black kite are common in Indian and Middle Eastern towns, and in parts of the Far East. The house crow first arrived in the dock area of Singapore in 1948, whether introduced or naturally is uncertain though it is a great wanderer and in India turns up as soon as any man-made settlement is created. It has gradually increased there as it has also done in Klang, Malaya, since it was first introduced in 1898.

In Britain, offal is usually deposited in dustbins to which only cats, and in some parts of London's suburbs foxes, can gain access, and the type of garbage available on dumps seems more suited to the gulls. It is of interest that in Mombasa and various other East African ports and also on the Lake of Geneva, the various races of black kite behave like gulls, which may also be present, by collecting garbage from the water surface, albeit clumsily (E. and A. Cruickshank, Ibis *106*: 253–4). In a recent book on *Pigeons and People*, Ordish and Binder have suggested that large numbers of pigeons are 'a luxury for wealthy food-rich nations – the "haves".' In fact, pigeons and other species dependent on man for food swarm to a much greater extent in the poverty-stricken areas of the Middle and Far East, numbers showing an inverse correlation with standards of hygiene and of living.

Feral pigeons occur in most towns in Europe and also, following introduction, those of the Far East, Australia and the U.S.A. Again it is notable that *Columba livia* can do better in Australian towns than any of the endemic pigeon species. In Africa, south of the Sahara, *C. livia* is replaced in the towns by the closely related speckled pigeon *C. guinea*. An unusual situation occurs in Addis Ababa according to Pitwell and Goodwin (1964) where *Columba guinea* co-exists with the white-collared pigeon *C. albitorques*, a bird confined to Eritrea and central Ethiopia. The white-collared pigeon seems to be as well suited to town living as the European feral pigeon; it nests in lofts and manages to collect food from smaller ledges than *guinea*. Otherwise both birds seem to share the same food and mode of life and it remains to be seen if one will eventually replace the other and what the fate of both species will be, if *livia* should become established. In the east from Semiretcheusk and the Russian Altai south through Turkestan and western Tibet, *Columba livia* is replaced by the allopatric blue hill pigeon *Columba rupestris* which becomes the common town bird. It may be conspecific with *livia* but the two both occur together in the capital of Mongolia, though *livia* is said to be more the bird of the town centre, being replaced by *rupestris* in the suburbs.

Cramp and Tomlins (1966) estimate that Inner London (defined as a rectangle with boundaries four miles east and west and two-and-a-half miles north and south of Charing Cross) supports between 10,000 and 20,000 pairs of feral pigeons and a similar number of house sparrows. They give evidence of a three-fold increase in the Bloomsbury district between 1951 and 1965. In 1951, pigeon numbers were barely one-sixth of those of the house sparrow but by 1965 were nearly 50% greater. This increase in the last fifteen years seems to be the result of more bread and other food being given by the public. It is in our cities that the paradoxes of our ambivalent attitudes to birds are seen. On the one hand, thousands of visitors feed the pigeons every year in Trafalgar Square while, early in the mornings, diligent local authorities do their utmost to catch and remove birds in the hope of reducing numbers in the interests of public hygiene. The authorities in Westminster alone trap about 6,000 annually, although our knowledge of population dynamics makes it fairly certain that if their efforts were discontinued the pigeon problem would not increase. The psychological response of man to animals provides a fascinating study in itself. That man's deep-rooted impulses may have ecological consequences for urban birds is demonstrated by the special care with which sickly or deformed individuals will often be fed and how white pigeons arouse more sympathy than black ones (black birds have long symbolised villainy). Tinbergen long ago showed that animals of rounded 'cuddly' outline most closely resembling human babies, release the deepest maternal and protective instincts in man. This is understandable, but it is less easy to appreciate why people readily accept the killing of drab-coloured animals like sparrows and rats but react strongly against the slaughter of brightly-coloured or 'pretty' species.

The feral pigeon is of course descended from the wild rock dove and the present day town flocks are partly a legacy of the days when the species was widely kept in semi-domestication by the lords of the manor as a source of winter food. The dovecote pigeon declined in importance during the late eighteenth century, when improvements in agriculture made the production of corn more valuable as a source of bread than of pigeon food, and farmers ceased to tolerate the plunderings of the squire's flocks. The rock dove was also a household bird in ancient Egypt and domestication certainly began even earlier, so it is highly probable that the species has always lived in close association with man. Like the house sparrow, it may well have spread north from the Mediterranean and Indian regions when the earliest Neolithic farmers also penetrated north to cultivate their corn and such weeds as fat-hen. Today rock doves living in the wild take a higher proportion of cultivated cereals than the closely related stock dove, even though both species compete for the same weed seeds.

Town pigeons are not merely a relic from earlier times, as they are well-adapted to their new environment. Their diet varies according to their location. Those in the dockland of Liverpool and Manchester obtain exotic seeds such as sorghum and maize, and also processed foods in the form of poultry crumbs and oil-seed products. The birds display considerable opportunism in their feeding and will rapidly descend on to a small moving lorry carrying bags of grain if some has been spilled. As soon as there is a lull in activity in the processing plants, the birds come down on to the conveyer to get at the grain being transferred from ship to silo. The conveyor belts move quite quickly and sometimes a hapless bird may be swept into the bins, eventually to add to the protein content of our bread. In Leeds, bread given by a bird-loving public is the staple diet – as Goodwin has said 'mutual recognition between individuals of *Homo* and *Columba* tends to be gratifying to the former and hence rewarding to the latter'. This diet is supplemented with cereal seeds and a few wild weed seeds. Weed seeds are partly collected on waste ground resulting from slum clearance schemes, and also from the fields outside the city boundary, which the birds visit when spring cereals are being sown or when ripe corn can be collected from the stubbles. Their diet is similar in London, as both Gompertz and Goodwin have shown, except that cereals are much less often obtained, although the birds do go 'fielding' to the parks and wasteland, where they get weed seeds.

My colleagues and I have found that three-quarters of the rock doves at Flamborough stop breeding in winter, their gonads being regressed from November–January. This enables them to deposit reserves of fat and conserve their energy over the most critical time of year for food supplies: in a seasonal environment it may be disadvantageous to stay in continuous breeding condition. Melanic varieties are significantly more prone to remain in a continuous breeding state and this enables them to reproduce throughout the year in town environments, where food stocks show little seasonal fluctuation (especially in dockland areas where grain cargoes are imported and processed). A reduced need for town birds to undergo a period of gonad quiescence could have enabled melanic morphs to be favoured. Pigeons breeding continuously no longer need long daylengths to remain reproductively active. But because fat deposition is usually photoperiodically controlled – at least in the northern pigeon species – this loss of photoperiodicity may have had more profound physiological repercussions which could not be tolerated by wild-living coastal populations. It is clear that the factors responsible for the selection against melanism in wild populations, whatever they may prove to be, are evidently absent in towns. Mainardi has studied in detail a process which assists this spread of melanism and has found that it is the result of birds' preference to pair with types resembling their parents. Such sexual selection in a group mating system must favour dominant characters (melanism) in the absence of any counter selection. Melanism also confers other advantages: black animals can absorb more heat from the environment, and feathers with heavy deposits of melanin are stronger than those without (this is why, in spite of the advantage of having white plumage, gulls have black wing tips where strength is essential). Hence, town pigeons seem to show a subtle type of industrial melanism of a kind known to occur in certain insects. This involves the emergence of a dominant gene which, even though it imposes superior fitness, cannot be expressed in the wild because it carries too many disadvantages. But before the matter can be taken much further these disadvantages must be explained.

The smaller doves are much less efficient town birds than the feral pigeons unless plenty of shrubs exist. The Indian turtle dove *Streptopelia chinensis* is a successful bird of cultivation and native settlements throughout most parts of its range in India, China and south-east Asia, and has replaced the barred ground-dove *Geopelia striata* as the town bird of Singapore (Ward, 1968). It was introduced to eastern Australia at the end of the nineteenth century where it has become a town bird found in city and suburban backyards, feeding with chickens and on bread given by the public. The smaller laughing or palm dove *S. senegalensis* is even more of a town or village bird throughout Africa, India and the Middle East (in Istanbul and Beirut) nesting on the ledges of buildings or in lofts as well as in trees and shrubs. It was introduced to Perth from the Zoological Gardens in 1898 and has since spread to colonise some of the local country towns. D. Goodwin tells me that the Indian turtle dove and feral pigeons may all be seen feeding together on the food placed in the open animal pens of Perth Zoo. The palm dove seems to be spreading in south-west Europe, but whether it originally reached Europe from Arabia and Palestine unaided is not certain. It has long been found in Turkey and records from the Balkans seem to be getting more frequent. In many ways its habitat preferences are the same as the collared dove *Streptopelia decaocto*, which (see page 22) has recently spread enormously in range. The palm dove is probably a more efficient town bird than the collared dove and it will be interesting to see whether it can spread further north in Europe, and how the two species manage to co-exist when they do occur together. None of these doves is a town bird as is the feral pigeon and their niche seems to be much the same as that occupied by the collared dove in Britain.

The collared dove seems much less flexible in its ecological tolerances than the feral pigeon, and it will rarely nest on buildings. Essentially it prefers planted areas such as parks, gardens and seaside roads, close to where grain is freely available; chicken-runs and small zoos are particularly favoured sites. Communal feeding at dockside warehouses (as at Avonmouth) and flour mills has long been recorded but the birds do not seem to be occupying the feral pigeon's place. For instance, according to Pashby and Cutts (1966), collared doves feed round the British Oil and Cake Mills works at Wilmington in the heavily industrialised section of the River Hull, and on an old bombed site close to Humber Dock Side, which is used by a firm of haulage contractors for its grain lorries. The birds flight one and a half miles to the docks from breeding areas in semi-suburban streets and a park, where they nest in the trees. The same is true in parts of Manchester. At the moment, collared doves do not seem to be causing any economic damage of consequence, and the chief cause for complaint is their monotonous calling which often irritates householders and visitors to seaside resorts.

I have already suggested that the ability of some pigeons to breed throughout the year has been an advantage in the urban environment. Virtually all temperate-zone species require daylengths to reach a specific threshold in order for their gonads to be stimulated into breeding condition, and in most a period of breeding activity is followed by an obligatory period of gonad regression, termed the refractory period (see page 137). This acts as a safety mechanism and inhibits the birds from attempting to breed at unfavourable times of the year when daylengths still stimulate the gonads. Unless a species can modify and change its inherent cyclical response to daylength, it may be seriously handicapped in towns, where the availability of man-made food supplies differs markedly from those found in the wild. This may limit the range of species which can succeed in artificial surroundings, and so far only the feral pigeon has entirely emancipated itself from the restrictions of a rigid photo-periodic response. Other town birds have reproductive cycles which either fit directly, or are able to adjust to urban conditions. The house sparrow, for instance, has evolved a long natural breeding season lasting from March until early August followed by a short refractory period of about one month. This physiological cycle is flexible enough to allow the bird to adapt to urban conditions. Even so, it could probably breed over a longer period than its physiological limitations permit. In some places, street lighting may add to the natural photoperiod.

The wood-pigeon's pituitary apparatus is sensitive to daylengths of about 11–12 hours' duration which renders it physiologically capable of breeding between March and September. In cultivated rural habitats it produces most of its eggs and young in August and September, when ripe cereals are plentiful. In London, the wood-pigeon breeds when tree buds and the seeds of the pasture weeds found in squares and parks, as well as bread, are most abundant; and it lays most of its eggs in May, although the laying season is extended as in rural habitats. The wood-pigeon can manage a breeding season appropriate to its food supplies in London because it has a long natural season of reproductive responsiveness and within this period it can adjust itself to suit the immediate conditions around it.

As an urban bird, the starling is an outsider compared with the house sparrow and feral pigeon. It breeds in spring on agricultural land and is too fixed by photoperiodic limitations to adapt to man-made food supplies. Starlings must live, feed and breed where their natural invertebrate food can be found – in gardens or town squares. But they do use our towns in a big way for roosting. This habit is a comparatively new one, which arose independently in various towns and countries, at the end of the nineteenth or early in the twentieth century. Outside Britain, urban starling roosts are found in many countries in Europe and also in Australia and the U.S.A. Except in North America and Britain, the birds seem to prefer a city's trees rather than its buildings. In Singapore, the glossy tree-starling *Aplonis panayensis* has had a large communal roost in trees near the cathedral for at least 70 years, according to Ward. Urban roosting has brought the starling to the notice of authority, on account of the noise, general disturbance and fouling caused by these dormitories. Most starling roosts in Britain are in reed beds, dense conifer thickets or the cover provided by evergreens such as rhododendrons or laurels. Roosting on cliffs has long been known in northern England and Scotland.

When Marples (1934) made a nation-wide inquiry in 1932–3 he recorded 285 roosts in Britain, but at this time there was very little urban roosting. At the turn of the century, Glasgow, Edinburgh, London, Dublin and Belfast had been the main centres. London is one of the best documented urban roosts, where the birds first roosted in trees and then transferred to buildings sometime between 1898 (when the birds still used the parks) and 1913. The habit of roosting in towns has spread at a remarkable rate, as Potts (1967) showed in a detailed inquiry made between 1962 and 1964, when 69 urban roosts were found in 39 conurbations. Complete definition of the changing pattern of urban roosting is complicated by the fact that in many towns the birds prefer to roost in trees and only move to buildings when the autumn leaves fall. Potts overcame this problem and that of allocating numerical values to the various roosts, by using a rating system. Roosts in urban areas in trees were scored 1; those on masonry outside urban areas and roosts inside buildings $1\frac{1}{2}$; roosts on industrial plants 2. Categories 3–5 were reserved for roosts in the centre of urban areas of under 10,000 birds, 10–15,000 birds and over 50,000 respectively. The results he plotted (see Fig. 39) show that the first roost in class 1 (containing over 50,000 birds) was established in 1897 since when there has been a geometric increase, as there has been in all classes of urban roosting. Potts points out that there was an 80% increase in the size of urban areas between 1900 and 1958 and that the process of expansion may have 'swallowed up' starlings roosting in natural sites. He considers that this would explain why large urban areas have acquired roosts sooner than smaller ones, even though the buildings may be of the same age. As Manzoni (1959) has suggested, any move towards rural roosting after autumn leaf fall would become more and more difficult as urban areas increase in size, unless the birds were prepared to move. These arguments imply that towns do not provide a positive attraction for starlings at first, but this may be only partly true (see below).

The increase in urban roosting may also reflect a general increase of the starling in Britain which (see Chapter 6) was relatively un-

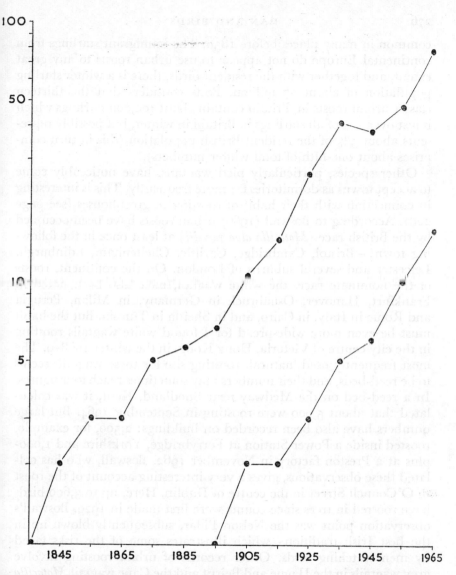

FIG. 39. Increase of urban starling roosts, upper graph based on the scoring method given in the text whereby roosts on masonry of over 50,000 birds score 5 and roosts on trees in urban areas or parks score 1 (see page 274 for full definition). Lower graph restricted to the growth of roosts on masonry (class 1 roosts) in the centre of urban areas excluding roosts on industrial plant, bridges, jetties, cranes, etc. Note the logarithmic scale. (After Potts 1967).

common in many places before 1850. The immigrant starlings from continental Europe do not appear to use urban roosts to any great extent, and together with the resident birds, there is a winter starling population of about 37 million. Potts considers that the thirteen class 1 urban roosts in Britain contain about 400,000 starlings which is just over 1% of all starlings in Britain in winter, but possibly represents about 5% of the resident British population (this in turn comprises about one-fifth of total winter numbers).

Other species, particularly pied wagtails, have noticeably come to accept towns as dormitories far more frequently. This is interesting in connection with their habit of roosting in greenhouses (see page 228). According to Boswall (1966) urban roosts have been occupied by the British race (*Motacilla alba yarrelli*) at least once in the following towns – Bristol, Cambridge, Carlisle, Cheltenham, Edinburgh, Leicester and several suburbs of London. On the continent, roosts of the nominate race, the white wagtail, have also been noted in Frankfurt, Hanover, Osnabruck in Germany, in Milan, Perugia and Rome in Italy, in Cairo, and in Sbeitla in Tunisia. But the habit must be even more widespread for I found white wagtails roosting in the city centre of Victoria, Hong Kong, in the winter 1968–9. The most frequently used 'natural' roosting site for these wagtails seems to be reed-beds, and their numbers may sometimes reach four figures. In a reed-bed on the Medway near Snodland, Kent, it was calculated that about 5,000 were roosting in September 1964. But large numbers have also been recorded on buildings: 2,500, for example, roosted inside a Power Station at Ferrybridge, Yorkshire and 1,000-plus at a Preston factory in November 1962. Boswall, who has collated these observations, gives a very interesting account of the roost in O'Connell Street in the centre of Dublin. Here, up to 3,600 birds have roosted in trees since counts were first made in 1929. Boswall's observation point was the Nelson Pillar, subsequently blown up in the best Irish tradition – which illustrates some of the risks faced by men watching birds. Other records of urban roosting involve grey wagtails in the Hague and Beirut and the Cape wagtail *Motacilla capensis* in South African towns. Jackdaws have roosted in Sofia and Stockholm. Ruttledge (1965) has recently reported a roost of goldfinches in Inner London, where about 100 birds slept in plane trees near the Natural History Museum between mid-winter and April.

The value of roosting near buildings has already been discussed in connection with greenhouse-roosting (page 228). Suggestions have been made that urban roosting gives the birds the advantage of the higher temperatures normally associated with towns compared with surrounding rural areas, or that it may give greater protection from predators. In an urban area the birds often seem to favour places like ventilators and industrial cooling-towers, which suggests that they enjoy the warmth. Brenner (1965) has measured the metabolic rate of starlings under laboratory conditions at different temperatures when the subjects were kept singly or in groups. At 2°–4° C, birds tested singly suffered a mean drop in internal body temperature of 2.7° C resulting in a state of hypothermia. The birds attempted to compensate for this by increasing their metabolic rate. If four birds were grouped together these adverse effects were reduced; subjects had a lower metabolic rate and heat loss, and the temperature range at which the lowest metabolic rate was experienced was lowered. Brenner considers that the starling has not evolved a physiological adaptation against cold; it does not become torpid at low temperatures and may therefore have adopted the habit of social roosting to reduce heat loss and maintain the metabolic rate at an efficient level. This suggests that there are big advantages in selecting urban sites.

When large numbers of birds roost in towns, whether they be starlings, pigeons or some other species, their accumulated droppings raise serious economic problems. The battle to keep buildings clean is an expensive one, especially when the older Gothic and classical revival styles of architecture are involved. Soon after the Crystal Palace was built it was realised that the structure provided a wonderful place for roosting birds. Consternation grew at the amount of fouling and after various unrewarding suggestions, the Duke of Wellington (according to Elizabeth Longford in *Victoria R.I.*, 1964) said to Queen Victoria, 'Try sparrowhawks ma'am.' Very much the same kind of advice has been given many times since (see page 290). Even the 'pyrotechnic display' which eventually solved the problem has since been employed on a lesser scale to disperse roosting starlings, and to deal with *Quelea* flocks in Africa. But another Fire of London and the extensive use of modern architecture, which is relatively unattractive to birds, is clearly not the answer in a country which rightly values its historic buildings, even though there is a marked absence of such bird problems in the rebuilt modern city centres of Plymouth and Coventry. In recent work to clean public buildings in Paris, the workmen sometimes removed layers of pigeon droppings a metre thick from the ledges of buildings. Bird droppings have a corrosive action on stonework, particularly limestone, and lodged in the crevices of valuable statues and stone-carvings they can cause immense and irreparable damage. Pavements and ledges fouled by droppings are slippery and dangerous to pedestrians and workmen, excreta mixed with nest material, stray feathers and detritus can block gutters and drains and provide a potential health hazard to man.

The problem of fouling by birds also arises in rural areas and some of the examples given emphasise what would also happen in towns if expensive remedial action were not constantly taken. At a roost near Holkham, Norfolk, starlings took over a small pine plantation of about two acres. At the beginning of the autumn pine needles and occasional patches of grass were visible on the ground. By the following March the ground was covered with a layer of ooze averaging 6 in. in depth. This was sufficient to kill the trees which were themselves coated with a layer of excreta as if some bizarre snowstorm had hit the area. Moulds and other fungi had sprung up which, with the stench, added to the atmosphere of death and foulness. At another roost near Stodmarsh, Kent, I was once bogged down in a four-wheel drive Land-Rover in a thick layer of starling droppings, which nearly reached the axles of the vehicle. Immense damage can be caused to woodland owners if birds choose to roost in a valuable stand of timber, as the accumulated droppings may eventually kill the trees, and even if these survive the weight of birds does much damage in snapping leading shoots and often branches. Mr Cyril Kirkland and D. Bevan of the Forestry Commission (see Bevan 1962) organised a survey of roosts in State forest conservancies from 1957–60 and had 38 forest roosts reported. Of these, 29 were in use in 1957 and 13 in 1960. In the other cases the birds either selected new sites within the forest or left the roost entirely. On average, roosts appeared to be occupied for about five years and covered a mean area of 4.6 acres, spruces being the most favoured tree. These authors did not consider that starling roosts were a very serious problem in large State forests. In any case it is fairly easy to disperse starlings if they choose a particularly valuable stand of timber. However, as the birds must go somewhere, control techniques should not be applied unnecessarily in situations where they do no damage.

The fouling of reservoirs and fish-ponds by roosting gulls and wildfowl worries the authorities from time to time, especially when the water is used for drinking. Pollution by droppings causes an increase of colon bacilli. Also the oxygen content of the water can be reduced through the oxidation of faecal matter, so enabling anaerobic bacteria to develop. With large volumes of water these effects are probably negligible and of no real economic importance.

There is undeniably some risk of disease transmission when large quantities of bird excreta are found near man. Considering the potential hazards there are relatively very few cases where the transmission of zoonoses can be proved, and most of these involve people like aviculturalists and pigeon fanciers who have frequent and close contact with birds. Lepine and Sautter (1951) showed that two-thirds of the feral pigeons in Paris are infected with psittacosis (ornithosis) and Hughes (1957) has similarly shown it to be present in domestic and feral pigeons in Liverpool. Haig and McDiarmid (1963) have also isolated a psittacosis virus from wood-pigeons shot on the Berkshire downs and consider that as the species is shot and handled on a large scale, and could also contaminate pasture and water troughs, it might well prove a source of infection for man and his livestock. The risk is hidden as the disease is usually asymptomatic in wild birds, while the acute form is usually restricted to young birds. The strain of psittacosis found in pigeons is much less serious than the virulent one from psittacine birds. All the same, it would be wrong to be too complacent about the risks, because at this stage far too little is known and many important outbreaks of infection may go unsuspected of any connection with birds. In Chicago in the winter of 1944–5 a large number of outbreaks of ornithosis were traced to the town pigeons (about 45% of the birds carried the disease), and it may be that many cases of ornithosis are still mistakenly diagnosed as virus pneumonia, as they were then and have been since.

Histoplasmosis, a pulmonary disease, seems to be increasingly important in veterinary and public health and men working in areas contaminated by starling faeces have been infected (Murdock, et al. 1962, Furcolow et al. 1961). Emmons (1961) isolated the causative fungus *Histoplasma capsulatum* from soil samples taken under a starling roost. There was a case in Missouri, U.S.A. in 1959 when 64 Boy Scouts helped to clean rubbish from the city park. Two weeks later four of the boys were ill with fever, high temperature and coughing, and histoplasmosis was verified by skin tests. This section of the park had apparently been a tangle of vegetation for nine years and was used as a roost by many starlings; their droppings saturated the ground.

Randhawa, Clayton and Riddle (1965) have isolated virulent strains of *Cryptococcus neoformans* from pigeon excreta collected from places frequented by the birds in London. This fungus causes a skin disease, cryptococcosis, which can also affect the lungs and central nervous system causing cryptococcal meningitis. Again there is little positive proof that infection comes directly from birds and in any case only a score or so cases have actually been recorded in Britain. In the U.S.A. there were two deaths in 1964 which could be traced to pigeons. There, the authorities are worried about causative organisms which may be freely distributed in the air in dried faecal dust. It is estimated that New Yorkers inhale three micrograms of this pigeon dust daily.

The diseases and parasites of birds are outside the scope of this book, though the monographs in this series on the house sparrow and wood-pigeon give some idea of these for two birds of economic importance. McDiarmid (1962) and Keymer (1958) should be consulted for wider reviews. This, however, is a convenient point to discuss briefly the role of wild birds in the dissemination and spread of disease among man and his plants and livestock. Again this field has given rise to much speculation, and conclusive evidence is generally lacking. Reviewing the subject in 1958, Keymer pointed out that primary epidemics of disease in wild birds seem to be uncommon and that there are few authentic reports of infection of domestic stock or man himself, apart from the classic example of psittacosis among Faroese women who handled infected fulmars. There have been many contrived experiments in which birds are artificially infected with a disease and shown to be capable of transmission. Thus Gustafson and Moses (1953) infected house sparrows with the causative virus of Newcastle disease (pseudo-fowl pest) and showed them to be capable of spreading the disease to other sparrows or chickens with which they were penned. They also reported the natural occurrence of the disease in a captured ailing sparrow and gave details of natural or unintentional infection in fifteen other species. Keymer failed to confirm the disease in a house sparrow found dead on premises where an outbreak had affected poultry, but quotes Gillespie (1952) as reporting the infection in a cock pheasant found dead in a field where domestic poultry on free-range were infected. He also quotes Wilson (1950) who isolated the virus from a gannet, and in the following year from cormorants and shags associated with epidemics in the Orkney Islands and Western Isles of Scotland. It was suspected that the islanders threw their diseased poultry over the cliffs into the sea where they were scavenged by seabirds, these in turn possibly being an important factor in the spread of the disease at the time.

Broadbent (1965) kept house sparrows in a cage with two separate groups of tomato plants, one of which was suffering from tomato mosaic virus. By flying back and forth and perching on the plants the sparrows infected 50 out of 262 of the healthy plants. No such infection occurred in a control experiment from which birds were omitted. It is clearly possible that wild birds can facilitate the spread of various plant and animal viruses, even though satisfactory proof is rarely forthcoming.

It has often been claimed that birds, particularly starlings, transmit foot and mouth disease, and Eccles (1939) showed that starlings ingesting the virus in contaminated food could excrete it for 10–26 hours, while it could persist for 91 hours on the plumage. The virus does not become established in the birds' tissues. While it remains conceivable that birds carry foot and mouth disease from one farm to another there is no definite evidence, contrary to the suggestion of Wilson and Matheson (1952), that migratory birds are responsible for bringing the disease into the country. It had for long been recognised that the first outbreaks of the disease of *unknown* origin – in the majority of cases the origin of an outbreak is known, being attributable to the importation of infected swill or to some other known factor – were concentrated on the English coast, mostly from Lincolnshire to Dorset. Partly because most of these outbreaks occurred in the September–January period the belief arose that migratory birds could be incriminated as the most important vector. A correlation was established between epidemics in the Low Countries and outbreaks in eastern England in the autumn at a time when birds could well have been involved. But a correlation was also discovered between outbreaks in France and those in southern England at seasons when migratory birds could not have been involved. In 1951, when a bad epidemic occurred in England, outbreaks in the autumn showed a distinct clustering round seaports which was not consistent with a pattern of broad front bird migration. The infection did not reach Britain during the war years 1940–4 in spite of an extremely high level of continental infection; birds still migrated but shipping and passenger traffic was reduced. For these and other reasons I concluded (1964) that the evidence so far available does not incriminate birds in the outbreaks of foot and mouth disease of 'obscure' origin in the English coastal counties.

The above does not deny that birds could transmit the disease, but it emphasises that relative to other factors they must be of minor importance. After my studies an unusually bad epidemic of foot-and-mouth disease occurred in Shropshire and surrounding areas in 1967–8 and the movements of starlings with special reference to this outbreak were investigated (Snow 1968). A hard weather west and south-west movement of starlings took place from the area of the outbreak without any associated new disease outbreaks. In fact, those new outbreaks which did occur were in the opposite direction from that taken by the birds. There was also a major starling roost centred in the outbreak area and it had no detectable influence on the spread of the disease. Indeed, the disease by-passed the roost in its spread to the north-east, and never affected the farms in the immediate vicinity of the roost. It proved possible to correlate the main features of the spread with prevailing strong winds, and the facts generally supported my earlier conclusions. The lesson is that knowing a bird to be capable of transmission and seeing it consorting with man or his livestock makes it a possible hazard, but does not prove that it really is one. It is all too easy to ascribe the blame to readily visible creatures, in the absence of proper information. The same reservation applies in the case of other diseases.

Accepting these reservations, birds may be important in the transmission of the following diseases either to man or to his lifestock or to both. Of bacteria, various forms of salmonellosis may be carried by birds but few of the samples examined have proved positive. Harbourne (1955) identified *Salmonella gallinarum* in rooks and considered that these could have been an important natural reservoir for local outbreaks of disease among domestic fowls. Pseudotuberculosis caused by *Pasteurella pseudotuberculosis* is common in birds, including the wood-pigeon, stock dove, magpie, tree sparrow, skylark, wren, jackdaw, rook, coot, partridge and pheasant and many others. More human cases are now being recorded and the disease may be of increasing importance; infection of green salad crops by birds is a distinct possibility. Of the virus infections, foot and mouth disease has already been mentioned. Equine encephalomyelitis seems to be spread by mosquitoes which have fed on blood from wild animal hosts suffering from early stages of the disease. The causative virus has been recovered from free-living pheasants, prairie chicken, purple grackle, magpie and redwinged blackbird in North America. Birds are probably the chief host in the enzootic areas, and it is possible that the infection of man or horses is only casual. Murray valley encephalitis or Australian X disease is primarily a disease of Australian wild birds, particularly water species like the night heron, musk duck, and various cormorants. It causes widespread sub-clinical infection in man but can occasionally lead to disease of the central nervous system.

Increasing knowledge indicates that wild birds are more important as natural harbourers of disease than was formerly suspected. Thus during an epidemiological study in the rice-fields of northern Italy, Babudieri (1960) was impressed by the large numbers of migratory birds, and found that 15 of 100 birds examined (mostly heron, little bittern, little egret, black tern and moorhen) were infected with *Leptospira bataviae*. In this area human leptospirosis (a variety of rat-bite fever) is very common, caused by a species of spirillum, and some of the birds, for example the moorhen, may be actual carriers of the serotype. It is not only suspected strongly that the birds provide a local reservoir for the disease, but it may also be significant that many of the species involved migrate to parts of Africa, e.g. Lake Chad, where the same bacterium has been reported. So far no fanatic has deliberately used migratory birds to spread a lethal virus, although the possibility has not been overlooked by the authorities, but a slightly Wellsian aura was introduced to ornithology when it was realised that certain migratory waders and ducks from Siberia were contaminated with strontium 90 from atmospheric nuclear explosions in the autumn of 1961. This was also shown to be the case with white-fronted geese by van den Hoek and Eygenraam (1965).

Birds' nests provide a rich source of ectoparasites, various coprophagous insects and other invertebrates, which are mainly important to birds using the nest. Concern for hygiene must be shown when birds like the house sparrow and pigeon build their nests inside granaries and food stores, as they provide a real refuge for various insect pests. Woodroffe and Southgate recognised three stages in the development of the fauna of a bird's nest, starting with its actual building and occupancy by the birds, when mainly ectoparasites are present. When the birds have deserted the nest, certain scavenging insects become dominant, many of which are important pests of stored products, including various clothes and house moths, Domestid and Ptinid beetles, silverfish and certain mites. The third phase is marked by decay, when a humus fauna of collembola, oribatid mites, earwigs, spiders, millipedes and woodlice appears. A notable feature is the constancy of the fauna of a bird's nest at any particular stage, colonisation not being a simple matter of chance.

BIRDS AND AIRCRAFT

The legend of Icarus and Daedalus epitomises the long-felt aspirations of man to emulate the flight of birds. Leonardo da Vinci (1452–1519) the scientist attempted to bring reality to the dream in a series of studied thoughts and drawings; da Vinci the poet still echoed the escapist ideal of conquering a new dimension: 'The great bird will make its first flight upon the back of the great swan filling the whole world with amazement, and all records with its fame; and it will bring eternal glory to the nest in which it was born.' In lighter moments J. B. S. Haldane would sometimes delight his students with dissertations on the size of pectoral muscles necessary to give an angel the power of flight; indeed, it was not until man abandoned the idea of flapping wings that the early pioneers managed to get a machine heavier than air to stay aloft. For a few years after the Wright brothers achieved the first controlled flight in 1903 man could share the airspace with the birds he had envied for so long. Pilots looked out of open cockpits and noted the height at which they saw birds – they could fly round the big ones if these did not get out of the way first. It took only forty years for high speed jets to emerge, for relative speeds to increase to a point where without instruments a pilot sees nothing until he hits it, and for birds to become a competitor and a positive hazard. This was the point reached in 1960 at Boston, U.S.A. when an Electra hit a flock of starlings soon after take-off and 62 out of the 72 people on board were killed in the resultant crash. Today the cost of bird strikes vastly exceeds any agricultural or other economic problem created by birds. Fatalities in civilian aviation have fortunately been few but there is certainly

PLATE 29. Rooks attracted from their rookery by a tape recording of their distress call being played through a loudspeaker system. The birds are being photographed with a polaroid camera so that their numbers can be counted.

PLATE 30. *Left,* feral pigeons live in closely integrated flocks, with each flock keeping to a very restricted area. The fouling of pavements, ledges and food stores by droppings is the main problem posed by this bird, as can be seen *right.* These birds belong to study population and some, e.g. the fourth bird from the bottom, have been marked with numbered wing tags.

no room for complacency: there have been many incidents which, but for the skill of the pilots concerned, could have been major human disasters.

Bird strikes may vary from a slight bump to severe damage requiring costly repair; or equally expensive labour charges in checking for possible damage after a pilot has reported a collision. It would be wrong for the public to be unduly alarmed at this hazard more than at any of the other risks involved in flying, just as it would be wrong for authorities not to do everything possible to reduce or eliminate the risks that do exist. Fortunately, once airborne, most civil aircraft operate well above the height at which bird-strikes are at all likely, and most of the danger is limited to the periods of landing and take-off. In contrast, military aircraft often fly at low altitudes and, to avoid radar detection, may even be specially designed for this purpose.

The number of bird strikes suffered by the military is not freely quoted for obvious reasons of security, but in Canada alone, seven F104 Star Fighter jets and possibly two others, each worth about £$\frac{3}{4}$ million, have been lost as a direct result of bird strikes – fortunately efficient ejector seats saved the pilots' lives in every case (Gunn and Solman 1968). Not all bird strikes are documented and it is difficult to collate satisfactory statistics, especially as the damage caused may range from nothing to the total loss of a plane or human life. The Canadian authorities have produced some useful information. Trans-Canada Airlines experienced a total of 486 strikes in five years. Until November 1968, twenty-three engines had to be changed because of birds and direct costs since 1959 have been reckoned at nearly $2 million. The Royal Canadian Air Force suffered 181 reported strikes between January 1957 and October 1963. Significantly, jets and turbo-prop aircraft, which flew 27% fewer hours than those with reciprocating engines, experienced 62% more strikes than the latter. Fifty-eight of the strikes were at take-off or landing and most occurred below 2,000 ft. The Royal Air Force is faced with an annual repair and replacement bill amounting to about £1 million as a result of birds (Stables and New 1968). The Royal Navy seems to suffer even more, primarily because many of the airbases are situated near the sea – where gulls are the chief menace – and also because naval air operations tend to be carried out at lower altitudes. It is of interest that most bird strikes involving carrier based planes occur on landing and not during take-off, because birds hover in the wake of a ship (Brown 1965). Between 1946 and 1963, 145 bird strikes were actually reported at civil aerodromes in the United Kingdom, the majority (96) occurring at take-off or at landing (28), but again these figures are probably an underestimate (Cooke-Smith 1965). According to Brown, B.E.A. experienced an average of nine strikes per month between June and September of 1967. Between 1958 and 1963, B.O.A.C. had to change 81 engines as a result of bird ingestion; of these, 40 had not been detected while the plane was in flight and were only discovered during routine maintenance inspections.

There are two basic types of bird strike: straight-forward collision with the airframe and superstructure, and ingestion into the engine. Jets suffer from the second type far more than propeller planes because the birds may be sucked directly into the engine's air intake, causing extensive damage to the turbine blades. At take-off the ingestion of a bird into an engine can cause overheating or complete power failure at the critical stage when full power is being used to get airborne. The large jets have a safety margin of power if one or even two engines fail, but the suddenness of the event can take a pilot by surprise. A host of other factors affect the risk of a bird strike; quite apart from such obvious ones as the location of an aerodrome, bird movements and weather conditions, other more subtle variables may be involved. For instance, there is evidence that the aerodynamics of aircraft like the VC10, with tail-mounted engines, causes fewer birds to be ingested than planes like the Comet 4, which has engines sited in the wings; the Boeing 707 which has pod-mounted engines is intermediate in this respect (Gulliver 1968).

The species of birds most likely to be involved in air strikes clearly depends on geographical and seasonal factors. In Europe, common, herring and black-headed gulls, lapwing and golden plover, feral and wood-pigeon, rook and starling are the most important. Kestrels have also caused several bird strikes in France. Some figures for Holland, derived from Hardenberg, are summarised in the following list to indicate the variety that may be involved (figures in brackets refer to the number of strikes):

Gulls	black-headed	(32)	Swift	(8)
	common		Mallard	(7)
	herring		Buzzard	(7)
Lapwing		(19)	Starling	(6)
Wood-pigeon		(10)	Carrion crow	(5)

Oystercatcher	(3)		
Partridge	(3)	Jackdaw	(2)
Chaffinch	(2)	Song thrush	(2)

and one each for house sparrow, owl, black-tailed godwit, feral pigeon, turtle dove, house martin, swallow, skylark, blackbird, golden plover, sparrowhawk, hobby and honey buzzard.

In Canada, gulls (herring, glaucous winged and ring-billed) were involved in 50 out of 135 strikes, waterfowl being next in importance (25 strikes) and starlings third (9 strikes).

Airfields can be attractive places for species which need open habitats and as such provide sites where interesting birds can live. For instance, Martlesham Heath in Suffolk long supported breeding stone curlews and inland nesting ringed plovers, the latter living in conditions similar to those enjoyed by the relic population of Breckland. Bridgeman (1965) who has documented the seasonal changes in bird numbers on three British airfields recorded a total of 43 species in one year of study.

There are many partial answers to the bird-strike problem. To some extent it is possible to design an aircraft to withstand a fairly high level of bird impact. None the less, a four-pound bird hitting an aircraft travelling at 500 m.p.h. is equivalent to the impact of a ton weight falling from 22 ft. – an impressive analogy quoted from Stables and New. Moreover, such an impact may be concentrated on an area of only a few square feet. It was to test windscreens for their resistance to such stresses that a modified ex-German V2 rocket launcher was designed and used to propel mock-ups of the front of aircraft at suspended bird carcases. It has now been proved that equally valid results are obtained if the bird is fired at a stationary windscreen (the effects of airflow round a travelling plane can be ignored at the relative speeds in question) and most of the research nowadays employs the so-called bird gun at the Royal Aircraft Establishment. This is a carefully engineered contraption which fires dead chickens by compressed air. Stables and New have reviewed the technological advances which have made safer windscreens possible – the use of treated plastic laminates incorporating polyvinyl butyral is an example. Considerable progress has been made, yet a completely bird-proof plane would probably prove to be too heavy to get off the ground.

Another approach is to avoid building airfields at sites where bird strikes are numerous. This seems obvious common sense, but it is surprising how often the authorities have neglected to obtain proper ornithological advice in the past. The case of the American naval base on Midway atoll in the Pacific is already well known. About 70,000 Laysan albatrosses and 7,000 black-footed albatrosses had traditionally nested here for countless years before man appeared on the scene to build a runway, and they continued to do so. In an area enclosed by the runways about 6,000 birds nested. In this same area, 6,266 adults and young were killed in 1957 and another 4,739 in 1958. By 1962 there were still 1,126 breeding pairs, which emphasises how inadequate such intensive slaughter can be, and strikes continued to occur at a rate of 300–400 per year (Kenyon et al. 1958, Robbins 1966). It would have been an even greater travesty of our need for a civilised approach to wildlife conservation, to have further intensified the slaughter campaign. With this experience, the proposal (now abandoned) to site an airbase on Aldabra Island north of Madagascar, where there is a large colony of frigate birds, was looked upon by conservationists with alarm. All the same, these are difficult problems because when issues of defence are involved it is not easy to reconcile conservation needs with short-term military expediency. Nearer home, ornithologists can foresee bird-strike problems if London's third airport is sited near the Thames marshes, which teem with birdlife. Yet airfields must be put somewhere and all risks from birds cannot be avoided in reality.

My colleague E. N. Wright is especially concerned with the problems posed by birds and aircraft, and is a strong advocate of the need for some degree of habitat control round airfields. For example, it is obviously possible to reduce the quantity of those soil-living invertebrates which attract large numbers of rooks and lapwings to the grassy areas surrounding runways. Wood-pigeons only feed on pastures when clovers are present, and attention should therefore be paid to the type of sward which is allowed to develop. Allowing grass to grow tall certainly makes an aerodrome less attractive to gulls, rooks, starlings and pigeons and although other species may then be encouraged their numbers may never approach the hazard level presented by large flocks of the gregarious species. In Holland, keeping the grass longer than 4 inches markedly reduced gull numbers and although redshanks increased, they were much less of a problem at 4–6 birds per 100 acres (Hardenberg 1965). Small rodents may increase in long grass and encourage predators like the short-eared owl, which happened at Vancouver Airport; but densities would not be expected to reach those achieved by wintering lapwings and starlings. Unfortunately, long grass has its disadvantages: it can make drainage less efficient, leading to runway deterioration, and if too near the runway, may obscure landing lights. Gulls are encouraged by garbage tips and large ones sited near an airfield are a problem, as was once the case at London Airport. The clearance of rubbish tips at some North American airports has produced immediate results.

Some of the attractions that aerodromes provide for birds are less tangible. Many species actually seem to prefer the paved surfaces of runways for resting. It is possible that these wide open spaces provide the bird with security from ground predators. It is also possible that such birds as the gulls are attracted by the warmth of these surfaces, as they can be 10° C above ambient temperature as a result of solar radiation, compared with adjacent grass areas (which can be 3–6° C below ambient temperature due to evaporation). Kuhring (1965) has some experimental evidence that herring gulls, at least, prefer warmer sites for resting if given a choice. In the case of aerodromes situated near estuaries or the coast, wading birds and gulls may use an airfield for roosting in the absence of a suitable shore or one covered at high tides; dunlin and semi-palmated sandpipers roosted at Boston Airport, Mass., U.S.A., and according to Drury, 160 sandpipers out of a flock of 1,500 were killed when a DC–8 landed amongst them. It seems to be the general experience that scaring birds which have come to an aerodrome to rest is easier than if they have come to feed, and easier again if an alternative resting place is available.

Most airports have a system of bird warning and scaring, operated through the air traffic controllers. The drill involved before takeoff or landing is rapidly becoming just as important as that of the fire-precaution service. Regular runway inspections are made and reports phoned to the control tower. If birds are present various scaring techniques may be used to disperse them. These range from the use of dogs, various noise machines, shellcracker cartridges and pyrotechnics such as Very lights, to bioacoustics involving the playback of recorded distress calls through a suitable loudspeaker system. As these scaring devices have a more general application in bird control they are considered in more detail in the next chapter. On the whole, they have the disadvantage that birds get used to them and their efficiency rapidly declines. One of the most effective means of scaring involves using the natural source of the birds' fear, namely a trained bird of prey, and it seems incongruous that the medieval sport of falconry should be given a jet-age fillip. Trained peregrine falcons have been used at Lossiemouth to keep the airfield clear of birds. Nevertheless, their use is limited, partly because specialist personnel are needed for successful training and flying, and partly because a widescale demand for birds of prey could not be met from wild stocks at a time when most raptors have suffered a serious decline. If supplies were available there would be scope for trying a wider range of hawks; gyr falcons, for example, prey naturally on the gulls and might be more effective than peregrines. Some experiments have been tried with a radio-controlled model shaped like a bird of prey but with limited success.

All in all, a variety of techniques exists for reducing bird hazards to aircraft and in combination may be considered to give cause for optimism, provided the risk from birds is treated seriously from the outset rather than as an incidental nuisance. The attitude now in planning and running airports is to consider bird problems as seriously as other hazards to flying. More and more operators are taking proper advantage of ornithological knowledge, and controllers can use short range radar to warn pilots of impending danger. Radar has become a revolutionary tool in the study of bird migration. Lack (1960) and, more recently, Eastwood and Rider (1965) have published radar observations which show that most bird movements over the North Sea occur below 5,000 ft. Lack occasionally noted echoes extending up to 9,000 ft. during spring passage, but only occasionally does the odd bird reach 21,000 ft. These figures emphasise once again that planes airborne and at operational height are not often likely to encounter birds. In Canada, Gunn and Solman have elaborated a system of bird forecasting by radar using hourly information of the radar intensity pattern of bird echoes for the previous 24 hours, supplemented by details of the pattern over the previous few days and by a knowledge of seasonal trends in the weather and its likely effects on bird movements. Their technique has many parallels with the methods used in meteorological forecasting, and they calculated that 77% of their forecasts were accurate and could be used effectively in flight planning and air traffic control to reduce bird strikes. If radar discloses a large flock of birds, pilots delay take-off just as they would if bad thunderstorms were imminent.

Birds, like people, are also undergoing an increasing risk from rising traffic speeds and road usage. In a survey of a two-mile stretch of arterial road in Northamptonshire in 1959, Hodson (1960) found that 288 birds of 26 species and 295 other vertebrates of 16 species were killed per year, the average traffic density being 101 vehicles per hour. House sparrows were the chief victims and many of these died in July and August when they were frequenting roadside corn-fields. But blackbirds, dunnocks, chaffinches, partridges and song thrushes also suffered badly. Road deaths were found to be highest from April until August, and involved many inexperienced young birds; peaks in road casualties coincided with Easter and Whit-sun Bank Holidays. One of the most important causes of road strikes seems to be the speed of the vehicles involved, so that any factor such as good weather which increases traffic speed, increases the number of deaths. Birds seem able to take avoiding action with vehicles travelling up to 25 m.p.h. Finnis (1960) also studied road deaths among birds, mostly in Kent, and similarly noted an increase in deaths in the summer months. He pointed out the uses made of roads by birds, for gritting, to get insects washed there during heavy rain, to use rain pools for drinking and bathing and of course to use the thermals created by surface heating. He states that in the winter of 1938 when a large number of skylarks moved across Kent, scores of birds came down to the snow-covered streets of towns to take the grit put down to help the traffic before they searched gardens and allotments for food. Many accidents occur at 'black spots' such as an open gate, a break in a hedge or wall, or where a good feeding site like a cornfield or patch of weeds lies across the road from a breeding or resting area. In further studies Hodson (1962) examined the conditions under which birds are killed. Like Finnis he found that the habits of some species such as the carrion crow, which descend to scavenge road corpses, make them specially likely to be hit. Song thrushes are at risk when they use kerb-stones as 'anvils' for breaking snail shells. He confirmed Finnis's list of 'black spots' and added the nearness of farm buildings to road junctions, while showing that roads through woodland were the least dangerous for birds.

Growing interest in the subject led to a national inquiry lasting from May 1960–April 1961, organised by Miss Terry Gompertz and reported by Hodson and Snow (1965). This produced details for 5,269 casualties covering 80 species on a total of 349 miles of road. From this it was calculated that the annual total of road deaths is probably about 2½ million, the average annual rate being 15.1 birds per mile but varying from 177.0 to 0.6 per mile. Road deaths may account for one-eighth of the total annual mortality of adult house sparrows. The adult population numbers about 10 million according to Summers-Smith, and 40% die each year. Possibly about half the sparrows killed each year are inexperienced juveniles but other species must be much less seriously affected by road deaths. Dunthorn and Errington (1964) tried to make some estimate of the importance of road deaths in relation to the size of the bird population at risk. By ringing nestlings they discovered that at least 11% of young song thrushes and similarly 12% of blackbirds, 3% of linnets and 4% of house sparrows died on the road.

Birds also collide with power and telephone lines, and if they are large birds like the swan, can cause considerable damage. Turček (1960) has also reviewed some of the other ways birds can cause trouble to overhead wires and poles. An unusual case involved goldfinches which extracted long threads of insulation material from a power line to use for nest-building. Later a female accompanied by newly fledged young indulged in the same behaviour, as also did a marsh tit. Wind action later caused the wires to short circuit. Turček also cites many instances of woodpeckers damaging telephone poles and other posts by their drilling causing weakening or actual breakage, and allowing access to the decomposing actions of fungi, insects or the weather. In Czechoslovakia, where about one wooden pole per mile is damaged, great-spotted and Syrian woodpeckers cause most of the trouble, green and grey-headed woodpeckers being much less important. In Britain, green woodpeckers seem to be more often involved, and this species can sometimes be particularly troublesome to roof shingles. In 1955, one or two green woodpeckers took to drilling holes through the steeple of a church in Surrey. The culprits were eventually caught roosting inside the steeple, after they had caused expensive damage. In 1966, I had details of a shingle spire being damaged in the same way at Kimbolton in Herefordshire. There is evidence that in some of these incidents the birds are attracted to insects and as a precautionary measure people with vulnerable roofs might be well advised to use suitable insecticides regularly. Dean (1949) records a green woodpecker in Yorkshire which took to drumming on the metal top of an electric pylon producing a sound like an automatic drill. It has often been suggested that woodpeckers are attracted to telephone poles by the humming of the wires, which supposedly resembles an insect sound. As no natural prey produces the appropriate noise it would be unlikely for the birds to have evolved such a non-adaptive response; they probably respond to such poles simply because they are dead trees. Woodpeckers do, however, drill through bee-hives to get at the occupants, but this is a different matter.

Great-spotted woodpeckers, particularly in Denmark, are known to open milk-bottles, but this extraordinary habit has really developed in the tit family. This and the habit of tearing paper, are interesting examples of how an extension of normal behaviour patterns can lead to economic problems, especially at times of high population density. In Britain, mostly blue, and about half as many great tits are involved in opening milk-bottles, although the coal tit, marsh tit, house sparrow, blackbird, starling, robin and other species are known to be capable of it. Fisher and Hinde (1949) state that the first known record of the behaviour dates from 1921, when tits prised open the wax-board tops of milk-bottles in Swaythling near Southampton. They trace the spread of the behaviour to 1947 when they could account for 89 records at places more than fifteen miles from any other place where the habit had been recorded. The spread of the habit is illustrated in Fig. 40 together with an indication of outbreaks in 1957 when there was a large tit irruption and increased incidence of the behaviour (Cramp, Pettet and Sharrock 1960). The tendency of tits not to move great distances, and the isolated and seemingly independent nature of new outbreaks, led Fisher and Hinde (1949) to the conclusion that different birds were individually acquiring the habit, rather than that it was spreading from an original single source. Nevertheless, although different birds at scattered localities may have individually learnt to open bottles, evidence suggested that the rapid spread of the habit around each centre was due to birds subsequently learning from each other. Cardboard caps are opened by a tearing action and metal foil ones by hammering movements. Hinde and Fisher (1951) pointed out that both movements are used during natural food searching and attributed the processes involved in opening milk-bottles to an extension of the food-searching behaviour. Tits naturally explore a wide variety of objects and if hollow may try to open them. Once rewarded by obtaining milk it might be expected that a bird would quickly learn the existence of a new food source and respond directly to the sight of a bottle.

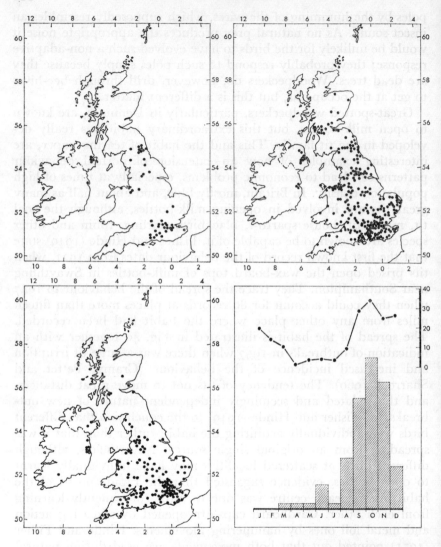

There is increasing evidence that birds acquire many of their feeding skills by watching and copying others, and this capacity, known as local enhancement or social facilitation, may be innate. Without such a mechanism birds could waste a lot of time in learning how to deal with a new food source. In experiments in which various baits such as tic beans are spread evenly on pastures where wood-pigeons are feeding on clover, we have seen this process in action. A bird finding a tic bean by chance stands still while it examines and swallows the new food, and then starts positively searching for others. Neighbouring birds often run forward to see what has been discovered, after which they begin searching for the new food using the modified searching behaviour adopted by the first bird. In this way a completely unexpected but profitable food source is rapidly exploited.

Paper-tearing, which can sometimes lead to serious damage inside houses, seems to be related to the opening of milk-bottles, although it is not rewarded by immediate food. It has a very much longer history as the following quotation which Cramp *et al.* noted shows. This comes originally from a poem published in 1693 by Father Jean Imberdis called 'Papyrus' which is devoted to paper-making (translation by Prof. E. Loughton).

> Small is this naughty Fowl, yet it can wreak
> No small Destruction with its claws and beak.
> For, when paper from afar it spies,
> Straightway through open Window in it flies.
> Its frequent blows the sheet do quickly tear
> Still sodden, and make Havoc everywhere . . .

FIG. 40. *Top* and *bottom left*. Distribution of opening milk bottles by tits. *Top left*, 1939; *right*, 1947; *bottom left*, 1957-8. Each dot represents an isolated outbreak of milk bottle opening and may involve many birds although it is considered that the habit has been learned by the birds independently in each area. (Data for 1939 and 1947 from Fisher & Hinde 1949; for 1957-58 from Cramp, Pettet & Sharrock 1960).
Bottom right. Seasonal incidence of paper-tearing by tits (columns) related to the frequency with which blue-tits search dead parts of trees for food, in which situation they frequently tear bark. (Data on paper tearing from Logan-Home 1953; on natural food searching from Gibb 1954).

During the 1957 outbreak of paper tearing by tits the following articles were involved (total records in brackets): Wallpaper (66) books (27), boxes (20), newspapers (17), lampshades (13), notices (9) labels (7), plus a further 57 incidents involving calendars, silver paper, letters, photo and picture frames, parcels, blotting paper, toilet rolls, tissue paper, razor blade packets. (Data from Cramp *et al* 1960).

To Gin and Snare it grows too soon inured,
And Carelessness is by Experience cured.
The Lime untouched, always the saucy Tit,
So keen its zest, to Paper straight will flit.

Paper-tearing became very common, as to a lesser extent did the habit of eating putty from window frames, during the 1957 tit irruption (Fig. 40). Although records of this occur in most years, such a large outbreak had not been recorded since 1949, when there was another irruption. During the 1949 outbreak of paper-tearing, in which tits (other species may also be involved but to a lesser extent) often entered houses to pull at wallpaper, labels on bottles, magazines, and other objects, Logan Home (1953) showed that incidents reached a peak in October, but were rather infrequent outside the August–December period. Some people attribute paper-tearing to food shortage, but Hinde's (1953) suggestion that it represents an expression of the normal food-searching drive seems to be the most plausible. Hinde quoted work by Gibb (later published in 1954) which showed that tits, particularly blue tits, naturally search the boles and dead branches of trees for insect food much more in the autumn and, in fact, the incidence of paper tearing coincides with that of this natural feeding pattern, as Fig. 40 shows. I think the high incidence of paper-tearing recorded in irruption years may simply be because there were many surplus birds outside their natural habitat, searching for food in the most appropriate environment they could find. This is not to deny that they may continue to search for food and so tear paper after they have satiated themselves on a nearby bird table, as is known to happen, because searching and feeding are separate behaviours. As Gibb has suggested, it will be advantageous for an animal to continue searching for food even when satiated, in order to avoid a hiatus between exhausting one food source and finding another. But on this view, paper-tearing does not have to be linked with food shortage or food abundance – it is simply a case of many tits in new habitats.

CHAPTER 12

WILD LIFE MANAGEMENT

TODAY Britain is such an overcrowded island that it is difficult to believe that demographers in the mid-1940s were seriously concerned at a decline in national fecundity. They prophesied grave economic consequences with too few people to maintain industry (automation was not anticipated) and to set the technical, cultural and moral standards for the rest of the world. These miscalculations should teach us to be cautious in making further prophecies, black though the prospects now appear. The population is expanding at a rate of 250,000 per annum, a million new cars appear on the road each year, urban expansion is currently commandeering 60,000 acres of rural land per year and in many areas over half the hedgerows have disappeared from farmland in the last five years. At the moment most people are unsophisticated in their leisure requirements, and seem satisfied to spend half their holidays shut in metal boxes for a brief respite of transistorised gregariousness in the crowds which throng the coast and deposit tons of litter over the countryside. All the same, an appreciation of other ways of relaxing is growing and is reflected, for example, in an 80% increase in the membership of sailing clubs in the last ten years which brings correspondingly greater pressure to bear on our estuaries, lakes, and coastal facilities. Today there are about 3 million anglers and over 100,000 naturalists, the fringe of a much bigger, but not easily measured, population that enjoys the countryside either for short pleasure trips (over half the population made such short trips during the Whitsun holiday of 1963) or as tourists. We no longer need to justify the role of wild life as part of this amenity.

The problems of planning and preserving man's whole environment on a world scale have been dealt with in a most stimulating book by Robert Arvill, *Man and Environment*, against the background of an expanding population and its future needs. The practical problems involved in conservation in Britain have been explored in a New Naturalist volume by Sir Dudley Stamp and it is unnecessary to deal with the subject in detail here. However, I should like to make three main points.

First, nature reserves and other protected areas are a vital aspect of wild life conservation because they are chosen to represent particular habitats containing characteristic species. They are, in a sense, living museums of evolution and must be preserved as such. Clearly the amount of access by the general public has to be restricted, as the animals and plants simply cannot tolerate unlimited disturbance or trampling. Even so, the success of the R.S.P.B.'s Operation Osprey shows what can be achieved by sensible management.

Second, small areas are not always satisfactory in that if the number of a bird species falls below a certain level, the population loses its viability and is liable to chance extinction. The loss of the Dartford warbler in Surrey (see page 41) provides a case in point and the value of conserving the New Forest to maintain a sufficiently large reservoir of the species is self-evident. Provided the habitat is not spoiled, most species can tolerate a reasonable level of disturbance. This means that if large areas of country are set aside for general amenity and are subject to controlled development they can support an interesting and varied wild life as well as provide other forms of relaxation. Within such National Parks, restricted reserves can be formed. Of course, these are the principles which are at present adopted by the Nature Conservancy. In this context it is not unreasonable to hope that much of Wales could be set aside as an amenity area for the Midland conurbations. Similarly, although man's ingenuity could open up the Highlands of Scotland for industrial productivity as many advocate, it is to be hoped that he will come to recognise its greater value as an outstanding amenity area for N.W. Europe. All this implies planning at a national and international level and once again I recommend the reader to Arvill's book.

Third, in his day-to-day life man must also have access to wild life. People need to participate in nature, not just view it as if through a glass case. Children need to pick flowers and collect frogs' spawn; there is a sense of discovery in tracking down a bird to its nest. Only by active participation can an understanding and sympathy with nature develop. This puts a premium on roadside verges, the rough corner of a field and the local common. Because so much of Britain is now taken up with agriculture, this is the habitat where most of our wild life is to be found, and nobody has the right to destroy it by thoughtless use of chemicals or the irresponsible felling of trees. Moore, Hooper and Davis (1967) have quoted some reasons why farmers destroy their hedges. In arable areas they are not needed to confine stock, as it is more easily done with a wire fence; up to $\frac{1}{2}$ acre suitable for growing crops can be reclaimed by removing a mile of hedge, which could cost up to £40 per year to maintain. They point out that on one farm the removal of $1\frac{1}{2}$ miles of hedges led to a decrease of from 66 to 8 in the number of reverse turns necessary at harvest, cutting by a third the time needed to harvest an acre. Economically it all makes sense. The question today is whether we can afford to stop short of absolute efficiency in order to reap greater, though less tangible, long-term rewards. Once again there is scope for planning and thought. No longer can man afford to sectionalise his interests to the extent of agriculture versus conservation with a philosophy of winner takes all; there is room for both in a planned environment, but for the most part it has to be a new environment and we cannot expect to revert to the conditions of the past.

It is because the need to strike a balance between the conflicting demands of pure agriculture, pest control, game management and wild life conservation is now widely recognised and appreciated, that many of the problems posed by some bird species remain intractable. So it is against this background that I shall conclude by considering the means available for dealing with the so-called pest species.

There are two basic approaches to the problem of bird damage: first, passive defence of the crop or situation at risk by siting it in a safe place or by giving it physical protection; second, active attack on the bird causing the problem. Our understanding of avian population dynamics and of the many examples cited throughout this book, makes it evident that very large numbers of certain species can be killed each year without reducing the numbers which will be present in the following year. This is because animals 'over-produce', resulting in an expendable surplus which has to be lost in some way, so that artificial killing may simply replace other natural causes of death. It follows that artificial population control will only be successful if more animals can be killed than would die for other reasons, or if the birth-rate can be made lower than the death-rate.

The fertility of a bird is defined in terms of the number of progeny which survive to reproduce. It was pointed out in Chapter 2 that changes in bird populations are primarily the result of changes in fertility, bearing in mind that this includes the mortality of young before they attain reproductive age. In a stable population the adult death-rate must balance the fertility rate and it follows that it must be low in species with a low reproductive output. The fertility rate (which includes juvenile mortality) can fluctuate within a limited range to compensate for annual changes in adult losses. Thus the average fertility of the wood-pigeon is 0.55 (this is the number of young from each female surviving to breed) but it has the potential to be three times as high if juvenile mortality is negligible. In contrast, the fertility of the fulmar is only about 0.10. If man could halve the present wood-pigeon population a doubling of the fertility would enable the population to increase again at a rate of 35% per annum. In the case of the starling, doubling the stable fertility rate would ensure a 50% increase, whereas the fulmar's increase would only be 4% per annum if the fertility rate were doubled. (This low figure partly depends on the late maturity characteristic of this species, as adults do not normally breed until they are 7 years old.) In other words, the artificial reduction of bird numbers by man is much more easily achieved and maintained in species with a low potential for population replacement. Such control is made even easier in species with colonial habits. So it was that man was able to reduce the fulmar and other seabirds, but with the present level of killing cannot reduce the wood-pigeon. This makes it pointless to contemplate the control of species with even higher fertilities (starling, house sparrow, bullfinch) without resorting to new and highly efficient techniques.

If it is accepted that a given level of killing makes no difference to the eventual size of a population, the next question to answer is whether the seasonal pattern of deaths among the species concerned is altered in such a way that some damage is prevented. In the case of the wood-pigeon it was found that winter roost shooting could not lessen the crop damage occurring after March. Shooting rooks at their rookeries is offset by the natural mortality occurring until early July, so that after this month it ceases to help in saving crops. Economic ornithology has done much in the past decade to define the circumstances in which artificial control is or is not feasible, and many other examples have already been discussed. Having defined the level of kill necessary in any situation, the next step is to relate the cost with that of the damage that would be prevented. Unfortunately, these two figures have often not been reconciled, partly

PLATE 31. Fouling by birds. *Above*, part of a winter roost of starlings in deciduous woodland, showing accumulated faeces adhering to the branches. The ground was covered with an 8 in. ooze of detritus and this eventually caused the death of many trees. *Below*, fouling caused by feral pigeons living inside a warehouse; fortunately the commodity was in protective bags but this is not always the case.

PLATE 32. Bird damage to aircraft. *Above left*, windscreen shattered by bird strike. *Right*, damage to turbine blades of Buccaneer by injected birds. *Below*, one of the culprits – a herring gull.

because political pressures have called for a show of remedial activity before its justification has been fully tested. In far too many of the cases where careful costings have been made, it has become evident that control costs more than does the damage if such legal and traditional techniques as shooting and trapping are employed.

It is salutary to remember that the traps available for catching birds today – the pigeon cage trap with bob-wires, the top-entry funnel trap for rooks, the Chardonneret trap, the ground entry funnel traps for sparrows – embody nothing new in principle that was not already known to the ancients and that cannot be matched in ingenuity by so-called primitive native tribes in existence today. Progress has come with improved efficiency rather than with new principles; with the replacement of crude coarse nets by Japanese mist-nets, of cross-bows and blunderbusses by the modern breech-loader. But, although mist-nets may produce spectacular catches on favourable days, there are many conditions, such as high winds and open backgrounds, in which they cannot be used. Incidentally, the cost of catching birds with rocket or cannon nets is almost always prohibitive, apart from the serious limitations attached to their use. Trapping, netting and shooting are all techniques which depend on a modicum of field-craft and skill, which are additional limiting variables. Some birds will enter a baited trap for food yet have no incentive to do so if it can be obtained more easily from its preferred habitat. In consequence, traps are often selective in catching individuals which are surplus to a balanced population and are forced to seek food in unusual places. This means that traps are usually seasonal in their effectiveness and are often biased towards the capture of naïve individuals. It is easy to catch young house sparrows when there is a post-breeding surplus, but very much more difficult to catch adults when this would really do good. It is true that in some circumstances the gregarious responses of a species can be exploited by using a decoy bird, but in the case of the bullfinch this method is biased towards the capture of young birds (see page 221).

The association of the shotgun with game-shooting has in turn made it a respected and favourite weapon for pest control. Unfortunately, it does not follow *a priori* that because some people prefer shooting, this is the best way to kill an animal, as shooting is extremely expensive. It is also unfortunate that the taboos associated with game-shooting are a positive hindrance in bird pest control, whether in the form of restricted seasons or codes of etiquette. Pigeon shooters find themselves denied access to estates during the game breeding season and later during the shooting season for game species. It is unrealistic to imagine that effective population control can be achieved in the remaining seasons. Scientific knowledge does not bring immediate change to this state of affairs, and so the long-term attitude must be one of education and the insurance that ineffective techniques do not become doggedly perpetrated as a palliative to those who are happy just so long as something seems to be done.

As these traditional methods are expensive and inefficient, we need to look for a better alternative. It is no coincidence, however, that the very methods which do offer the prospect of killing large numbers of birds cheaply and efficiently have been outlawed by the various Bird Protection Acts to the extent that even their investigation by responsible research organisations is curtailed. No responsible person would seriously contemplate using tethered decoys or bird-lime, but poisoning cannot be so easily dismissed. This does not mean a return to the undesirably crude methods of our predecessors: a letter in the *Essex Weekly Times* (27 April 1917) read: 'A pint of wheat dressed with strychnine will destroy thousands of sparrows at a cost say of 2s. It can be safely prepared by any chemist. A friend of mine told me that his men picked up over 1,800 in three days. All that is necessary is a little care in keeping it out of reach of chickens.'

Chemicals which stupefy rather than kill directly can be used under Government licence within the terms of the Protection of Birds Act (1954), and research into their use has progressed, partly to overcome the problems involved in using direct poisons. The idea of using stupefying agents is by no means new. *The Complete Farmer*, published by A Society of Gentlemen in 1766, relates how pigeons from a farmer's loft were causing damage to a neighbour. The owner recommended that the neighbour should 'pound them, if you catch them trefpaffing'. But the neighbour improved on the hint and 'steeped a parcel of peas in an infufion of coculus indicus, or fome other intoxicating drug, and ftrewed them upon his ground'. When the birds were stupefied the neighbour threw a net over them and called for the owner to come and collect, not being permitted to kill the birds, however much of a nuisance they were.

In theory, protected birds which become affected by any drug can be allowed to recover and be released unharmed. In practice, wild victims may ingest anything from a sub-narcotic to a lethal dose and so a certain number of accidental deaths is inevitable. The number of deaths during field trials differs for different species because sensitivity to a comparable dose (measured in mg per kg body weight) varies according to the species; stock doves and feral pigeons are much more sensitive to alpha-chloralose than partridges or wood-pigeons once differences in body weight are allowed for. For many years cautious field experiments have been conducted by staff of the Ministry of Agriculture working in close liaison with organisations concerned with game preservation and bird protection. It was soon discovered that baits of wheat or barley could be laid on fields and attract wood-pigeons, but they proved hopelessly indiscriminate and of every 100 birds caught, only 57 were wood-pigeons, 16 were game-birds and 4 were small protected species. With a change to large baits using peas and tic beans, far more selectivity was achieved, so that of every 100 birds caught 88 were wood-pigeons, 5 game-birds and less than one small protected bird was affected (in both these examples the remaining birds caught were species like rooks and starlings listed under Schedule II of the Protection of Birds Act). A direct poison would kill in these circumstances, but because stupefying chemicals were used, only 14% of the game-birds were actually killed, the remainder being released unharmed. The protected birds caught are usually common species such as blackbird and skylark (these are even more common than the wood-pigeon), so it becomes evident that in this context 'protected' is an emotive word and that in reality there can be no real risk to wild life, other than to game-birds.

When any research project reaches this stage the matter becomes political rather than scientific, in the sense that a decision must be made to relate the merits of damage prevention to other conservation and country interests. To reconcile many and often conflicting interests is far from easy, especially as no single authority exists for allocating priorities. It is for reasons such as these that economic ornithologists have failed to find much in the way of tangible answers to bird problems. The difficulties do not end at this stage, because farmers often disagree among themselves on the extent to which certain species pose problems, and this is reflected in their degree of co-operation in nationally recommended schemes for action. Again, under the legacy of our feudal past, a tenant farmer is often prevented from acting against a pest because this would endanger game animals which, though they eat his crops, legally belong together with the shooting rights to the owner of the estate. The dangers to other forms of wild life are considerably less when stupefying baits are used in urban environments, where their use is legal under a Government licence; Thearle has recently reviewed the current position.

A central theme of the research done into the use of stupefying baits has been the attempt to develop selective methods of bait presentation. This seems to offer more promise of success than the discovery of specific poisons for certain species such as an avian equivalent of the rat poison Warfarin. It is quite feasible that these await discovery and that something could be found empirically. All new drugs, particularly in the United States, are subject to an enormous screening process to discover their potential for a multiplicity of uses. When it was discovered that Warfarin caused haemorrhage in rodents, but for practical purposes was harmless to man and a wide range of other animals, its value as a selective rodent poison could be developed. To initiate and subsidise a research programme to discover specific drugs for each species would, nevertheless, be out of the question, because of the enormous costs involved without guarantee of success. In such circumstances, the sensible course is to accumulate as much knowledge about an animal's ecology and physiology as possible so that if a suitable agent is screened it can quickly be put to use, with at least two points in mind. First, the case of thalidomide has emphasised that inadequately tested drugs may possess unsuspected secondary dangers, and the same lesson comes from the experience of organo-chlorine insecticides. Second, even if secondary risks are negligible, selection may lead to the emergence of resistant strains. This in turn highlights the need to use chemical weapons strategically – and not by way of unsubtle blanket applications.

Given selective baiting procedures and accepting these reservations, it would be feasible, assuming a change in the law, to use direct poisons and other antiphysiological agents rather than stupefying substances which have disadvantages in the costs involved in collecting and killing affected subjects. One twentieth-century idea is to feed problem birds a contraceptive pill. The pros and cons of reproduction inhibition cannot be dealt with fully here, especially as many of the arguments must be theoretical in the absence of field trials. Suffice to remark that the reproductive rate of such birds as the feral pigeon so exceeds the needs of replacement that one must envisage reductions of over 80% in productivity, unless the output from untreated individuals is to cancel out the effects of sterility in treated birds. This implies an extremely efficient level of treatment for success and the attainment of this level is made even more difficult because the agents available are only effective for limited periods (6–9 months). Permanent sterilants would help to solve difficulties in administration and could have cumulative benefits, but unfortunately those agents which are effective longer tend at present to be the more dangerous chemicals, and could not be used in a densely populated island like Britain. Indeed, whenever the use of drugs or poisons is envisaged it still has to be accepted that they must be applied intensively enough over wide areas to affect more individuals than would die through natural causes. Operations on this scale imply a highly organised administration rather than dependence on *ad hoc* voluntary support, which may only be forthcoming when people think they have a problem. In the absence of strong incentive, there must be a large measure of co-operation in any programme hoping to achieve population control of common and fecund species like the house sparrow, rook, feral and wood-pigeon.

Instead of killing birds directly, it is sometimes possible to make the habitat unsuitable for them. This of course becomes increasingly difficult the more closely adapted the species concerned is to the problem situation. It is possible that there would be fewer wood-pigeons on farmland in the absence of hedges, but there would be fewer farmland birds – a loss which would outweigh the gain. It is clearly foolish to position rubbish tips which attract gulls at the end of aerodrome runways, and habitat control in this context would seem to be common sense; but hitherto authorities have done just this kind of thing, which makes it necessary to state the obvious. Soil has been sterilised and herbicides have been used round airport runways in attempts to reduce the number of birds dependent on soil-invertebrates and ground herbage, and in these special cases the technique may be sound. On a wide scale this approach is clearly incompatible with conservation. The planting of deciduous trees in conifer mono-cultures, in order to encourage insectivorous birds, has been mentioned (page 95), as has the expediency of providing alternative sites to attract problem birds away from the areas in which they cause harm (page 217). This last can be a dangerous procedure, because it is more likely to lead to a larger bird population than would otherwise be possible and to cause a risk of grave damage if the alternative site loses its attraction for any reason, such as loss of food stocks.

If it is shown that widespread or even local population control is not feasible, the remaining solution to bird damage is to protect the crop at risk. The most direct way of doing this is by protective cages. It is surprising how often people who claim to be suffering exorbitant bird damage year after year consider the costs involved to be too high. There can be no doubt that this is the only answer when very valuable crops are being grown, as for instance plots of cereals undergoing genetical trials at experimental farms, where sparrows can cause damage out of all proportion to what they eat. Wire netting enclosures are admittedly expensive, but recently a firm has marketed a system whereby bamboo poles slot into appropriate holes in small balls to make a lightweight frame of any proportions over which nylon netting can be laid. Farmers and horticulturists operating on large acreages cannot use these methods, but there is no excuse for the gardener who neglects the judicious use of black cotton on his peas or *Polyanthus*, or who cannot be bothered to net his blackcurrants. It is usually the lazy man who calls out for something to be done about the garden birds, while the man with initiative is already using his wife's nylon stockings as sleeves to protect the cherries.

Noise machines and scarecrows have been in vogue for ages. Gunther pointed out one of their drawbacks in a *Report on Agricultural Damage by Vermin and Birds* in 1917 when he wrote 'But scaring is unsound economically, for the birds will feed somewhere, and immunity is secured for well-protected crops at the expense of the poorer or less energetic farmers: the loss to the country is just the same.' Admittedly, this is not always true as it is sometimes possible to frighten birds off a valuable crop on to one of lesser importance but the point always needs bearing in mind. One aspect of the task of scaring is to ensure that no particular grower suffers more than his neighbours. In Africa, where flocks of *Quelea* do immense damage to native cereals, boys are constantly kept on guard at strategic points to frighten off any intruders, using drums, rattles and flashing tins; the boy is usually positioned in some high vantage point with strings leading from it to various noise-making devices in the fields. It is recognised that the *Quelea* will eventually settle and do damage somewhere; the aim is to ensure that no one person suffers disproportionately, and the same attitude was adopted in England in earlier years.

Birds will often avoid a new object or sound at first but unless their fear is reinforced by some unpleasant experience they quickly get used to the new situation, just as they do to traffic noise, aircraft engines and other everyday experiences which have no serious consequences. Thus bangers and other noise machines and strange looking objects may initially cause a bird to prefer a field without such an object, but in the absence of any choice hunger quickly overcomes any fear and it will ignore the device. Wright has described an experiment in which ten automatic bird scarers producing loud explosions by the combustion of acetylene in a pressure chamber, were sited on either side of an airfield runway. These proved effective for one week, after which birds even started perching on them. This waning of response to a new stimulus was appreciated by J. Worlidge (1716). To scare rooks from corn he recommended digging holes about two feet deep and four feet in diameter and placing long crow feathers round the circumference and in the bottom, claiming that crows would not feed near such places: 'I prefume the Reafon is, becaufe whilft they are feeding on the ground, the terrifying object is out of their fight; which is not ufual in other Scare-Crows, wherewith in a little time they grow familiar, by being always in view.'

Various colours are sometimes stated to have repellent properties depending on the species concerned. Kalmbach and Welch (1946) considered that birds would avoid green-coloured rodent baits, Haviland (1892) believed that a sparrow showed antipathy to purple and others have argued that pigeons avoid red-coloured objects. It is true that birds will show colour discrimination in free-choice trials, but the interpretations that can be made from such contrived experiments are very limited. In any case, it is an integral feature of the 'feeding-image' that birds will discriminate between two objects if offered the choice. There are some circumstances in which birds do exhibit innate colour preferences, for instance young game-birds (Murton and Thearle, in prep.) and the ducklings of various wildfowl (Kear) prefer green: this presumably helps these nidicolous species to locate aphids and various green algae respectively, soon after birth. This early colour preference is modified by subsequent learning so that the birds will rapidly adjust to feeding on any coloured object that provides food. In this way Croze trained carrion crows to seek out pieces of meat which were hidden under mussel shells painted red and distributed over the shore at Ravenglass. Batesian and Mullerian mimicry rely on birds learning to associate unpleasant taste experiences with features of visual recognition, including the pattern, form and colour of the insect concerned.

Unusual objects which have no significance in the normal life of a bird are unlikely to arouse more than a short-term fear response and the best hope of success seems to be in objects to which birds have evolved adaptive responses. Fear of predators suggests one approach and this is, of course, the basis of the scarecrow modelling a man. Whether or not a small bird is frightened by a hawk partly depends on the circumstances in which it is seen. A hunting raptor may elicit strong escape behaviour, whereas one engaged in breeding behaviour may be recognised as harmless, and small birds (sparrows, pied wagtail) may themselves build in the foundations of a nest occupied by a bird of prey. Lorenz (1939) and Tinbergen (1951) showed that birds have an ability to distinguish fine points of recognition; in their classic experiments a silhouette of a goose made to fly overhead brought little response from captive wildfowl, but when pulled in reverse it looked like a hawk and released fear responses. However, it is now known that this fear of a hawk-shape is similar to the fear shown towards any new object and that its expression partly depends on the subject's earlier experiences within its environment, and not on a pure innate recognition of raptors. Thus, mallard ducklings reared in complete isolation were equally frightened by a hawk or goose shape when presented over their cage for the first time (Melzack, Penick and Beckett 1959).

Mobbing is one aspect of the anti-predator response given to a non-flying predator and is an expression of the bird's tendency to behave in incompatible ways; to investigate, to attack and to flee. Both Hinde and Marler have shown how a small change in the bird's environment will elicit investigation while a major change promotes fear. Because of this, chaffinches and great tits will keep their distance from real owls or good imitation models, but will approach and investigate those embodying only a few owl-like characteristics. Hinde has shown how the mobbing response of chaffinches wanes in a complicated manner because more than one decremental process must be involved and he assumes that the change depends on a balance between processes leading to decreases and those leading to increases in responsiveness, each being independent of the others.

The mobbing responsiveness of the chaffinch increases if the stimulus is removed and is then re-presented, but with intervals of re-presentation of up to 24 hours the response is still reduced. The degree or waning can be lessened if a new object is shown at the second exposure, but this depends on how long the first object is exposed. The practical lesson which follows from this kind of research is the need to make model predators as life-like as possible, to reinforce them with other noxious stimuli and to alter their mode and frequency of presentation as much as possible – how often a farmer just leaves a scarecrow to fall down.

Models of flying hawks, which can be suspended on balloons above an orchard, and other ingenious and realistic devices are likely to give better results than ill-conceived silhouettes of motionless predators stuck up in unlikely places; attempts to make a model hawk on the basis of a radio-controlled aeroplane must be limited when the result looks patently like an aeroplane. It is not surprising that one of the most successful means of scaring birds from airfields in Britain involved the use of a live peregrine falcon. After copying birds and learning to fly, man has now turned to birds to keep his runways clear. From experiments it has been concluded that flying a falcon at least once a day could keep an airfield clear of birds, but that such clearance did not last more than one or two days. This degree of effectiveness has to be set against the trouble and costs involved in training and rearing falcons (assuming these can be obtained) and the fact that falcons are relatively ineffective in wooded country or under bad weather conditions.

Birds give warning of the approach of predators by making alarm calls, and these provoke flight and the seeking out of shelter. The characteristics of these calls show convergence between species because, unlike the case of normal song which brings reproductive isolation, it is an advantage for different species to avoid the same danger by responding to a common alarm call. Alarm calls do not last long and have properties which make the bird difficult to locate. Marler has shown them to be of high frequency so that phase differences in the ears of a predator cannot place the source of the sound. Nor can binaural comparisons of the arrival time of the sound be of much help to a predator because the calls are continuous and have no sudden start or finish. Finally, the use of sound shadow (the difference of intensity in the sound received by the two ears) is only helpful if the width of the head exceeds the wave-length of sound, and with alarm calls this is not the case as they have short wave-lengths. The alarm call of the chaffinch (the 'seet' note) when seeking cover has all these properties and causes other birds to respond by fleeing to shelter. On the other hand, when mobbing an owl, the chaffinch employs the low frequency 'chink' call which is easily placed.

The innate response of birds to appropriate alarm calls has been used as a scaring device by playing recorded calls through a suitable tape-recorder and loud-speaker system, a technique first developed by Frings and Jumber in 1954 in the United States but since developed by other workers, in particular Busnel and Giban in France and Brough in England. If held in the hand and presented with particularly frightening stimuli, some species will occasionally give a so-called 'distress' call, a number of which have been recorded. The principle may well have been known to the ancients. An Egyptian tomb painting from Thebes dating to the eighteenth dynasty depicts bird-hunters in canoes in the papyrus swamps of the Nile. One holds a live cormorant and a boomerang and the other has just thrown his weapon and killed a bird rising from its nest in the colony. The decoy, which is held by its legs, gives the appearance of a bird in distress which suggests that its calls were being used to attract others within range.

There is sometimes confusion over what should be termed a distress call, and whether they differ in kind or only in degree from other alarm calls. For instance, German workers raised a short staccato alarm call from starlings when they dragged a fox past the nesting site of a pair, and the recording proved very effective in frightening starlings. It is perhaps analogous with the mobbing-type alarm call of the chaffinch. On the other hand, the true distress call of the starling is a long drawn-out scream, which probably serves a rather different function, although it too is very effective in frightening birds and has been used to disperse roosts (see data in Brough 1968). Normally the distress call of a bird seems to be given when it is actually caught by a predator, and its emission causes other members of the species to come to the sound source and possibly mob. This has not been proved and the difficulties in observing it would clearly be considerable, but it is known that gulls respond to a distress call played from an airfield vehicle by approaching and mobbing the sound source. If this is normally the case, mobbing of a predator by numerous other members of the species might allow the captured bird to escape, and though not proven, this seems to be a reasonable supposition of its function on the evidence so far available. In the case of certain alarm calls, Perrins has recently noted a ventriloquial quality which may temporarily cause a predator to look away, perhaps just long enough for the prey to escape. Certainly the sudden note caused Perrins to look away from subjects he had caught in a mist-net, and other observers have had similar experiences.

When the distress call of a gull species, rook, jackdaw or lapwing is played over a loudspeaker, other members of the species at first fly up, drift towards the sound source and then disperse. Not all species have distress calls which evoke this kind of response (e.g. oystercatcher and wood-pigeon), although they may have other alarm notes. It is likely that the range of alarm calls which a species possesses, including true distress, escape-inducing, shelter-seeking, aggressive mobbing, will vary according to their survival value. Thus a top predator such as an eagle may have experienced no selective pressure to evolve a distress call. Hence, for the purposes of applied work each species must be considered on its own merits. In a series of field trials Brough has established that recorded distress sounds are more effective if they can be reinforced with other noxious stimuli, and his experience does suggest that they are cheaper and more effective than using a combination of fire-crackers, rockets and loud bangs. Wright has reported that repeated use of gull distress calls kept an airfield clear of birds for about twelve months with little evidence that the birds were becoming used to them, whereas in the experiment mentioned above, habituation to acetylene bangers occurred after only two days.

Other variables influence the effectiveness of distress calls. For instance, Gramet and Hanoteau found that it was easier to scare rooks from their breeding colonies during the nest-building period than when they started brooding, and easier if the colonies were small. Winter roosts were much more easily dispersed than breeding colonies, as the birds joined other roosts or formed new ones. Scaring corvids from crops also proved feasible, and a system of two loudspeakers protected up to 20 hectares for as long as 59 days. None the less, constant repetition of the same signal at the rate of 1–10 per hour did make the birds pay less attention to the sound source, and they flew away less often and returned more rapidly. Changing the recording seemed to provide sufficient difference to re-establish the initial response.

The idea of using high frequency sound waves, i.e. ultrasonics, to scare birds has attracted much attention and research effort. There is little evidence to suggest that birds can detect sound waves much above the frequency detectable by man (their upper limit of detection is probably about 20 kc) or that again these high frequency sounds have any significance for them. Experiments using sounds from 16–40 kc have produced unconvincing results, as either there was no scaring effect or only subjects a few feet from the sound source were affected, a response which is open to other interpretations. The propagation of high-frequency sounds requires large amounts of power and it is extremely difficult to project the sounds over long distances. All in all, there would be little prospect of making the technique generally available, even if it worked.

Attempts have been made, particularly by French workers, to isolate the components of the distress call which have the most effect, in the hope that these may be used to produce super-stimuli. So far this has had little success as birds seem to respond to the whole signal and not to particular components. As with alarm calls, the distress calls appear to possess many physical characteristics in common and this convergence leads to a common interspecific value. The distress calls of black-headed and herring gulls affect both species, and to a lesser extent carrion crow, rook and jackdaw. The Larid gulls respond to the distress signal of jay and jackdaw. On the other hand, the call of the common gull is far more peculiar to the species, according to Busnel who found that other gulls were hardly affected by its emission. The quality of a recording and playback has a profound influence on the effectiveness of a distress call, and earlier suggestions that American herring gulls had subspecific differences which made their calls ineffective in Europe were probably due to the poor quality of the tapes. Current work in Britain is concerned with improving the technical quality of recordings and of finding ways of playing the calls over long distances without loss of quality and effectiveness. Future developments are likely to centre on finding the most effective and economic combinations of sound and other stimuli which will lead to the slowest practical rate of habituation.

Much research has been concentrated on finding what Duncan, Wright and Ridpath call a chemical scarecrow – an olfactory or gustatory repellent substance which will prevent birds eating a crop to which it is applied. Obviously such a substance must not contaminate the crop in any way. Much confusion and conflicting evidence has arisen in this field for a variety of reasons. To start with, it has often been assumed that substances which are particularly foul-smelling or which have unpleasant taste for humans evoke similar repulsions in birds. Yet there is no *a priori* reason why birds should have evolved adaptive responses to substances which have no significance in their natural lives. All the same, chemicals like beta naphthol, naphthalene, di-phenyl-guanidine, tetra-methyl-thiuram-di-sulphide (thiram) or Morkit, which is a commercial bird repellent with over three-quarters of anthraquinone, have been held to be repellent, although when Wright applied them to gooseberry buds in controlled experiments no evidence of repellence could be obtained so far as damage by bullfinches was concerned. Wright (1962) also found that neither thiram nor anthraquinone applied at the rate of either five or ten per cent by weight of maize seed deterred rooks from feeding on the newly sown grain, though some success in deterring grackles and cowbirds from eating newly sown maize in Mexico by using thiram has been claimed by Young and Zevallos (1960).

One of the problems is that in cage tests birds will discriminate between food objects and will often show a preference for the untreated samples. The same avoidance of treated food does not necessarily occur in the field because here the same conditions of choice do not exist. For instance, it was found during cage trials that feral pigeons would distinguish between normal maple peas and those coated with a technical white oil, which is used as a sticker for alpha-chloralose, and would not eat the food treated with this oil. Under field conditions this observation has no significance, unless treated and untreated baits are laid out side by side. So far, all critically conducted field trials of so-called repellent chemicals have yielded negative results, and none could be sincerely recommended as a means of combating bird damage (this does not apply to mammals where the sense of smell is highly developed and of importance in the life of the animal).

Birds have well-developed olfactory organs, particularly such species as the oilbird, turkey vulture and kiwi, which might be suspected to rely on odour detection, but in other species which have been subjected to controlled experimentation the evidence indicates that the sense of smell is poorly developed and of little consequence in the normal life of the bird. This may reflect how inappropriate the test conditions are; after all, why should birds respond to cheap human perfumes? Similarly, blowing tobacco smoke at a bird from a hide has no significance for a bird and evokes no response so far as we can tell.

Earlier failures with repellent agents led Duncan to investigate the sense of smell and taste of pigeons. Birds possess very few taste buds (about 100 on the posterior end of the pigeon's tongue as against 9,000 in man distributed all over the tongue). Yet when tested with a wide range of chemicals in drinking water, pigeons and domestic fowls displayed an ability to detect and reject a very wide range of chemical substances, often at extremely low concentrations. Fowls, for example, showed a marked preference for a solution combining two parts per thousand of a compound tasting of butter. The extraordinary degree of convergence shown by some mimetic insects emphasises the high powers of visual discrimination which birds possess, in this case brought about by a need to avoid distasteful models. Such observations make it unreasonable to expect that any crude smell or object would provide meaningful scaring mechanisms, however repulsive they may be to us, and the same arguments apply to auditory repellents.

TABLES

Table 1.   Census returns for grey partridges and red-legged partridges on 3,000 acres in Norfolk

		No. of breeding adults	Ratio of young to old in August	Total August population	Percentage loss from August–Spring			Calculated post-breeding population of young*	% loss of young from spring to autumn	% change in breeding population in next season
					Shot	Other loss	Total loss			
1952	G	1364	2.02	4175	40	25	65	6752	59	+ 5
	R	68	2.06	214	121	+ 77	(44)			+ 76
1953	G	1438	0.35	1982	0	32	32	7118	93	– 7
	R	120	0.34	174	0	11	11			+ 27
1954	G	1344	1.11	2930	8	55	63	6653	77	– 19
	R	154	1.28	359	27	38	65			– 18
1955	G	1092	2.07	3407	26	36	62	5405	58	+ 17
	R	126	1.48	321	56	+ 15	(41)			+ 49
1956	G	1276	0.61	2112	0	44	44	6316	87	– 7
	R	188	0.77	349	0	50	50			+ 7
1957	G	1188	2.22	3910	21	49	70	5881	54	+ 2
	R	174	2.64	652	37	33	70			+ 14
1958	G	1210	0.48	1832	0	54	54	5990	90	– 31
	R	198	0.69	355	0	41	41			+ 6
1959	G	840	3.44	3758	28	42	70	4158	30	+ 34
	R	210	3.92	1053	61	+ 0.5	(60.5)			+ 96
1960	G	1124	3.68	5282	37	35	72	5564	25	+ 28
	R	412	3.72	1975	54	27	81			– 8

* Assumes an average chick production of 9.89 per pair of adults (data from Middleton and Huband 1966)

	No. of breeding adults	Ratio of young to old in August	Total August population	Percentage loss from August–Spring			Calculated post-breeding population of young*	% loss of young from spring to autumn	% change in breeding population in next season
				Shot	Other loss	Total loss			
1961 G	1444	1.91	4202	36	35	71	7148	61	− 16
R	378	2.07	1160	66	+ 2	64			+ 10
1962 G	1210	0.43	1730	0	51	51	5990	91	− 30
R	414	0.66	687	0	37	37			+ 4
1963 G	846	0.35	1142	0	27	27	4188	93	− 2
R	432	0.15	544	0	+ 1	(1)			+ 27
1964 G	832	1.12	1764	14	44	58	4118	77	− 11
R	548	1.00	1096	26	25	51			+ 4
1965 G	740	0.97	1460				3663	80	
R	528	0.24	654						

* Assumes an average chick production of 9.89 per pair of adults (data from Middleton and Huband 1966)

Table 2.   Relation between number of red grouse dispersing in winter and the number known to be taken by predators

	No. of live grouse in autumn	No. of grouse dispersing	No. killed by predators	No. of raptors seen per 100 h.
Low area				
1956–7	341	172	44	8
1957–8	597	207	161	12
1958–9	637	414	182	10
1959–60	302	144	45	5
1960–1	468	117	87	4
High area				
1957–8	659	274	107	8
1958–9	541	356	92	9
1959–60	246	103	40	2
1960–1	558	191	43	5

From Jenkins, Watson and Miller 1964

Table 3. Percentage of different prey in the diet of the peregrine, goshawk and sparrowhawk in the breeding season

	Peregrine England, Wales and S. Scotland	Scottish Highlands Inland	Scottish Highlands Coastal	Goshawk	Sparrow-hawk
Grouse and other large game birds	4	21	1	10	
Waders	9	18	16	1	
Gulls and terns	} 1	} 4	15		
Puffins and other auks			30		
Rock dove			15		
Feral pigeon	25	17	5	19	
Wood-pigeon	2	3	T	18	
Other large birds	} 2	} 9	} 13	4	
Corvids					1
Medium birds (thrush–woodpecker)	47	19	4	14	9
House sparrow					32
Other small passerines	10	9	T	11	57
Rabbit and hare				15	
Other small mammals				1	T

Peregrine records from Ratcliffe 1963

Goshawk and sparrowhawk records of plucking remains from the territories of birds near Hamburg based on Brüll 1964

T = trace

Table 4. Number of nest boxes occupied by various species of insectivorous birds in the Forest of Dean

	Number of nest boxes occupied by:					†*Amount of defoliation by caterpillars*
	Pied flycatcher	*Redstart*	*Great tit*	*Blue tit*	*All species	
1950	87	15	37	37	180	M
1951	100	14	31	54	201	S
1952	98	11	22	41	172	S
1953	85	10	17	38	152	N
1954	76	10	27	48	161	H
1955	67	15	17	35	135	H/M
1956	60	12	25	50	149	H
1957	54	4	75	79	215	S
1958	71	12	28	49	160	S
1959	71	11	36	55	174	S
1960	58	10	20	49	141	S/N
1961	62	3	45	72	188	S/N
1962	59	18	21	46	146	N
1963	58	19	16	42	136	S
1964	57	13	23	46	141	S/N

* Other species included in total area are coal tit, marsh tit, nuthatch

† Defoliation figures: H = heavy; M = moderate; S = slight; N = negligible are based on Betts (1955), R. E. Crowther and notes by B. Campbell (adapted from Campbell 1968)

Table 5. Bird density per 100 acres of English farmland as shown by the British Trust for Ornithology, Common Bird Census

	Returns for 9,980 acres scattered throughout Britain in 1962	Returns for 5,432 acres of Midland farms mostly examined in 1966
Mallard		1.0
Red-legged Partridge	0.8	0.4
Grey Partridge	4.0	3.2
Pheasant		1.2
Moorhen	2.4	0.2
Lapwing	2.8	1.2
Curlew	0.4	
Stock Dove	0.2	0.1
Turtle dove	0.6	0.8
Cuckoo	n	n.8
Little owl	0.4	0.2
Tawny owl		0.2
Green woodpecker	0.2	0.1
Skylark	12.8	18.2
Swallow	1.6	1.0
Carrion Crow	1.6	2.0
Jackdaw		0.2
Jay		0.2
Magpie	0.8	2.0
Great tit	2.4	7.0
Blue tit	3.8	10.4
Coal tit		0.1
Marsh tit		0.2
Willow tit		0.2
Long-tailed tit		0.4
Treecreeper		0.2
Wren	6.6	8.0
Mistle thrush	1.0	0.8
Song thrush	8.8	10.2
Blackbird	16.6	30.6
Redstart	0.6	0.1
Robin	7.0	16.6
Reed warbler	0.6	0.2
Sedge warbler	0.8	1.8
Blackcap	0.2	1.2
Garden warbler	0.4	0.6
Whitethroat	7.2	11.2

	Returns for 9,980 acres scattered throughout Britain in 1962	*Returns for 5,432 acres of Midland farms mostly examined in 1966*
Lesser whitethroat	0.4	1.6
Willow warbler	2.6	3.0
Chiffchaff	0.8	1.4
Spotted flycatcher	0.6	0.6
Dunnock	9.0	22.4
Meadow pipit	0.8	0.1
Pied wagtail	0.6	0.4
Yellow wagtail	0.6	1.0
Greenfinch	2.8	6.4
Goldfinch	1.2	2.4
Linnet	5.2	10.0
Bullfinch	0.4	3.0
Chaffinch	10.2	16.2
Yellowhammer	5.4	10.6
Corn bunting	0.8	2.0
Reed bunting	1.8	3.0
Tree sparrow	3.8	6.6

Column one is from Williamson and Homes 1964 who give figures for number of singing males per 100 acres. These figures have been doubled on the assumption that each male had a female

Column two derived from Williamson 1967

Table 6. Average density of birds per 100 acres of farmland at sites in Cambridgeshire (Carlton) and Oxfordshire

	Summer population	Cambs	Oxon		Winter population	Cambs	Oxon
R	Wood-pigeon	43	6	R, wv	Skylark	64	19
R	Rook	36	14	R	Wood-pigeon	47	7
R	House sparrow	33	7	R	House sparrow	43	31
R	Skylark	30	4	R, wv	Tree sparrow	42	—
R	Tree-sparrow	22	—	R, wv	Starling	38	98
R	Linnet	22	11	R, wv	Chaffinch	35	32
R	Partridges	11	1	R, wv	Lapwing	28	8
R	Blackbird	10	36	R, wv	Rook	26	10
R	Song thrush	9	17	R, wv	Blackbird	20	35
R	Yellow hammer	8	8	R, wv	Linnet	14	19
R	Starling	7	5	R	Partridge	13	8
sv	Swallow	6	—	wv	Redwing	11	6
R	Robin	5	9	R	Yellow hammer	11	15
sv	Turtle Dove	5	—	wv	Fieldfare	10	23
sv	Whitethroat	4	11	R, wv	Greenfinch	10	5
R	Pheasant	4	—	R	Dunnock	8	3
R	Dunnock	4	7	R	Song thrush	6	14
R	Chaffinch	4	21	R	Pheasant	6	—
R	Goldfinch	3	0	R	Robin	4	13
R	Lapwing	3	5	R	Wren	3	3
R	Meadow pipit	3	—	R	Blue tit	3	7
R	Greenfinch	3	2	R	Bullfinch	3	—
R	Wren	3	5	R	Long-tailed tit	3	4
R	Blue tit	3	2	R	Great tit	2	2
R	Bullfinch	2	—	R	Goldfinch	2	2
R	Corn bunting	2	—	R	Green woodpecker	1	1
sv	Willow warbler	2	2	R	Jackdaw	1	—
R	Great tit	2	1	R	Jay	1	1
R	Long-tailed tit	2	2	R	Marsh tit	1	—
R	Stock dove	1	—	R	Stock dove	0.5	—
R	Marsh tit	1	—	R	Meadow pipit	0.5	3
sv	Blackcap	1	—	R	Corn bunting	0.5	2
R	Jay	1	0	R	Moorhen	0.5	—
R	Moorhen	0.5	—	wv	Golden plover	0.5	—
P	Common gull	0.5	—	P	Common gull	0.5	—
sv	House martin	0.5	—	P	Black-headed gull	0.5	
R	Jackdaw	0.5	—	R	Little owl	0.5	—
R	Magpie	0.5	1	R	Tawny owl	0.5	—

	Summer population	Cambs	Oxon	Winter population	Cambs	Oxon
R	Willow tit	0.5	—	Great spotted		
sv	Lesser whitethroat	0.5	I	woodpecker	0.5	—
sv	Spotted flycatcher	0.5	—	Magpie	0.5	I
R	Reed bunting	0.5	R	Mistle thrush	0.5	2
R	Tree creeper	0.5	R	Tree creeper	0.5	—
R	Mistle thrush	0.5	I	Willow tit	0.5	—
R	Kestrel	0.2	R	Reed bunting	0.5	—
R	Little owl	0.2	R	Kestrel	0.5	—
R	Tawny owl	0.2	R	Heron	0.2	—
P	Heron	0.2	P	Snipe	0.2	—
P	Mallard	0.2	P	Woodcock	0.2	—
P	Herring gull	0.2	P	Lesser-black		
sv	Swift	0.2		backed gull	0.2	—
R	Green woodpecker	0.2	I P	Coal tit	0.2	—
P	Carrion crow	0.2	2 R	Pied wagtail	0.2	—
P	Wheatear	0.2	R	Carrion crow	0.2	2
sv	Tree pipit	0.2				
R	Pied wagtail	0.2				

Carlton figures due to Westwood and Murton (unpubl.)

Oxfordshire figures from Chapman 1939

Status at Carlton shown as R= resident, sv = summer visitor, P = passage visitor, wv = winter visitor

Table 7. Bird density in deciduous woodland. (First three columns in number of birds per 100 acres, last column relative frequency of contact.) data derived from:

	Bevan 1963	Williamson 1964	Williamson and Homes 1964	Yapp 1962
Robin	133	131	64	(78)
Blue tit	68	82		(39)
Wren	73		51	(70)
Whitethroat	—	65	11	
Willow warbler	53	59	29	(56)
Great tit	48	45		(39)
Blackbird	43	64	42	(65)
Chaffinch	35	55	13	(87)
Song thrush	18	30	24	(35)
Dunnock	13	64	9	
Garden warbler		30		(22)
Starling		27		(4)
Wood-pigeon		30		(48)
Coal tit		18		
Chiffchaff	13	23		(31)
Pheasant		14		
Jay		9		(22)
Marsh tit		9		
Nuthatch		9		
Tree pipit		9		(22)
Great spotted woodpecker		5		
Mistle thrush		5		(22)
Redstart		5		(22)
Grasshopper warbler		5		
Linnet		5		
Jackdaw				(22)
Blackcap				(22)
Cuckoo				(35)

Bevan's data refer to a Surrey oak wood.

Williamson and Homes to 265 acres of mixed woodland sampled by the Common Bird Census

Williamson to mixed woodland in Berkshire

Yapp to lowland pedunculate oak woodland

Table 8.   Percentage of nests started which produce one or more
fledged young depending on habitat

	Woodland	Farmland	Suburban/urban
Blackbird	12	28	50
Song thrush	12	26	53
Dunnock	21	35	38
Chaffinch	11	27	20

After Snow and Mayer-Gross 1967

Table 9.   Number of rook nests in Nottinghamshire in relation to
acreage of farm crops

	Total all crops and grass	Total grass	Total cereals	Total nests	Nests per sq. mile
1928	423,633	219,260	93,171	6,576	7.8
1932	415,581	225,525	82,515	6,113	7.2
1944	400,022	187,137	124,442	10,306	12.2
1958	396,144	195,316	142,280	17,028	20.2
1962	392,439	194,631	149,036	10,609	12.6

After Dobbs 1964

Omitting the data for 1962 for the reasons given in the text, the correlation
between the number of rook nests per sq. mile and the acreage of cereals
is $r_2 = 0.947$

Table 10.   Annual and seasonal variations in mean clutch of rook
related to earthworm availability

	1964	1965	1966
Mean clutch size in March	4.0 (51)	3.3 (25)	4.1 (21)
Mean clutch size in April and May	3.6 (9)	3.5 (23)	3.5 (13)
Earthworm index in March	2.95	1.18	3.51
Earthworm index in April	5.07	3.49	3.71

Table 11. Clutch size of the rook in England

| Clutch size | Number of clutches | | | |
| | Near Oxford | | Cambridgeshire | |
	Early	Late	Early	Late
1	—	—	3 (2)	2 (1)
2	6	2	11 (4)	4 (2)
3	20	10	19 (14)	13 (6)
4	56	5	36 (29)	21 (11)
5	57	3	23 (18)	4 (1)
6	11	—	4 (4)	1 (1)
7	1	—	1 (1)	—
Total	151	20	97 (72)	45 (22)
Mean	4.3	3.5	3.8 (4.0)	3.5 (3.5)

The Oxford data are from Lockie 1955

Eggs laid before 31 March are classed as 'early' those laid after this date as 'late'

The figure in brackets omit data for 1965 which was an exceptionally late year for breeding

Table 12. Number of young rooks produced per clutch depending on clutch size

	Clutch size	Number of clutches	Total number of young fledged	Average number of young fledged per clutch
Early nests				
	1	3	0	} 0.7
	2	11	10	
	3	19	25	1.3
	4	34	75	2.2
	5	22	40	1.8
Late nests				
	1	2	1	} 0.5
	2	4	2	
	3	13	33	2.5
	4	21	48	2.3

Table 13.   Breeding success and juvenile survival of rook in relation to earthworm availability

	1964	1965	1966
Number of eggs laid in March	204	83	85
% hatched	56	69	59
% young fledged of those hatched	64	91	76
Number of young produced per brood (number of broods in brackets)	2.4 (31)	2.7 (19)	2.4 (16)
Mean earthworm index in April	5.07	3.49	3.71
Number of eggs laid in April	32	81	46
% hatched	69	64	78
% young fledged of those hatched	64	94	100
Number of young produced per brood	1.8 (8)	2.7 (18)	3.3 (11)
Mean earthworm index in May	6.25	4.64	1.15
Mean clutch size for whole season	3.93	3.42	3.85
Mean % young fledged of eggs laid	37	62	56
Number of young raised per clutch	1.45	2.12	2.16
Ratio of adults to young at fledging	1:0.73	1:1.06	1:1.08
Ratio of adults to young in June	1:0.28	1:0.30	1:0.07
% change in proportion of juveniles between fledging and June	− 62	− 72	− 94
Mean earthworm index in June	1.65	0.79	0.56
* Index of total adult breeding population	310	304	235

* The numbers of eggs laid and figures derived therefrom are based on only a sample of nests which could be reached by climbing. The index of breeding population is the best estimate of the total population and is based on the number of occupied nests. It was possible to count all nests and it was assumed that the ratio of occupied to empty was the same as for those which could actually be examined.

Table 14. Comparison of the estimated breeding population of common birds in Illinois in 1909 and again in 1957 after agricultural development

Numbers in millions

1909		1957	
House sparrow	5.3	Redwinged blackbird	8.4
Redwinged blackbird	5.1	House sparrow	6.1
Common grackle	4.1	Horned lark	5.6
Meadowlark (spp.)	4.0	Meadowlark (spp.)	3.8
Mourning dove	2.5	Common grackle	3.6
Yellow-shafted flicker	2.3	Dickcissel	3.4
Field sparrow	2.1	Starling	3.1
Robin	1.9	Mourning dove	2.0
Brown-headed cowbird	1.8	Bobolink	1.9
Dickcissel	1.7		
Brown thrasher	1.6		
Blue jay	1.6		
Red-headed woodpecker	1.3		
Common crow	1.2		
Bobolink	1.2		
Indigo bunting	0.9		
Horned lark	0.8		
Bobwhite	0.8		
Approximate total	40.2		37.9

After Graber and Graber 1963

Table 15. Major foods of grain-eating birds when living off farmland. Unless otherwise stated the names refer to seeds

	Jan–Mar	*Apr–June*	*July–Sept*	*Oct–Dec*
Greenfinch	*Polygonum* *Arctium* Brassicas Cereals	*Taraxacum* *Senecio* *Stellaria*	Brassicas Cereals *Arctium*	*Arctium* Brassicas *Polygonum*
Goldfinch	*Arctium* *Dipsacus* Thistles *Senecio*	*Taraxacum* *Senecio* Thistles	Thistles *Senecio*	Thistles *Arctium* *Senecio*
Linnet	Brassicas *Polygonum* *Chenopodium*	Brassicas *Stellaria* *Taraxacum*	Brassicas Thistles *Rumex*	Brassicas *Chenopodium* *Polygonum*
Bullfinch	Buds *Rumex* *Chenopodium*	*Stellaria* *Taraxacum* *Capsella*	Brassicas *Rumex* *Sonchus*	*Chenopodium* *Rumex* *Rubus* *Urtica*
Chaffinch	Cereals *Chenopodium* Brassicas *Polygonum*	Invertebrates *Stellaria*	Cereals Brassicas *Chenopodium*	Cereals *Chenopodium* Brassicas *Polygonum*
Wood-pigeon	Clover Weed leaves Cereals	Clover Tree and weed flowers (Brassicas) Seeds of pasture weeds *Cerastium* *Viola*	Cereals Legumes Brassica flower and leaves	Cereals Tree fruits Roots Clover
Stock dove	Cereals *Polygonum* Brassicas *Chenopodium*	Brassicas *Stellaria* Brassica flower-buds	Cereals Legumes Brassicas	Cereals *Polygonum* Brassicas *Chenopodium*
Turtle dove		*Fumaria* *Stellaria* Brassicas Grass seed	*Fumaria* *Stellaria* Cereals	

	Jan–Mar	*Apr–June*	*July–Sept*	*Oct–Dec*
Grey partridge	Grass Grass seed *Polygonum*	Grass seed Grass *Stellaria* *Cerastium*	Grass seed *Cerastium* *Stellaria* Flower-buds including Brassicas	*Polygonum* Cereals Roots Grass

Data for finches, from Newton 1967; for pigeons, from Murton, Westwood and Isaacson 1964; and for partridge, from Middleton and Chitty 1937.

Table 16.   Estimated seed crop of ash, judged by the spring pollen count, and bullfinch damage in following winter

	Pollen count for Ash*		Degree of bullfinch damage†	
1957/58	832	(4)	Severe	(8)
1958/59	692	(6)	Slight	(1)
1959/60	12	(11)	Moderate	(6)
1960/61	2942	(1)	Slight	(1)
1961/62	34	(10)	Severe	(8)
1962/63	2450	(2)	Absent or slight	(1)
1963/64	290	(9)	Severe	(8)
1964/65	568	(7)	Considerable	(7)
1965/66	1020	(3)	Low	(4)
1966/67	756	(5)	Low	(4)
1967/68	476	(8)	Severe	(8)

* Data from Hyde (1963) kindly extended *in litt.*

† Based on information collated for south-east England by D. D. B. Summers *in litt.*

Figures in brackets are ranking orders.

Table 17.   Incidence of bird damage to ripe apples and pears in orchards in southern England

	% of fruits damaged of those examined*		
	1961	*1962*	*1963*
Cox	2.6	0.3	0.1
Worcester Permain		1.3	0.7
Laxton's Fortune		1.2	1.8
Lord Lambourne	6.6	0.5	0.5
Conference	3.1	4.1	1.8
Laxton's Superb		3.4	
Williams		1.0	
Mean % damaged	4.1	1.7	1.0

* The total number of fruits examined was approximately 188,000 from Wright and Brough 1966

Table 18. Mean number of cockles per tenth of a square metre in experimental plots set out on the Llanrhidian Sands, Burry Inlet, South Wales

	Netted areas where oystercatchers and fishermen excluded			Control areas where oystercatchers and fishermen present			Control areas where fishermen excluded but oystercatchers present		
	Plot D			Plots C and E			Plot A		
	1st W.	2nd W.	Older	1st W.	2nd W.	Older	1st W.	2nd W.	Older
Nov. 1960	71	95	5	282	67	6	546	91	6
Feb. 1961	88	86	4	127	4	1	255	5	4
May 1961	75	76	6	137	2	2	257	3	3
Aug. 1961	24	21	2	86	2	1	222	6	—
	Plot K			Plots J and L			Plot A		
Nov. 1961	118	143	7	170	160	8	111	118	8
Jan. 1962	70	139	10	45	15	5	75	7	4
Mar. 1962	30	76	6	32	8	4	100	5	2
May 1962	23	78	5	22	3	5	91	2	3
July 1962	15	55	4	19	3	4	87	—	—

(These data have been simplified from Hancock and Urquhart 1965, who should be consulted for full details and statistical analysis.)

Table 19. Smolt production from known plantings of hatchery-reared underyearling salmon in a 10-mile experimental area of the Pollett River, Canada

	Year of planting	Number of under-yearlings planted	Parr one year after planting	Total smolts produced from planting
No bird control	1942	16,000	3,000	2,000
	1943	16,000	2,000	1,000
	1945	249,000	12,000	5,000
	Av. (light and heavy plantings)	6,000	3,000
Control of goosanders and kingfishers	1947	273,000	25,000	22,000
	1948	235,000	45,000	14,000
	1949	243,000	39,000	19,000
	1950	246,000	57,000	24,000
	Average	249,000	43,000	20,000

BIBLIOGRAPHY

This is a selected bibliography. In certain cases only a recent paper by an author is given if this in turn gives details of earlier work. References are not repeated if already given once for earlier chapters unless they are of particular significance for the text.

CHAPTER I

BOURNE, W. R. P. 1968. Oil pollution and bird populations. In 'The Biological effects of oil pollution on littoral communities'. (Eds. J. D. Carthy and D. R. Arthur.) *Field Studies* 2, suppl. 2: 99–121.

BOURNE, W. R. P. 1970. Special review – after the 'Torrey Canyon' disaster. *Ibis* 112: 120–8.

CARSON, R. 1962. *Silent Spring*. Boston, Houghton Mifflin Co.

COLLIAS, N. E. and SAICHUAE, P. 1967. Ecology of the red jungle fowl in Thailand and Malaya with reference to the origin of domestication. *Nat. Hist. Bull. Siam Soc.* 22: 189–209.

COTT, H. B. 1953. The exploitation of wild birds for their eggs. *Ibis* 95: 409–49.

COULSON, J. C. 1963. The status of the kittiwake in the British Isles. *Bird Study* 10: 147–79.

FISHER, J. 1966. *The Shell Bird Book*. London, Ebury Press & Michael Joseph.

FISHER, J. and PETERSON, R. T. 1964. *The World of Birds*. London, MacDonald.

FRIEDMANN, H. 1946. *The Symbolic Goldfinch*. Washington, The Bollingen Series VII Pantheon Books.

GURNEY, J. H. 1921. *Early annals of ornithology*. London, Witherby.

JEFFERIES, D. J. 1967. The delay in ovulation produced by pp¹–DDT and its possible significance in the field. *Ibis* 109: 266–72.

MELLANBY, K. 1967. *Pesticides and Pollution*. London, Collins.

PARSLOW, J. L. F. 1969. The 'Torrey Canyon' incident and the seabirds of Cornwall. *Ann. Rep. Cornwall Bird-watching and Preservation Soc.* 1967: 78–89.

RATCLIFFE, D. A. 1967. Decrease of eggshell weight in certain birds of prey. *Nature* 215: 208–10.

STATON, J. 1943. Some birds at Nottingham Sewage Farm in 1942. *Brit. Birds* 36: 242–3.

TAVENER, J. H. 1963. Further notes on the spread of the eider in Great Britain. *Brit. Birds* 56: 273–85.

TROW-SMITH, R. 1951. *English Husbandry*. London, Faber & Faber.

TUDOR, R. O. 1964. Birds in Art, pp. 63–5 in *A New Dictionary of Birds*. Ed. Sir Landsborough Thomson. London, Nelson.

ZEUNER, F. E. 1963. *A History of Domesticated Animals*. London.

CHAPTER 2

BLANK, T. H., SOUTHWOOD, T. R. E. and CROSS, D. J. 1967. The ecology of the partridge. I. Outline of population processes with particular reference to chick mortality and nest density. *J. Anim. Ecol.* 36: 549–56.

BULL, P. C. 1957. Distribution and abundance of the rook (*Corvus frugilegus* L.) in New Zealand. *Notornis* 7: 137–61.

CARR-SAUNDERS, A. M. 1922. *The population problem: a study in human evolution*. Oxford.

CHOATE, T. S. 1963. Habitat and population dynamics of white-tailed ptarmigan in Montana. *J. Wildl. Mgmt.* 27: 684–99.

DOUGLAS, M. 1966. Population control in primitive groups. *Brit. J. Sociology* 17: 263–73.

ELTON, C. S. 1958. *The ecology of invasions by animals and plants*. London, Methuen.

FITTER, R. S. R. 1965. The breeding status of the Black Redstart in Great Britain. *Brit. Birds* 58: 481–92.

HARRISON, T. H. and HOLLOM, P. A. D. 1932. The great crested grebe enquiry, 1931. *Brit. Birds* 26: 62–92, 102–31, 142–55, 174–95.

HOLLOM, P. A. D. 1959. The great crested grebe census 1946–1955. *Bird Study* 6: 1–7.

JENKINS, D. 1961. Population control in protected partridges (*Perdix perdix*). *J. Anim. Ecol.* 30: 235–58.

JENKINS, D., WATSON, A. and MILLER, G. R. 1963. Population studies on Red Grouse, *Lagopus lagopus scoticus* (Lath.) in north-east Scotland. *J. anim. Ecol.* 32: 317–76.

KLOPFER, P. H. and MACARTHUR, R. H. 1960. Niche size and faunal diversity. *Amer. Nat.* 94: 293–300.

LACK, D. 1954. *The natural regulation of animal numbers*. Oxford.

LACK, D. 1966. *Population studies of birds*. Oxford.

LIDIKER, W. J. 1962. Emigration as a possible mechanism permitting the regulation of population density below carrying capacity. *Amer. Nat.* 96: 29–33.

MACARTHUR, R. and MACARTHUR, J. 1961. On bird species diversity. *Ecology* 42 (3): 594.

MAGEE, J. D. 1965. The breeding distribution of the stonechat in Britain and the causes of its decline. *Bird Study* 12: 83–9.

MAYR, E. 1951. Speciation in birds. *Proc. Xth Int. Orn. Congr. 1950*: 91–131.

MIDDLETON, A. D. and HUBAND, P. 1966. Increase in red-legged partridges (*Alectoris rufa*). *Game Res. Ass. Ann. Rep.* 5: 14–25.

MONK, J. F. 1963. The past and present status of the wryneck in the British Isles. *Bird Study* 10: 112–32.

MURTON, R. K., ISAACSON, A. J. and WESTWOOD, N. J. 1964. A preliminary investigation of the factors regulating population size in the woodpigeon *Columba palumbus*. *Ibis* 106: 482–507.

NICHOLSON, E. M. 1955. Special review. Lack on the natural regulation of animal numbers. *Brit. Birds* 48: 38–42.

PARRINDER, E. R. 1964. Little ringed Plovers in Britain during 1960–62. *Brit. Birds* 57: 191–8.

PEAKALL, D. B. 1962. The past and present status of the red-backed shrike in Great Britain. *Bird Study* 9: 198–216.

PEITZMEIER, J. 1956. Neue Beobachtungen über Klimaschwankungen und Bestandsschwankungen einiger Vogelarten. *Vogelwelt* 77: 181–5.

PERRINS, C. M. 1963. Survival in the great tit, *Parus major*. *Proc. Int. Orn. Congr.* 13: 717–28.

PRESTT, I. and MILLS, D. H. 1966. A census of the great crested grebe in Britain 1965. *Bird Study* 13: 163–203.

STAFFORD, J. 1962. Nightjar enquiry, 1957–58. *Bird Study* 9: 104–15.

SOUTHWOOD, T. R. E. 1967. The ecology of the partridge. II. The role of pre-hatching influences. *J. Anim. Ecol.* 36: 557–62.

TUBBS, C. R. 1963. The significance of the New Forest to the status of the Dartford warbler in England. *Brit. Birds* 56: 41–8.

WILLIAMSON, K. 1959. The September drift-movements of 1956 and 1958. *Brit. Birds* 52: 334–77.

WYNNE-EDWARDS, V. C. 1962. *Animal dispersion in relation to social behaviour*. Edinburgh.

WYNNE-EDWARDS, V. C. 1963. Intergroup selection in the evolution of social systems. *Nature* 200: 623–6.

CHAPTER 3

ALEXANDER, G., PETERSON, J. E. and WATSON, R. H. 1959. Neo-natal mortality in lambs. *Aust. Vet. J.* 35: 433.

ARMOUR, C. J. and THOMPSON, H. V. 1955. Spread of myxomatosis in the first outbreak in Great Britain. *Ann. appl. Biol.* 43: 511–18.

BERRY, S. S. 1922. Magpies versus livestock: an unfortunate new chapter in avian depredations. *Condor* 24: 13–17.

BOLAM, G. 1913. *Wildlife in Wales*. London.

BURGESS, D. 1963. Carrion crows in Northern England. *Agriculture* 70: 126–9.

ERRINGTON, P. L. 1946. Predation and vertebrate populations. *Quart. Rev. Biol.* 21: 144–77, 221–45.

GAUSE, G. F. 1934. *The struggle for existence.* Baltimore.

HARVIE-BROWN, J. A. 1906. *A fauna of the Tay Basin and Strathmore.* Edinburgh.

HOLLING, C. S. 1965. The functional response of predators to prey density and its role in mimicry and population regulation. *Mem. Ent. Soc. Can.* 45: 1–60.

LEOPOLD, A. 1933. *Game management.* New York.

LEVER, R. J. A. W. 1959. The diet of the fox since myxomatosis. *J. Anim. Ecol.* 28: 359–75.

LOCKIE, J. D. 1964. The breeding density of the golden eagle and fox in relation to food supply in Wester Ross, Scotland. *Scot. Nat.* 71: 67–77.

LOCKIE, J. D. and RATCLIFFE, D. A. 1964. Insecticides and Scottish golden eagles. *Brit. Birds* 57: 89–102.

LOCKIE, J. D. and STEPHEN, D. 1959. Eagles, lambs and land management on Lewis. *J. Anim. Ecol.* 28: 43–50.

LOTKA, A. J. 1925. Elements of physical biology. Baltimore.

MCCOY, J. W. 1941. Injuries to Texas cattle caused by starlings. *Veterinary Medicine* 36: 432–3.

MCCREATH, J. B. and MURRAY, R. D. 1954. A survey of an Argyll hill-farming district. *Rep. No. 26 of Economics Dept., West of Scotland College of Agric.*

MOOK, L. J. 1963. Birds and the spruce budworm. *In* The dynamics of epidemic spruce budworm populations, ed. R. F. Morris. *Mem. Ent. Soc. Can.* 31: 268–72.

MOORE, N. W. 1957. The past and present status of the buzzard in the British Isles. *Brit. Birds* 50: 173–97.

PRESTT, I. 1965. An enquiry into the recent breeding status of some of the smaller birds of prey and crows in Britain. *Bird Study* 12: 196–221.

RATCLIFFE, D. A. 1962. Breeding density in the peregrine *Falco peregrinus* and raven *Corvus corax. Ibis* 104: 13–39.

RATCLIFFE, D. A. 1963. The status of the peregrine in Great Britain. *Bird Study* 10: 56–90.

RICE, D. W. 1956. Dynamics of range expansion of cattle egrets in Florida. *Auk* 73: 259–66.

RUDEBECK, G. 1950–51. The choice of prey and modes of hunting of predatory birds with special reference to their selective effect. *Oikos* 2: 65–88; 3: 200–31.

SANDEMAN, P. W. 1957. The breeding success of golden eagles in the southern Grampians. *Scot. Nat.* 69: 148–52.

SCHORGER, A. W. 1921. An attack on livestock by magpies. *Auk* 38: 276–7.

SMITH, I. D. 1964. Ovine neo-natal mortality in Western Queensland. *Proc. Aust. Soc. Anim. Prod.* 5: 100.

SMITH, K. D. and POPOV, G. B. 1953. On birds attacking desert locust swarms in Eritrea. *Entomologist* 86: 3–7.

SNOW, D. W. 1968. Movements and mortality of British Kestrels (*Falco tinnunculus*). *Bird Study* 15: 65–83.

SOLOMON, M. E. 1949. The natural control of animal populations. *J. Anim. Ecol.* 18: 1–35.

SOUTHERN, H. N. and WATSON, J. S. 1941. Summer food of the red fox (*Vulpes vulpes*) in Great Britain: A preliminary report. *J. Anim. Ecol.* 10: 1–11.

TINBERGEN, L. 1960. The natural control of insects in pine woods. I. Factors influencing the intensity of predation by songbirds. *Arch. Néerl. Zool.* 13: 265–343.

VAN SOMEREN, V. D. 1951. The red-billed oxpecker and its relation to stock in Kenya. *E. Afr. Agric. J.* 17: 1–11.

VESEY-FITZGERALD, D. F. 1955. Birds as predators of the red locust (*Nomadacris septemfasciata* Serv.). *Ostrich* 26: 128–33.

VOLTERRA, V. 1926. Variazioni e fluttuazioni del numero d'individui in specie animali conviventi. Reprint at pages 409–48 in Chapman, R. N. 1931. *Animal Ecology*, New York. *Mem. Acad. Naz. Lincei* 2: 31–113.

VOUTE, A. D. 1946. Regulation of the density of the insect-populations in virgin-forests and cultivated woods. *Arch. Néerl. Zool.* 7: 435–70.

WATSON, A. 1957. The breeding success of golden eagles in the north-east Highlands. *Scot. Nat.* 69: 153–69.

WATSON, J. 1893. *Ornithology in relation to agriculture and horticulture.* Allen 1893.

CHAPTER 4

BERLEPSCH, FRHR. VON 1926. *Der gesamte Vogelschutz.* 11th ed. Neudamm.

BETTS, M. M. 1955. The food of titmice in oak woodland. *J. Anim. Ecol.* 24: 282–323.

BOSSEMA, I. 1968. Recovery of acorns in the European jay (*Garrulus g. glandarius* L.) Koninkl. Nederl. *Akademie Van Wetenschappen—Amsterdam* C71: 1–5.

BRIAN, M. V. and BRIAN, A. D. 1950. Bird predation of defoliating caterpillars. *Scot. Nat.* 62: 88–92.

BRUNS, H. 1960. The economic importance of birds in forests. *Bird Study* 7: 193–208.

CAMPBELL, B. 1955. The breeding distribution and habitats of the pied flycatcher (*Muscicapa hypo leuca*) in Britain. Part 3. Discussion. *Bird Study* 2: 179–91.

CAMPBELL, B. 1968. The Dean nest box study, 1942–64. *Forestry* 41: 27–46.

DOWDEN, P. B., JAYNES, H. A. and CAROLIN, V. M. 1953. The role of birds in a spruce budworm outbreak in Maine. *J. econ. Ent.* 46: 307–12.

GIBB, J. A. 1960. Populations of tits and goldcrests and their food supply in pine plantations. *Ibis.* 102: 163–208.

GIBB, J. A. and BETTS, M. M. 1963. Food and food supply of nestling tits (Paridae) in Breckland pine. *J. Anim. Ecol.* 32: 489–533.

HÄHNLE, H. 1946. *Das Schutzgebiet Behr-Steckby (Anhalt) des Reichs bundes für Vogelschutz.* Geingen (Brenz).

HASEGAWA, H. and ITO, Y. 1967. Biology of *Hyphantria cunea* (Lepidoptera: Arctiidae) in Japan. I. Notes on adult biology with reference to the predation by birds. *Appl. Ent. Zool.* 2: 100–10.

HELMINEN, M. 1963. Composition of the Finnish populations of capercaillie, *Tetrao urogallus*, and black grouse, *Lyrurus tetrix*, in the autumns of 1952–61, as revealed by a study of wings. *Pap. Game Res. Riistat. Julk* 23: 1–124.

HERBERG, M. 1959. Erfahrungen bei der biologischen Bekampfung waldschadlicher Inseklen durch Ansiedlung von Höhlenbrütern in Vogelschutzgebiet Steckby. *Vortrag auf der Zentralen Tagung für Ornithologie in Erfurt.*

HOFFMAN, R. S. 1961. The quality of the winter food of blue grouse. *J. Wildl. Manag.* 25: 209–10.

HOLTMEIER, F.-K. 1966. Die ökologische Funktion des Tannenhähers im Zirken-Lärchenwald und an der Waldgrenze des Oberengadins. *J. Orn., Lpz.* 107: 337–45.

JOHNSTONE, G. W. 1967. Blackgame and capercaillie in relation to forestry in Britain. pp. 68–77 in *Wildlife in the Forest: Rep. of 7th Discussion Meeting, Cirencester 1967, Forestry Suppl.* Oxford University Press.

KAASA, J. 1959. On the knowledge of the food of the black grouse (*Lyrurus tetrix* (L.)) in Norway. *Norwegian State Game Res.* 2: 1–112.

KENDEIGH, S. C. 1947. Bird population studies in the coniferous forest biome during a spruce budworm outbreak. *Bull. Dep. Lands and For. Ontario, Canada Div. Res. Biol.* 1: 1–100.

KEVE, A. and REICHART, G. 1960. Die Rolle der Vögel bei der Abwehr des amerikanischen Bärenspinners. *Falke* 7: 20–6.

KLUIJVER, H. N. 1951. The population ecology of the great tit *Parus m. major* L. *Ardea* 38: 99–135.

LINDROTH, H. and LINDGREN, L. 1950. On the significance for forestry of the capercaillie, *Tetrao urogallus* L., feeding on pine-needles. *Suomen. Riista* 5: 60–81.

MACKENZIE, J. M. D. 1952. Fluctuations in the number of British tetraonids. *J. Anim. Ecol.* 21: 128–53.

MANSFIELD, K. 1956. Zur Vertilgung behaarter Raupen durch Sing vögel. *Waldhygiene* 1: 160–4.

MELLANBY, K. 1968. The effects of some mammals and birds on regeneration of oak. *J. appl. Ecol.* 5: 359–66.

MORRIS, R. F., CHESHIRE, W. F., MILLER, C. A. and MOTT, D. G. 1958. The numerical response of avian and mammalian predators during a gradation of the spruce bud-worm. *Ecology* 39: 487–94.

NEF, L. 1959. Protection des bourgeons de pins contre les attaques du Tétras lyre (*Lyrurus tetrix* L.). *Bull. de la Société Royale Forestière de Belgique*, 3–10.

OWEN, D. F. 1956. The food of nestling jays and magpies. *Bird Study* 3: 257–265.

PENNIE, I. D. 1950–51. The history and distribution of the Capercaillie in Scotland. *Scot. Nat.* 62: 65–87, 157–78; 63: 4–17, 135.

PENNIE, I. D. 1963. Article on capercaillie in '*The Birds of the British Isles*'. Bannerman & Lodge Vol. 12. Edinburgh, Oliver & Boyd.

PERRINS, C. M. 1965. Population fluctuations and clutch-size in the great tit, *Parus major* L. *J. Anim. Ecol.* 34: 601–47.

REICHART, G. 1959. Birds destroying the eggs of *Hymantria dispar* L. *Aquila* 66: 315–17.

ROYAMA, T. 1966. Factors governing feeding rate, food requirement and brood size of nestling great tits *Parus major*. *Ibis* 108: 313–47.

SEISKARI, P. 1958. Metsiemme kehityksen vaikutuksesta riistalajien elinmahdollisuuksiin. *Suomen. Riista* 12: 21–42.

SEISKARI, P. 1962. On the winter ecology of the capercaillie *Tetrao urogallus*, and the black grouse, *Lyrurus tetrix*, in Finland. *Pap. Game Research* 22: 1–119.

SIIVONEN, L. 1957. The problems of the short-term fluctuations in numbers of tetraonids in Europe. *Pap. Game Res. Riistat Julk.* 19: 1–44.

SIIVONEN, L. 1958. Basic reasons for tetraonid lows and the application of the results obtained. *Suomen. Riista* 12: 43–54.

SOUTHWOOD, T. R. E. 1967. The ecology of the partridge. II. The role of prehatching influences. *J. Anim. Ecol.* 36: 557–62.

TINBERGEN, L. and KLOMP, H. 1960. The natural control of insects in pine woods. II. Conditions for damping of Nicholson oscillations in parasite-host systems. *Arch. Néere. Zool.* 13: 344–79.

TURČEK, F. J. 1948-51. A contribution to the function of forest bird-population from the point of view of biocoenology and forest managements. *Aquila* 55-8: 51–73.

TURČEK, F. J. 1954. The ringing of trees by some European woodpeckers. *Ornis Fenn.* 31: 33–41.

TURČEK, F. J. 1968. Die Verbreitung der Vogelkirsche in den Wäldern durch Vögel. *Waldhygiene* 7: 129–32.

VOOUS, K. 1960. *Atlas of European Birds.* London, Nelson.

ZEHETMAYR, J. W. L. 1954. *Experiments on tree-planting on peat.* Bull. For. Comm. Lond. 22. 110 pages.

ZWICKEL, F. C. 1966. Sex and age ratios and weights of capercaillie from the 1965–66 shooting season in Scotland. *Scot. Birds* 4: 209–13.

ZWICKEL, F. C. 1966. Winter food habits of capercaillie in north-east Scotland. *Brit. Birds* 59: 325–536.

CHAPTER 5

ALEXANDER, W. B. 1932. The bird population of an Oxfordshire farm. *J. Anim. Ecol.* 1: 58–64.

ASHMOLE, M. J. 1962. The migration of European thrushes: a comparative study based on ringing recoveries. *Ibis* 104: 314–46, 522–59.

BEVEN, G. 1963. Population changes in a Surrey oak wood during fifteen years. *Brit. Birds* 56: 307–23.

CHAPMAN, W. M. M. 1939. The bird population of an Oxfordshire farm. *J. Anim. Ecol.* 8: 286–99.

CODY, M. L. 1966. The consistency of intra- and inter-continental grassland bird species counts. *Amer. Nat.* 100: 371–6.

COLQUHOUN, M. K. 1941. The birds of Savernake Forest, Wiltshire. *J. Anim. Ecol.* 10: 25–34.

COLQUHOUN, M. K. and MORLEY, AVRIL 1941. The density of downland birds. *J. Anim. Ecol.* 10: 35–46.

DAVIES, P. W. and SNOW, D. W. 1965. Territory and food of the song thrush. *Brit. Birds* 58: 161–75.

DAVIS, B. N. K. 1967. Bird feeding preferences among different crops in an area near Huntingdon. *Bird Study* 14: 227–37.

GLUE, D. E. 1967. Prey taken by the barn owl in England and Wales. *Bird Study* 14: 169–83.

GOOCH, W. 1811. *General view of the agriculture of the county of Cambridge.* London, Phillips.

HARTLEY, P. J. T. 1954. Wild fruits in the diet of British thrushes. A study in the ecology of closely allied species. *Brit. Birds* 47: 97–107.

HOLYOAK, D. 1968. A comparative study of the food of some British Corvidae. *Bird Study* 15: 147–53.

LACK, D. 1935. The breeding bird population of British heaths and moorland. *J. Anim. Ecol.* 4: 43–51.

LACK, D. and VENABLES, L. S. V. 1937. The heathland birds of South Haven Peninsula, Studland Heath, Dorset. *J. Anim. Ecol.* 6: 62–72.

LACK, D. and VENABLES, L. S. V. 1939. The habitat distribution of British woodland birds. *J. Anim. Ecol.* 8: 39–70.

LOCKIE, J. D. 1956. The food and feeding behaviour of the jackdaw, rook and carrion crow. *J. Anim. Ecol.* 25: 421–8.

MOORE, N. W., HOOPER, M. D. and DAVIS, B. N. K. 1967. Hedges. I. Introduction and reconnaissance studies. *J. appl. Ecol.* 4: 201–20.

SMITH, STUART 1950. *The Yellow Wagtail.* New Naturalist Monog. Collins, London.

SNOW, D. W. 1955. The breeding of the blackbird, song thrush, and mistle thrush in Great Britain. Parts 2 & 3. *Bird Study* 2: 72–84; 169–78.

SNOW, D. W. 1965. The relationship between census results and the breeding population of birds on farmland. *Bird Study* 12: 287–304.

SNOW, D. W. 1966. Population dynamics of the blackbird. *Nature* 211: 1231–3.

SNOW, D. W. and MAYER-GROSS, H. 1967. Farmland as a nesting habitat. *Bird Study* 14: 43–52.

TICEHURST, N. F. and HARTLEY, P. H. T. 1948. Report on the effect of the severe winter of 1946–7 on bird-life. *Brit. Birds* 41: 322–34.

VENABLES, L. S. V. 1937. Bird distribution on Surrey Greensand heaths: The avifaunal–botanical correlation. *J. Anim. Ecol.* 6: 73–85.

WILLIAMSON, K. 1964. Bird census work in woodland. *Bird Study* 11: 1–22.

WILLIAMSON, K. 1967. The bird community of farmland. *Bird Study* 14: 210–26.

WILLIAMSON, K. and HOMES, R. C. 1964. Methods and preliminary results of the common bird census, 1962–63. *Bird Study* 11: 240–56.

YAPP, W. B. 1962. *Birds and Woods.* London O.U.P.

CHAPTER 6

BURNS, P. S. 1957. Rook and jackdaw roosts around Bishop's Stortford. *Bird Study* 4: 62–71.

COOMBS, C. J. F. 1960. Observations on the rook *Corvus frugilegus* in south-west Cornwall. *Ibis* 102: 394–419.

COOMBS, C. J. F. 1961. Rookeries and roosts of the rook and jackdaw in south-west Cornwall. Part I. Population, distribution and rookeries. *Bird Study* 8: 32–7.

COOMBS, C. J. F. 1961. Rookeries and roosts of the rook and jackdaw in south-west Cornwall. Part II. Roosting. *Bird Study* 8: 55–70.

COULSON, J. C. 1960. A study of the mortality of the starling based on ringing recoveries. *J. Anim. Ecol.* 29: 251–71.

DAVIES, J. L. 1949. The breeding status of the starling in west Wales. *Brit. Birds* 42: 369–75.

DOBBS, A. 1964. Rook numbers in Nottinghamshire over 35 years. *Brit. Birds* 57: 360–4.

DUNNET, G. M. 1955. The breeding of the Starling *Sturnus vulgaris* in relation to its food supply. *Ibis* 97: 619–62.

DUNNET, G. M. 1956. The autumn and winter mortality of starlings *Sturnus vulgaris*, in relation to their food supply. *Ibis* 98: 220–30.

DUNNET, G. M. and PATTERSON, I. J. 1968. The rook problem in north-east Scotland. pp. 119–39 in *The Problems of Birds and Pests* ed. R. K. Murton and E. N. Wright. Instit. of Biol. Symp. 17. London, Academic Press.

EVANS, A. C. and GUILD, W. J. M. 1948. Studies on the relationships between earthworms and soil fertility. 5. Field populations. *Ann. appl. Biol.* 35: 485–93.

GERARD, B. M. 1967. Factors affecting earthworms in pastures. *J. Anim. Ecol.* 36: 235–52.

GOODACRE, M. J. 1959. The origin of winter visitors to the British Isles. 4. Starling (*Sturnus vulgaris*). *Bird Study* 6: 180–92.

HALDANE, J. B. S. 1955. The calculation of mortality rates from ringing data. *Proc. XI Int. Orn. Cong.* 1954: 454–8.

HENDERSON, MARY 1968. The rook population of a part of West Cheshire 1944–1968. *Bird Study* 15: 206–8.

KALMBACH, E. R. 1922. A comparison of the food habits of British and American starlings. *Auk* 32, No. 2: 189–95.

KLOMP, H. 1951. Over de achteruitgang van de keivit, *Vanellus vanellus* (L.), in Nederland en gegevens over het legmechanisme en het eiproductie-vermogen. *Ardea* 39: 143–82.

KRAAK, W. K., RINKEL, G. L. and HOOGERHEIDE, J. 1940. Oecologische bewerking van de Europese ringgegevans van de Kievit (*Vanellus vanellus* (L.)). *Ardea* 29: 151–75.

LACK, D. 1943. The age of some more British birds. *Brit. Birds* 36: 193–7, 214–21.

LACK, D. 1948. Natural selection and family size in the starling. *Evolution* 2: 95–110.

LACK, D. and SCHIFFERLI, A. 1948. Die Lebensdauer des Stares. *Orn. Beob.* 45: 107–14.

LISTER, M. D. 1964. The lapwing habitat enquiry, 1960–61. *Bird Study* 11: 128–47.

LLOYD, B. 1950. Further notes on the breeding status of the starling in west Wales. *Brit. Birds* 43: 142–3.

LOCKIE, J. D. 1955. The breeding and feeding of jackdaws and rooks with notes on carrion crows and other Corvidae. *Ibis* 97: 341–69.

LOCKIE, J. D. 1956. Winter fighting in feeding flocks of rooks, jackdaws and carrion crows. *Bird Study* 3: 180–90.

LOCKIE, J. D. 1959. The food of nestling rooks near Oxford. *Brit. Birds* 52: 332–4.

LOMAS, P. D. R. 1968. The decline of the rook population of Derbyshire. *Bird Study* 15: 198–205.

MURTON, R. K. and VIZOSO, M. 1963. Dressed cereal seed as a hazard to wood-pigeons. *Ann. appl. Biol.* 52: 503–17.

MYRBERGET, S. 1962. (On the geographical distribution of the Lapwing *Vanellus vanellus* (L.), in Norway.) *Sterna* 5: 1–14.

NICHOLSON, E. M. 1938–9. Report on the lapwing habitat enquiry, 1937. *Brit. Birds* 32: 170–91; 207–29, 255–9.

OWEN, D. F. 1959. The breeding season and clutch-size of the rook *Corvus frugilegus. Ibis* 101: 235–9.

PARSLOW, J. L. F. 1967. Changes in status among breeding birds in Britain and Ireland. *Brit. Birds* 61: 49–64.

PINOWSKI, J. 1959. Factors influencing the number of feeding rooks (*Corvus frugilegus frugilegus* L.) in various field environments. *Ekologia Polska* 7: 435–81.

RAW, F. 1959. Estimating earthworm populations by using formalin. *Nature* 184: 1661–2.

STEVENSON, H. 1870. *The Birds of Norfolk.* 3 vols. London and Norwich.

TISCHLER, W. 1955. Effect of agricultural practice on the soil fauna. pp. 215–28 in *Soil Zoology* ed. D. K. McE. Kevan. London, Butterworths.

VAN KOERSVELD, E. 1958. A few data on the reproduction of the rook *Corvus f. frugilegus* L. *Ardea* 46: 58–62.

VENABLES, L. S. V. and U. M. 1953. Rooks breeding in Shetland. *Brit. Birds* 46: 265–6.

CHAPTER 7

BRAY, R. P. 1968. Mortality rates of released pheasants. *Game Res. Ass. Ann. Rep.* 7: 14–33.

BROAD, P. D. 1952. The occurrence of weed seeds in samples submitted for testing by the O.S.T.S. *J. Nat. Inst. Agric. Botany* 6: 275–86.

BUMP, G. 1958. *Red-legged partridges of Spain.* U.S. Dept. of Interior, Fish & Wildl. Service, Special Scientific Report: No. 39.

BUNTING, A. M. 1960. Some reflections on the ecology of weeds. In *The Biology of Weeds.* Symp. British Ecological Soc. ed. J. L. Harper. Blackwell, Oxford.

BUXTON, E. J. M. 1953. The use of Delfware pots as nesting-holes for house sparrows. *Brit. Birds* 46: 272.

EBER, G. 1956. Vergleichende untersuchungen über die Ernarhrung einiger Finkenvögel. *Biol. Abh.* 13/14: 1–60.

EVANS, P. R. 1966. Autumn movements, moult and measurements of the lesser redpoll *Carduelis flammea cabaret. Ibis* 108: 183–216.

GODWIN, H. 1960. The history of weeds in Britain. In *The Biology of*

Weeds. Symp. British Ecological Soc. ed. J. L. Harper. Blackwell, Oxford.

HAMMER, M. 1948. Investigations on the feeding habits of the house-sparrow (*Passer domesticus*) and the tree-sparrow (*Passer montanus*). *Danish Rev. Game Biol.* 1: 1–59.

HOWELLS, G. 1963. The status of the red-legged partridge in Britain. *Game Res. Ass. Ann. Rep.* 2: 46–51.

HUDSON, R. 1965. Summary of foreign-ringed birds in Britain and Ireland during 1906–63. *Brit. Birds* 58: 87–97.

INGRAM, C. 1953. The use of earthenware pots as nesting-holes for house sparrows. *Brit. Birds* 46: 352.

KENT, A. K. 1964. The breeding habitats of the reed bunting and yellow hammer in Nottinghamshire. *Bird Study* 11: 123–127.

MEIKLEJOHN, M. F. M. 1954. The use of earthenware pots as nesting-holes for starlings and house sparrows. *Brit. Birds* 47: 95–6.

MEISE, W. 1953. The use of Delfware pots as nesting-holes for house-sparrows. *Brit. Birds* 46: 36.

MIDDLETON, A. D. and CHITTY, H. 1937. The food of adult partridges, *Perdix perdix* and *Allectoris rufa* in Great Britain. *J. anim. Ecol.* 6: 322–36.

MURTON, R. K., ISAACSON, A. J., and WESTWOOD, N. J. 1963. The food and growth of nestling wood-pigeons in relation to the breeding season. *Proc. Zool. Soc. Lond.* 141: 747–82.

MURTON, R. K., WESTWOOD, N. J. and ISAACSON, A. J. 1964. The feeding habits of the woodpigeon *Columba palumbus*, stock dove *C. oenas* and turtle dove *Streptopelia turtur*. *Ibis* 106: 174–188.

NEWTON, I. The breeding biology of the chaffinch. *Bird Study* 11: 47–68.

NEWTON, I. 1967. The adaptive radiation and feeding ecology of some British finches. *Ibis* 109: 33–98.

PETTERSSON, M. 1956. Greenfinches and *Daphne mezereum*. *Bird Study* 3: 147–8.

PETTERSSON, M. 1961. The nature and spread of *Daphne*-eating in the greenfinch, and the spread of some other habits. *Anim. Behav.* 9: 114.

ROBINSON, D. W. 1964. Weed control in horticulture – a review. *7th Brit. Weed Cont. Conf.* 3: 994–1010.

SEEL, D. C. 1964. An analysis of the nest record cards of the tree sparrow. *Bird Study* 11: 265–71.

SEEL, D. C. 1970. Nestling survival and nestling weights in the house sparrow and tree sparrow *Passer* spp. at Oxford. *Ibis* 112: 1–14.

SOUTHWOOD, T. R. E. and CROSS, D. J. 1969. The ecology of the partridge. III. Breeding success and the abundance of insects in natural habitats. *J. Anim. Ecol.* 38: 497–509.

SUMMERS-SMITH, D. 1963. *The House Sparrow*. New Nat. Monog. Collins, London.

SVÄRDSON, G. 1957. The 'invasion' type of bird migration. *Brit. Birds* 50: 314–43.

TAST, J. 1968. Changes in the distribution, habitat requirements and nest-sites of the Linnet, *Carduelis cannabina* (L.) in Finland. *Annls. Zool. fenn.* 5: 159–78.

WOODFORD, E. K. 1964. Weed control in arable crops. *7th Brit. Weed Cont. Conf.* 3: 944–64.

CHAPTER 8

BOYD, H. and ELTRINGHAM, S. K. 1962. The whooper swan in Great Britain. *Bird Study* 9: 217–41.

CAMPBELL, B. 1960. The mute swan census in England and Wales 1955–6. *Bird Study* 7: 208–23.

CHURCH, H. F. 1956. The mute swan population of the eastern Borders. *Bird Study* 3: 212–17.

ELTRINGHAM, S. K. 1963. The British population of the mute swan in 1961. *Bird Study* 10: 10–28.

GILLHAM, M. E. 1956. Feeding habits and seasonal movements of mute swans on two south Devon estuaries. *Bird Study* 3: 205–12.

JONES, N. G. B. 1956. Census of breeding Canada geese 1953. *Bird Study* 3: 153–170.

KEAR, J. 1963. The agricultural importance of wild goose droppings. *Wildfowl Trust Ann. Rep.* 14: 72–7.

KEAR, J. 1963. Wildfowl and agriculture. pp. 315–28 in *Wildfowl in Great Britain*. ed. G. L. Atkinson-Willes, Monog. No. 3 Nature Conservancy, London, H.M.S.O.

KEAR, J. 1964. *Wildfowl and agriculture in Britain. In* Proceedings of the M.A.R. Conference. I.U.C.N. Publication New Ser. 3: 321–31.

KEAR, J. 1965. Recent changes in Scottish barley acreages and the possible effect on wild geese. *Scot. Birds* 3: 288–92.

KEAR, J. 1965. The assessment by grazing trial of goose damage to grass. *Wildfowl Trust Ann. Rep.* 16: 46–7.

KEAR, J. 1967. The feeding habits of the Greylag goose *Anser Anser* in Iceland, with reference to its interaction with agriculture. *Proc. VIIth Int. Cong. Game Biol.* 7: 615–22.

KINSEY, C. 1959. Spring grazing autumn-sown cereals. *N.A.A.S. Quart. Rev.* 46: 88–92.

MURTON, R. K., ISAACSON, A. J. and WESTWOOD, N. J. 1966. The relationship between wood-pigeons and their clover food supply and the mechanism of population control. *J. appl. Ecol.* 3: 55–96.

PERRINS, C. M. and REYNOLDS, C. M. 1967. A preliminary study of the mute swan, *Cygnus olor*. *Wildfowl Trust Ann. Rep.* 18: 74–84.

PILCHER, R. E. M. and KEAR, J. 1966. The spread of potato-eating in whooper swans. *Brit. Birds* 59: 160–1.

RAWCLIFFE, C. P. 1958. The Scottish mute swan census 1955–56. *Bird Study* 5: 45–55.

TICEHURST, N. F. 1957. *The Mute Swan in England*. London, Cleaver-Hume Press.

VAN KOERSVELD, E. 1955. Damage to crops by birds and mammals, and methods for the prevention of such damage. *Wildlife Repellents, I.T.B.O.N. Arnhem* 32: 9–76.

CHAPTER 9

BECKER, P. and GILBERT, N. D. H. 1958. Selective bird damage on pears in winter. *J. Roy. Horticultural Soc.* 83: 509–15.

BOSWALL, J. 1966. Pied wagtails roosting inside greenhouses. *Brit. Birds* 59: 100–6.

BROUGH, T. 1963. The problem of bird damage in horticulture. *Sci. Hort.* 16: 35–41.

BROWN, E. B. 1961. Linnet damage to strawberry fruit. *Plant Pathology* 10: 41–2.

BROWN, R. G. B. 1969. Seed selection by pigeons. *Behaviour* 34: 8–131.

COHEN, E. 1960. Unusual roosting site of pied wagtails. *Brit. Birds* 53: 315.

CRAMP, S., PETTET, A. and SHARROCK, J. T. R. 1960. The irruption of tits in autumn 1957. *Brit. Birds* 53: 49–77; 99–117; 176–92.

HAWKINS, J. E. and BULL, P. C. 1962. Controlling redpolls in Otago orchards. *The Orchardist New Zealand*, May 1962.

LACK, D. and LACK, E. 1958. The nesting of the long-tailed tit. *Bird Study* 5: 1–19.

MINTON, C. D. T. 1960. Unusual roosting site of pied wagtails. *Brit. Birds* 53: 132–3.

MOUNTFORT, G. 1957. *The Hawfinch*. New Nat. Monog. Collins, London.

NEWTON, I. 1964. Bud-eating by bullfinches in relation to the natural food supply. *J. appl. Ecol.* 1: 265–79.

NEWTON, I. 1967. The feeding ecology of the bullfinch (*Pyrrhula pyrrhula* L.) in southern England. *J. Anim. Ecol.* 36: 721–44.

NEWTON, I. 1967. Attacks on fruit buds by redpolls *Carduelis flammea*. *Ibis* 109: 440–1.

NEWTON, I. 1968. Bullfinches and fruit buds. In *The Problems of Birds as Pests*. Symposium 17 Instit. of Biol. ed. R. K. Murton and E. N. Wright, London, Academic Press.

ROACH, F. A. 1963. The Bullfinch—its past and present position relative to damage to fruit crops. Proceedings of Bird Damage to Fruit Crops Conference, N.F.U. London. Nov. 1962.

TESNHOUSE, D. 1962. A new habit of the redpoll *Carduelis flammea* in New Zealand. *Ibis* 104: 250–2.

SUMMERS, D. D. B. 1968. pp. 234 in *The Problems of Birds as Pests*. 17 Symp. Institute of Biol. ed. R. K. Murton and E. N. Wright, London, Academic Press.

WRIGHT, E. N. 1959. Bird damage to horticultural crops. *J. Roy. Horticultural Soc.* 84: 426–34.

WRIGHT, E. N. 1961. Use of traps to control bullfinches. *Exp. Horticulture* 4: 55–62.

WRIGHT, E. N. and BROUGH, T. 1966. Bird damage to fruit. Fruit Present and Future. *Roy. Hort. Soc.* 1966: 168–80.

WRIGHT, E. N. and SUMMERS, D. D. B. 1960. The biology and economic importance of the bullfinch. *Ann. appl. Biol.* 48: 415–18.

CHAPTER 10

ASHMOLE, W. P. 1963. The biology of the wideawake or sooty tern *Sterna fuscata* on Ascension Island. *Ibis* 103b: 297–364.

BARNES, J. A. G. 1952. The status of the lesser black-backed gull. *Brit. Birds* 45: 3–17.

BARNES, J. A. G. 1961. The winter status of the lesser black-backed gull, 1959–60. *Bird Study* 8: 127–47.

BOSWALL, J. 1947. Herring gulls nesting on buildings. *Brit. Birds* 40: 255.

BOSWALL, J. 1960. Observations on the use by sea-birds of human fishing activities. *Brit. Birds* 53: 212–15.

BROWN, R. G. B. 1967. Breeding success and population growth in a colony of herring and lesser black-backed gulls *Larus argentatus* and *L. fuscus*. *Ibis* 109: 502–515.

BRUYNS, M. F. M. 1958. Gulls which are a menace to other species. The herring gull problem in the Netherlands. *Bull. Internat. Comm. Bird. Pres.* 7: 103–7.

BUXTON, J. and LOCKLEY, R. M. 1950. *Island of Skomer*. London, Staples.

BUXTON, E. J. M. 1961. The inland breeding of the oystercatcher in Great Britain, 1958–59. *Bird Study* 8: 194–209.

COULSON, J. C. 1963. The status of the kittiwake in the British Isles. *Bird Study* 10: 147–179.

COULSON, J. C. and MACDONALD, A. 1962. Recent changes in the habits of the kittiwake. *Brit. Birds* 55: 171–7.

COULSON, J. C. and WHITE, E. 1957. Mortality rates of the shag estimated by two independent methods. *Bird Study* 4: 166–71.

COULSON, J. C. and WHITE, E. 1958. Observations on the breeding of the kittiwake. *Bird Study* 5: 74–83.

CULLEN, E. 1957. Adaptations in the kittiwake to cliff-nesting. *Ibis* 99: 275–302.

DARE, P. J. 1966. The breeding and wintering populations of the oystercatcher (*Haematopus ostralegus* Linnaeus) in the British Isles. *Fishery Invest. Lond., Ser. 2*, 15 (5): 69 pp.

DAVIDSON, P. E. 1967. A study of the oystercatcher (*Haematopus ostralegus* L.) in relation to the fishery for cockles (*Cardium edule* L.) in the Burry Inlet, South Wales. *Fishery Invest., Lond. Ser. 2*, 15 (7): 28 pp.

DAVIDSON, P. E. 1968. The oystercatcher—a pest of shellfisheries. pp. 141–55 in *The Problems of Birds as Pests*. 17 Symp. Inst. of Biology ed. R. K. Murton and E. N. Wright. London, Academic Press.

DAVIS, T. A. W. 1958. The breeding distribution of the great black-backed gull in England and Wales in 1956. *Bird Study* 5: 191–215.

DEWAR, J. M. 1908. Notes on the oystercatcher (*Haematopus ostralegus*) with reference to its habit of feeding upon the mussel (*Mytilus edulis*). *Zoologist* 12: 201–12.

DRINNAN, R. E. 1957. The winter feeding of the oystercatcher (*Haematopus ostralegus*) on the edible cockle (*Cardium edule*). *J. Anim. Ecol.* 26: 441–69.

DRINNAN, R. E. 1958. Observations on the feeding of the oystercatcher in captivity. *Brit. Birds* 51: 139–49.

DRINNAN, R. E. 1958. The winter feeding of the oystercatcher (*Haematopus ostralegus*) on the edible mussel (*Mytilus edulis*) in the Conway Estuary, North Wales. *Fishery Invest., Lond. Ser. 2*, 22 (4): 15 pp.

DRURY, W. H. 1965. Results of a study of herring gull populations and movements in southeastern New England. pp. 207–17 in *Colloque le problème des oiseaux sur les aérodrome*, Nice 25–27 novembre, ed. R-G. Busnel and J. Giban.

EDWARDS, R. L. 1958. Movements of individual members in a population of the shore crab *Carcinus maenus* L., in the littoral zone. *J. Anim. Ecol.* 27: 37–45.

ELSON, P. F. 1962. Predator-prey relationship between fish-eating birds and Atlantic salmon. *Bull. Fish. Res. Bd. Can.* 1933: 87 pp.

FISHER, J. 1966. The fulmar population of Britain and Ireland, 1959. *Bird Study* 13: 5–76.

GREENHALGH, C. M. 1952. Food habits of the Californian gull in Utah. *Condor* 54: 302–8.

GREGORY, T. C. 1948. Colony of tree-nesting cormorants in Kent. *Brit. Birds* 41: 185–6.

GRIBBLE, F. C. 1962. Census of black-headed gull colonies in England & Wales, 1958. *Bird Study* 9: 56–71.

HAMILTON, F. D. 1962. Census of black-headed gull colonies in Scotland, 1958. *Bird Study* 9: 72–80.

HANCOCK, D. A. and URQUHART, A. E. 1965. The determination of natural mortality and its causes in an exploited population of cockles (*Cardium edule* L.) *Fishery Invest. Lond. Ser. 2*, 14 (2): 40 pp.

HANCOCK, D. A. and URQUHART, A. E. 1966. The fishery for cockles

(*Cardium edule* L.) in the Burry Inlet, South Wales. *Fishery Invest., Lond. Ser. 2*, 15 (3): 32 pp.

HARRIS, M. P. 1964. Recoveries of ringed herring gulls. *Bird Study* 11: 183–91.

HARRIS, M. P. 1965. The food of some *Larus* gulls. *Ibis* 107: 43–53.

HARRIS, M. P. 1967. The biology of oystercatchers *Haematopus ostralegus* on Skokholm Island, S. Wales. *Ibis* 109: 180–93.

HICKLING, R. A. O. 1957. The social behaviour of gulls wintering inland. *Bird Study* 4: 181–92.

HICKLING, R. A. O. 1960. The coastal roosting of gulls in England & Wales. *Bird Study* 7: 32–52.

HICKLING, R. A. O. 1967. The inland wintering of gulls in England, 1963. *Bird Study* 14: 104–13.

HIGLER, L. W. G. 1961. De census van de kokmeeuw (*Larus ridibundus* L.) in Nederland, België en Luxemburg in 1961. *Limosa* 35: 260–5.

HOLLOM, P. A. D. 1940. Report on the 1938 survey of Black-headed Gull colonies. *Brit. Birds* 33: 202–21, 230–44.

HOLMER, M. 1955. [Notes on the biology of the Goosander (*Mergus merganser*) at the Indal River.] *Vår Fågelv.* 14: 231–5.

HULSCHER, J. B. 1963. Oyster-catchers and lamellibranchiates in the Wadden Sea. (Eng. transl.) *De Levende Natuur.* 67: 80-5.

HUNTSMAN, A. G. 1941. Cyclical abundance of birds versus salmon. *J. Fish Res. Bd. Canada* 5 (3): 227–35.

KADLEC, J. A. and DRURY, W. H. 1968. Structure of the New England herring gull population. *Ecology* 49 (4): 644–76.

KORTLANDT, A. 1942. Levensloop, samenstelling en structuur der Nederlandse aalscholverbevolking. *Ardea* 31: 176–280.

LUMSDEN, W. H. R. and HADDOW, A. J. 1946. The food of the shag (*Phalacrocorax aristotelis*) in the Clyde sea area. *J. Anim. Ecol.* 15: 35–42.

MACPHERSON, H. A. 1892. *A vertebrate fauna of Lakeland.* Edinburgh.

MADSEN, J. and SPÄRCK, R. 1950. On the feeding habits of the Southern cormorant. *Dan. Rev. Game Biol.* 1: 45–75.

MILLS, D. H. 1962. The goosander and red-breasted merganser as predators of salmon in Scottish waters. *D.A.F.S. Freshwater and Salmon Fisheries Research* 29.

MILLS, D. H. 1965. The distribution and food of the cormorant in Scottish inland waters. *Freshwater & Salmon Fish. Res.* 35: 1–16.

MYLNE, C. K. 1960. Predation of Manx shearwaters by great black-back gulls on Skomer. *Bird Notes* 29: 73–6.

NAYLOR, E. 1962. Seasonal changes in a population of *Carcinus maenas* (L.) in the littoral zone. *J. Anim. Ecol.* 31: 601–9.

NORMAN, R. K. and SAUNDERS, D. R. 1969. Status of little terns in Great Britain and Ireland in 1967. *Brit. Birds* 62: 4–13.

NORTON-GRIFFITHS, M. 1967. Some ecological aspects of the feeding behaviour of the oystercatcher *Haematopus ostralegus* on the edible mussel *Mytilus edulis*. *Ibis* 109: 412–24.

NORTON-GRIFFITHS, M. 1969. The organisation, control and development of parental feeding in the oystercatcher (*Haematopus ostralegus*). *Behaviour* 34: 55–114.

PHILLIPS, G. C. 1962. *Survival value of the white colouration of gulls and other seabirds*. D. Phil. thesis, Oxford.

POULDING, R. H. 1954. Some results of marking gulls on Steepholm. *Proc. Bristol Nat. Soc.* 29: 49–56.

RADFORD, M. C. 1960. Common gull movements shown by ringing returns. *Bird Study* 76: 81–93.

RADFORD, M. C. 1962. British ringing recoveries of the black-headed gull. *Bird Study* 9: 42–55.

SNOW, B. 1960. The breeding biology of the shag *Phalacrocorax aristotelis* on the island of Lundy, Bristol Channel. *Ibis* 102: 554–75.

STEVEN, G. A. 1933. The food consumed by shags and cormorants around the shores of Cornwall (England). *J. Mar. Biol. Ass. U.K.* 19: 277–92.

STONEHOUSE, B. 1967. Feeding behaviour and diving rhythms of some New Zealand shags, *Phalacrocoracidae*. *Ibis* 109: 600–5.

STRONG, R. M. Further observations on the habits and behaviour of the herring gull. *Auk* 40: 609–21.

SUSHKINA, A. P. 1932. *Some data on the biology of the cormorant with reference to the harm it inflicts on fisheries*. Astrakhan.

TINBERGEN, N. and NORTON-GRIFFITHS, M. 1964. Oystercatchers and mussels. *Brit. Birds* 57: 64–70.

TOOK, G. E. 1955. Nesting of herring gulls on roof-tops in Dover. *Brit. Birds* 48: 88–9.

VAN DOBBEN, W. H. 1952. The food of the cormorant in the Netherlands. *Ardea* 40: 1–63.

WHITE, H. C. 1957. Food and natural history of mergansers on salmon waters in the maritime provinces of Canada. *Bull. Fish. Res. Bd. Can.*, 116: 63 pp.

CHAPTER 11

BABUDIERI, B. 1960. Wild birds as carriers of pathogenic leptospira. *In* Leptospirae and leptospirosis in man and animals. *Polish Acad. Sci. Problem Ser.* 19: 88–92.

BEVAN, D. 1962. Starling roosts in woodlands. *J. Forestry* 56: 59–62.

BOSWALL, J. 1966. The roosting of the pied wagtail in Dublin. *Bull. Brit. Orn. Cl.* 86: 131–40.

BRENNER, F. J. 1965. Metabolism and survival time of grouped Starlings at various temperatures. *Wilson Bull.* 77: 388–95.

BRIDGMAN, C. J. 1965. Seasonal variations in bird numbers on airfields. pp. 103–10 in Busnel & Giban 1965.

BROADBENT, L. 1965. The epidemiology of tomato mosaic. 9. Transmission of TMV by birds *Ann. appl. Biol.* 55: 67–9.

BROWN, J. G. W. 1965. Birds on aerodromes the problems to the airline operator. pp. 31–2 in Busnel and Giban 1965.

BUSNEL, R-G. and GIBAN, J. 1965. *Colloque le problème des oiseaux sur les aérodromes.* Nice 25–27 novembre 1963. Instit. National Researche Agronomique.

BUSNEL, R-G. and GIBAN, J. 1968. Prospective considerations concerning bio-acoustics in relation to bird-scaring techniques. pp. 17–28 in Murton and Wright 1968.

COOK-SMITH, R. A. W. 1965. The nature of bird strike incidents occurring at civil airfields in the United Kingdom. pp. 17–21 in Busnel and Giban 1965.

CRAMP, S. and TOMLINS, A. D. 1966. The birds of Inner London 1951–65. *Brit. Birds* 59: 209–33.

DEAN, F. 1949. Green woodpecker 'drumming' on metal cap of electric pylon. *Brit. Birds* 42: 122–3.

DEXTER, R. W. 1952. Banding and nesting studies of the eastern nighthawk. *Bird Banding* 23: 109–14.

DUNTHORN, A. A. and ERRINGTON, F. P. 1964. Casualties among birds along a selected road in Wiltshire. *Bird Study* 11: 168–82.

EASTWOOD, E. and RIDER, G. C. 1965. Some radar measurements of the altitude of bird flight. *Brit. Birds* 58: 393–426.

ECCLES, M. A. 1939. Le rôle des oiseaux dans la propagation de la fièvre aphteuse. *Bull. Int. Office Epizootics* 18: 118.

EMMONS, C. W. 1961. Isolation of *Histoplasma capsulatum* from soil in Washington D.C. *Publ. Hlth. Rep., Wash.* 76: 591–5.

FINNIS, R. G. 1960. Road casualties among birds. *Bird Study* 7: 21–32.

FISHER, J. and HINDE, R. A. 1949. The opening of milk bottles by birds. *Brit. Birds* 42: 347–57.

FITTER, R. S. R. 1945. *London's Natural History.* New Nat. Collins, London.

FURCOLOW, M. L., TOSH, F. E., LARSH, H. W., LYNCH, H. J. and SHAW, G. 1961. The emerging pattern of urban histopolasmosis. *New Engl. J. Med.* 264: 1226–30.

GIBB, J. 1954. Feeding ecology of tits, with notes on treecreeper and goldcrest. *Ibis* 96: 513–43.

GOMPERTZ, T. 1957. Some observations on the feral pigeon in London. *Bird Study* 4: 2–13.

GOODWIN, D. 1960. Comparative ecology of pigeons in Inner London. *Brit. Birds* 53: 201–12.

GULLIVER, J. R. 1968. pp. 42 in Murton and Wright 1968.

GUNN, W. W. H. and SOLMAN, V. E. F. 1968. A bird-warning system for aircraft in flight. pp. 87–96 in Murton and Wright, 1968.

GUSTAFSON, D. P. and MOSES, H. E. 1953. The English sparrow as a natural carrier of Newcastle disease virus. *Amer. J. vet. Res.* 14: 581–5.

HAIG, D. A. and MCDIARMID, A. 1963. Occurrence of ornithosis in the wood pigeon. *Nature* 200: 381–2.

HARDENBERG, J. D. F. 1965. Clearance of birds on airfields, pp. 121–6 in Busnel and Giban 1965.

HINDE, R. A. 1953. A possible explanation of paper-tearing behaviour in birds. *Brit. Birds* 46: 21–23.

HINDE, R. A. and FISHER, J. 1951. Further observations on the opening of milk bottles by birds. *Brit. Birds* 44: 393–6.

HODSON, N. L. 1960. A survey of vertebrate road mortality 1959. *Bird Study* 7: 224–31.

HODSON, N. L. 1962. Some notes on the causes of bird road casualties. *Bird Study* 9: 168–73.

HODSON, N. L. and SNOW, D. W. 1965. The road deaths' enquiry, 1960–61. *Bird Study* 12: 90–99.

HOMES, R. C. 1964. *The Birds of the London Area*. Revised ed. publ. for The London Nat. Hist. Soc. by Hart-Davis, London.

HUGHES, D. L. 1957. Man and his animals. *Vet. Rec.* 69: 1061–5.

KENYON, K. W., RICE, D. W., ROBBINS, C. S. and ALDRICH, J. W. 1958. *Birds and aircraft on Midway Islands. November 1956–June 1957 Investigations.*. U.S. Dept. Interior, Fish and Wildlife Service, Special Sci. Rep. No. 38.

KEYMER, I. F. 1958. A survey and review of the causes of mortality in British birds and the significance of wild birds as disseminators of disease. *Vet. Rec.* 70: 713–20; 736–40.

KUHRING, M. S. 1965. Equipment used in Canada for dispersing birds. pp. 301–4 in Busnel and Giban 1965.

LACK, D. 1960. The height of bird migration. *Brit. Birds* 53: 5–10.

LEPINE, M. P. and SAUTTER, V. 1951. Sur l'infection des pigeons parisiennes par le virus de l'ornithose. *Bull. Acad. natn. Md.* 135: 332–8.

LOFTS, B., MURTON, R. K. and WESTWOOD, N. J. 1966. Gonadal cycles and the evolution of breeding seasons in British columbidae. *J. Zool. Lond.* 150: 249–72.

LOGAN-HOME, W. M. 1953. Paper tearing by birds. *Brit. Birds* 44: 16–20.

MAINARDI, D. 1964. Effetto evolutivo della selezione sessuale basata su imprinting in Columba livia. *Riv. ital. Orn.* 34: 213–16.

MANZONI, H. 1959. Man versus the starling. *New Scientist* 5: 1283–5.

MARPLES, B. J. 1934. The winter starling roosts of Gt. Britain 1932–33. *J. Anim. Ecol.* 3: 187–203.

MCDIARMID, A. 1962. *Diseases of free-living wild animals*. F.A.O. Agricultural Studies No. 57. F.A.O., Rome.

MURDOCK, W. T., TRAVIS, R. E., SUTLIFF, W. D. and AJOLLO, L. 1962. Acute pulmonary histoplasmosis after exposure to soil contaminated by starling excreta. *J. Am. med. Ass.* 179: 73–5.

MURTON, R. K. 1964. Do birds transmit foot and mouth disease? *Ibis* 106: 289–98.

MURTON, R. K. and WRIGHT, E. N. 1968. *The Problems of Birds as Pests.* 17 Symp. Instit. of Biol. London, Academic Press.

PASHBY, B. S. and CUTTS, D. B. 1966. Some observations on the feeding flights of the collared dove in Hull. *The Naturalist* 1966: 53–4.

PITWELL, L. R. and GOODWIN, D. 1964. Some observations on pigeons in Addis Ababa. *Bull. Brit. Orn. Cl.* 84: 41–5.

POTTS, G. R. 1967. Urban starling roosts in the British Isles. *Bird Study* 14: 25–42.

RANDHAWA, H. S., CLAYTON, Y. M. and RIDDELL, R. W. 1965. Isolation of *Cryptococcus neoformans* from pigeon habitats in London. *Nature* 208: 801.

ROBBINS, C. S. 1966. *Birds and aircraft on Midway Islands 1959–63 Investigations.* U.S. Fish and Wildlife Ser. Special Sci. Rep. Wildlife No. 85.

RUTTLEDGE, W. 1965. Goldfinch roost in Inner London. *Brit. Birds* 58: 442–3.

SNOW, D. W. 1968. Birds and the 1967–68 foot-and-mouth epidemic. *Bird Study* 15: 184–90.

STABLES, E. R. and NEW, N. D. 1968. Birds and Aircraft: The Problems. pp. 3–16 in Murton and Wright 1968.

SUTTON, G. M. and SPENCER, H. H. 1949. Observations at a nighthawk's nest. *Bird Banding* 20: 141–8.

TURČEK, F. J. 1960. On the damage by birds to power and communication lines. *Bird Study* 7: 231–6.

VAN DEN HOEK and EYGENGRAM, J. A. 1965. Radioactive contamination in a wild bird population. *Ardea* 53: 1–8.

WARD, P. 1968. Origin of the avifauna of urban and suburban Singapore. *Ibis* 110: 239–55.

WILSON, W. W. and MATHESON, R. C. 1952. Bird migration and foot and mouth disease. *J. Min. Agric.* 59: 213–28.

WOODROFFE, G. E. and SOUTHGATE, P. J. 1951–2. Birds' nests as a source of domestic pests. *Proc. Zool. Soc. Lond.* 121: 55–62.

WRIGHT, E. N. 1965. A review of bird scaring methods used on British airfields. pp. 113–19 in Busnel and Giban 1965.

CHAPTER 12

BROUGH, T. 1968. Recent developments in bird scaring on airfields. pp. 29–38 in Murton and Wright 1968.

BROUGH, T. 1969. The dispersal of starlings from woodland roosts and the use of bio-acoustics. *J. appl. Ecol.* 6: 403–10.

BUSNEL, R-G. 1965. Études experimentales sur l'interspécificité des signaux acoustiques de divers Laridés et Corvidés. pp. 247–58 in Busnel and Giban 1965.

BUSNEL, R-G. and GIBAN, J. 1965. *Le Problème des Oiseaux sur les Aérodromes.* Nice 25–27 novembre 1963. Instit. National de la Recherche Agronomique.

BUSNEL, R-G. and GIBAN, J. 1968. Prospective considerations concerning bio-acoustics in relation to bird-scaring techniques. pp. 17–28 in Murton and Wright 1968.

DUNCAN, C. J. 1964. Articles on Taste and Smell in birds in *A New Dictionary of Birds* ed. Landsborough Thomson. London, Nelson.

DUNCAN, C. J., WRIGHT, E. N. and RIDPATH, M. G. 1960. A review of the search for bird-repellent substances in Great Britain. *Annals des Epiphytes* No. 11ère. service uniq—ra

FRINGS, H. and JUMBER, J. 1954. Preliminary studies on the use of a specific sound to repel starlings (*S. vulgaris*) from objectionable roosts. *Science* 110: 318–19.

GRAMET, P. and HANOTEAU, J. 1965. Le problème de l'accoutumance des Corvidés et Laridés aux signaux de détresse. pp. 267–72 in Busnel and Giban 1965.

HAVILAND, G. D. 1892. A sparrow's antipathy to purple. *Nature* 46: 394.

HINDE, R. A. 1954. Factors governing the changes in strength of a partially inborn response, as shown by the mobbing behaviour of the chaffinch (*Fringilla coelebs*) *Proc. Roy. Soc.* B142: 306–58.

KALMBACH, E. R. and WELCH, J. F. 1946. Coloured rodent baits and their value in safeguarding birds. *J. Wildl. Mgmt.* 10: 353.

KEAR, J. 1966. The pecking response of young coots *Fulica atra* and moorhens *Gallinula chloropus. Ibis* 108: 118–22.

LORENZ, K. 1939. Vergleichende Verhaltens forschung. *Zool. Anz. Suppl. Bd.* 12: 69–102.

MARLER, P. 1957. Specific distinctiveness in the communication signals of birds. *Behaviour* 11: 13–39.

MELZACK, R., PENICK, E. and BECKETT, A. 1959. The problem of 'innate fear' of the hawk shape: an experimental study with mallard ducks. *J. comp. Physiol. Psychol.* 52: 694–8.

MURTON, R. K. and WRIGHT, E. N. 1968. The Problems of Birds as Pests. 17 Symp. Instit. of Biology. London, Academic Press.

PERRINS, C. 1968. The purpose of the high-intensity alarm call in small passerines. *Ibis* 110: 200–1.

THEARLE, R. J. P. 1968. Urban bird problems. pp. 181–97 in Murton and Wright 1968.

TINBERGEN, N. 1951. *The Study of Instinct.* London, O.U.P.

WORLIDGE, J. 1716. *A complete system of Husbandry and Gardening or the Gentleman's Companion, in the business and pleasures of a country life.* London.

WRIGHT, E. N. 1962. Experiments with anthraquinone and thiram to protect germinating maize against damage by birds. *Ann. Épiphyties* 13: 27–31.

WRIGHT, E. N. 1965. A review of bird scaring methods used on British airfields. pp. 113–119 in Busnel and Giban 1965.

YOUNG, W. R. and ZEVALLOS, D. C. 1960. Studies with chemical seed treatments as bird repellents for the protection of germinating maize in the Mexican tropics. *F.A.O. Plant Prot. Bull.* 8: 37–42.

INDEX

Birds are indexed only under their group vernacular names (e.g. tit, thrush) unless this name is a single word (e.g. sparrowhawk, not hawk, sparrow). Scientific names have not been given in the text, but are instead listed here after the vernacular names: scientific names are not indexed separately. Trinomial nomenclature has only been used in the few special cases where subspecific identity is important for the text.